Necktie Parties

10/13/05

Necktie Parties

A History of Legal Executions
in Oregon, 1851-1905

Diane L. Goeres-Gardner

Diane L Goeres-Gardner
10/13/05

CAXTON PRESS
Caldwell, Idaho
2005

ISBN 0-87004-446-x

Library of Congress Cataloging-in-Publication Data

Goeres-Gardner, Diane L.
  Necktie parties : a history of legal executions in Oregon, 1851-1905
/ by Diane L. Goeres-Gardner.
      p. cm.
  Includes bibliographical references and index.
  ISBN-13: 978-0-87004-446-5
  1. Executions and executioners--Oregon--History. 2. Executions
(Administrative law)--Oregon--History. I. Title.

  HV8699.U5G64 2005
  364.66'09795'09034--dc22

                                        2005011734

Lithographed and bound in the United States of America by
CAXTON PRESS
Caldwell, Idaho
172679

v

Contents

In memory of
Helen Hampton Lyklama
1949–2003

With the hope that someday the
killing will stop.

CONTENTS

Section Three —Sensational Journalism, 1896-1905

Illustrations

Southern Oregon Historical Society, #2422
Jacksonville gallows used to hang Lewis O'Neil in 1886.
(See story on page 123)

INTRODUCTION

Welcome to the world of frontier justice. *Necktie Parties* records, in chronological order, the individual stories of the men who climbed the gallows steps and faced the hangman's noose in Oregon's early days.

Oregon's history of hangings during the nineteenth century is a history of ordinary people who committed extraordinary acts. In many cases, the condemned enjoyed their notoriety, at least up to the moment the rope was tightened around their necks.

No other book covers these events in a case-by-case description. Besides the details of the hangings themselves, background information lays the foundation for understanding the community and culture surrounding the events. *Necktie Parties* uses trial records, witness testimony, newspaper reports and other historical records in an effort to make this part of Oregon's legal history comprehensible to the general public, lawyers and historians. By emphasizing the event (what took place) over text (the legal analysis) it is easier to study law's effect on society. Each case is a story in itself, yet also part of a larger historical context. Each is a window into how ordinary citizens experienced the legal process as the law was implemented.

Hangings are by necessity stories about the law, because the law provides the format and structure of how the case was handled. Homicides that result in hangings are, by their very nature, particularly suited for the narrative voice.[1] Each case has a beginning, middle and an end. The sequence of events provides the setting of when, where, and why events occurred. The narrative approach makes the legal issues easier to understand and allows the inclusion of cultural nuances surrounding each case.

There are some factors the reader needs to know before delving into the specifics of each case history. These factors include the early history of hangings in Oregon, an overview of execution ritual, understanding the media's influence and the history of penitentiary escapes.

Early Hanging History

The notion of hanging, or executing a murderer, has a long tenure in English history. Immigrants coming to Oregon carried more than just families and supplies with them. They also brought their social and cultural expectations, ethics and legal traditions. Hanging was a punishment brought from England, and practiced in the colonies long before the Revolutionary War.

The settlers who made their way across the Great Plains supported the concept of righteous revenge and punishment for individual crimes. The *Old Testament* quote, "An eye for an eye and a tooth for a tooth," wasn't just a religious ideology: it was practiced as a legal tradition all along the Oregon Trail—from Missouri to the Pacific Ocean. Society and the state's legal right to take the life of a convicted murderer was not only the practical way to keep society safe; it was the culturally expected way.

The Cornoyer and Moreland family diaries speak to this ideology when they relate their experiences in a wagon train coming to Oregon. On Wednesday, June 30, 1852 the train passed seven graves in one day. That day the wagon train left two additional graves of its own. The inscription on the first grave read: "Charles Botsford; murdered June 28, 1852. The murderer lies in the next grave." Several feet away, the second inscription read: "Horace Dolly, hung June 29, 1852."[2]

These family diaries describe the mechanics of the murderer's trial and execution. The group chose two men to serve: a judge—a man respected and admired: and a sheriff—a man with enough physical strength and vigor to implement whatever punishment might be necessary. The judge and sheriff chose a twelve-man jury. The jury heard the evidence, departed a safe distance to reach their decision and returned twenty minutes later with their verdict. After Dolly was declared guilty, a crude scaffold was immediately constructed by pushing two wagons together, with their tongues raised as high as possible, and tied together. The immigrants looped a noose around the convicted man's neck and he was pushed off the wagon seat. He strangled to death while the audience watched.

The Moreland diary mentions three hangings taking place during their trip to Oregon, while the Kern family diary notes that five murders occurred during their journey. If a hanging took place after every murder, one could conclude that the executions did not have much preventative influence on potential murderers.

Such hangings were considered morally acceptable, if not exactly legal. Of course the settlers needed an applicable legal structure first, and that wasn't established until after Oregon became an established territory of the United States.

Hangings outside the law did occur in Oregon. By definition a lynching was an illegal or extra-legal hanging. According to David Hazen, who wrote a column for the *Oregonian* in 1917, the first lynching in Oregon took place on June 1, 1813.[3] A group of fur traders were on their way to Astoria when they met some Indians, one of whom stole a "valuable silver goblet". The lead trader was so incensed that he laid a trap for the thief. The next evening they caught one of the Indians trying to steal some more of their belongings. When the whole village was gathered the traders dragged the culprit out and hanged him from a hastily erected gallows. Their intent was to teach the whole tribe a lesson about what happens when Indians steal from the whites.

Besides providing moral instruction, lynchings also served as an alternate form of punishment when communities didn't trust the available legal structure. That is what happened during two intense periods of vigilante action in Oregon's history. The first occurred from 1863-1865 at the end of the Civil War, when twenty-seven men faced the justice of "Judge Lynch". The second period began in 1882 in the desert and cattle country around Prineville and ended with the 1884 election of James Blakely to the office of Crook County sheriff.[4] At least nine men ended up hanging from a makeshift gallows during those two years.[5] Oregon had a lynching as late as 1909 when Oliver Snyder was lynched in Wasco County.[6] Lynching gradually disappeared as legal remedies became more consistent and uniform. For an interesting example of a semi-legal hanging see Berry Way's hanging in 1863 at Canyon City in Appendix A.[7]

When the victim was well-known and well-liked in the community, public condemnation of the accused could be devastating. Or in some cases, if the accused was part of a hated ethnic group, public antipathy could be overwhelming.[8] In these instances the legal authorities often had to use ingenious and judicious methods to thwart men intent on lynching the accused. Another circumstance that stirred public anger was if the crime was particularly heinous, cold-blooded, or involved sexual assault.

White men were lynched less often than Indians. Indians were regarded as living outside legal justice and therefore more likely to suffer from lynch law, much like Blacks in the South. As a hated and feared ethnic group, the Indians had first-hand experience with hangings. The very first legal hangings in Oregon were of the five Cayuse Indians convicted of murdering Marcus and Narcissa Whitman and eleven others in 1847. With much public fanfare the Native Americans were hanged in public view in Oregon City on June 6, 1850.[9]

Native Americans living in the Oregon Territory were not only subjected to hangings as punishment, but they soon utilized it for their own purposes. The Oregon City *Spectator* related the story of an Indian brave hanging his wife. When asked why he did such a thing, he replied, "She would not stay at home, and to break her of this habit he thought he would beat and hang her awhile, after the custom of the civilized whites."[10]

Besides its punitive emphasis, observing a hanging was believed to have great moral instruction. Public officials and even parents used executions to reinforce acceptance of authority. Matilda Sager recounts, in an interview with Fred Lockley, how her foster father exposed her to a hanging in order to teach her discipline. As an eight-year old orphan, she witnessed the loss of her two brothers and foster parents in the Whitman massacre in 1847. She describes the hanging she witnessed a few years later with an abusive foster father:

> We rose to where a crowd had assembled. Presently the officers brought out a man and hanged him. I was horrified. He (the foster father) said, 'I brought you to see the hanging to impress on your mind what happens to people who do not mind their elders and do exactly what you are told.' It took me months to forget the horrible sights I had seen when the Indians killed Doctor and Mrs. Whitman and my brothers and the others, and now for weeks I woke up at night covered with the sweat of terror at seeing the man hanged in my dreams. I could see him twitch and his tongue hang out and his protruding eyes.[11]

It's difficult to imagine the terror Matilda must have felt at the deaths already witnessed. It is understandable how witnessing another killing could have compounded her trauma.

In the early days in the West, people believed that hanging murderers was an absolute necessity. Hanging was the only method society had to deal with those convicted of first-degree murder. The concept of rehabilitation wouldn't become part of public policy in Oregon until early 1900. The necessity of hanging, as well as the belief that it served as deterrence for would-be-criminals, was reflected in the following 1879 newspaper editorial:

> Society is simply protecting itself, and this it has a right to do . . . Having no moral sensibility they (the murderers) are not affected by disgrace, and deprivation of liberty is not such punishment as will deter them and their kind from crime . . . But above all, should the penalty be commuted, the punishment they would receive would convey no lesson to the reprobate class who laugh at prisons and fear only the gallows.[12]

Execution Details and Rituals

When discussing execution rituals, it's important to remember one thing—it's all in the details. From spiffy new black suits to grisly autopsies, conducting a successful hanging was the result of experience and precise planning. After the accused was tried and the sentence pronounced, it was the county sheriff's duty to carry out the law's demands. Their effectiveness in doing so influenced their re-election possibilities. Therefore, the better the hanging—the higher the likelihood of re-election.

Early on, the sheriff's major responsibility was to stand on the gallows and pull the pin, a small metal bar, which unlatched the floor of the gallows and, in effect, precipitated the final moments of a man's life. The execution warrant stated that the event had to take place between certain hours, usually between noon. and 4 p.m. The sheriff had the ultimate discretion to choose the exact time within the parameters set by the judge. The warrant allowed some leeway in case a hitch developed in the proceedings, and of course there were occasional hitches.

For instance, there was the time a sheriff had to take a poll of the audience whether to wait for the reprieve, that he knew was on the way, or to go ahead and hang the convict now. Then there were the garrulous men who, while standing on the gallows, thought that if they talked long enough everyone would just give up, go home and let them go. But worst of all was a convict committing suicide while still in the cell and depriving the spectators of the planned entertainment. Sheriffs had to be ready for and anticipate anything that might happen.

Another major concern was preparing the gallows for the big event. There was a science that revolved around how far a man should fall.[13] If he fell too far, his head would be ripped off and there would be a bloody mess. If he didn't fall far enough, he would slowly strangle to death instead of having his neck snapped for a nice clean kill. A sheriff's experiences soon lead to perfection in this area.

As the potential psychological harm that could result from viewing a hanging was recognized, the sheriffs were given the additional responsibility of keeping women, children and assorted riff raff from viewing the spectacle. Although hangings had been removed from public viewing as early as 1835 in New York and 1868 in England,[14] it was not until 1879 that Oregon began requiring counties to build high fences or stockades around the hanging site. The walls didn't have to be any particular height as they varied from twelve feet to forty feet high. The fences managed to keep the crowds from gathering inside the enclosures, but they did nothing about the crowds that waited outside.

The county sheriff sometimes dispensed engraved invitations to whoever he wanted to attend the event. Some sheriffs interpreted that to mean everyone who wanted to attend could attend (except women and children, of course), while other sheriffs let only newspaper reporters, law officers and a dozen witnesses observe the event.

Various innovations were developed over time to make the sheriff's job easier. Electricity was used to release the trap door pin. False ropes were rigged to disguise the real person pulling the trapdoor open. The hangman's knot was perfected and the placement made more scientifically exact. Special ropes became available that didn't stretch so much—making the necessity of hanging a man twice less likely. Even special gallows were constructed that could be broken down, shipped across the state and used again—an early example of waste management.

The sheriff was also in charge of the murder investigation. The era of modern forensic investigation was yet to come. The microscope wasn't used until the late 1890s. Fingerprinting was still to be discovered and certainly no one had dreamed of DNA. However, county sheriffs used what they had to full advantage. Logic, examination of motivation, opportunity and knowledge of the people living in his jurisdiction were the main weapons a county sheriff used to find his murderer.

Although modern forensic science was not yet born, the sheriffs often proved to be innovative in their investigations. In 1852, Polk County Deputy Sheriff James Nesmith created his own forensic investigation by firing a shot through a shirt and comparing it to the original to disprove Adam Wimple's contention that he killed his wife in self-defense.[15] Sheriffs examined footprints left at the scene for their size and condition, comparing them to suspect's shoes. They even analyzed horseshoe prints to track killers down. A sheriff looked for his killer in the person with opportunity and the most to gain. It isn't a coincidence modern day detectives have the saying, "Follow the money". They learned it from their predecessors.

Media Influence

Newspapers were the basic means of communication between and within Oregon communities, and the owners and writers felt this responsibility keenly. While they seemed to understand the kind of power they had to shape public opinion, they didn't yet understand how much they also revealed about the culture of the times. For us, newspapers offer the most accessible pictures of what was happening in a community at the particular time a murder trial or a hanging was taking place. Trial transcripts and legal files give the basic facts about a felony case but only hint at the surrounding social and cultural nuances taking place concurrently. By using both sources we are provided a broader understanding of each case.

By 1865, city newspapers began reporting every detail of the convicted men's lives while they waited in jail for their executions. The prisoners were offered many special exemptions not allowed the regular convicts. Their meals were specially catered and what they ate, or didn't eat, right before their hanging was splashed across newspaper headlines. Visitors were allowed to visit at leisure. Instead of working all day like the others, convicts awaiting hanging were allowed to read, knit, play cards, perform music or do whatever they desired. One even participated in a snowball fight the day before his hanging. Important people came to interview and examine them. Many of these intimate details are recorded in the individual cases. Even after hangings were confined behind tall stockade walls, the executions themselves were described in "lip-smacking detail" by local newspapers.[16]

More press was always given to the condemned rather than the victim(s). Even today, in our modern world, that remains true. The victim was dead and gone—old news. The murderer was still alive and provided fresh copy for competing newspapers. From 1850 through the 1870s, newspaper articles about hangings ranged from seven lines to three inches. By 1890 news articles covered the front page and part of a second. Complete manuscripts of trials were printed. While competing newspapers might try to scoop each other by discovering various tidbits about the convict and his crime, there was surprisingly little disagreement about whether the jury's verdict should or should not be carried out.

There are hints that not everyone believed in capital punishment. Petitions begging the governor to commute the convict's sentence were organized, signed and presented. Occasionally, letters to the editor were printed protesting various aspects of how executions were performed. However, there were no citizen uprisings or protests against capital punishment during this time period.

From the kind of rope used, to what kind of clothing the convict wore, every detail was an integral part of the atmosphere created at these events. The ceremony provided guidelines and a structure for everyone involved, and usually the ritual was performed quite satisfactorily. So when the condemned failed to confess his guilt and ask the community's forgiveness, the audience was understandably disappointed. Or if the sheriff failed to stretch the rope properly, and the condemned landed alive and kicking on the ground below the trap-door, the public was justifiably scandalized.

While readers today may find these same details insignificant, the readers at the time of the hangings demanded them—right down to how many heartbeats it took for a man to die. The body was often laid out for public viewing, this window into death offering full confirmation that the condemned was truly deceased and had suffered the final consequences of his actions.

Hangings were meant to be a public display of contrition and consequence, a moral lesson against civil disorder. This public display and festival atmosphere reached its peak in 1879 when 8,000 people, including women and children of all ages, came to watch a double hanging in Portland. Larger cities weren't the only place huge crowds gathered. Even smaller communities had problems. An 1878 article in the Roseburg *Plaindealer* captured the drama exactly.

> *Dramatic hangings or necktie parties, as they are called, are the rule now-a-days. The convicted murderer steps upon the scaffold with a state bearing and just a little tremor—stage fright—and makes a little speech replete with injured innocence to a select audience of unlimited numbers. Next morning we read in the dailies all the disgusting particulars of the execution, embellished in the finest reportorial language in which the condemned man characterized his conviction as a damned conspiracy. A more recent occurrence of such damned conspiracies, and less publicity of such horrible details seems to be demanded in order to check the homicidal epidemic. It is high time that this promiscuous killing should be stopped and a more wholesome sentiment is a subject to be cultivated.*[17]

The executions gradually lost their moral example as crowds became larger and more unruly, and officials began to advocate a more sedate atmosphere.

Oregon's newspapers used the phrase "necktie parties" to describe the atmosphere and expectations of all participants.[18] Its slightly frivolous, sarcastic and mocking connotation defined the public's attitude toward these events. An article in an 1878 Portland newspaper proclaimed the headline just before a hanging, "A Necktie Sociable Will Occur".[19]

Gradually, the public aspects of the penalty eroded. It wasn't until the latter part of the century, when hangings became more private and a more solemn atmosphere was encouraged, that the term "necktie parties" fell out of usage. Most of the laws in Oregon were evolving and changing during this time period, but the conviction of first-degree murder was always the same—it was a sentence to hang. Many of the ceremonies changed, but the essential element—death—remained constant.

History of the penitentiary

It's impossible to examine Oregon's hanging history without also discussing the state penitentiary. The need to keep order on the frontier was paramount, as the earliest pioneers were mostly made up of rowdy single men between the ages of 18 and 40. It is thought that because these men were without mothers, wives and sisters nearby, they were more susceptible to alcohol, gambling, violence and murder.[20] The very first institution established in the Oregon Territory wasn't a hospital, or a courthouse. It was a one-room, log-style jail built in Oregon City in 1845 for $875.[21] The Oregon Legislature passed a bill in 1851 requiring a larger territorial prison be built in Portland, but no money was appropriated for it until 1857.

The larger prison wasn't much good at keeping convicts inside its walls. The newspapers were constantly reporting escapes. In January 1860, four prisoners escaped.[22] In July 1860, there were three more escapes.[23] Deciding that it was impossible to create a secure environment on that location, the Legislature moved the prison to Salem. A modern building was constructed and all the convicts were moved in 1866. However, the escapes persisted. Within a few months, nine convicts escaped from the new building.[24] From the time the prison was built until 1883 there were at least fifty-one escapes.[25]

By March 1879, there were 170 convicts housed in the Oregon Penitentiary and every cell was full. The cost of holding such a large group was an enormous expense for the new state. The concept of supervised parole didn't become popular until 1911, so Oregon Governor W. W. Thayer came up with a novel idea—he simply let them go. During the first three months of 1879, he pardoned fourteen convicts and commuted the sentences of ten more.[26] The sheer number of men escaping from the prison and the absolute certainty that no man would ever serve a life sentence profoundly influenced the men serving on local juries to vote for first-degree murder instead of second-degree murder convictions. Such first-degree convictions would always result in a sentence to hang.

By the end of the century the penitentiary had reduced its number of escapees, started requiring the prisoners to operate a jute mill, and reestablished the public's trust. People began to believe that the penitentiary could actually perform its required function of holding convicted criminals within its stone walls until their sentence was up.

Then two events outside the prison profoundly affected what was to happen inside its walls.

In 1902 the antics at the double hanging of John Wade and B. H. Dalton enraged the authorities. Not only were the crowds inside and outside the stockade a menace, but the mocking performance of Wade playing with the rope just before his hanging didn't give the whole event the desired somber atmosphere.[27] Also in 1902 there was a tragic and deadly escape from the prison when Harry Tracy and David Merrill killed three guards, three sheriffs, and a civilian before the deadly spree ended.[28] Both events influenced the Legislature to pass a law on February 16, 1903, that stated, "all executions should take place within the walls of the penitentiary, out of hearing and out of sight of all except officials."[29] It went into effect on May 18, 1903.

There was one point of confusion—the wording of the bill did not deal with men arrested, or tried before 1903, and sentenced to hang after April 1903. Front pages of the *Oregonian* and the *Journal* alarmed readers with predictions that killers would go free and the legal system would fail. A compromise was quickly reached and additional wording was added. The new law now continued: "Any warrant issued prior to the taking effect of this measure, shall be executed by the sheriff. The act shall not be construed to affect the execution of any warrant issued prior to the taking effect of this measure."[30] Because the act specifically excluded warrants issued prior to May 1903, three more hangings took place outside the penitentiary: June 5, 1903, January 21, 1904, and July 21, 1905. These were the last hangings to take place outside the penitentiary walls.

Harry D. Egbert, from Harney County, was the first man hanged inside the Oregon State Penitentiary on January 29, 1904.[31] Ironically, Egbert's death heralded the most gruesome outcome of all. It was rumored that after the hanging his body was skinned and used to make a lampshade for the warden. Between 1903, when the law was implemented, and 1914, thirty-seven men were sentenced to hang inside the penitentiary walls. Twelve received executive clemency and twenty-four paid the ultimate penalty on the Salem gallows.[32] The gallows was used for the last time in 1923 when James E. Kingsley, age 25, was hanged. [33]

In 1914 the death penalty was abolished by constitutional amendment. Six years later, after two particularly gruesome murders and a great deal of publicity, the citizens of Oregon passed a referendum reinstating the death penalty. Capital punishment remains under the control of the state and continues to limit the number of people allowed to view the final event.

References

Albany Democrat (Albany, Oregon) December 5, 1895.

Blakely, James. As told to Herbert Lundy, "Finale . . . When the Juniper Trees Bore Fruit." *Oregonian* (Portland, Oregon) March 26, 1939.

Bowen, William. *The Willamette Valley.* Seattle: University of Washington Press, 1978.

Brogan, Phil F. *East of the Cascades.* Portland: Binfords & Mort, 1964.

Crockatt, Ernest L. *The Murder of Till Taylor.* Philadelphia: Dorrance & Company, 1970.

Dicken, Samuel N. *The Making of Oregon: A Study in Historical Geography.* Portland: Oregon Historical Society, 1979.

Dodge, Orville. *Pioneer History of Coos and Curry County.* Salem: Capital Printing, 1898.

Friedman, Lawrence. *Crime and Punishment in American History.* NY: Basic Books, 1993.

Gross, Ariela. "Beyond Black and White: Cultural Approaches to Race and Slavery." *Columbia Law Review,* 101, #3, April 2001.

Helm, Mike. *Conversations With Pioneer Women by Fred Lockley.* Eugene: Rainy Day Press, 1981.

Himes, George H. "Scrapbook #76", p. 111, Oregon Historical Society, Portland, Oregon.

Johnson, Sgt. J. R. "The Penitentiary, Our First Institution." *Oregon Historical Quarterly*, Vol. 2, 1956.

Judd, Frank. *Marion County History.* Vol. 4, 1958.

Kelley, John W. "When Oregon Went Berserk: Vigilante Justice." *Oregonian* (Portland, Oregon) September 18, 1936.

Laythe, Joseph Willard. "A Cycle of Crisis and Violence: The Oregon State Penitentiary, 1866-1968." A masters thesis, Portland State University, 1992.

Leeson, Fred. *Rose City Justice.* Portland: Oregon Historical Society, 1998.

Long, William R. *A Tortured History, The Story of Capital Punishment in Oregon.* Eugene: The Oregon Criminal Defense Lawyers Association, 2002.

Maxwell, Ben. "Frontier Hangings Were Gala Occasions in Salem." *Capital Journal* (Salem, Oregon) January 30, 1952.

Moreland, Jesse, Rev. "Overland Journeys to the Pacific Collection, 1852." Oregon Historical Society, Portland, Oregon, Mss. 1508.

Mountain Sentinel (Union, Oregon) May 25, 1893.

Moynihan, Ruth. *Rebel for Rights, Abigail Scott Duniway.* Boston: Yale University Press, 1983.

Oregonian (Portland, Oregon) March 19, 1866, August 31, 1866, February 6, 1879, February 7, 1879, February 10, 1879, March 3, 1879, March 29, 1879, April 8, 1879, May 6, 1879, March 3, 1883, March 27, 1903, April 1, 1903, April 14, 1963, September 10, 2001.

Plaindealer (Roseburg, Oregon) September 7, 1878.

Register Guard (Eugene, Oregon) April 4, 1976.

Schultz, Janice. *The Logic of Women on Trial*. Carbondale, Illinois: Southern
   Illinois University Press, 1994.
Scott, Harvey. *The History of the Oregon Country, Vol. III*. Cambridge: The
   Riverside Press, 1924.
Spectator (Oregon City, Oregon) May 1, 1851.
Statesman (Salem, Oregon) January 31, 1860, January 30, 1952.
The Dalles Weekly Chronicle (The Dalles, Oregon) December 31, 1909.

Notes

1 Ariela Gross, "Beyond Black and White: Cultural Approaches to Race and Slavery", *Columbia Law Review*, 101, #3 April 2001, p. 643.

2 Harvey Scott, *The History of the Oregon Country, Vol. III* (Cambridge: The Riverside Press, 1924) pp. 277-8. See also Ruth Barnes Moynihan, *Rebel for Rights, Abigail Scott Duniway* (Boston: Yale University Press, 1983) p. 37. Moynihan mentions the same incidents as Scott.

3 George H. Himes, "Scrapbook #76", p. 111. Oregon Historical Society, Portland, Oregon.

4 James Blakely, as told to Herbert Lundy, "Finale . . . When the Juniper Trees Bore Fruit", *Oregonian*, March 26, 1939.

5 Phil Brogan, *East of the Cascades* (Portland: Binfords & Mort, 1964) p. 154.

6 *The Dalles Weekly Chronicle* (The Dalles, Oregon) December 31, 1909.

7 See Appendix A.

8 For more details see Case #24.

9 Fred Leeson, *Rose City Justice* (Portland: Oregon Historical Society Press, 1998) p. 9. Some sources say three were hanged.

10 *Spectator* (Oregon City, Oregon) May 1, 1851.

11 Mike Helm, ed., *Conversations with Pioneer Women by Fred Lockley* (Jefferson: Rainy Day Press, 1981) pp. 10-11. The hanging she witnessed was that of Creed Turner on December 4, 1851 in Hillsboro, Washington County, Case #2.

12 *Oregonian*, February 7, 1879.

13 For more information on the art of hanging see the rare book, "A Handbook on Hanging" by Charles Duff, London: Putnam, 1928. It even has a table coordinating the client's weight with the height of the trap to produce the best results.

14 Friedman, pp. 75-76, and Duff, p. 12

15 For more details see Case #4.

16 Friedman, p. 170.

17 *Plaindealer,* September 7, 1878.

18 *Spectator* (Oregon City, Oregon) May 1, 1851

19 For more details about these two hangings see Cases #5/6.

20 Friedman, p. 177.

21 Sgt. J. R. Johnson, "The Penitentiary, Our First Institution, " *Oregon Historical Quarterly*, Vol. 2, 1956, pp. 6–13.

22 *Statesman* (Salem, Oregon) January 31, 1860.

23 *Statesman*, July 3, 1860.

24 *Oregonian*, August 31, 1866. The paper named the individuals who escaped: Mat Bledsoe, Ed Mitchell, Ludarm, Lambert, Wright, Daniels, Williams, Douglas and White. On June 8, 1866 two more convicts escaped.

25 Joseph Willard Laythe, "A Cycle of Crisis and Violence: The Oregon State Penitentiary, 1866-1968" (A masters thesis, Portland State University, 1992) p. 26.

26 *Oregonian*, April 8, 1879.

27 For more details see Cases #43/44.

28 Laythe, pp. 76-77.

29 *Register Guard* (Eugene, Oregon) April 4, 1976.

30 *Oregonian*, April 1, 1976.

31 *Statesman,* January 30, 1952.

31 Ernest L. Crockatt, The Murder of Till Taylor (Philadelphia: Dorrance & Company, 1970) p. 182.

32 *Oregonian*, April 14, 1963.

Open to the Public, 1851–1866

Chapter One

Territory of Oregon v. William Kendall 1851

The first official hanging in Oregon's history occurred on April 18, 1851 and Oregon wouldn't become the thirty-third state of the Union until eight years later on February 14, 1859. The major territorial newspaper was the Oregon City *Statesman* and was primarily concerned with national politics. It reported very little about what happened locally. However, on April 18, 1851 it made an exception. The *Statesman* published the entire testimony of the historic trial on the front page of the newspaper the day William Kendall was hanged.

William Kendall was a stubborn Missouri frontiersman homesteading in Oregon. He had been feuding with another farmer, William Hamilton, for several months over the ownership of some hogs and several acres of land that Hamilton was leasing from Kendall. According to various sources Hamilton no longer wanted to live on the property and had made arrangements for his sister Melissa Taylor and her husband, William, to live on the property until the lease expired.[1] Kendall believed Hamilton should give up the lease.

Besides arguing about the lease Kendall believed Hamilton had stolen some of his hogs. Pigs were allowed to run loose and fend for themselves during the year until it was time to round them up for butchering. Often they just disappeared or went feral joining the wild bands living in the forests.[2] Hamilton denied knowing the whereabouts of any Kendall hogs.

On the morning of January 7, 1851 Kendall was butchering hogs at Henry Smith's home, about six miles from Salem when William

Hamilton's brother, John, showed up with a message for Kendall from William.[3] Butchering was a difficult project and it was common for neighbors to work together. Cooperation helped the job go faster and several families were able to share the meat before it spoiled. John told Kendall that his brother wanted to meet with him the next day and settle the problem. Kendall belligerently refused, and the two men nearly came to blows before Smith could separate them.

"Tell your brother to leave me and my property alone or it won't be good for his health," Kendall yelled as Hamilton rode away.

John immediately rode to the home of Mary Ann Mott where he relayed Kendall's defiant message to his brother. Mary Ann was a 30-year-old widow with seven children living a mile down the road. William Hamilton had been named administrator of her dead husband's estate and guardian of her children. Her family was totally dependent upon Hamilton's ability to manage their finances. At that time in Oregon's history, mothers and wives could not legally be guardians of their own children or manage money their children inherited.

About 5 p.m. John and Mary Ann walked down the road as William got on his horse and headed the other way. A few minutes later, the couple heard a shot. They ran back to the road and found William Hamilton lying dead on the ground.

No one saw who shot William Hamilton, but his neighbors, Sarah and Hiram Taylor, a farm family with six children, remembered talking to Kendall about 3:30 p.m. when he came looking for Hamilton. They suggested that Kendall go to Mary Ann Mott's house and watched him walk away. Five days earlier Kendall had been at their house discussing Hamilton and declared, "I'm going to give him a round. As mean a man as him ought not to live."

William Gilham, the Marion County coroner, and Joshua McKinley, a 36-year-old Canadian, arrested Kendall about 10 p.m. the night of the murder at Jesse and Ruby Looney's house, where he had eaten dinner. The grand jury hearing began on March 26, 1851, in Salem, capital of Marion County—a day late on account of high water and bad roads—not an uncommon problem in early Oregon history. William Strong was the presiding circuit court judge. Amory Holbrook was the prosecutor, while W. G. T'Vault and B. F. Harding were appointed defense attorneys.[4] Evidence and testimony was heard and the grand jury returned an indictment against William Kendall on March 27, charging him with first-degree murder.

On March 29, 1851, Kendall entered a plea of "not guilty" and asked for a change of venue, declaring that he could not receive a fair trial based on the prejudice of Marion County's residents.[5] Judge

Strong denied the motion, but it took two days to finally swear in a panel of twelve impartial jurymen. At 2 p.m. on April 2, the trial finally started. Witnesses testifying for the prosecution included the following: John Hamilton, Henry Smith, Hiram and Sarah Taylor, Mary Ann Mott, Coroner William Gilham, P. O. Riley, Marion County Sheriff William John Herren, G. H. Bridges (another worker at Smith's on the day of the murder), and John Davis (a 28 year-old boarder at Taylor's). Hiram Taylor gave the most damaging testimony against Kendall. Taylor was married to Hamilton's sister.

Hiram had been working in a field between his home, Kendall's house, and Mary Ann Mott's house on the day of the murder. He saw Kendall take out his gun, fire off a test round, load it again, and head down the road toward Mott's. Twenty minutes later he heard a shot and people started screaming "murder".

Attorney William T'Vault based his defense on the fact that no one had actually witnessed the shooting; therefore it was only a guess that Kendall was the guilty party.[6] Only three witnesses testified for the defense: Joseph Waldo, Thomas Bayley, also at Looney's when Kendall was arrested, and John Roe, another farmer working at Taylor's on the day of the murder.[7] All three men tried to place Kendall too far away to have committed the murder.

Kendall was arrested and prosecuted based on the history of his threats, the Taylors' testimony, and boot tracks found near Hamilton's body. Mapping out the countryside and walking distance between the houses certainly made his presence possible at the time of the shooting.

The jury withdrew for a half an hour before returning with a verdict. On April 4, Judge William Strong pronounced the defendant guilty of first-degree murder and sentenced him to hang fourteen days later on April 18, 1851 between 10 a.m. and 4 p.m.[8] Judge Strong later noted that disputes about land ownership were the basis of most of the homicides he presided over in his courtroom.[9]

Marion County didn't have a courthouse or a jail in 1851, so the prisoner was placed in irons and boarded in Benjamin Munker's house until the day set for the hanging. Between the trial and the date of the hanging, Kendall thought about starving himself to death, but soon realized two weeks wasn't enough time to do the job right. The day before he died, he was allowed to spend the afternoon eating and drinking to his heart's content in Baker's Tavern. Justice was an expensive proposition in 1851. The Marion County Sheriff, John Herren, was paid a $100 fee plus $50 for incidental expenses. The total cost of prosecuting, lodging and feeding Kendall amounted to $1,951—a huge sum at that time. The county sold Kendall's property for $898 to pay part of the expense. In the end, it cost the county tax-payers $1,053 to house, hold and hang William Kendall.[10]

The gallows was erected on the corner of what is now Church and Trade Streets in Salem. Before the noose could be set, Kendall made an effort to lunge forward and prematurely strangle himself, but Sheriff Herren stopped him. Kendall declared himself innocent right up to the second the rope ended his life. As only 13,323 people lived in the Oregon Territory at the time, the execution served as a great excuse for people to gather together.[11] A "large concourse of people" was present for the execution.[12]

John Hamilton, as administrator of his brother's estate held a public auction on March 22. A complete list of items sold, how much was paid and who bought it is included in the estate file. Prices paid ranged from Jacob Woodsides paying 6 1/4 cents for two panes of broken glass to Mr. Murphy paying $65 for a roan colt. The auction netted $347.81 for the family, which added to the gold, stock, and payable notes owed Hamilton created an estate worth $4,194.56, not including his Marion County land claim of 640 acres.[13] The estate records provide a remarkably clear picture of how business was transacted between residents during that era. Without banks, credit unions, or the convenience of paper money, people relied on each other and an agreed upon barter system to conduct commerce. Value was assigned to produce, such as 200 bushels of wheat, and notes for such were passed back and forth. A man's word was his most precious possession because that was the only way he could get credit or buy supplies. According to the probate records Hamilton was a very wealthy man in 1851.

William Taylor, husband of William's sister Melissa, was named guardian to Hamilton's only son, William J. Hamilton, on June 7, 1852. Taylor and his brothers, Hiram and John, put up a bond of $5,000 against his ability to honestly administer the estate. In 1868 Hiram Smith, a local lawyer, filed a court suit against Taylor alleging that Taylor had refused to pay for the boy's education or expenses for the past fifteen years. Taylor also hadn't supplied the court with an accounting of the estate since he was named guardian. As young Hamilton was now over 14 years old, he requested that Hiram Smith be named guardian instead. Smith and Taylor agreed that Taylor would pay $3,100 to Smith as part of the boy's estate. Taylor would immediately pay $200 cash, and sign two real estate mortgages for the balance. One was worth $1,000 at 12 percent interest due immediately and the other due in two years for $1,900 at 12 percent interest. The final accounting from Taylor showed that he'd loaned the majority of his ward's money to his brother, Hiram, who failed to repay it, and accepted a land mortgage against Hiram Taylor's donation land claim No. 58 in his own name. Instead of managing the boy's money so it increased, William Taylor had practically thrown it away. Whether he actually paid the $1,900 is not noted.

The day Kendall was hanged the Oregon City *Spectator* published an appropriate comment,

> *"What an unlucky name the name of William has been this year in Oregon. If I had a son by that name I think I should change it. William Kendall killed William Hamilton and is to be executed tomorrow. William Kean killed William Cook and his trial commences on the 22nd. You had better look out sweet William."*[14]

Later he could have added that William Taylor had defrauded William Hamilton out of his rightful estate.

References

Bowen, William A. *The Willamette Valley*. Seattle: University of Washington Press, 1978.

Genealogical Material in Oregon Provisional Land Claims Abstracted from Applications, Vols. I-VIII, 1845-1849, Vol. 6, p. 138.

Maxwell, Ben. "Frontier Hangings Were Gala Occasions in Salem." *Capital Journal* (Salem, Oregon) January 30, 1952.

Marion County Estate Records, William J. Hamilton, #0029, 1851; and James Hamilton, #0411, 1870, Oregon State Archives, Salem, Oregon.

Marion County Guardianship Records, William J. Hamilton, #0057, 1852, Oregon State Archives, Salem, Oregon.

Oregon Statesman (Oregon City, Oregon) April 4, 1851, 18 April 18, 1851, April 25, 1851.

Peterson del Mar, David. *Beaten Down: A History of Interpersonal Violence In The West*. Seattle: University of Washington Press, 2002.

Territory of Oregon v. William Kendall, Marion County Circuit Court Register and Fee Book, 1849-1890, Book 1, p. 25. Oregon State Archives, Salem, Oregon.

The Spectator (Oregon City, Oregon) January 14, 1851, January 16, 1851, April 10, 1851, April 17, 1851, April 25, 1851.

Chapter 1 notes

1 *The Spectator* (Oregon City, Oregon) January 14, 1851.

2 Wild pigs were exceptionally capable of surviving in the Willamette Valley. Few settlers attempted to pen the animals inside fences, instead relying on the honesty of their neighbors to distinguish ownership. William Bowen. *The Willamette Valley* (Seattle: University of Washington Press) 1978, p. 87.

3 *Oregon Statesman* (Oregon City, Oregon) April 18,1851. The *Oregon Statesman* was later moved to Salem, Oregon.

4 *Oregon Statesman*, April 4, 1851.

5 *Oregon Statesman*, April 18, 1851.

6 *Oregon Statesman*, April 25, 1851. T'Vault's entire speech was printed on the front page.

7 See Case #7 where John Roe is found guilty of murdering his wife.

8 *Oregon Statesman*, April 18, 1851.

9 David Peterson del Mar. *Beaten Down: A History of Interpersonal Violence in The West,* Seattle: University of Washington Press, 2002, p. 222.

10 *Salem Statesman*, January 30, 1952.

11 *The Spectator*, April 10, 1851.

12 Ben Maxwell, "Gala Occasions in Salem", *Statesman* (Salem, Oregon) January 30, 1952.

13 Marion County Estate File of William Hamilton, #0029, 1851, Oregon State Archives, Salem, Oregon. See also *Genealogical Material In Oregon Provisional Land Claims Abstracted from Applications, Vols. I – VIII,* 1845-1849, p. 163. All three Hamilton brothers, William, John and Joseph claimed land adjacent to each other on November 10, 1847.

13 *The Spectator*, April 17, 1851.

Chapter Two

Territory of Oregon v. Creed Turner 1851

In 1848, the U.S. Congress triumphantly passed the measure giving Oregon its own territorial government. By 1851 ten counties had been created, with the five smallest located in the top northwest corner of the state. There was no Multnomah County yet; instead the area around Portland was divided between Clackamas County with Oregon City as county seat, and Washington County with Hillsboro (a.k.a. Hillsborough) as county seat. Hamilton's murder and Kendall's execution in Marion County had been a real shock to the Territory's inhabitants. Unfortunately, six months later another murderer stood in front of a judge.

Edward A. Bradbury was the 24-year-old son of a wealthy Cincinnati, Ohio, mill owner.[1] C. M. Bradbury, Esquire, was the owner of Bradbury's Mills and a powerful man in his hometown. Edward had come west to explore the new land opening in Oregon and to visit his older brother, Charles Bradbury, whose wife had recently given birth to a son. He arrived in Portland with his friend, Captain Loring, and was soon to start working in Loring's general store. However, instead of becoming enamored with the land, he got involved with a woman, the daughter of Farmer John Bonser living on Sauvie's Island outside Portland.[2] Hotels or motels didn't exist in those days so instead visitors boarded with families and Edward boarded with them.

John and Elizabeth Bonser had arrived in Oregon in 1847 with a large family—three boys and three girls still living at home in 1850.[3] Their middle daughter, Martha, was 15 years old and a beauty.

Creed Turner, an even earlier immigrant from Kentucky, was also boarding with the Bonser family and had his eye on Martha. We know Turner had arrived prior to May 1847 because his signature is on a set of resolutions passed by a large group of Clackamas County landowners on May 27, 1847, along with 150 other well-known Oregon pioneers.[4] According to early Clackamas County records, Turner signed ownership of fifty head of American cattle over to Thomas M. Chambers while Turner was traveling back to the eastern states. Besides the cattle agreement Turner also signed a power of attorney over to Chambers dated May 24, 1847.[5]

On Sunday morning, October 19, 1851, the Bonser family and Edward Bradbury were all together in the Bonser home.[6] Turner entered the room, stepped up to Bradbury's side and without any known provocation pulled a small "dirk" knife out of his pocket. He gutted Bradbury with five long swipes across his abdomen, two across his chest, more cuts on both arms and his left side. Bradbury died the next day. Witnesses testified that the murder was unjustified and the jealous survivor a cowardly criminal.

Reverend Kingsley served as chaplain at the grave on Tuesday morning as Bradbury was buried in the Portland City Cemetery.[7]

Washington County Sheriff William Hardin Bennett was also a Kentucky native but had little sympathy for Turner. He immediately arrested Turner and the next day the grand jury returned an indictment against him for first-degree murder. Turner was neither repentant nor dismayed at his action. He told the authorities that his only regret was that he was unable to kill himself.

The trial was held on October 24, 1851, in Hillsboro. Besides Martha Bonser, those subpoenaed to testify were James Bonser, John Bonser, Stephen Bonser, Doctor R. P. Wilson, William Warren, Doctor Davenport, John B. Lindsay, Ellis Walter, Stephen Johnston, and Luval Johnston. A. Campbell served as the District's prosecuting attorney and the firm of Frank Tilford and Matthew P. Deady defended Turner.[8] Twelve men were chosen to serve as jurors: Lewis C. Cooker, George Webbert, John S. White, John Harrison, William Wilson, E. B. Soatt, John Gilmour, Martin Gillihan, Wilson Hoyt, Charles Steward, William Baylee, and T. G. Naylor, foreman.

On November 4, 1851, Creed Turner stood in front of the Judge O. C. Pratt and was sentenced to hang on December 4.[9]

Forty-six days after the murder of Edward Bradbury, the residents of Hillsboro turned out to see the execution. Turner had spent the last week of his life writing madly on his biography. Visitors to the jail heard him mumbling to himself, "No! They have not done me justice —an innocent man has to die. I'm coming to myself now, and life is getting sweeter and sweeter to me; it's hard. Some have taken me for a grand scoundrel of the first water, and that I aimed to get a big name. I wasn't smart enough to act insane." As many men had realized before Turner, he was at last overcoming the anger and fury that initiated his grand action against Bradbury, and savoring the last few hours of his remaining days.[10]

He ate a large meal the evening before he was to die and had his face clean-shaven the next morning. He requested to be baptized but it was too late to make the arrangements. As his hands were tied behind his back he complained to the sheriff, "it need not be tied so tight as he had large hands and it would not slip."[11] According to witnesses no black cap was pulled over Turner's head before the hanging.

Nearly 250 people waited on Thursday, December 4 to see the condemned man climb the scaffold.[12] About 10:30 a.m. Sheriff Bennett led Turner out of the jail and up the scaffold steps. Stepping to the front of the trap Turner gave a short speech to the people standing below.

"I committed the deed and now I'm paying for it. If I had to do it over again I would. I leave my written words for you all to read." This referred to the manuscript he'd written explaining his conduct.[13]

Reverend John S. Griffin and Elder James McBride gave a short sermon from the top of the scaffold. The sun broke through the clouds shortly before the execution and the reporter from the *Statesman* felt it was an omen of God's pleasure at the upcoming execution. At precisely 11 a.m. the sheriff slipped the pin and Creed Turner died. This was the first and last hanging in Hillsboro, Washington County, Oregon.

Two years later, in 1853, Martha Jane Bonser married Marquis DeLayfette Armstrong.

References

1850 Federal Census, Clatsop, Marion and Washington County, Oregon.

Clackamas County Land Claim, Vol. 4, pp. 305 and 307, Creed Turner, May 24, 1846.

Genealogical Material in Oregon Provisional Land Claims Abstracted from Applications, Vols. I-VIII, 1845-1849. pp. 55, 59, 72, 114, Oregon State Archives, Salem, Oregon.

Himes, George H. "Scrapbook #60", p. 59, Oregon Historical Society, Portland, Oregon.

Oregon Statesman (Oregon City, Oregon) December 9, 1851.

Provisional and Territorial Government Records. Creed Turner Land Claim, Vol. 4, p. 305 and 307, May 24, 1847, Oregon State Archives, Salem, Oregon.

Spectator (Oregon City, Oregon) May 7, 1847, October 28, 1851, November 4, 1851, December 9, 1851.

Territory of Oregon v. Creed Turner, U. S. District Court Case Records, 1851,Washington County, #93A-025, Box #13. Oregon State Archives, Salem, Oregon.

The Weekly Times, (Portland, Oregon) October 28, 1851, October 30, 1851, December 6, 1851

Chapter 2, notes

1 *The Weekly Times* (Portland, Oregon) October 23, 1851.
2 Sauvie's Island was named for Jean Baptiste Sauvie who established a dairy there about 1834.
3 1850 Federal Census, Washington County, Oregon.
4 *Spectator* (Oregon City, Oregon) May 7, 1847.
5 Provisional and Territorial Government Records. Creed Turner Land Claim, Vol. 4, p. 305 and 307, May 24, 1847, Oregon State Archives, Salem, Oregon.
6 *Spectator*, October 26, 1851.
7 *The Weekly Times*, October 23, 1851.
8 *The Weekly Times*, October 30, 1851.
9 Ibid.
10 *Oregon Statesman* (Oregon City, Oregon) December 9, 1851. *The Oregon Statesman* says that 500 men women and children watched the execution. That would be nearly a quarter of the entire population living in Oregon.
11 *Oregon Statesman*, December 9, 1851. The news article also says that Turner "was equipped in his shroud" before he was taken to the place of execution. Perhaps the word is used simply to mean the garments he wore were the ones he was to be buried in. It seems unlikely that he was wrapped in sheets of white linen and carried to the scaffold.
12 *Spectator*, December 9, 1851.
13 Ibid. Such manuscripts were common during this time. Unfortunately Turner's manuscript has been lost over time. See also Case #10, State of Oregon v. Andrew Pate, for further discussion.

Chapter Three

Territory of Oregon v. Return William Everman 1852

hree hundred spectators jammed Cynthian (present day Dallas), the county seat of Polk County on May 11, 1852.[1] On the gallows stood Return William Everman, a 24-year-old Kentucky carpenter, convicted of first-degree murder.[2] The county officials weren't very expert at hanging people and misjudged the drop needed to break a man's neck. They ended up strangling Everman. It was an agonizing spectacle.

The events leading up to the hanging began six months earlier. Cyranus (Cyrus) S. Hooker made two very serious enemies before his death. He accused Will Everman of breaking into his house and stealing an expensive gold watch. He also alienated Everman's friend, Enoch Smith, who was so angry he offered to pay a bounty of $250 to anyone who would kill Hooker. The records don't indicate why Smith hated Hooker.

Will Everman was an adventurous man, about 5' 10" tall with large blue eyes and rather bald. His brother, Hiram Everman, age 28, was 6' tall, with a long beard and a distinctive scar running down the side of his face near his mouth.[3] The brothers had lived in Washington County for two years before arriving in Polk County in December 1852. Unfortunately, about the time they arrived in Cynthian, the number of robberies skyrocketed and residents associated the two events rather closely. There was little industry in Oregon at that time and young men with limited prospects often found it difficult to earn an honest living.

Deciding to make a little money and get revenge on the man who besmirched his name all in one shot, Will took advantage of plans to travel to the California gold mines. On February 12, 1852, Hiram Everman, Enoch Smith, and David James Coe packed up their possessions and headed south.

Before joining them on the trip, Will left his boarding house, hid behind a rail fence near a field Cyrus Hooker was harrowing just outside Rickreall and waited. On the morning of February 13, Hooker showed up with his horses ready to work the field. When he was about thirty yards away, Everman shot him with a musket crammed with buckshot and slugs, putting three gaping holes in Hooker's back. As the poor victim lay bleeding on the ground, Everman walked up and shot him again—this time with a revolver, which blew his brains out.

Hooker's neighbors found his body that afternoon and started an investigation. The footprints running around the body and back to the hiding place told the story of a murderer lying in wait and shooting in cold blood. Many people had heard Hooker accusing Everman of the theft and Everman threatening to shoot Hooker for besmirching his name. A group hurried to Goff's boarding house, where Everman was living, to question him, only to discover he had already left for California. A large posse gathered and rode after the men. They caught up with Hiram Everman and Enoch Smith that night and arrested them as material witnesses.

Unfortunately, Will Everman and David James Coe hadn't remained with the main party, but continued south by themselves. A smaller posse composed of James Foster,, J. W. Burch and S. Goff, saddled up, and after sixty hours of hard riding caught up with the two men on Monday, February 16 at Deer Creek (near the city of Roseburg), in Douglas County. The wanted men were spending the night at the home of William Wallace Walker. Walker and the Everman brothers were friends when they lived in Missouri and had come over the plains together in 1850.[4] Traveling a little more slowly the posse and their captives returned to Cynthian on Saturday.

An inquest was held on February 17, 1852, at the home of John Barrows in Polk County. The inquest jury, Walt Ford, Joseph Embree, James S. Foster, Cary D. Embree, and George Evans, found reason to believe Hiram Everman was aware that his brother killed Hooker and helped him escape. Hiram was officially arrested and held under a bond of $500 until a trial could be held on April 14, 1852.[5]

Cyrus Olney, a member of the 1857 Constitutional Convention and later to become a respected Oregon judge, defended Everman at the trial. Reuben P. Boise, who also became a respected judge, was the prosecutor.[6] Hiram pled guilty to being an accessory after the fact and was sentenced to three years of hard labor in the penitentiary. As such a thing didn't yet exist in the territory, and no one wanted to build a penitentiary just to hold one man, the citizens had to come up with an alternative solution. On the day of William's execution an auction was held and Hiram was sold to Theodore Prather, who became his defacto jailor for the next three years.[7] Prather was an honest man who gave Hiram a horse, a saddle and $20 when his time was up. Hiram later married, raised a family and became a conscientious citizen living in Douglas County.[8]

David James Coe was tried as an accessory to murder, acquitted and released from custody. Coe turned against his former friend and testified against Will at the trial.

Courtesy Oregon State Sheriffs' Association
Polk County Sheriff
Benjamin F. Nichols

Enoch Smith was 30 years old, overweight with blonde hair and blue eyes. He was charged as an accessory before and after the fact.[9] The jury couldn't agree on a verdict, eleven voting him guilty of murder in the first degree and one voting him guilty of murder in the second degree, so a second trial was ordered. Because of the notoriety a change of venue was granted and the trial moved to Yamhill County.

To Sheriff Benjamin F. Nichols' everlasting embarrassment, before Smith could be transferred he slipped the irons off his legs and escaped out the Polk County jail's second story window. He was later recaptured hiding and ill in Solomon Allan's barn located partway between Cynthian and Lafayette. This time the jury found him guilty of first-degree murder and sentenced him to hang on June 18, 1852. A petition asking the governor to commute Smith's death sentence to three years imprisonment was circulated and presented to the governor. To the astonishment of Oregon's citizens, Territorial Governor Jubal P. Gaines, apparently motivated by a personal and political animosity toward the presiding judge, signed an unconditional pardon and set Enoch Smith free on June 7, 1852.[10] In 1855 he married Mahala Ann Johnson and filed for a Donation Land Claim in Lane County. Smith retained his approval and appreciation of executive pardons as his signature shows up on a pardon petition in 1854 for John Harms and in 1857 for William Eddings.[11]

Return William Everman was tried and convicted of first-degree murder on April 20, 1852 and sentenced to hang on Tuesday, May 11, 1852.[12] Smith Gilliam was the executioner.[13]

A few days before the execution, Everman led authorities to the banks of the Rickreall River and unearthed Hooker's gold watch he had hidden there. He also wrote a full confession, which was published in the *Oregon Statesman* on May 25, 1852.[14]

Cyrus Hooker's brother, Parmenus P. Hooker, was named sole heir and administrator of his brother's estate. He gave a $500 reward to the members of the posse that captured Everman. James S. Foster, Cary D. Embree, and James Harris were appointed by the Polk County court to appraise the estate. After paying the reward, a bill for a $10 coffin, and various other bills, Hooker netted $1,188.88 on October 17, 1853.[15]

References

1850 Federal Census, Washington County, Oregon.

Donation Land Claim No. 84, Cyranus S. Hooker in Polk County.

Donation Land Claim No. 1894, Enoch Smith in Lane County.

McArthur, Scott. "Greed and Sex Lead to Six Hangings in County." *Great Events II*, Special Edition of Polk County History by *Sun-Enterprise* Newspaper, Monmouth, Oregon, Craig Lockwood, Editor.

Oregon Historical Quarterly, Vol. 61, 1960, p. 295.

Oregon Statesman (Oregon City, Oregon) February 28, 1852, March 3, 1852, March 9, 1852, March 10,1852, April 20, 1852, April 27,1852, May 4, 1852, May 25, 1852, June 22, 1852.

Polk County Observer (Dallas, Oregon) February 2, 1900.

Polk County Probate File, Cyranus S. Hooker, #0259, 1852, Oregon State Archives, Salem, Oregon.

Territorial Government Documents #3456-65, #7125, #9163, #10858, Oregon State Archives, Salem, Oregon.

Territorial Government. Secretary Executive Journal of Official Actions of the Governor, March 3, 1849–January 12, 1859. See p. 86, Enoch Smith's pardon of June 7, 1852. Oregon State Archives, Salem, Oregon.

Territory of Oregon v. Hiram Everman, Polk County Circuit Court Index, Case File #322, filed April 14, 1852, Oregon State Archives, Salem, Oregon.

Territory of Oregon v. R. W. Everman, Polk County Circuit Court Index, Case File #16, filed April 14, 1852, Oregon State Archives, Salem, Oregon.

Umpqua Trapper, Fall, 1975, pp. 68-69.

The Weekly Times (Portland, Oregon) February 28, 1852, May 1, 1852, May 8, 1852.

Chapter 3 notes

1 *Oregon Statesman* (Oregon City, Oregon) May 25, 1852.

2 1850 Federal Census, Washington County, Oregon.

3 *Oregon Statesman*, February 24, 1852.

4 *Oregon Statesman*, May 25, 1852.

5 Territory of Oregon v. Hiram Everman, Polk County Circuit Court Index, Case File #322, filed April 14, 1852, Oregon State Archives, Salem, Oregon.

6 Reuben P. Boise was elected prosecuting attorney for the first and second districts (comprising all the counties lying on the west of the Willamette River) in 1853 by the territorial legislature.

7 *Oregon Historical Quarterly*, Vol. 61, 1960, p. 295.

8 On July 11, 1853 Judge O. C. Pratt wrote a letter to George Curry. Apparently Curry had asked Pratt about the possibility of pardoning Hiram Everman. Pratt declined to give his opinion and suggested Curry contact Reuben Boise and J. W. Nesmith. See #10858, Territorial Government Documents, Oregon State Archives, Salem, Oregon.

9 Ibid., p. 195.

10 *Oregon Statesman*, June 22, 1852. This pardon was a symptom of the extreme confusion and conflict pervading the state at the time.

11 Territorial Government Documents #7125 and #9163.

12 *Oregon Statesman*, February 24, 1852.

13 *Polk County Observer* (Dallas, Oregon) February 2, 1900.

14 *Oregon Statesman*, May 25, 1852.

15 Polk County Probate File, Cyranus S. Hooker, #0259, 1852, Oregon State Archives, Salem, Oregon.

Chapter Four

Territory of Oregon v. Adam Wimple 1852

A dam E. Wimple crossed the plains in 1845[1] from Oneida, New York,[2] intending to make a new home in Oregon. On May 22, 1847 he filed on a 640-acre donation land claim near Mary's River and worked for three years to improve it.[3] After hearing about gold in California he packed up and headed for the gold mines in the fall of 1848. He returned to Oregon in the spring of the next year with nearly $10,000 in gold.[4]

On his return he sold his land and moved to Portland where he bought a boarding house and a tavern. On July 4, 1850, he helped the little town celebrate its first Fourth of July by serving a big dinner at his boarding house.[5] In the fall he built a store on the Tuality Plains in Washington County where he sold general merchandise.

To celebrate his newfound wealth Wimple started looking for a good wife to cook and clean for him. Women were hard to find in those days on the Oregon frontier and mighty particular about their men, but Wimple persevered and his pot of gold was a considerable asset.

David Allen and his family lived about thirteen houses away from Wimple's store in Washington County. Allen thought Wimple would like his stepdaughter, Mary, and introduced them to each other. One week after they met, she agreed to marry Wimple and preparations were made for the wedding, which included buying $40 worth of clothes for the young bride.

Mary Allen was the out-of-wedlock daughter of 30-year-old Elizabeth Alfrey Allen. Matilda Jane Sager Delaney remembers playing with Mary Allen and how she was beaten by her foster father because of Mary's "illegitimacy".[6] Mary was 13 years old and Adam was 35, old enough to be her father.[7] Adam and Mary were married on January 5, 1851, and they settled into a rented cabin in Washington County. In the spring, David Allen persuaded his rich new son-in-law to move in with the family. Relations didn't go very well between the new couple and the bride's parents, and Wimple soon decided to move back to his home in Portland, taking Mary with him. The Allen's weren't happy to see their meal ticket leave and soon persuaded Mary to move back to her stepfather's home leaving Wimple alone in Portland.

By the end of that summer Wimple was fed up with the situation, instituted legal proceedings and convinced Mary to return to him. In November 1851 he bought land in Polk County near Mary's Uncle Lee, in what is now called Cooper's Hollow. Here the couple put up a two-room cabin and started to make a home. They were still unhappy and Wimple decided to move back east hoping that the distance from his in-laws would solve all their problems. He sold most of his property and the couple traveled back to the Allen home to say one last good-by. All went well until they started home and Mary got angry with Adam. They exchanged verbal insults and Mary's childish anger changed to physical violence when she yanked out a bunch of Adam's hair. She announced her decision to stay in Oregon. Adam Wimple didn't want to leave his little wife so he stayed too.

Sunday, August 1, 1852, dawned a warm and glorious Oregon day.[8] Several of Wimple's neighbors came by for a Sunday morning visit. It went well until people started gathering up their belongings and preparing to leave.

"Well, how are you two getting along out here all by yourselves?" Mr. Cox asked Adam.

"I ain't had a minute's peace since I married that woman!" Adam replied with a great deal of vehemence. Mary, overhearing the remark, glared angrily at him.

The company left at 11 a.m. and the Wimples waved to their friends as they rode away.

About 1 p.m. that afternoon the closest neighbors noticed smoke spiraling up from the area of the Wimple cabin and rode as fast as they could to the clearing. By then the cabin was nearly burned to the ground and there wasn't much anyone could do to stop the fire. All that was left were some smoldering logs from the walls. Neither Adam nor Mary was anywhere to be found. However, Adam's prize mare was missing.

Polk County Sheriff Benjamin Franklin Nichols was notified and a thorough search was made of the burned out ruins. To no one's surprise human bones and flesh were discovered in the northwest corner of the basement. The gruesome remains weighed about eight pounds and looked like part of a hip.[9] Also found were various rings and beads belonging to Mary Wimple lying in what were thought to be human entrails.

Friends and neighbors of the deceased recalled how a year earlier, in November 1851, Wimple had threatened on two different occasions to shoot Mary Wimple, her friends and then himself if she ever tried to leave him again.[10]

Two weeks later James Nesmith found Wimple wandering on foot in the woods. Wimple's horse had freed itself from his hobbles and left Wimple alone. Nesmith arrested him, tied him up and brought him back to Cooper's Hollow. During the ride back Adam made a full confession and told what happened after the visitors left that terrible Sunday morning. He seemed relieved to finally get the story out in the open.

"After everyone left Sunday, Mary was spitting mad at me. She didn't want to live with anyone who talked about her like I did—telling the neighbors I didn't have any peace since we got married. She called me the meanest man in the world and said I deserved cuckolding every day of my life,"[11] he said.

"She admitted spending time with a man when we were separated. But I forgave her for that." Wimple paused and a pained expression crossed his face. "I don't see why she said I deserved that."

He went on, "Mary ran out of the house but I dragged her back. She tore my shirt and bit me on my arm. When I went into the other room to change my shirt, she came to the door with a pistol in her hand. 'Damn you! I can shoot as well as you!'[12] she said and fired. The pistol ball went through my sleeve. I lost my head 'bout then. I grabbed the pistol and struck her twice on the head with it before she fell on the floor." He pantomimed hitting Mary on the head.

"She cried and pleaded for her life. She said she would go east with me if I wanted. Blood was coming out of her eyes, ears and nose. I felt sorry for her, poor thing. I figured she would die anyway and I might as well finish her off, so I hit her a good one again. She died right after that."[13]

Wimple was anxious that Nesmith understood how his sympathy and concern for his wife was the cause for the fatal blow. After killing her, he dragged her body in front of the fireplace, took off the planks, which covered a cellar and threw her down below.

After washing the blood off his hands, he gathered up his "horse," pistol, powder, slugs, knife, blankets and food to make his escape.[14] Before leaving he went back to make sure she was dead. He thought she was. It was later discovered that her body was found in the opposite corner of the cabin from where he threw her so it's assumed she was only stunned when he threw her into the cellar. In order to cover his crime he started a fire with some rags in a wooden chest, shut the door to the cabin and rode off.

"Only then did I become conscious of what I had done. I thought to myself—I have killed my poor wife. I wouldn't have done it for 'ten thousand thousand worlds'![15] I determined to kill myself but discovered that I had no caps for the pistol. I tried to poison myself with plants but that just made me sick. I had just decided to come back and give myself up when you found me."

A week after his arrest, on Thursday, August 20, 1852, Wimple escaped the Polk County sheriff's custody.[16] Somehow Wimple had filed off his irons three days earlier and pretending they were still locked waited for his chance. That night, when the guard was alone with him, Wimple complained that he was ill and persuaded the guard to make him some tea. While the guard was outside gathering wood for a fire, the murderer discarded his shackles, climbed up on the roof and hid. For the next two days and nights he wandered the area around his burned out cabin until finally desperate for food he entered a neighbor's house, gave himself up and asked for breakfast.[17]

The Dallas community was so incensed by Mary Wimple's murder that there was talk of a lynching.[18] In order to ensure a fair trial, a change of venue was granted and the trial was moved from Polk County to Oregon City in Clackamas County.

On Monday, September 11, 1852, the trial started. Campbell and Thornton served as the county prosecutors. Mr. Wood and Matthew P. Deady were appointed to defend Wimple. Deady later became Associate Justice of the Territorial Supreme Court and a prominent Democratic politician. Judge Thomas Nelson, a resident of Oregon City, presided over the two-day affair.[19] The twelve jurors were: Hardin Gammon, teamster; William F. Highfield, watchmaker; Ronald Crawford, wharf boat keeper; William Gird, grocer; Jonathan M. Bacon, farmer, William Barlow, town proprietor; Thomas Waterbury, farmer; William Hawkins, farmer; David Burnsides, mechanic; and Orville Risley, farmer.[20] Most of the testimony covered Wimple's confession and various neighbors' observations of the couple's animosity toward one another.

The Clackamas County sheriff, William C. Dement, conducted his own forensic experiments with the pistol and Wimple's shirt, proving rather conclusively that it had been torn and powder smeared on it rather than having a slug fired through it. The shirt was passed around to the jury for their examination and the sheriff testified how it should have looked if a shot had truly been fired through it. It was pretty obvious that Wimple had imagined at least part of his story.

Before the jury recessed to consider their verdict, Judge Nelson addressed the twelve men:

"If Adam Wimple committed the crime in a moment of passion and rage caused by the deceased, then the jury was to find him guilty of second degree murder or manslaughter. If the prisoner had time to think—even for a minute—between the provocation and the act, then he was guilty of first-degree murder."[21]

Judge Thomas Nelson continued with his judicial instructions, "The prisoner has the right to have his whole confession considered, but the jury has the right to reject such parts of the confession they think false and believe the parts they think true."[22]

The audience noted the judge's compassion for the murdered girl when he reminded the men that Mary's virtue was not in question. Even if her general character were "infamous", it would not justify the act of murder.

In order to convict Adam of first-degree murder the jury had to answer yes to each of the following four questions: Was Mary Wimple dead? Did the defendant cause her death by some bodily injury? Was the defendant capable of distinguishing between right and wrong and knew what he was doing to be an offense against God and nature? Did the defendant kill the deceased purposely and of deliberate and pre-meditated malice?

The jury retired to another room for an hour before returning with their own question. They wanted to know if premeditation was evidence of malice? The judge was very direct. Yes, the jury could infer malice if the defendant had time to premeditate the killing. A short time later the jury returned with their verdict—guilty of murder in the first degree.

When Adam was asked if he had anything to say before the sentencing, he replied no. However, Judge Nelson did have something to say and his words were explicit and to the point:

She whom you have killed was young, it may be, thoughtless. You had arrived at that period of life when passion should be subject to reason. She was a female—you were a man. She was your wife whom you had sworn to cherish and protect, and yet your arm that should have been ever raised in her defense, struck her down in death. To her pleading for life, if we are to believe your own statements, you turned an unlistening ear, and with remorseless cruelty when she was lying before you, helpless, prostrate, bleeding, and with beseeching cries entreating you to spare her life—you, her legal guardian, her husband and professing sentiments of warm affection for her, gave her the fatal blow which hurried her into eternity.[23]

Adam Wimple was sentenced to hang back in Dallas on October 8, 1852, between 9 and 11 a.m.

Friends who came to Oregon in 1845 with Wimple frequently alluded to him as that "Crazy Wimple."[24] He was an eccentric man and many people believed Wimple was "soft in the upper story".[25] One story told how he walked seventy miles to Oregon City to buy a tin cup and fifty cents worth of sugar when the same thing could have been purchased in Polk County for a few cents more and sixty-nine miles closer. Sixty-nine miles were a long way to walk or ride a horse when few roads existed and those that were available were mighty rough at best. When he was offered a good horse to ride, he declined the offer for the reason that the horse would be too much trouble to him. Friends say he sometimes went without food for thirty-six hours, eating the young tree balsam rather than walk a mile to a house to get his meals.[26] He was considered to be of "unsound mind" by many of his neighbors long before the murder.[27]

The *Oregon Statesman* printed a long confession written by Wimple and given to the Polk County sheriff. Attached to the confession was a letter addressed to Wimple from his sister, Adeline Wood. She was looking forward to his return with his bride after being gone for ten years and informed him that his mother had died on July 19, 1852. Adeline didn't know her young sister-in-law was dead and her brother was sentenced to hang.

On October 8, 1852, Adam Wimple, commonly known to be "crazy as a bedbug", climbed the steps of the hangman's scaffold. He died 68 days after he killed Mary, the little 13-year-old bride, whom he loved more than "ten thousand thousand worlds".

References

1849 Map of Oregon Territory from Oregon State Archives, Salem, Oregon.

1850 Federal Census, Washington County, Oregon.

Helm, Mike, ed. *Conversations With Pioneer Women by Fred Lockley.* Eugene: Rainy Day Press, 1981.

The Morning Oregonian (Portland, Oregon) August 21, 1852, August 25, 1852, September 11, 1852, September 25, 1852, August 14, 1895.

Oregon Historical Quarterly, Vol. 61, 1960, p. 295.

Oregon Statesman (Oregon City, Oregon) August 14, 1852, September 1, 1852, September 11, 1852, October 9, 1852, October 24, 1852.

Polk County Land Claim Vol. 4, p. 305, Adam E. Wimple, May 22, 1847,
    Oregon State Archives, Salem, Oregon.
Polk County Observer (Dallas, Oregon) February 2, 1900.
Scott, Harvey. *History of the Oregon Country, Vol. II*. Cambridge: The
    Riverside Press, 1924.
Territory of Oregon v. Adam E. Wimple, Polk County Index, Case #14, Oregon
    State Archives, Salem, Oregon.
The Weekly Times (Portland, Oregon) July 31, 1852, September 11, 1852,
    September 18, 1852.

Chapter 4 notes

1 *Morning Oregonian* (Portland, Oregon) August 14, 1895.
2 1850 Federal Census, Washington County, Oregon. Oneida, New York became the home of the Oneida Community in 1848. It was the most extreme socialist/communist experiment that ever took place in the United States.
3 Polk County Land Claim, Vol. 4, p. 305, Adam E. Wimple, May 22, 1847, Oregon State Archives, Salem, Oregon.
4 *Oregon Statesman* (Oregon City, Oregon) September 11, 1852.
5 Harvey Scott, *History of the Oregon Country, Vol. II*, (Cambridge: The Riverside Press, 1924), p. 313.
6 Mike Helm, ed., *Conversations With Pioneer Women by Fred Lockley* (Eugene: Rainy Day Press, 1981) p. 10.
7 Ibid.
8 *Morning Oregonian*, September 25, 1852.
9 Ibid.
10 Ibid.
11 Ibid. "Cuckolding" was an extremely negative term meaning the wife had an affair with another man.
12 Ibid.
13 Ibid.
14 Ibid.
15 Ibid.
16 *Oregon Statesman*, September 1, 1852.
17 Ibid.
18 Violent crimes against women and children usually created great public animosity during this time in Oregon's history.
19 *Morning Oregonian*, September 11, 1852.
20 *Oregon Statesman*, September 11, 1852. Jurors named in the newspaper, while their occupations were found in the census.
21 *Morning Oregonian*, September 25, 1852.
22 Ibid.
23 Ibid. Here Judge Nelson emphasizes the nineteenth century concern for control over emotional excess. See Lawrence M. Friedman, *Crime and Punishment in American History*, (NY: Basic Books, 1993) p. 145.
24 *Morning Oregonian*, August 14, 1895.
25 Ibid.
26 Ibid. Tree balsam is the tender new growth under the bark of young saplings.
27 Harvey Scott, p. 313.

Chapter Five

Territory of Oregon v. Indian George and Indian Tom 1854

Hangings were not limited to white Oregon residents. The native Indian population soon experienced this new kind of death. In all but two isolated cases Indian hangings were part of general warfare between the new and the old residents.

For instance, on November 29, 1847, a group of frustrated Indians rushed the Whitman settlement and massacred Doctor and Mrs. Marcus Whitman and 11 other residents. Eventually, the Cayuse tribal leaders turned over five members of their own tribe to stand trial. On June 3, 1850 five Indians were hanged in Oregon City in retaliation for the Whitman Massacre.[1]

Two years later, in September 1852, the Modocs of the Klamath River basin massacred an emigrant train of sixty-five people. Four Modoc Indians were hanged on October 3, 1853, at Fort Klamath as a result of the Modoc War.

After the Modoc Indians were hanged trouble continued brewing in southern Oregon. News articles soon began appearing in Oregon like the following that was printed in the Oregon City *Spectator*.

The Indians in the Illinois Valley have been quite troublesome. Two men were shot on the Illinois River and one of them, Mr. Tedford, expired after three or four days (of) severe suffering. A Mr. Rouse was severely injured by a blow from an axe across the face, but I am informed he has nearly recovered. The Indians burned Miller's house some two weeks since, and made an attempt to burn Rhodes'. They shot some cattle on Peck's ranch and succeeded in driving off thirty or forty head of cattle and horses from the ranch owned by Mr. Mooney.

Much as we may deplore the fate of the Indians we are irresistibly impelled to the conclusion that nothing but the white man's arm felt in its power and vengeance will render our property and our lives safe in Northern California and Southern Oregon.[2]

The farmers of Oregon mostly honored the rights of the original inhabitants as the settlers expected to live in their homes with their families for many years. The miners had no such expectations. They weren't burdened with wives and children or thoughts of living in the area for the rest of their lives. The consequences of alienating the local Indians were considered minimal.[3] In December 1853, David Logan, a prominent lawyer and member of the Oregon Constitution Convention, faced no repercussions after raping an Indian woman on the main street of Jacksonville with a crowd of white men and women watching. The poor woman screamed for help the entire time.[4]

A month earlier several white men were killed, including two miners by the names of James Kyle and Richard Edwards. The killings weren't considered part of any specified Indian war, so are included here. The Modoc chiefs tried to appease the whites by offering up the offenders to white man's justice. Indian George, Indian Tom and probably Indian Thompson were brought to Jacksonville and arrested by Jackson County Sheriff Thomas Pyle.

Not many records remain documenting the hanging of Indian George and Indian Tom. The few records that remain suggest that a third Indian, only referred to as Indian Thompson, may also have been hanged at the same time.[5] The Jackson County court case files from that date have been lost, and the entries in the Judgment Book are ambiguous.

On Monday, February 6, 1854, the Jackson County grand jury presented a single combined indictment against both Indian Tom and Indian George for the murder of James C. Kyle committed a year earlier. The next day D. B. Brenan and P. P. Prim were appointed to defend the men and C. Sims was Jackson County's prosecuting attorney. Twelve local white men were chosen as jurors: S. D. VanDyke, Edward McCarty, Thomas Gregory, L. A. Davis, Robert Hargadine, A D. Lake, James Hamlin, Samuel Hall, Fredrick Alberdein, Fredrick Heber and Robert Hendersen.[6] Louis Denois and Mr. Culver were appointed language interpreters.

It took a full day to hear the testimony and reach a verdict. The next day the two (or three) men were sentenced to hang four days later on Friday, February 10, 1854. The Jacksonville Judgment Book reads as follows:

Courtesy Oregon State Archives
White Owl and Quit-A-Tumps were hanged in Pendleton in 1879.

You, Indian George, have been indicted and tried for one of the highest crimes known to our laws to wit, the crime of murder. You have had a fair and impartial trial as much as if you had belonged to our own race. You have had the benefit of counsel who did every thing for you that was possible, but an intelligent and upright jury upon a fair and dispassionate examination of the evidence given against you not only by those whom you supposed to be unfriendly towards your people but by the chiefs of your own tribe have found you, Indian George, guilty in manner and form as you stand indicted of having on the night of the seventh of October 1853 deliberately and with premeditated malice shot James C. Kyle and as there was no provocation on the part of Mr. Kyle which could justify you in the use of violence towards him they have said that you were guilty of murder in the first degree, an offence which by our laws is punishable with death.[8]

The judge's message only named Indian George although the grand jury indictment and formal sentencing document list both Indian George and Indian Tom.

A separate indictment appears on page 12 of the Jackson County Judgment Book against Indian Thompson although no sentence is recorded later. It's possible that Indian Tom and Indian Thompson are the same person because no separate trial records exist for Indian Tom. W. J. Plymale, an early Oregon newspaper columnist, wrote that United States Judge O. B. McFadden presided over the trial of Indian Tom and Tompson and only gave them three days from

25

conviction to execution of February 10.[9] He doesn't mention Indian George.

On Wednesday, February 8, 1854, a jury convicted Indian Thompson of killing Richard Edwards. Jurors who served at his trial were William Kahler, Fredrick Alberdein, A. D. Lake, George F. Vining, D. T. Cursey, Morris Howell, Samuel Hall, S. D. VanDyke, Robert Hendersen, Fredrick Heber, L. A. Davis and E. E. Gore.[10] Seven of the men served on both juries. The prosecution attorneys were paid $75 and the defense attorneys were paid $100.[11]

Jackson County Sheriff Thomas Pyle held the men in jail until the appointed day. Welborn Beeson, a resident of Jacksonville wrote about the hanging in his journal of February 11, 1854:

"I heard they hung three Indians at Jacksonville for killing a man of Shyle (Kyle) some three months ago. Most of our neighbors went to see them hung. I could not bear to see them hung, poor things".[12]

Clashes between the Indians and the settlers continued. Seven Indians were hanged in southern Oregon between 1853 and 1857.[13]

In 1858 Colonel Wright chased a group of Coeur d'Alene and Spokane Indians after they attacked a government pack train. After pursuing them up into Washington Territory, Wright captured them, held an immediate trial and sentenced them to death. They were executed by standing them in a cart, throwing a rope over a tree limb and hanging them.[14]

On October 3, 1873, four more Modoc Indians were hanged in Jacksonville according to the Portland *Oregonian* of October 6, 1873. The hangings didn't seem to have much impact on Oregon Indian activities because the Indian wars continued.

The proceedings of 1854 were almost exactly repeated in January 1879 when three Indians were hanged in Pendleton as a result of "Joseph's War".[15] White Owl and Quit-a-tumps were hanged for the murder of George Coogan, a prominent Portland resident. Aps, another Indian also convicted of murder, was hanged seven days later. The first two men admitted killing Coogan but Aps claimed to be innocent right up to the end. Their friend Yuma testified against his friends at the trial and betrayed them. Al Bunker, who was shot at the same time as Coggan identified White Owl as Coogan's killer. The jury deliberated for an hour before returning a guilty verdict. All three were reservation Indians who took part in the 1877 Indian War when nearly fifty white people were killed. The army arrested several of the tribal chieftains and held them hostage until the tribe surrendered the real culprits.

Umatilla County Sheriff John L. Sperry supervised the execution. Nearly 100 persons, including ten Indians, watched the hangings.

Frank C. Middleton (Mido), the *Oregonian* correspondent, returned to Portland with photographs of the hangings and the original hangman's noose used to end the life of White Owl.[16]

In most cases violence by the Indians was an attempt to defend their land and their way of life against invaders. The violence by the settlers against the Indians was used to subjugate and terrify the native population.[17] There were hundreds of Indians hanged, shot, beaten and starved to death all across Oregon between 1850 and 1900. Although the Indians were held accountable for any attacks on white settlers, there wasn't much justice for them if they were victims. During the 1870's there were twenty-eight Nez Perce killed by white men. Only one white man was ever indicted for murder.[18]

References

Daily Oregonian (Portland, Oregon) October 6, 1873, January 13, 1879, January 16, 1879, January 18, 1879, January 20, 1879, February 4, 1879.

The Daily Standard (Portland, Oregon) November 19, 1878.

Dicken, Samuel N. *The Making of Oregon: A Study in Historical Geography.* Portland: The Oregon Historical Society, 1979.

Douthit, Nathan. *Uncertain Encounters.* Corvallis, Oregon: Oregon State University, 2002.

Hegne, Barbara. *Settling The Rogue Valley–The Tough Times, The Forgotten People.* Medford: The Southern Oregon Historical Society, 1995.

Himes, George H. "Scrapbook #43", p. 18, Oregon Historical Society, Portland, Oregon.

Johnson, David A. *Founding the Far West: California, Oregon, and Nevada, 1840 1890.* Berkley: University of California Press, 1992.

Lavender, David. *Land of Giants.* Garden City: Doubleday, 1956.

Laythe, Joseph W. *Bandits and Badges: Crime and Punishment in Oregon, 1875–1915.* (A PhD. Dissertation, University of Oregon, 1996).

Oregon Spectator (Oregon City, Oregon) November 19, 1853, December 3, 1853.

Territory of Oregon v. Indian George and Indian Tom, Jackson County Judgment Book, February 6, 1854–February 9, 1854, pp. 10-13, Jackson County Courthouse, Medford, Oregon.

Territory of Oregon v. Indian Thompson, Jackson County Judgment Book, February 8, 1854.

Chapter 5 notes

1 Fred Leeson, *Rose City Justice* (Portland: OHS Press, 1998), p. 9. Leeson gives the date of the hanging as June 6, 1850. Rev. H. K. Hines, the author of *The History of Oregon*, (Chicago: The Lewis Publishing Co., 1893), gives the date of the hanging as June 3, 1850.

1 *Oregon Spectator* (Oregon City, Oregon) December 3, 1853.

2 Samuel N. Dicken, *The Making of Oregon: A Study in Historical Geography* (Portland: The Oregon Historical Society, 1982) p. 90.

3 David A. Johnson, *Founding the Far West: California, Oregon, and Nevada, 1840–1890* (Berkeley: University of California Press, 1992), p. 426.

4 Bert and Margie Webber, *Jacksonville, Oregon: The Making of a National Historic Landmark* (Fairfield: YeGalleon, 1982) pp. 117-18.

5 Territory of Oregon v. Indian George and Indian Tom, Jackson County Judgment Book, February 6, 1854, pp. 10–12, Jackson County Courthouse, Medford, Oregon.

6 Bert and Margie Webber, p. 14.

7 Territory of Oregon v. Indian George and Indian Tom.

8 George H. Himes. "Scrapbook #43", p. 18, Oregon Historical Society, Portland, Oregon.

9 Territory of Oregon v. Indian Thompson, Jackson County Judgment Book, February 8, 1854, pp. 12 - 13, Jackson County Courthouse, Medford, Oregon.

10 Barbara Hegne, *Settling The Rogue Valley–The Tough Times, The Forgotten People* (Medford: The Southern Oregon Historical Society, 1995) p. 12.

11 Ibid.

12 Nathan Douthit, *Uncertain Encounters* (Corvallis: Oregon State University Press, 2002) p. 166.

13 David Lavender, *Land of Giants* (Garden City: Doubleday, 1956) p. 315.

14 Joseph W. Laythe, *Bandits and Badges: Crime and Punishment in Oregon, 1875-1915* (A Dissertation, University of Oregon, 1996) p. 140.

15 *Daily Oregonian* (Portland, Oregon) February 4, 1879. No record remains of the mentioned photo-graph.

16 David Peterson del Mar, *Beaten Down: A History of Interpersonal Violence In the West* (Seattle: University of Washington Press, 2002) p. 30.

17 David Lavender, p. 368. He has the most inclusive summary of Indian hangings that I've been able to find. See in particular Chapter Four, "Pangs of Adjustment" and Chapter Five, "Extravaganza".

Chapter Six

Territory of Oregon v. Charles John Roe 1859

At a time when superlatives were standard in newspapers, the words "atrocious murder" hardly raised an eyebrow. However, the C. John Roe case was indeed an incredibly appalling and "atrocious murder".

Charles John Roe was an employee of the Hudson Bay Company and arrived in the Oregon Territory about 1834. He was one of thirty white men living in Oregon in 1838. Roe was thrilled when the Methodist Missionary, Jason Lee, arrived because he could then marry Nancy McKay, the half-breed daughter of Captain Thomas McKay.[1] So on July 16, 1837, a triple wedding was held when Jason Lee married Anna Marie Pittman, Cyrus Shepard married Susan Downing and Charles Roe married Nancy. Records are unclear but he had at least one child with his first wife.[2]

After the Hudson Bay Company left the Oregon Territory, the trappers who remained established a defined and culturally homogenous community in Marion County. The families were united by nationality, language, religion and blood.[3] In 1856, after his first wife died, John Roe married Angelica Carpentier and had a child a year later.[4] Angelica was the orphaned daughter of Charles Carpentier, a French trapper, and an Indian mother. She and her sister, Sophia, were placed in the Methodist Mission School near Salem for several years when their mother died. After leaving the mission Angelique seems to have had a number of lovers or husbands. The *Oregonian* reported "she had lived with a Negro and a Kanaka and had children by both."[5]

Angelica's niece and her husband, W. B. Cook, were visiting the couple the evening of February 11, 1859.[6] Roe was especially jealous of his beautiful wife that night and accused her of having an affair with another man. She denied it, saying that it was "a lie and he could not prove it". Roe flicked his pocketknife open, grabbed her hair with his right hand, tipped her head back and slashed her throat from ear to ear. Their two-year old son was sitting in his mother's lap and was deluged in hot red blood. Instantly Angelica leaped out of her chair, opened the front door and a few moments later died in the street.

Roe didn't try to escape. He was arrested by Deputy Sheriff Chandler, put in irons and locked up in the new Marion County jail. The next morning Chandler brought Roe to John Boon's store where Justice of the Peace Purdy publicly questioned him.[7] Roe acknowledged killing his wife, saying, "He loved his wife as he did his own soul, and he had killed her to keep anyone else from enjoying her."[8]

After confessing he climbed into bed, asked people to leave him alone and went to sleep. The guard noted that he seemed to sleep soundly with little concern for his child or his dead wife.

Judge Reuben Boise presided at the trial on February 24, 1859 and heard Roe's confession read in open court.[9] He sentenced Roe to hang on Saturday, April 2, 1859.[10] The scaffold was built next to the jail door facing Church Street. It was estimated that between 800 and 1,500 people showed up that Saturday afternoon.[11] Many of them were women and children.

Roe's defiance had evaporated by the day of his execution and he made a very repentant speech to the audience. Between the time of the murder and his execution he was baptized and proclaimed his religious conversion. Reverend William Roberts and Reverend A. F. Waller walked with the condemned man up on the gallows platform. Speaking in an audible but firm voice Roe gave his farewell speech. He told the audience that he anticipated a heavenly pardon and recognized that he had been "a hell-deserving sinner for a long time before I committed this deed for which I am about to suffer."[12]

Marion County Sheriff Narcisse A. Cornoyer pulled the pin unlocking the floor of the gallows at 12:12 p.m., an hour after they first mounted the scaffold, and finally put an end to the entertainment. Roe was the first man hanged in Oregon after it became a state on February 14, 1859.

References

1842 Oregon State Census, Oregon State Archives, Salem, Oregon.

1850 Federal Census, Washington County, Oregon.

Bowen, William. *The Willamette Valley: Migration and Settlement on the Oregon Frontier*. Seattle: University of Washington Press, 1978.

Carey, Charles H. *A General History of Oregon*. Portland, Binfords & Mort, 1922. pp. 292-3.

Maxwell, Ben. "Frontier Hangings Were Gala Occasions in Salem." *Capital Journal* (Salem, Oregon), January 30, 1952.

Oregonian (Portland, Oregon) February 19, 1859.

Oregon Inhabitants Prior to 1839, www.oregonpioneers.com

Peterson, David. "Eden Defiled: A History of Violence Against Wives In Oregon." A Dissertation (unpublished), Department of History, University of Oregon, June 1993. Located at the Oregon State Archives, Salem, Oregon

Salem Statesman (Salem, Oregon) January 30, 1952.

Territory of Oregon v. Charles J. Rowe, Marion County Circuit Court Register and Fee Book, 1849-1890, Journal Book 2, pp. 345–6, Oregon State Archives, Salem, Oregon.

Chapter 6 notes

1 Thomas McKay was the stepson of John McLoughlin, the most powerful man in Oregon at this time. His mother, Marguerite McKay, was the widow of Alexander McKay and daughter of a Swiss trader and a Cree Indian mother. Thomas worked for his stepfather and became a famous trapper and scout. (p.119) Three of McKay's sons accompanied Jason Lee back east in 1838. (p. 193). See *Land of Giants* by David Lavender. (Garden City, N.Y.: Doubleday, 1956).

2 1842 Oregon State Census: Charles Rowe–2 males over 18, 2 females over 18, 1 child, 85 acres under improvement, 100 bushels of wheat in 1842, 60 bushels of grain in 1842, 9 horses, 9 neat stock, 0 sheep, 10 hogs.

3 William Bowen, *The Willamette Valley* (Seattle: University of Washington Press, 1978), p. 43.

4 *Salem Statesman* (Salem, Oregon) January 30, 1952.

5 Oregon Inhabitants Prior to 1839, www.oregonpioneers.com.

6 1860 Marion County Census lists the following: W. B. Cook, age 36, b. MO, carpenter, wife- L. (Indian) b. Oregon; L. A. age 15, male b. VA; M. J. age 12, male b. W.T.; H. A. age 8, male b. Oregon; C. L. age 6, male, b. Oregon; W. A. age 3, male b. Oregon.

7 *Oregonian* (Portland, Oregon) February 19, 1859.

8 Ibid.

9 In 1858 Reuben Boise was elected circuit court judge and continued to serve in various judicial and legal capacities until he retired in 1904. His courtroom sentences carried ten men to the gallows.

10 Territory of Oregon v. Charles J. Rowe, Marion County Circuit Court Register and Fee Book, 1849-1890, Journal Book 2, pp. 345-6, Oregon State Archives, Salem, Oregon.

11 *Salem Statesman*, January 30, 1952.

12 Ibid.

Chapter Seven

Territory of Oregon v. Danford Balch 1859

The story of Danford Balch begins on October 1, 1850, when he and his wife, Mary Jane, settled on a 345.92-acre donation land claim situated in what is now the Willamette Heights district of Portland. By 1858 they had become the parents of nine children, ages 16 years to 15 months—Anna, Hosea, Thomas, Emma Caroline, John, Danford Jr., Louis, Celestia and Celinda.[1]

To help with the farm work a young man named Mortimer Stump lived with the family. He and the oldest daughter, Anna, took a liking to each other and Mortimer asked her father if they could get married. Balch was disgusted with the idea and kicked the young man out of his house. Against Balch's wishes the two young people eloped across the Columbia River to what is now Vancouver, Washington. It's unclear why Balch disliked Stump so much.

Two weeks later, on November 18, 1858, Balch was drinking in downtown Portland and ran into Mortimer Stump, Ad Stump, and Stump's father outside Starr's Tin Shop.[2] After exchanging nasty words with each other, Balch took his double-barreled shotgun and followed the men to the Stark Street ferry where the Stump family was loading a wagon full of supplies. No bridges crossed the Willamette in 1858 but Jimmy Stephens provided regular ferry service.[3]

Danford Balch's drinking impaired his memory of that day, but the description he gave of his emotional, physical and psychological state sounded more like a man describing the loss of a lover than a daughter. Perhaps that explains what happened next. Balch saw his lost daughter standing on the ferry and he headed around the wagon toward her. Whether he was being threatened or fired accidentally is hard to know, but a few minutes later Mortimer Stump was dead with a load of buckshot in his face and neck.

Balch was held in the Multnomah County Jail without bail until April 28, 1859, when he escaped with three other prisoners. He was re-arrested at his own house by Portland City Marshal J. H. Lappeus on July 23, 1859.[4]

On August 17, 1859, the district court was convened and a trial was held with Judge A. E. Wait presiding.[5] The firm of David Logan and Williams represented the defense. Colonel Kelly assisted Mr. Douthitt, the district attorney. The trial lasted four days until Balch was found guilty and sentenced to hang on Monday, October 17, 1859.[6]

Multnomah County Sheriff Addison M. Starr erected the gallows in an open area on Front and Salmon Streets. Danford Balch, age 39, died on a wet dreary Monday morning at 11 a.m. while 500–600 witnesses watched, including the entire Stump family.[7] It was a come one, come all affair. No effort was made to shield the event from innocent eyes. Some sources say his daughter, the young Widow Stump, watched her father hang. The *Weekly Oregon* published Balch's confession on October 22, 1859. Doctor A. M. Loryea, a partner in the Hawthorne Insane Asylum, pronounced Balch dead.[8]

Balch tried to make certain his children received their share of his land after his death. By a series of legal shenanigans on the part of their mother, her new husband, John A. Confer, and their guardian, C. S. Silver, four of the children lost that inheritance. The children's portion of Balch's estate was sold to John H. Mitchell. It wasn't until June 25, 1883, that the Oregon Supreme Court restored the land to four of the children: Emma, John, Danford Jr. and Louis.[9] The other four had signed their rights away before the court's decision was handed down.

References

1850 Federal Census, Washington County, Oregon.

Hazen, David W. "When Portland Staged Its First Legal Hanging." *Oregonian* (Portland, Oregon) August 14, 1938.

Himes, George. Scrapbook #21, p. 85, Oregon Historical Society, Portland, Oregon.

Humbird, Jim. "When Hangings Were A Major Pastime." *Weekly Oregonian* (Portland, Oregon) September 3, 1939.

Lambert, Francis. Sheriff of Multnomah County, Oregon, letter of February 9, 1962.

Miller, Edward M. "That Was An Eventful Day in Portland." *Oregon Journal* (Portland, Oregon) January 26, 1958.

Oregon Journal (Portland, Oregon) January 16, 1949.

Pement, Jack. "A Hanging Matter." *Oregon Journal* (Portland, Oregon) November 14, 1975.

Sentinel (Jacksonville, Oregon) January 28, 1860.

Scott, Harvey W. *History of the Oregon Country, Vol. III.* Cambridge: Riverside Press, 1924.

State of Oregon v. Danford Balch, Multnomah County Journal Book 1, Case #817, p. 150, August 20, 1869, Portland, Oregon.

Swing, William, "Willamette Heights Pioneer Was Hanged As Murderer." *Oregonian* (Portland, Oregon) October 15, 1961.

Weekly Oregonian (Portland, Oregon) November 20, 1858, July 2, 1859, July 30, 1859, August 27, 1859, October 15, 1859, October 22, 1859.

Chapter 7 notes

1 1850 Federal Census, Washington County, Oregon. And Harvey W. Scott, *History of the Oregon Country, Vol. III* (Cambridge: The Riverside Press) 1924, p. 352.

2 *Weekly Oregonian* (Portland, Oregon) October 22, 1859.

3 James B. Stephens began operating the Stark Street Ferry in the early 1850's. He sold the ferry to Joseph Knott in 1861. Percy Maddux, *City on The Willamette* (Portland: Binfords & Mort, 1965) p. 175.

4 *Weekly Oregonian*, July 30, 1859.

5 *Weekly Oregonian*, August 27, 1859.

6 State of Oregon v. Danford Balch, Multnomah County Journal Book 1, Case #817, p. 150, August 20, 1859, Portland, Oregon.

7 William Swing, "Willamette Heights Pioneer Was Hanged As Murderer" *Oregonian*, October 15, 1961.

8 George Himes, Scrapbook #21, p. 85, Oregon Historical Society, Portland, Oregon.

9 Harvey W. Scott, *History of the Oregon Country, Vol. III* (Cambridge: Riverside Press, 1924) p. 352.

Chapter Eight

State of Oregon v. Matthew Moss 1860

Matthew Moss was a 28-year-old bachelor who lived with another bachelor, George Brown, near present day Falls City and worked at Sharp's sawmill about eight miles southwest from Dallas on the Luckiamute River.

Just a gunshot's distance away was the cabin belonging to Mr. and Mrs. George Harper. Mrs. Harper had left the area for several months but recently had returned. She complained to her husband that Matthew Moss's disagreeable attentions had caused her to leave and she wanted her husband to do something about it when she came back.

On Thursday night, January 12, 1860, several men were gathered at Samuel Gothard's cabin, which was also nearby, when Harper confronted Moss about "interfering" with his wife. Harper pulled a gun and ordered Moss to leave.[1] Moss left quietly, but stopped at another neighbor's cabin and asked to borrow a gun so he could go hunting the next day. Instead of going home he turned around carrying his new weapon and walked back to Gothard's cabin. He spotted Harper through the window, took aim and shot him dead.

Moss was feared by everyone in the neighborhood and considered a desperate and dangerous character. Some neighbors were convinced he had killed another man in the South before coming to Oregon.[2] Because of his neighbor's fears he wasn't arrested until a warrant was issued on Friday morning. Sheriff James S. Holman and a large group of men got together, rode out to his cabin and arrested him.

The grand jury returned an indictment against Moss on January 12, 1860, with a charge of first-degree murder. Robert Burns and E.

W. Evertz filed the original complaint charging Moss with Harper's murder. Benjamin Whiteaker was the grand jury foreman.[3]

Three material witnesses, Charles Sterns, John Holdridge, and Robert Burns paid a bond of $100 each to be released until the trial. Other witnesses called to testify were Elizabeth Shirley, John Thorp, William Ford, Joseph Smith, Mr. and Mrs. William Willis, E. W. Evertz, Wilson Lee, Robert Farley and J. B. Sytes.[4] The trial was held February 6 with Judge Reuben Boise presiding, James Nesmith, and Wilson prosecuting, and Hayden defending. The jury found Moss guilty of first-degree murder within a few minutes after leaving the courtroom.

While waiting for his execution he made good use of his time by writing his autobiography with the hope that someone would publish it after his death. Crime pamphlets extolling young men to live lawfully and claiming repentance were moneymaking propositions in 1860.

On Tuesday, March 20, 1860, Matthew Moss marched to the gallows accompanied by Polk County Sheriff James Holman and two clergymen. About 1,200 spectators surrounded the scaffold and gathered together to hear his confession.[5] The official witnesses were John Sheldon, John O. Shelton, Jackson Lovelady, John Hines, James Townsend, and Clark Gest.[6]

Moss fulfilled his audience's expectations with a speech full of repentance and guilty admissions. He confessed to a life full of villainy and misdeeds, killing Harper, and assassinating a man in Kentucky. He met his death quietly with the hope of reaching heaven after exhorting his listeners to view his body after death and "to profit by the exhibitions of the results of his crimes".[7]

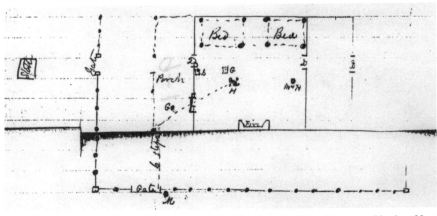

Trial record, State of Oregon v. Matthew Moss

Floor plan of Gothard's cabin, where Moss shot Harper.

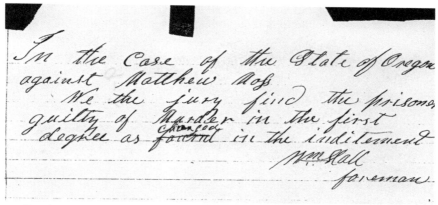

Jury's verdict in State of Oregon v. Matthew Moss, Polk County, 1860.

References

1860 Federal Census, Polk County, Oregon, Mortality Schedule.

McArthur, Scott. "Greed and Sex Lead to Six Hangings in County." *Great Events II*, Special Edition of Polk County History by *Sun-Enterprise* Newspaper, Monmouth, Oregon. Craig Lockwood, Editor.

Oregon Argus (Oregon City, Oregon) January 18, 1860, March 31, 1860.

Polk County Circuit Court Index, Oregon State Archives, Salem, Oregon.

Sentinel (Jacksonville, Oregon) January 28, 1860.

State of Oregon v. Matthew Moss, Polk County Circuit Court Case File #325, Oregon State Archives, Salem, Oregon.

Statesman (Salem, Oregon) January 17, 1860, January 24, 1860, February 14, 1860, March 20, 1860, 27 March 1860.

Weekly Oregonian, (Portland, Oregon) March 27, 1860, March 31, 1860.

Chapter 8 notes

1 *Statesman* (Salem, Oregon) 17 January 1860.
2 Ibid.
3 State of Oregon v. Matthew Moss, Polk County Circuit Court Case File #325, Oregon State Archives, Salem, Oregon.
4 Ibid.
5 *Statesman*, March 27, 1860.
6 State of Oregon v. Matthew Moss.
7 *Weekly Oregonian* (Portland, Oregon) March 27, 1860.

Chapter Nine

State of Oregon v. William Casterlin 1860

On December 3, 1859, William Casterlin, a 42-year-old cooper (a maker of wooden barrels) from Illinois, returned from Jacksonville to the house he shared with Samuel Mooney, his partner.[1] Hiram Abbott and Doctor George Elliott came with him. Mooney and Casterlin had come to Oregon together, served together in the Indian Wars and up to that day were the best of friends. After drinking together all evening, Mooney and Casterlin started arguing. While Abbott and Elliott tried to defuse the situation, Mooney left the house and Casterlin became so enraged that he grabbed a gun and fired out the door after him. When the men went outside they found Mooney's body lying on the ground. He had been shot between the eyes.

Only 51 years old, Mooney left three children in Wapato County, Iowa. His only heirs were his wife, who had left him to live with another man, and his children: Merrit, Jack and Elizabeth, who married Andrew Gibson.[2] Besides his personal possessions, only worth $68.13, he had a note worth $794.50, dated November 7, 1857, against the U. S. government for supplies sold to the Second Regiment Oregon Mounted Volunteers and the Ninth Regiment Oregon Mounted Militia army garrisons. Mooney had come to Oregon sometime between 1853 and 1855 and settled on a donation land claim near Deer Creek (later named Roseburg) in Douglas County. Later he sold the land, served in the Indian wars of 1855 as a mounted volunteer in Captain O'Neal's Company E, and moved to Jackson County.[3]

The Corvallis editor of the *Weekly Union* was quite adamant in demanding something be done about all the murders occurring in Oregon:

> *Murders are becoming rampant in the southern portion of our state, as well as in the north. Life is held entirely too cheap on the Pacific coast, and it requires at the hands of our courts the adoption of some means to prevent the destruction of human life.*[4]

When he wasn't drinking William Casterlin was such a pleasant fellow that he became a favorite of the Jackson County jailors. The grand jury met on Monday, March 26, 1860, and voted to indict Casterlin for first-degree murder.

Judge P. P. Prim ruled over the trial on March 28. H. G. Burnett was the prosecuting attorney while William G. T'Vault and B. F. Dowell served as Casterlin's defense attorneys. The twelve jurors appointed to hear the trial were Joshua Kellison, Bennett Million, F. M. Chapman, Morgan W. Davis, Samuel Williams, Lafayette Gall, Joseph H. Davis, E. Dillette (also spelled E. Dillett and C. E. Tillette), George W. Walker, John L. Carter, Daniel Rathbun and Thomas Pyle (the ex-county sheriff who hanged Indian George and Indian Tom in 1854). After a protracted deliberation they brought back a verdict of "guilty of first-degree murder."[5] The court also imposed a judgment against Casterlin's land, goods, and chattels for the cost and expenses of the trial. The public sale netted $497.50 used to pay for his burial and his living expenses while in jail.[6]

After he was convicted of first-degree murder the execution date was set for Friday, May 11, 1860.[7] Meanwhile Jackson County Sheriff Legrand J. C. Duncan held Casterlin in the Jacksonville Jail.

Friends and neighbors of Casterlin petitioned Governor John Whiteaker for a reprieve, but he refused to sign the order changing the verdict to life imprisonment.[8] While some wanted Casterlin to go to prison, others felt differently. The *Oregon Argus* in Oregon City printed a letter from a correspondent from Jackson County:

> *. . . some are trying to have his sentence commuted, as was done with Bowen. But I trust they will not succeed, for the evidence is too plain for any other punishment than death. It seems to me that the people here are rather tenderhearted in punishing crime. Frankly yours, H-D-K.*[9]

At 11:30 a.m. on May 11, the condemned man was escorted from the jail to the waiting gallows. Reverend Driver gave a short sermon and led the audience in singing a hymn. Casterlin stepped forward and calmly confessed to a life of sin and abuse of "spirituous drink" and wished his audience to shun the evil way, which had led him to his unfortunate fate. He remembered nothing from the afternoon before the shooting until he woke up in jail the day after the shooting. In the same calm manner he had displayed all through the arrest, trial and incarceration, he talked directly to the crowd saying that he hoped all would learn from his terrible example.

Ten minutes after climbing the steps, at exactly 11:20 p.m., Sheriff Duncan pulled the black cap over the prisoner's head, tied his arms and legs together, and flipped the trapdoor pin.[10] There was a horrible writhing and heaving of the body for several minutes as the man struggled to breathe. The hanging was such a sad affair one of the sheriff's deputies nearly fainted.[11]

References

1860 Federal Census, Jackson County, Oregon.

Hegne, Barbara. *Settling The Rogue Valley – The Tough Times, The Forgotten People*. Medford: The Southern Oregon Historical Society, 1995.

Jackson County Probate Records, Samuel Mooney Case #0772, August 8, 1861, Oregon State Archives, Salem, Oregon.

Oregon Argus (Oregon City, Oregon) May 12, 1860.

Oregon Statesman (Salem, Oregon) March 20, 1860, April 17, 1860, May 1, 1860, May 22, 1860, May 29, 1860.

State of Oregon v. William Casterlin, Jackson County Journal Book, March 26, 1860 – May 11, 1860, pp. 118, 128, 130, 150, 158, Jackson County Courthouse, Medford, Oregon.

Weekly Union (Corvallis, Oregon) December 12, 1859, May 22, 1860.

Chapter 9 notes

1 1860 Federal Census, Jackson County, Oregon.

2 Jackson County Probate File, Samuel Mooney, #0772, August 8, 1861, Oregon State Archives, Salem, Oregon.

3 Barbara Hegne, *Settling the Rogue Valley – The Tough Times, The Forgotten People*, Eagle Point, Oregon (Medford: The Southern Oregon Historical Society, 1995) pp. 43-44.

4 *Weekly Union*, 1December 12, 1859.

5 State of Oregon v. William Casterlin, Jackson County Journal Book, March 26, 1860–May 11, 1860, pp. 128, 130, Jackson County Courthouse, Medford, Oregon.

6 Barbara Hegne, p. 44.

7 *Oregon Statesman* (Salem, Oregon) May 1, 1860.

8 *Oregon Statesman*, May 22, 1860. The newspaper doesn't give the reason why Gov. Whiteaker refused to grant the reprieve. Information about this case is extremely sparse.

9 *Oregon Argus* (Oregon City, Oregon) May 12, 1860.

10 *Weekly Union*, May 22, 1860.

11 *Oregon Statesman*, May 29, 1860.

Chapter Ten
State of Oregon v. Phillip George 1860

Corvallis was a small but growing farm community in 1860 with a large German population. Two German residents, Phillip George, about 50 years old, and his partner, John Clark, had moved to Corvallis eight months earlier from Jackson County. They bought an old home and opened a boarding house and horse stable, which they named "American House". Clark was responsible for overall management of the enterprise and George was responsible for the cooking.[1]

The three-year partnership wasn't a happy one. The partners were constantly fighting—usually about money. Over time, the disagreements got more and more violent. On Sunday, May 10, 1860, their final fight ended in death.[2]

George had spent all day partying and getting drunk until he passed out, so at two o'clock in the afternoon when Ulrey woke him up because he needed to get his horse, he was suffering from a nasty hangover. Going out to the stable he found teamsters William Preston and Despain buying hay from John Clark. Apparently, George didn't want Clark to sell the hay and the partners got into a fistfight. The two men knocked each other around and scuffled in the barn and barnyard. Clark died a few minutes later as he staggered from the barn to the house porch. Witnesses were shocked over George's refusal to fetch a doctor, and his total indifference over Clark's death.

"The damned cuss ought to die!" George declared and calmly pulled Clark's pocketbook out of his pants and took out the money. "It's partnership money and I'm entitled to it."

Phillip George was arrested and the Benton County Coroner, Doctor T. J. Right, held an immediate inquest. It was difficult to tell what caused Clark's death because there was no evidence of obvious violence on the body. The next day, Sunday, May 11, Doctors Coombs, Hayley and McAffee performed an autopsy, and finally determined that Clark had died from a head wound—probably from a small rock thrown by George.

Doctor Right was named administrator of Clark's estate while M. Stock, A. Roberts and Lemuel A. Classe were appointed to appraise his property. According to the property appraisal on file all he owned was one change of clothes, a watch and a small journal worth a total of $22.00.[3]

The Benton County District Attorney J. Q. Thornton immediately charged George with first-degree murder. The foreman of the grand jury, Lemuel A. Clark, signed the indictment on April 11, 1860.

George's trial was held in Benton County Circuit Court on April 4 when he was convicted of first-degree murder and sentenced to hang on May 25, 1860.[4] The Honorable R. E. Stratton was the presiding judge. Five witnesses testified: N. P. Briggs, William Preston, Doctor J. R. Hayley, Doctor J. S. Coombs and Doctor T. J. Right.[5] By 1860 Benton County had a jail built to house their criminals and George was held there under tight security until the assigned day arrived.

On May 25, 1860, George mounted the scaffold and bravely faced from 1,500 to 2,000 spectators who had gathered to hear his dying speech.[6] Just as he finished declaring his innocence in very broken English with a heavy German accent and stepped forward to face his death, Sheriff Sheldon B. Fargo made a surprise announcement. Governor John Whiteaker had refused to sign a petition commuting George's sentence to life imprisonment, but did grant him a thirty-day reprieve—enough time for the Supreme Court to hear his plea for a new trial.[7] Unfortunately, the reprieve still needed to be signed by the Secretary of State, Lucien Heath, in Salem—a round trip of sixty-five miles from Corvallis, or six hours of hard horseback riding. Unwilling to make the decision on his own whether to honor the not-quite-legal reprieve or to ignore it and hang George anyway, the sheriff asked the audience to vote.[8] It must have been an excruciating few minutes as the condemned man listened to people debating his fate. Instead of going forward with the hanging, human compassion prevailed and George was taken back to the jail.

On June 15, 1860, the Corvallis *Weekly Union* published George's entire scaffold speech given a month earlier and J. Q. Thorton's reply. Thorton was the Benton County District Attorney and was furious after George's speech:

Having as counsel for the State prosecuted the prisoner, and made myself thoroughly acquainted with all the circumstances and direct facts giving an irresistible strength to the conviction that the killing was deliberate, premeditated and malicious, I was appalled as I stood there in the shadow of the apparatus of death and heard him uttering his slanders with a countenance which seemed to radiate falsehood and every feature of which was in contradiction.[9]

Twenty-eight days later the court upheld the conviction and another date was set for George's execution. At noon on Friday, June 22, 1860, Phillip George was driven in an open wagon from the jail to the site of his death, and again climbed the scaffold steps.[10] Reverends Rayner and Avery accompanied him. This time he faced a smaller crowd, which also included a great number of women and children. Benton County Sheriff Fargo stood beside him ready to put George's head in the noose. Just before George's hands were tied he handed a package to the sheriff to deliver to a friend in Albany. He gave another long speech declaring his innocence, his conversion to Christianity and begging people not to scorn his 16 year-old son. Showing the same brave calm exhibited during his trial, Phillip George stepped into death, breaking his neck as the rope jerked tight.[11] He hanged from the scaffold for twenty-five minutes before Doctor Right and Doctor McAfee pronounced him dead.[12]

The gallows at the end of Second Street remained standing for years until finally weather and time eventually eroded the sad reminder.

References

Benton County Probate File, John Clark, #0085, May 7, 1860, Oregon State Archives, Salem, Oregon.

Oregon Argus (Oregon City, Oregon) March 17, 1860.

Oregon Democrat (Albany, Oregon) July 3, 1860.

Oregon Statesman (Salem, Oregon) March 20, 1860, April 24, 1860, May 29, 1860, June 6, 1860, June 26, 1860, July 3, 1860.

Oregonian (Portland, Oregon) March 17, 1860, July 3, 1860.

State of Oregon v. Phillip George, Benton County Circuit Court Case file #282, Oregon State Archives, Salem, Oregon.

Weekly Union (Corvallis, Oregon) March 13, 1860, May 22, 1860, May 29, 1860, June 5, 1860, June 26, 1860.

Chapter 10 notes

1 *Weekly Union* (Corvallis, Oregon) March 13, 1860.
2 *Oregon Statesman* (Salem, Oregon) March 20, 1860.
3 Benton County Probate File, John Clark, #0085, May 7, 1860, Oregon State Archives, Salem, Oregon.
4 State of Oregon v. Phillip George, Benton County Circuit Court Case File #282, Oregon State Archives, Salem, Oregon.
5 State of Oregon v. Phillip George.
6 *Weekly Union* (Corvallis, Oregon) May 29, 1860. The *Oregon Statesman* of May 29, 1860 says that "1200 persons were present–300 females".
7 *Oregon Statesman*, June 6, 1860.
8 *Weekly Union*, May 29, 1860.
9 *Weekly Union*, June 5, 1860.
10 *Weekly Union*, June 26, 1860.
11 *Oregon Statesman*, June 26, 1860.
12 State of Oregon v. Phillip George.

Chapter Eleven

State of Oregon v. Andrew J. Pate 1862

M urder Creek, three miles north of Albany in Linn County, got its name from an incident that happened on February 8, 1862.[1] The Robert Conn family heard a shot and a man shouting. When they went to investigate, they found the body of George Lamb floating in the water. It was easy to track the murderer by following his footsteps in the snow.

Andrew J. Pate was found in Albany wearing one of his own shoes and one of Lamb's. Apparently, Lamb had been a very industrious and prudent young man. He had saved nearly $500 (a great deal of money in 1862) and was getting ready to propose to a local young lady.[2] Pate wanted Lamb's money and his girl, so he killed him.

A hearing was held on Tuesday, April 8, 1862, in Linn County Circuit Court where Pate entered a plea of "not guilty". The firm of Thornton & Powell represented Pate and J. G. Wilson was the prosecuting attorney for the county. The trial started on Thursday, April 10. Twelve good and lawful men were sworn in as jurors—Levi Douglas, J. A. Dunlap, W. N. Gotha, James Keeny, W. R. Kirk, Miller Morgan, David Myers, T. M. A. G. Parrish, William Steele, Jonathan Wassom, E. L. Watter, and Jefferson Huff, foreman.[3] The jury found the defendant guilty of murder in the first degree. He was sentenced to hang on Tuesday, May 27, 1862.[4]

In an ironic footnote to history, Pate's lawyers were awarded all his stolen money and personal property by order of Judge Reuben Boise on April 12, 1862.[5]

After the trial an enterprising newspaperman, George N. Spears, persuaded Pate to tell him about the murder and had the resulting confession printed by A. L. Stinson and P. W. Haley in Albany. Crime pamphlets were very popular on the east coast and usually included the murder's confession, a short biography and occasionally a minister's execution sermon. Even on the Oregon frontier readers were curious about the killer's background, motives and emotions. Besides serving as editorial exhortations against the evil life, the pamphlets often used bloody descriptions to fascinate their readers.[6]

Pate's confession is a prime example of a typical crime pamphlet. It mentions very little about the actual murder, but does give a profound view of life as experienced by an unskilled and self-serving young man in the middle 1800s. He was born in Nashville, Tennessee in 1834 and ran away from an abusive drunken father at age twelve. For the next eight years he wandered around the Midwest, usually chopping wood, but rarely working for more than a few months at any location. Every job ended with Pate being cheated, getting in a fight or being abused by someone. In 1854, at age 20, he met up with a group of young men headed to California and joined the westward migration. His California mining experience was a litany of catastrophes. Eventually, he wandered north and by 1861 landed in Winchester, Oregon with David Owens, John Winship and George Lamb. Pate and Lamb heard about a job in Albany and continued heading north. They joined Henry Pratt and Peter Settle cutting logs into rails for fences and boarded with the Crow family.

After a series of quarrels with Lamb (none of which were Pate's fault), Pate shot his friend in the back, cut his throat and tried to hide the body in Murder Creek. Linn County Deputy Sheriff Looney C. Bond arrested him a few hours later in Albany at the shoe shop. The printed confession served as Pate's memorial, a testament blaming everyone in the world, except himself, for the consequences he faced.[7]

Two thousand people crowded around the gallows on May 27.[8] Like a king attending a coronation, Pate rode in a carriage from the jail to the site and waved to everyone he saw. After leaving the carriage escorted by Linn County Sheriff Timothy A. Riggs, Pate shook hands with various friends and walked slowly down the aisle that opened ahead of him. The six-foot drop came at 12:54 p.m. and Pate died instantly. His body hung for 25 minutes before being cut down and buried.

Andrew J. Pate was the first man hanged in Linn County.[9]

References

Belknap Collection, "A Rare Pamphlet of Pate's Confession," in vault at Oregon Historical Society, Portland, Oregon.

"Confession of Andrew J. Pate, the murderer of George Lamb and two others who was executed at Albany, Oregon on Tuesday the 27th day of May 1862. I, Andrew J. Pate, do certify that I have read my confession after it was placed in type and that the same has been truly and correctly given in print as originally written by Mr. George N. Spears and narrated to him by myself. This 27th day of May 1862, witnesses Looney C. Bond and Newton Bond, Albany, Oregon, and printed by A. L. Stinson and P. W. Haley, 1862."

Harrison, Glenn. *Linn County Historical Society Newsletter*, March 2001.

McArthur, Lewis A. *Oregon Geographic Names*. Portland: Oregon Historical Society, 1974.

"Oregon Geographic Names." *Oregon Historical Quarterly*, Vol. 46.

Oregonian (Portland, Oregon) February 12, 1862.

State of Oregon v. Andrew J. Pate, Linn County Circuit Court Journal, Vol. 2, pp. 31, 39, 40, 46, Oregon State Archives, Salem, Oregon.

Weekly Oregon Statesman, (Salem, Oregon) June 2, 1862.

Chapter 11 notes

1 "Oregon Geographic Names," *Oregon Historical Quarterly,* Vol. 46. P. 345.

2 Glenn Harrison, *Linn County Historical Society Newsletter*, March 2001.

3 State of Oregon v. Andrew J. Pate, Linn County Circuit Court Journal, Vol. 2, p. 39, Oregon State Archives, Salem, Oregon.

4 State of Oregon v. Andrew J. Pate, p. 40-41.

5 Ibid. p. 46.

6 Patricia Cline Cohen, *The Murder of Helen Jewett*, (NY: Vintage Books, 1999) p. 27.

7 Belknap Collection, "A Rare Pamphlet of Pate's Confession", in vault at Oregon Historical Society, Portland, Oregon.

8 *Weekly Oregon Statesman* (Salem, Oregon) June 2, 1862.

9 "Oregon Geographic Names," p. 345.

Chapter Twelve

State of Oregon v. Henry Deadmond 1865

In August 1864, George W. Meek, age 39, of Lane County and a hired man, Henry Deadmond, drove a herd of cattle from Lane County southeast over the Canyon City Trail, through the mountains to the gold camps of eastern Oregon and western Idaho. Meek may have hired Deadmond because the latter was very familiar with the area.[1]

After selling the cattle Meek and Deadmond headed home with their saddlebags full of gold. Cranford Isabell, age 28, of Yreka, California met up with the pair and asked to ride with them as they traveled back to Lane County. Meek agreed.

They left Canyon City on September 2 and camped the first night on Indian Creek. The trio camped the next evening on the banks of Willow Creek in Wasco County. Isabell started a fire and began to fix supper, Meeks went up the creek a little ways to get water, and Deadmond herded the horses across the creek.

The large amount of money Meek was carrying with him must have been an irresistible temptation to Deadmond. After leaving the camp he returned and shot his two companions. Meek fell with a bullet in the head as he was getting water at the spring and Isabell was shot in the chest as he sat by the campfire.[2] Apparently, the murderer didn't know Isabell also had money with him. One of the men who discovered the bodies, Jesse Cox, found $1,100 hidden on Isabell's body, which was later returned to the dead man's family.[3] Isabell was still wearing a loaded revolver in the holster strapped to his waist. His loaded rifle lay on the ground next to him. Neither victim had a chance to fire a single round.

William Pennington received a letter from his friend, Henry Deadmond, dated September 8, 1864, as Deadmond recovered from his "ordeal" in Eugene City. In it he detailed his supposed escape from the bushwhackers that killed Meek and Isabell. The letter seems chillingly absent of emotion or concern when he describes his friend's death. Deadmond also mentions lending $120 to buy eight head of cattle for "them". Pennington was George Meek's friend. Schuyler Meek, George's son, married William's daughter, Mary Ellen Pennington, in 1895.

Meek's family immediately started an investigation. It took a week for Samuel Meek, George's brother, and a small posse to find the bodies 160 miles east of Eugene. George Meek left his wife, Margaret, and seven children: Isibel, Emily, Samuel, Sarah, Alice, G. W. and a little one not yet named.[4] According to the probate file, Meek was heavily in debt, $12,260.53, most of it owed to his brother Samuel. The court appointed administrator, James Howard, was only able to pay 11.75 percent of the bills against the estate.[5]

Deadmond and his friend, William Eddings, left Eugene right after the posse left, supposedly to join the posse, but never caught up with it. Suspicion immediately fell on Deadmond when the death scene revealed that the supposed thieves hadn't even searched the bodies. Only the saddlebags carrying the money from the cattle sale were gone.

Deadmond and Eddings were arrested October 10 at the Bridge Creek lodging house in Wasco County.[6] At first the authorities suspected that Eddings was a partner in the scheme, but he was eventually exonerated. (In an interesting turn of events William Eddings was later convicted of killing William P. Thomason on July 26, 1883, and sent to prison.[7])

At that time in Oregon's history, "road agents" were a serious problem east of the Cascades. They preyed on anyone traveling the trails and roads winding through the mountains and deserts severely limiting the pack trains bringing supplies to the mining towns of eastern Oregon. By 1865 nearly 19 million dollars in gold had been mined in Oregon, and that was a mighty big temptation.[8] Deadmond was rumored to belong to one of the road agent gangs. However, Deadmond was also an established miner in the Canyon City area. Joaquin Miller noted that Deadmond traveled with his party to Eastern Oregon in the spring of 1864. After they left camp on Bridge Creek, Deadmond was shot in the face by a band of hostile Indians. The shot tore away part of his jaw.[9] This was only a few months before Meek and Isabel were killed. Perhaps this incident gave Deadmond

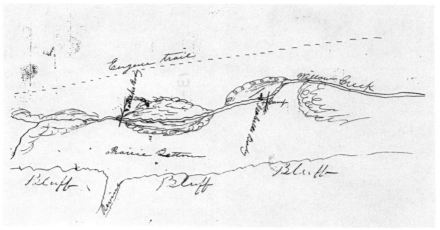

Trial record, State of Oregon v. Henry Deadmond
Map of Willow Creek camp where Deadmond shot Meek and Isabell.

the idea of attacking a traveling party and pretending it was someone else.

The Wasco County grand jury returned two indictments for first-degree murder against Deadmond. The trial was held in The Dalles from Wednesday, December 21, to Friday, December 23, 1864, when Deadmond was found guilty of first-degree murder.[10] J. G. Wilson was the presiding Circuit Court Judge. James A. Odell was appointed special prosecuting attorney, and G. W. Gates served as defense counsel. Jurors were Jeremiah Dougherty, A. O. Phelps, R. F. Gibbons, Z. Donnell, James D. Taylor, Reece H. Wood, William P. Abrams, Nathaniel W. Wallace, Samuel C. Tomlinson, Anthony Snyder, Henry Heppner and James Fulton, foreman.[11]

There were twenty-two witnesses summoned by the prosecution: Alex F. Stormant, John W. Stormant, A. F. Reynolds, William Pennington, Allison Pennington, Jesse Cox, Isaac Ledbetter, Joseph Carter, Orville Olney, Nathan Olney, Joseph Teal, Albert Bethel, William Tomlinson, J. D. May, Frank Coleman, Henry St. Clair, Perry Maupin, P. Emery, J. D. Borland, Edwin Powers, Angus McGowen, and Samuel Meek.[12]

Six witnesses were summoned for the defense: Pomery Emery, James Ingels, John W. James, Bluford and Riley Deadmond, and William Eddings. On Saturday, Christmas Eve, Deadmond was sentenced to hang on Friday, February 17, 1865, between 10 a.m. and 4 p.m. and to pay the costs of the prosecution.[13]

Deadmond didn't own much property, but the authorities believed he should pay his way with what he had, so on January 7, 1865, a public auction was held. Judge Wilson had issued a judgment against Deadmond for $832.46, the cost of his trial, right after his conviction.[14] One bay horse sold for $131.00 and a sorrel for $60.00. A pair of gloves sold for $.50. Saddlebags brought in $4.00. A revolver and "flash" sold for $14.50 and a bridle sold for $1.50. After expenses for feeding the horses, sheriff's costs for serving court summons and so forth, the county received a total of $154.18.

A year earlier, on February 1, 1864, Deadmond had sold his cabin and half interest in four mining claims for $400 cash and $1,100 to be paid later by William T. Lillard of Canyon City. The claims were located near Canyon City on the upper line of the claims of F. Dunsher and Company and below the claims of Moss and Company,. and better known as the "Price Claims".[15] The $1,100 that Lillard still owed Deadmond was subsequently used to pay the remainder of the prisoner's trial bill.

The week before the hanging a detachment of soldiers were dispatched from Pendleton and garrisoned in The Dalles to insure a peaceful execution. Authorities feared that the other members of Deadmond's gang and his brother, Riley, might try to break him out of jail. A year later on February 10, 1866, Stephen Gardner shot Riley Deadmond to death, during an altercation in the Eugene Long Tom Saloon.[16]

Father Vermass of the Catholic Church visited with the convict several times in the week before the execution and accompanied him as he walked to the scaffold. Sheriff Charles White purchased Deadmond a new outfit—a stylish black coat with matching trousers and a pair of white gloves.

Even though the mud in front of the jail was ankle deep, a large crowd gathered outside the jail on the morning of February 17, 1865. The army garrison, with about ninety soldiers, formed a human shield around the convict as he exited the jail. The sheriff and his deputies marched Deadmond out of the jail and everyone climbed into a wagon that was waiting outside. About 300–400 men followed along behind them. The sheriff took great care in selecting the site, just off the road leading to the army garrison, to make sure families living in the area would not be able to view the execution. After a short prayer at the foot of the scaffold, Deadmond climbed to the top, asked for a drink of water, and made a short speech.

" Gentlemen, I'm now on the scaffold, and am about to die. Let my fate be a warning to you all. I expect to see heaven and will pray for you all. I forgive all and ask to be forgiven by all."

Sheriff White tied the man's hands and feet and adjusted the rope around his neck. There was a pause as Deadmond stepped forward and spoke again.

" I want to say good-buy to all. I hope to meet you all in Heaven. I expect to go to Heaven—if there is such a place in this world." He turned to the Sheriff. "How far do I have to fall?"

"About six feet?"

"Will my feet touch the ground?"

"No," Sheriff White answered softly.

The black cap was pulled over his head and at 1:20 p.m. the pin was pulled and the trap opened. Unfortunately, his neck was not broken and it took eighteen agonizing minutes for Deadmond to strangle to death. After Doctor A. M. Belt pronounced the prisoner dead, the body was buried in The Dalles Catholic Cemetery.

Nearly a 1,000 people watched, including 150 women and children. The editor of the Eugene *Oregon State Journal* had much to say about that: "we think (they) would have acted more becoming the sex if they had remained at home and attended to some domestic work. We do not think it is at all becoming in parents to bring their children—male and female, to witness such a scene as was enacted yesterday; we are of the opinion that it does not redound either the benefit of the parents or children."[17]

This was the first "legal" hanging in Wasco County, famous for its wild ways and vigilante activities.

References

Daily Oregonian (Portland, Oregon) September 26, 1864, February 15, 1866, February 20, 1866.

Deady, M. P. Scrapbook #112, p. 127, Oregon Historical Society, Portland, Oregon.

Dicken, Samuel N. *The Making of Oregon: A Study in Historical Geography.* Portland: The Oregon Historical Society, 1979.

Douglas Independent (Roseburg, Oregon) July 26, 1883, July 28, 1883, August 4, 1883, October 13, 1883, October 20, 1883, January 26, 1884.

Eugene City Review (Eugene, Oregon) September 24, 1864.

Lane County Probate File, George W. Meek, #0181, February 21, 1865, Oregon State Archives, Salem, Oregon.

Lewman, Charles. Central Point, Oregon, November 2001 interview.

Oregon Intelligencer (Jacksonville, Oregon) October 1, 1864.

Oregon State Journal (Eugene, Oregon) September 17, 1864, September 24, 1864, February 25, 1865.

Oregon Statesman (Salem, Oregon) October 3, 1864, October 10, 1864, December 31, 1864.

State of Oregon v. Henry Deadmond, Wasco County Circuit Court Case File. Criminal cases filed alphabetically by defendant, Oregon State Archives, Salem, Oregon.

Chapter 12 notes

1 Charles Lewman, Meek biographer, puts his birth date in 1825 making Meek about 39 years old. *The Oregon Intelligencer* (Jacksonville, Oregon) October 1, 1864, indicated Meek was about 52 years old.

2 *Oregon State Journal* (Eugene, Oregon) September 24, 1864.

3 State of Oregon v. Henry Deadmond, Wasco County Circuit Court Case File. Criminal cases filed alphabetically by defendant, Oregon State Archives, Salem, Oregon.

4 Per Lewman, George Washington Meek may also have been a bigamist. Besides his wife, Margaret Renner, whom he married in 1851, he also had six, possibly seven, children with Lydia Johnson.

5 Lane County Probate File, George W. Meek, #0181, February 21, 1865, Oregon State Archives, Salem, Oregon.

6 *Oregon Statesman* (Salem, Oregon) October 10, 1864.

7 *Douglas Independent* (Roseburg, Oregon) January 26, 1884.

8 Samuel N. Dicken, *The Making of Oregon: A Study in Historical Geography* (Portland: The Oregon Historical Society, 1979), p. 85.

9 This interesting tidbit was brought to my attention by Margaret Guilford-Kardell who publishes the "Joaquin Miller Newsletter".

10 State of Oregon v. Henry Deadmond.

11 Ibid.

12 Ibid.

13 Ibid.

14 Lane County Probate File, George W. Meek, #0181, February 21, 1865, Oregon State Archives, Salem, Oregon.

15 State of Oregon v. Henry Deadmond.

16 *Daily Oregonian* (Portland, Oregon) February 20, 1866.

Chapter Thirteen

State of Oregon v. George Beale
State of Oregon v. George Baker
1865

D aniel Delaney immigrated to Oregon in 1843 with many other prominent Oregonians—the Nesmiths, the Waldos, the Applegates and the Looneys. He was a very wealthy and successful Tennessee plantation owner who brought five sons, William, David, George, James and Daniel Jr., and a considerable amount of money with him.[1] The family settled near Turner, a small town south of Salem, and built a beautiful new home. Besides his immediate family, he also brought at least one female slave, Rachel Beldon, who gave birth to a part-white son in 1857. His name was Jack DeWolf.[2]

George Beale was another member of the 1843 wagon train that brought the Delaney family to Oregon. However Beale returned to Missouri and on September 10, 1852, arrived for the second time in Salem. His first wife, Sarah, died on August 17, 1855, and he married 12 year-old, Mariah S. Taylor in 1857 in Marion County.[3] By 1864 Beale was 41 years old, a mildly successful saloon owner in Salem, and the father of two sons, ages eight and seven.

Daniel Delaney thought Beale was his good friend. He didn't realize how much Beale hated and resented him for his wealth and good fortune. Between 1843 and 1864 Beale often stayed at Delaney's house when he visited his claim located a few miles away.[4] During those visits Beale was able to check out the various places Delaney might have hidden his money. These visits inflamed Beale's burning jealousy, anger and greed.

Banks didn't exist in Oregon yet, so settlers hid their money in various places on their property. When George Beale heard that Delaney had sold a herd of cattle and received a lot of cash, he came up with a plan to steal it. He suspected that Delaney, age 72, was hiding his money in a keg of nails under a bed. Needing a partner he blackmailed a local butcher into helping him.[5] George Baker, age 57, his wife Nancy, and two children had lived in Salem for at least five years.[6] Beale let Baker drink on credit in his saloon until he had Baker so far in debt to him the man felt he had no choice except to help him.

Beale was already well known for his loose talk and get rich quick schemes, which always seemed to go awry. In March 1864 he had been charged and found guilty of renting out a billiard table without a license. After pleading guilty he was fined $50 and the cost of the trial.

The newspaper articles, trial testimony, and eventual confessions reveal a clear story of what happened next.

On the evening of Monday, January 9, 1865, Daniel Delaney was home alone as his wife was ill and staying at her son's home. The two thieves used lampblack or coal to blacken their faces and disguise themselves as Delaney was known to be friendly to black people and arrived at a pre-arranged spot to wait for dark. Baker had his shotgun and Beale had a pistol. Beale also brought a large bottle of whiskey for Baker to drink to give him plenty of "good courage and that there would be no back out in me."[7]

When it was quite dark the men walked to Delaney's front gate and Beale hollered three or four times at the house saying they were lost and needed directions. Delaney opened the door and when he stepped out Beale ordered Baker to shoot, which he did. Delaney's dog started to attack the men so Baker shot it, too. Delaney had fallen to his hands and knees and now started to get up and return to the house. Beale jumped over the fence and ran up to the old man.

"I know you Beale. For God's sake don't kill me and I'll give you all the money I've got."

"Old man," Beale replied, "dead men tell no tales." And with that Beale shot the old man in the head.

Meanwhile little Jack DeWolf, who had seen the whole thing, grabbed the wounded dog and ran back into the house. Inside he quickly shut and barred the door against the two men. That didn't protect him though, because the men grabbed a wood log, about three feet long and eight or ten inches wide, which they used to break down the door. Once inside Beale shot at the little boy three or four times but only superficially wounded him. Baker stayed outside on guard. After awhile Beale called Baker inside and both men tore the house apart looking for Delaney's money. Beale later gave Baker $500 in gold pieces as his share of the loot. Unknown to Baker, Beale kept

$1,400. Delaney's money immediately became a story of legend. No one believed that the men only found $1900. Delaney's sons estimated that their father had hidden between $50,000 and $70,000 somewhere in the house.

After the initial excitement of breaking into the house, the burglars relented and let little Jack live. The next morning, still wearing his bloody and shot-ridden clothes, Jack ran to David Delaney's house and reported the murder. Marion County Sheriff Sam Headrick was notified and with a small group of men they rode to Turner to investigate. At the scene they discovered a lost hatband, and tracked the murderers' horses back to Salem. By Saturday, January 14, the sheriff had completed his investigation and arrested George Beale and George Baker and charged them with first-degree murder.

The 1865 Oregon Census states that besides 16 horses and 20 head of cattle, Delaney owned 975 acres of land valued at $4,000 and personal property valued at $1,500. Gold nuggets and gold dust valued at $20,370.76 were hidden in the house. A U.S. Treasury bond worth $6,362.01 was also discovered in the house.[8] His wife, Elizabeth, and children William, age 40, Daniel, age 38, David, age 36, George, age 32, and James, age 29, survived him. Everyone lived in Marion County except George and James who lived in Union County. William was named administrator of the estate and spent the huge amount of $20 on a coffin and $50 on a headstone for his father's grave. After paying all the estate's bills, $31,049.86 was the final balance left to divide among the six heirs.[9]

The double trial started on Tuesday, March 21, 1865, with Judge Reuben Boise presiding and Rufus Mallory and Richard Williams prosecuting. The firm of David Logan, Caton and Curl served as defense attorneys for both defendants. The attorneys quickly agreed to a jury, only calling forty names before finishing. The jury consisted of Eli C. Cooley, Green C. Davidson, Anderson Dehaven, Wright Forshin, Fred W. Geer, King L. Hibbard, L. D. Hall, S. L. Kenworthy and four others not named.[10]

When little Jack was called to testify the defense objected on the ground that under the law Negroes could not testify in a criminal case where a white man was on trial. Judge Boise over-ruled that objection.[11] Defense lawyer David Logan then objected on the grounds that Jack wasn't intelligent enough to understand the questions or the consequences of his answers. Prosecuting Attorney Mallory argued the opposite. After asking the boy some questions meant to judge his intelligence, Judge Boise ruled in favor of the defense and Jack wasn't allowed to tell what he had seen the night of January 9 because "he did not understand the obligation of the oath".[12] The judge determined this by asking Jack if he knew anything about hell. The boy replied, yes "that was where most of them were going."[13] While the boy's testimony wasn't allowed at the trial, everyone in the community already knew what he had told the sheriff and district attorney.[14]

The Swarts brothers, Simon, Alonzo and Levi, were prosecution witnesses at the trial, each swearing that they had not seen the accused men on the day of the murder although both men tried to use them as alibis. This wasn't the only time the Swarts brothers were involved in murder. In 1884 their brother, David Swarts, was murdered, and in 1895 Alonzo Swarts was sent to prison for life after being convicted of second-degree murder.

After a week of hearing mostly circumstantial evidence, on Saturday, March 25, 1865, the jury foreman, F. W. Geer, read the verdict out loud to the silent courtroom. "We the jury find the prisoners guilty as charged in the indictment."[15]

A few days before the hanging both men signed written confessions, which were quickly printed by Frederick G. Schwatka. During the hanging he loudly harangued the crowd to buy one of his pamphlets as the proceeds were going to the poor men's widows.

On May 17, 1865, Beale and Baker were taken to a scaffold set up among a clump of oak trees near the bridge over the creek on South Church Street in Salem.[16] The convicted men were escorted from the jail and conveyed to the scaffold with a detachment of twenty to thirty Marion County Riflemen guarding them. Families came from miles around, setting up picnic lunches and enthusiastically watching the proceedings. The condemned men sat with their assigned guardians on chairs during the ceremonies.

Beale was quite debonair and self-confident in his black gloves, white stockings and gaiters. He gave an eloquent little speech repenting his crime and after reading from the Ninety-Eighth Psalm tossed his Bible into the crowd. He presented quite the spectacle pressing a silver crucifix against his chest and embracing the sheriff as he finished.

Baker was much more penitent and depressed. He needed assistance climbing the scaffold steps and shuddered visibly as he gazed at the hangman's rope swinging slightly in the wind. Quickly he turned away and searched the crowd. He asked that his wife, Nancy Duncan Baker, and his two sons, ages 20 and 16, would not suffer at the hands of his neighbors for his mistakes.

Sheriff Headrick tied the men's legs together, placed black caps over their heads and gave the signal to drop the trap.[17] The rope broke Baker's neck, but cut Beale's jugular vein making a bloody mess of his debonair clothing.

They hung there for twenty minutes before Doctor McAfee pronounced them dead. Baker's relatives claimed his body and took him away to be buried. No one wanted to bury Beale in a local cemetery until Daniel Waldo, a local resident, volunteered to bury the body on his property. Waldo had a rather individualistic nature and was outraged that the righteous Christians didn't have pity for a dead man. Twenty years later in 1885 another man, Joseph Drake, was hanged in Salem and was also buried in the Waldo Cemetery near Beale's grave.

In a strange turn of events Matilda Jane Sager, tragically orphaned when her parents died and again when Indians killed her foster parents, Doctor and Mrs. Marcus Whitman, married David Delaney. She not only witnessed those murders, but also the hanging of Creed Turner in Hillsboro at age ten and now the hanging of Beale and Baker for the murder of her father-in-law.

For many years rumors circulated around the community as people tried to locate the stolen money. William Delaney filed a suit against the defendant's lawyers, Caton and Curl, in the belief they knew where the money was buried. Others searched the property and nearby streams for a strong box in which many thought Delaney might have hidden his money. If anyone found it they kept the fact to themselves.

Kate Pringle Miller, daughter of Clark Pringle and Catherine Sager Pringle, recalls watching men build the gallows for Beale and Baker. "Hangings were public in those days and people drove in from twenty miles around to see Beale and Baker hanged . . . I saw the crowd assembled on Mill Creek. It was as big a crowd as a circus would have brought out, only they were quieter."[18]

References

1860 Federal Census, Marion County, Oregon.

1865 Oregon State Census, Marion County, Oregon.

Deady, M. P. "Scrapbook #112", pp. 121, 133, 135. Oregon Historical Society, Portland, Oregon.

Helm, Mike, ed. *Conversations With Pioneer Women by Fred Lockley.* Eugene: Rainy Day Press, 1981.

Judd, Frank. "Salem's First Hangings." *Marion County History,* Vol. 4, 1958, pp. 55-57.

Marion County Probate File, Daniel Delaney, #0262, February 8, 1865, Oregon State Archives, Salem, Oregon.

Maxwell, Ben. "Frontier Hangings Were Gala Occasions in Salem." *Capital Journal* (Salem, Oregon) January 30, 1952.

McLagan, Elizabeth. *A Peculiar Paradise.* Portland: Georgian Press, 1980.

Mertz, Sarah Jane Bennett. "The Hanging of Uncle George" and "The Delaney Murder Trial." 15427 Treemont Place, La Pine, Oregon, 97739.

Oregon Statesman (Salem, Oregon) March 27, 1865, May 17, 1865.

Scrapbook 226d, pp. 23, 24, 25, Oregon Historical Society, Portland, Oregon.

State of Oregon v. George P. Beale, Marion County Circuit Court Register & Fee Book, 1849-1890, Judgment Book 2, p. 358, No. 1363, Oregon State Archives, Salem, Oregon.

State of Oregon v. George P. Beale and George Baker, Marion County Circuit Court Register & Fee Book, 1849–1890, Judgment Book 3, p. 417, No. 1415, Oregon State Archives, Salem, Oregon.

Steaves, Sarah Hunt. *Book of Remembrance of Marion County Oregon Pioneers 1840–1860.* Portland: The Berncliff Press, 1927.

Steber, Pat. "Salem's First Hanging." *Enterprise Herald* (Independence, Oregon) June 25, 1975.

Chapter 13 notes

1 Pat Steber, "Salem's First Hanging", *Enterprise Herald* (Independence, Oregon) June 25, 1975.

2 He "purchased Rachel for $1,000 and brought her to Oregon where she worked in the fields, maintained the household and garden, and nursed Mrs. Delaney, who was an invalid for many years." Elizabeth McLagan, *A Peculiar Paradise,* (Portland: Georgian Press Company, 1980) p. 85.

3 Sarah Jane Bennett Mertz, "The Hanging of Uncle George." 15427 Treemont Place, La Pine, Oregon.

4 Scrapbook 226d, p. 24 Oregon Historical Society, Portland, Oregon.

5 Frank Judd, "Salem's First Hangings." *Marion County History,* Vol. 4, 1958, p. 54. *The Salem Statesman* of 30 January 1952 had a story written by Ben Maxwell that says Baker was a butcher.

6 1860 Federal Census, Marion County, Oregon.

7 Sarah Jane Bennett Mertz, "Delaney Murder Trial." La Pine, Oregon.

8 M. P. Deady, Scrapbook #112, p. 121, Oregon Historical Society, Portland, Oregon. The article states that $64,000 in gold was found in the house and the killers made off with $6,000.

9 Marion County Probate File, Daniel Delaney, #0262, February 8, 1865, Oregon State Archives, Salem, Oregon.

10 Sarah Jane Bennett Mertz, "Delaney Murder Trial" from confession of George Baker.

11 Elizabeth McLagan, p. 64. "A code of civil procedure approved in 1862 made no mention of race, and allowed black people to be witnesses in the courts of the state, although they could not (yet) act as jurors."

12 M. P. Deady, "Scrapbook #112" pp. 133, 135. Oregon Historical Society, Portland, Oregon.

13 Ibid. p. 135.

14 Many sources have perpetuated the story that Jack's testimony helped convict Beale and Baker. The legal documents are very clear in this regard. Jack was not allowed to testify. Even an 8 year-old white child's testimony would have been viewed with caution.

15 State of Oregon v. Beale and Baker, Marion County Circuit Court Register & Fee Book, 1849-1890, Judgment Book 3, p. 417-418, No. 1415, Oregon State Archives, Salem, Oregon.

16 Frank Judd, p. 56.

17 *Oregon Statesman* (Salem, Oregon) May 17, 1865.

18 Mike Helm, ed., *Conversations with Pioneer Women* by Fred Lockley. (Eugene: Rainy Day Press, 1981) p. 229.

Chapter Fourteen

State of Oregon v. William Kane 1865

In 1862 gold was discovered in the mountains surrounding Canyon City, a small town in what was then part of Umatilla and Wasco Counties. The gold rush that followed brought hundreds of miners, prospectors, and Chinese laborers into the area. On October 14, 1864, Canyon City became the county seat for the newly created Grant County.

One of the many men looking to strike gold was an old Irish sailor, William Kane (often spelled Cain). He arrived in Canyon City in the fall of 1864 and began working for Andy Watson who was running a sluice mining operation. Kane worked faithfully all winter for Watson as the mine owner repeatedly came up with excuses about not being able to pay Kane until the spring. Besides the $40-$50 he had already saved and deposited with a local Canyon City businessman, Kane was terribly excited about having so much money at one time and planned to buy some land. Kane waited impatiently all through the long winter for his promised $100.[1]

Kane was an unassuming fellow, small in stature and something of a social misfit—even in that society of eccentric men. He was described as half demented, uneducated and more ape-like than human looking, but sober and honest. Watson, on the other hand, was well liked in the community. He was a big man and strong—both physically and socially. Unfortunately, he also liked to drink and gamble.

Finally, in early June 1865 Kane found out that Watson had received the long anticipated money. Kane went to him and demanded his pay so that he in turn could pay the merchants who had extended him credit on food and supplies all winter. Instead of paying him in gold, Watson gave the old man the new fangled money called "greenbacks". It was an unspeakable insult to a man who had just spent all winter digging gold. "At that time in Oregon, paper money was only worth 40 cents on the dollar and wasn't accepted in stores or saloons, nor could it be traded for gold dust or coin."[2] The concept of paper money was still very new. Stacy J. Edson was the inventor who, in 1857, discovered the green ink necessary to print currency that was nearly impossible to counterfeit.[3]

Having no ability or knowledge of how to force the man to pay his debt honestly, Kane resorted to the use of violence. Taking his revolver with him he confronted Watson at the mine and threatened to shoot him if he didn't pay up. When Watson refused, Kane shot him. As Watson fell backwards into the water flume used to dig ore out of the hillside Kane fired two more shots. The body disappeared into the water, floated under some logs and eventually down the river.

Kane handed over his pistol to a man standing nearby and gave himself up to Grant County Sheriff M. P. Berry. There was some talk of lynching but Sheriff Berry was able to calm things down long enough to have a trial. The grand jury handed down an indictment on June 13, 1865, and Kane was tried in the circuit court. He was found guilty of first-degree murder on June 15, 1865 and sentenced to hang on August 3, 1865.[4]

The day of his hanging hundreds of spectators jammed the little town of Canyon City to witness the big event. The scaffold was erected at the east end of the town cemetery so Kane and his coffin were loaded into a wagon and transported together from the jail to the waiting gallows.

Irving Hazeltine of Canyon City described the scene in a way that elevated Kane's hanging to a thing of legend. "When they took him to the gallows, why he was playing solitaire on his coffin with a deck of cards. He was handcuffed and his legs were shackled but he could still manipulate the cards. Some young people were running along, getting ahead of the buckboard or rig that was taking him up the hill and he hollered at them and said, 'Don't be in a hurry, because there won't be anything doing until I get up there."[5]

His last words on the gallows maintained that he was insane when he killed Watson. His skull is on display in the Grant County Museum.[6]

References

"Affiliated Societies-Grant County Historical Society." *Oregon Historical Quarterly*, Vol. 54, June, p. 154.

Nedry, H. S. "Early History of Grant County." *Oregon Historical Quarterly*, Vol. 53, pp. 251-2.

Oregonian (Portland, Oregon) June 5, 1863.

Oregon State Journal (Eugene, Oregon) August 12, 1865.

Weekly Mountaineer (Canyon City, Oregon) July 14, 1865.

Chapter 14, notes

1 *Weekly Mountaineer* (Canyon City, Oregon) July 14, 1865. C. H. Miller wrote a scathing letter to the newspaper defending Kane's actions and the fraud that was committed against him.

2 "Affiliated Societies-Grant County Historical Society," *Oregon Historical Quarterly*, Vol. 54, June, p. 154.

3 *Oregonian* (Portland, Oregon) June 5, 1863.

4 Nedry, H. S., "Early History of Grant County", *Oregon Historical Quarterly*, Vol. 53, pp. 251-252.

5 "Affiliated Societies-Grant County Historical Society" p. 154.

6 "Affiliated Societies-Grant County Historical Society" p. 154. It's probable that Franklin Kane, listed in the 1860 Wasco County Federal Census is the same person here described as William Kane. He was listed as a 32 year-old Englishman working as a teamster and living with John Boughton and John Bills.

Chapter Fifteen

State of Oregon v. Thomas Smith 1866

Sidney and Barbara Presley Smith were murdered on Friday, March 9, 1866, on their farm six miles west of the city of Brownsville.[1] Sidney was 42 years old and Barbara was 30. They were married in Marion County on Valentine's Day in 1849 and had four children—Rhoda Ann, age 16, Leora, age 10, Mary, and baby Edward.[2]

When a neighbor, James Cunningham, rode up that Friday morning, Sidney's brother, Thomas, claimed that Sidney had gone crazy, killed his wife and then killed himself. It was a particularly frightening and bloody murder.

Part of the story came out later during the trial. Earlier that day Thomas and Sidney had a brief argument and at the end Thomas declared, "Well, this will not do me," as he left the house.

Inside the living room Sidney sat by the fireplace smoking his pipe, Barbara sat on the couch holding the baby, and Rhoda Ann sat on a chair with her back to the door. She heard a shot and saw her father fall forward with a bullet hole between his eyes. Rhoda Ann turned and saw her Uncle Tom standing in the door with a pistol. He fired again, this time the shot flew past the baby's head and hit Barbara in the right breast. In shock and fright she laid the baby on the floor and ran past Thomas, attempting to escape into the orchard. He followed and dragged her back to a woodpile near the house where she begged Rhoda Ann to help her. Uncle Tom grabbed his sister-in-law's wrist and pulled her into the smoke house where he brutally slashed her face and hands. In the end she was stabbed in the neck "like a pig".[3] The children were not injured but witnessed the entire affair. Thomas threatened to kill them all if they didn't swear to say that father killed mother and then shot himself.

Thomas might have gotten away with it but the two oldest girls eventually overcame their fear and asked, "How could Papa kill Mama when he was dead already?"

That seemed to put a different light on things and it soon became apparent that Thomas was the murderer of Barbara Smith, not her husband. By then the coroner and the sheriff had noticed that the bullet hole in Sidney's head didn't have any powder burns around it indicating that the shot had come from a distance and he couldn't possibly have shot himself.

A possible motive soon surfaced. Sidney had recently returned from the Idaho gold fields with a significant amount of gold, which he hid on his farm. Thomas had stayed home to run the farm while Sidney was gone and rumors suggested that he wasn't too happy to see his brother come home, plus he wanted some of the gold. Thomas had never been as successful as his brother and Sidney's new wealth just underscored that difference. There were also rumors flying around the neighborhood that the murderer was having an incestuous relationship with his oldest niece.

Thomas Smith was arrested the next Saturday and questioned by Justice Ellis of Brownsville on Monday, March 19, 1866.[4] He was indicted by the Linn County grand jury for both murders on May 1, 1866.[5] Although a small man, he was securely chained and transported to Albany for trial. Rufus Mallory was the prosecutor, while Cranor and Helm of Albany and J. D. Thornton defended Smith. Judge R. P. Boise presided. The trial date of Thursday, March 29, 1866, was set for the first indictment charging Thomas with the murder of Barbara Smith. The trial was held in the Albany courthouse and lasted two days. Twelve jurors were sworn in: James M. Reed, Nathan Newton, A. B. Morris, William A. Paul, Samuel F. Jones, Strowder Froman, John Parrell, Robert Foster, William Shepherd, David Sherer, William P. Anderson and E. H. Randall, foreman.[6]

Rhoda Ann and Leora testified at the trial. It was decided that Mary and Edward were too young. All had seen Thomas drag their mother into the smoke house and heard her dying screams when he killed her. After he was found guilty of murdering Barbara Smith, the indictment charging him with his brother's death was set aside.

Smith was chained in a first floor room of the courthouse with riveted (rather than locked) manacles secured around his ankles to prevent any escape attempt. These were the same manacles used to lock up Andrew Pate in 1862 before he was hanged.[7] Even inside the cell the chain from the manacles was looped through an iron staple pounded into the floor. He could move only a few feet from the cot in the room. He was 35 years old, a short man, about 5' 6" tall with blue eyes, dark hair and whiskers. During the trial and confinement Smith presented quite the disreputable appearance and was described as " a small man, with a bad physiognomy; a man that made some pretensions to religion and was a member of the Methodist church."[8]

In the end Smith confessed that he did indeed kill his brother and sister-in-law. He denied it was about the money, instead confirming the rumors that he was having an affair with his 16 year-old niece, Rhoda Ann.

She'd confessed the affair to her mother and eventually Barbara told her husband after he returned from the gold fields. Sidney wanted Rhoda to confess in front of Thomas and on the morning of March 9 he set up the confrontation. Rhoda defied her father and refused to confess, so Sidney tied her hands and started beating her in front of Thomas. Her pleas for help and Thomas' prior determination to kill his brother and sister-in-law came together to precipitate the final murderous act. The publication of the confession in the Albany newspaper put the case to rest. There was no doubt that Thomas Smith deserved to hang.

The hanging was set for Thursday, May 10, 1866.[9] That morning Linn County Sheriff O. W. Richardson read Smith a newspaper article describing the suicide of Calvin, his brother, in Placerville, Idaho. Within a few short months all three Smith brothers were dead.

The sheriff tied the prisoner's arms behind him and loaded him into a wagon. Following the tradition Pate had established four years earlier, they all proceeded to a level spot southwest of town.

"The gallows stood prominent above the mass of human heads crowded about in every direction."[10] A huge crowd of 3,000 people surrounded the open scaffold.[11] On his last day Smith was fashionably dressed in highly polished leather boots and a black frock coat. Smith sat on a bench during the proceedings, even as the black cap was pulled over his head and the knot was tightened about his neck. Finally the prayers and speeches were over, and Sheriff Richardson asked Smith to stand up, step forward and stand on the trap. A moment later the bolt was pulled and the condemned man fell seven feet to his death. The case set a record in Oregon history: only sixty-two days from murder to execution.

Some time later the children were playing near their house and found a rawhide bag filled with $25,000 in gold hidden under a wooden drain outside the house.[12] This was eventually used to support and educate the orphaned youngsters.

References

Brownsville Times (Brownsville, Oregon) June 16, 1905.

Carey, Margaret Standish, and Patricia Hoy Hainline. *Halsey, Linn County's Centennial City.* Brownsville: Calapooia Publications, 1977.

Democrat (Albany, Oregon) May 12, 1866.

Gazette (Corvallis, Oregon) May 12, 1866.

Linn County Historical Newsletter, Vol. 1, No. 40, October 2003, pp. 2-5.

Oregon State Journal (Eugene, Oregon) March 17, 1866.

Oregonian (Portland, Oregon) March 13, 1866, March 20, 1866, March 28, 1866, April 10, 1866, April 11, 1866, May 16, 1866.

State of Oregon v. Thomas Smith, Linn County Circuit Court Journal, Vol. 2, p. 218, Oregon State Archives, Salem, Oregon.

Chapter 15 notes

1 *Oregonian* (Portland, Oregon) March 13, 1866.

2 Margaret Standish Carey and Patricia Hoy Hainline, *Halsey, Linn County's Centennial City* (Brownsville: Calapooia Publications, 1977), p. 12.

3 *Oregonian*, March 13, 1866.

4 *Oregonian*, March 20, 1866.

5 State of Oregon v. Thomas Smith, Linn County Circuit Court Journal, Vol. 2, p. 218, Oregon State Archives, Salem, Oregon.

6 Ibid.

7 *Oregonian*, May 16, 1866.

8 Margaret Standish Carey, p. 13.

9 State of Oregon v. Thomas Smith.

10 *Oregonian*, May 16, 1866.

11 *Gazette* (Corvallis, Oregon) May 12, 1866. The Albany *Democrat* of May 16, 1866, says there were 3,000 people from out of town plus the local townspeople. The *Oregonian* of May 16, 1866, says there were 5-6,000 people there.

12 Margaret Standish Carey, p. 14.

Chapter Sixteen

State of Oregon v. William Kay Neil 1877

Seth Whipple Hayes and his brother, Ebenezer Hayes, donated land to the Oregon & California (O & C) Railroad in 1871 and created a depot for the railway, which formed the town of Halsey. Seth Hayes and others helped incorporate the town and proceeded to set up a charter that prohibited the consumption or sale of liquor within the town limits.

Hayes had some hired men working for him who occasionally imbibed too much alcohol and couldn't work when he needed them. As a result of his workers being too drunk to work and his personal feelings against alcohol, Hayes started speaking against a nearby saloon and its owner. His wealth and prominence gave him a great deal of influence in the community, and the local liquor dealers were afraid of him.

A 34-year-old saloonkeeper by the name of William Kay Neil moved into town in the fall of 1876 and set up shop. The new saloon was conveniently located a block northeast of the railroad depot. It quickly gained a bad reputation for being noisy, exceptionally violent and a gathering place "for persons of low, dissipated and vicious habits".[1] Neil was furious when he heard what Hayes was saying about him and decided to confront the man.

Hayes was repairing a well near Neil's saloon on the afternoon of Wednesday, November 1, 1876, when the two men started arguing and shouting insults at each other. The feud heated up when Hayes accused Neil of keeping "a low-down doggery". Neil suddenly drew a knife and stabbed Hayes three times, puncturing his chest once and his stomach twice.[2] According to the honor code of 1876, Neil believed that such an insult required a violent and homicidal reply.[3]

Hayes died three hours later that evening. He was 51 years old and the father of six children. He and his first wife, Polly Stillwell, were married on February 15, 1843, and moved to Oregon in 1852 with two sons, Daniel and David. Two years after Polly's death, on November 1, 1865, he married his second wife, Sarah Vawter, and together they had four children, Stephen, Frank, Gertrude and Irving.[4] Sarah married Jesse Ribelan after Hayes' death.

Neil's friend, George W. Miller, offered Neil his horse immediately after the stabbing. Fortunately, the horse objected to having a murderer on his back and bucked the killer off. Neil ran on foot toward Brownsville for three miles before an impromptu posse caught up with him and brought him back to Halsey. Linn County Sheriff James R. Herren arrived just in time to escort him to Albany, the Linn County seat. Because Hayes was such a prominent, wealthy and respected member of the community, there was considerable talk of a lynching, but common sense prevailed. Miller was also arrested as an accomplice but was later released.

Neil was indicted for first-degree murder on Friday, November 3, 1876.[5] James K. Weatherford served as defense counsel, and District Attorney George Burnett, J. C. Powell and N. B. Humphrey worked for the state. The trial began on Wednesday, November 8, 1876, in front of Judge Reuben Boise, as Neil pleaded self-defense. Twelve jurors were chosen: Jesse Barr, H. Eckerman, Isaac Hayes, James B. Houston, M. F. Hyde, Isaac Meeker, John Millard, A. S. Nanny, Joseph Nixon, James Turner, Cyrus Westlake, and Milton Hale, foreman.[6] The trial was short and quick, lasting a single day. The jury only needed about an hour to return with a guilty verdict.

On November 10, 1876, a record crowd, including a very large number of ladies, gathered inside the Linn County Courthouse to hear the sentence pronounced.[7] Neil was sentenced to hang on December 22, 1876.[8]

On December 22, a small item appeared in the local newspaper, *The States Rights Democrat*–"Execution Postponed. The execution of W. K. Neil for the murder of Mr. Hays has been postponed until the 20th of next month, for the purpose of allowing his relatives, who live in California, time to get here before his death." The execution was actually delayed until Friday, January 26, 1877.

Tuesday, January 23, the prisoners in the Linn County Jail organized an impromptu music concert. Neil and four other prisoners were let out into the exercise yard and soon started making a horrendous racket. Neil, playing the bones, made the worst noise of all. Sheriff

Herren and the other jailors became suspicious and quickly locked them back in their individual cells. George Cline, a guard, and the sheriff found a hole dug almost through the wall in the privy. It took a little persuasion before Neil gave up his digging tool, a half-inch framing chisel, ground down to a very sharp point.[9]

Neil was escorted to the gallows by Reverend Robert L. Stevens of the Episcopal Church, Reverend S. G. Irvine, of the United Presbyterian Church, Sheriff James R. Herren and Deputy George W. Humphrey. Waiting on the scaffold were: Lane County Sheriff Stewart B. Eakin, Benton County Sheriff Solomon King, Benton County Deputy Sheriff J. M Hamilton, Doctor O.P.S. Plummer, and Doctor J. L. Hill. The scaffold was only ten feet square and crowded with so many men standing on it.[10] Hundreds of spectators from all over the county and neighboring counties had gathered to watch the event.

The frightened prisoner could barely stand up by himself and had to be held upright by the sheriff and his deputy as he climbed the gallows steps. On the top he stepped forward and made a short speech barely heard by the crowd.

"Ladies and gentlemen, I am to be executed, I want you to listen to me. I have been improperly convicted. I ain't, I ain't. . . I did not do this murder of which I am charged." As the rope was adjusted around his neck, he mumbled, "God help me!"[11]

Even though this was the second hanging in Linn County, it was Sheriff Herren's first and as a result there was a little hitch in the proceedings. A diary entry of Z. T. Bryant relates the events of January 26, 1877, in Albany with several hundred people watching.

> The sheriff came out and fixed the rope and a wagon drove up with his coffin and soon brought out Neil. He could not walk without help; it was that he was drunk. He started to say something but mumbled and soon he stepped on the trap-door and black cap put on his head and face, and rope fixed, and the door sprung and he fell and his feet touched the ground, and the sheriff and another man or two raised him up and put a twist in the rope and something in the loop. They got him dead.[12]

Kay Neil had to be hanged twice, but they finally got the job done. His body was put in a coffin and taken to Mrs. McMechan, his aunt's house, who shipped his body back to his parents in California.

References

1870 Federal Census, Linn County, Oregon.

Albany Register (Albany, Oregon) November 3, 1877.

Champoeg Pioneer, No. 13, February 1957.

Dunn, Pat, "Diary of Z. T. Bryant, 1876." Glenn Harrison, Harrison@cmug.com

Himes, George H., Scrapbook #76, p.88, Oregon Historical Association, Portland, Oregon.

Lang, H. O. ed. *History of Willamette Valley*. Portland: Himes and Lang, 1885, p. 768.

Linn County Marriage Records, Oregon State Archives, Salem, Oregon.

Oregonian (Portland, Oregon) November 4, 1876, January 27, 1877.

Peterson del Mar, David. *Beaten Down: A History of Interpersonal Violence in the West*. Seattle: University of Washington Press, 2002.

State of Oregon v. William K. Neil, Linn County Circuit Court Journal, Vol. 5, p. 124, Oregon State Archives, Salem, Oregon.

States Rights Democrat (Albany, Oregon) November 10, 1876, November 17, 1876, December 15, 1876, December 22, 1876, January 26, 1877, February 2, 1877.

Chapter 16 notes

1 *Oregonian* (Portland, Oregon) January 27, 1877.

2 *States Rights Democrat* (Albany, Oregon) November 10, 1876.

3 David Peterson del Mar, *Beaten Down: A History of Interpersonal Violence in the West* (Seattle: University of Washington Press, 2002) p. 53. Peterson emphasizes the violence that occurred in the west as a result of real and perceived verbal insults.

4 1870 Federal Census, Linn County, Oregon. (The Linn County Marriage records give the marriage date as September 7, 1865.)

5 State of Oregon v. William K. Neil, Linn County Circuit Court Journal, Vol. 5, p. 124, Oregon State Archives, Salem, Oregon.

6 State of Oregon v. W. K. Neil.

7 *States Rights Democrat*, November 10, 1876.

8 *States Rights Democrat*, November 17, 1876.

9 *States Rights Democrat*, January 26, 1877.

10 *Oregonian*, January 27, 1877.

11 Ibid.

12 Pat Dunn, "Diary of Z. T. Bryant, 1876", provided by Glenn Harrison, Harrison@cmug.com.

Modern Inventions Improve Executions, 1878–1894

Chapter Seventeen

State of Oregon v. Sevier Lewis 1878

C oquille City was known as a pleasant and peaceful place to live in the early years of Oregon's history. The peace was only occasionally marred by acts of violence, one of which occurred on Monday, May 22, 1876.[1]

Zachariah Lewis was disturbed by information Sylvia Lewis, his young niece, had confided in him. Zack, at age 25, was quite a bit younger than her father, his half-brother, and his niece thought of him more like an older brother than an uncle. Asking for help, the girl told him that her father, Sevier Lewis, was forcing her to have sex with him and she was going to have a child. Zack confronted his half-brother and warned him to stop or he would tell the whole family. Zack helped the sixteen-year old girl move in with her grandparents to escape from her father. He told Sevier that if he tried to retrieve Sylvia that he'd kill him.

Furious, Sevier loaded his pistol, grabbed his yager (a sharp hand hoe) and told his oldest son, age 15, to come with him with the remark that they "might see some game before they returned".[2] Picking up his gun he went to his father's field near Coquille and shot his half-brother to death. He fired twice, killing Zack instantly. The young man had been plowing about a mile from his father's (Hiram H. Lewis) house. The Lewis family had moved from the interior of Oregon to the Coquille area just two years earlier and they were working hard to prepare as much land as possible for planting.

In Empire City, Coos County District Attorney C. W. Fitch brought evidence to the Coos County Grand Jury on May 27, 1876. They issued an indictment charging Sevier Lewis with the May 22, 1876, murder of Zachariah Lewis. Sevier was charged with shooting Zach with a pistol once in the stomach and once in the left side. Witnesses were Robert Lowe, James A. Simons, Willoughby Lewis and Hiram H. Lewis.[3]

After the murder, Sevier Lewis left the county and hid from the law. A large reward was offered for his arrest. A month later Lewis was recognized by a farmer, Mr. Riddle, who lived near Canyonville. Riddle wrote a letter to Sheriff Livingston describing a very nervous hired hand who only worked two or three days before leaving unexpectedly. A search failed to locate the mysterious stranger and the sheriff finally gave up the chase.

It was nearly two years before Sevier Lewis was arrested in Seattle on December 10, 1877.[4] A Mr. Perkins thought he recognized Lewis drinking in the bar room of the American House Hotel. Alerting the owner, Mr. Haley, the two men followed Lewis to the Vanity Fair Saloon where they drank some beer with him. When Lewis left the bar they followed him to the Oriental Hotel. One man stayed on watch and the other went to fetch Seattle Sheriff Wycoff. The three men arrested the wanted man and notified the authorities in Oregon. Sevier Lewis was soon escorted back to Oregon.

Lewis' trial began on May 27, 1878 after Coos County Sheriff Andrew "Glenn" Aiken and Deputy W. R. McCormack served subpoenas on J. A. Simon, Samuel Wager, M. S. Simons, M. H. Lewis, Yelverton M. Lowe (a resident of Beaver Slough), M. S. Hanscom, David Drew (a machinist and blacksmith), C. H. Lewis, Willoughby Lewis, Hiram H. Lewis and Sylvia Jane Lewis.

Sevier's attorneys, J. M. Siglin, David L. Watson and T. G. Owen, issued subpoenas on May 18, May 30 and June 5 to Charles P. Fox, James A. Waller, Daniel Bridges, William Morras (resident of Beaver Slough), J. B. Lewis, D. C. Lewis and Alonzo Lewis to testify at court for him. Sheriff Aiken was unable to find Charles P. Fox or D. C. Lewis.

In an affidavit filed on May 30, 1878 by J. M. Siglin, Sevier swore that he wanted a continuance to postpone the trial because he had been without counsel or money to pay for an attorney, and hadn't been able to issue subpoenas for witnesses. The district attorney's reply to the request revealed some pretty angry and disgusted public servants. County Clerk M. A. Jackson swore that Lewis hadn't ever asked to issue requests for any witnesses until May 18. Sheriff Aiken swore that he had talked with Lewis many times about his rights to request witnesses between January and May. Lewis never gave him any names or requested subpoenas be issued for the trial. He verified that Siglin had been conferring with Lewis since January. Jailor W. H. S.

Hyde swore that he had admitted Siglin into Lewis's jail cell many times in the past five months. Judge Watson denied Lewis's request to delay the trial and it went ahead as scheduled.

Jury foreman Isaiah H. Atkinson stood in front of the Coos County courtroom on June 13, 1878, and read the verdict, "We the jury find the defendant guilty as charged in the indictment."[5]

Judge J. F. Watson sentenced Lewis to hang on August 9, 1878, and charged him with $830.10 court costs. The defense lawyers applied for a postponement to Oregon Governor T. F. Chadwick until Judge Watson could return to Coos County and rule on their appeal application. Governor Chadwick signed the order changing the hanging date to Friday, August 30, 1878.[6]

Trial record, State of Oregon v. Sevier Lewis
Certification of witnesses that Sevier Lewis was hanged August 13, 1878.

Sevier Lewis was marched to the scaffold on August 30, 187,8 at Empire City, in front of 250 spectators.[7] Coos County District Attorney Silas H. Hazard, Lewis's attorneys, Sheriff Aiken, and Deputy McIntosh escorted the convict to the top of the scaffold.

After Lewis' hands and feet were tied, he stepped forward and gave a rather rambling speech.

I am going to die, I know that—I know that it was all brought on by a low-lived branch of the family. I know that your minds are all influenced against me . . . I believe in God Almighty, and I believe some of the family will suffer worse than I will . . . I was punished just as bad before as I was after they arrested me, because I was separated from my family. It is all I live for and I am going to die for them. If I could die a thousand times and save my daughter I would do it. If I could save her I

*would be satisfied to die. You have been deceived in this trouble;
I could not help it; I went over that day to try and settle it with
them. No, sir, I did not go over there with the intention of killing
him. They know that I went over there to try to settle with them
without trouble. John knows and so does my son that I started
from home with that motive. They have convicted me; all of them
have threatened my life.*[8]

Lewis was 53 years old, about 5'10" tall and weighed about 175 lbs.
Defiant, stubborn and vindictive, he finally forced Sheriff Aiken to
manhandle him closer to the hanging rope. Even as the black cap was
pulled over his head and he was being pushed forward, he yelled,
"What in the hell are you doing that for? I am not afraid to die." [9] The
hanging was quick and clean. Doctors Golden and Steel pronounced
Lewis dead ten minutes after he fell at 3:50 p.m.

This hanging was the first time witnesses, called bona-fide elec-
tors, were appointed to legally swear that the execution had taken
place. Witnesses named were J. M. Siglin, T. G. Owen, Doctor D. L.
Steel, Doctor Charles B. Golden, A. P. Owen, R. G. Anssans, Gilbert
Hall, John T. Moulton, C. C. Tominson, Daniel Bridges, John
Flanagan, and Joseph B. Gilbert.

Judging from the newspaper articles there was little sympathy
expressed for Lewis by anyone in the county.

References
Coos Bay News (Empire City, Oregon) May 31, 1876.
Coos Bay News (Marshfield, Oregon) December 19, 1877.
Dodge, Orville. *Pioneer History of Coos and Curry Counties.* Salem: Capital
  Printing Company, 1898, pp. 240 and 404–405.
Oregonian (Portland, Oregon) January 1, 1876, June 1, 1876, June 26, 1876,
  September 9, 1878.
Plaindealer (Roseburg, Oregon) September 7, 1878.
State of Oregon v. Sevier Lewis, Coos County Circuit Court, May 30, 1878,
  Coos County Courthouse, Coquille, Oregon.

Chapter 17 notes
1 State of Oregon v. Sevier Lewis, Coos County Circuit Court, 30 May 1878, Coos County Circuit Court
  Case Files, Coos County Courthouse, Coquille, Oregon.
2 *Coos Bay News* (Empire City, Oregon) May 31, 1876.
3 State of Oregon v. Sevier Lewis.
4 *Coos Bay News* (Marshfield, Oregon) December 19, 1877.
5 State of Oregon v. Sevier Lewis.
6 State of Oregon v. Sevier Lewis.
7 *Plaindealer* (Roseburg, Oregon) September 7, 1878.
8 *Oregonian* (Portland, Oregon) September 10, 1878.
9 *Plaindealer*, September 7, 1878.

Chapter Eighteen

State of Oregon v. James Cook
1879

On Sunday afternoon, December 1, 1878, George Craig and James Cook were preparing to leave the Wasco County Jail for the state penitentiary. Craig and Cook had been convicted of "larceny in a store" after they stole a watch from Timothy Baldwin's saloon the previous September. Craig was the twenty-one year old son of Doctor Polhemus Craig, a prominent physician and druggist in The Dalles.[1]

After his arrest in Portland Craig implicated Cook in the theft. It was rumored that Cook had gone to Boise, Idaho, but Deputy Marshal Haine was suspicious of a big box sitting in the house Cook shared with an Indian woman. When the officers flipped the box over, Cook flipped out. After Cook's trial, Judge McArthur sentenced them each to seven years in the penitentiary. The two partners had been on the outs since the trial, where Cook had vehemently denied his guilt and was convicted primarily on George Craig's testimony.

That afternoon Sheriff James B. Crossen let Craig and Cook out of their separate cells along with two other prisoners for a little exercise in the jail corridor. As James Cook was very muscular and well known for his Herculean strength, he was heavily "ironed" with shackles on his feet.[2] He was also very agitated, clanking his irons and stomping back and forth in the waiting room. Suddenly he stopped, whirled and grabbed his young accomplice. Holding on to Craig's hair with one hand he swiped at the man with a pilfered razor in his other, nearly severing the head from the body. The young man was dead before anyone could even try to stop the killing.

Sheriff Crossen immediately interrogated Cook, "Who gave you the razor?"

"You did," Cook smirked.

Crossen pulled his pistol from its grip and jammed it in Cook's ear. "Now, tell me who gave you that razor."

"You did. Go ahead and shoot. I'd rather hang or have you shoot me than spend seven years in the penitentiary."

It was later decided that the Indian woman who had been living with Cook must have given him the weapon.[3]

John Michell, a Wasco County justice of the peace, was also the acting coroner. He rounded up six men to serve on the coroner's jury and after listening to the testimony they all agreed that George Craig had come to his death at the hands of James Cook. It cost the county $17.50 to hold the hearing.[4]

By December 27, 1878, James Cook was convicted of first-degree murder and sentenced to hang on Friday, February 7, 1879, between 10 a.m. and 3 p.m.[5] L. L. McArthur was the presiding judge, L. B. Isom was the district attorney and George H. Durham was the court appointed defense counsel. Trial witnesses were William H. Miller, George Edgar, Doctor J. P. Tieman, Robert Earl, Henry Clarist, John McQuate, Joseph Simon and Charles Williams. The two prisoners in the jail at the time of the murder, A. Thorp and Ah Coon, "a pock-marked Chinese cook at the Walla Walla Hotel", were also subpoenaed.[6] Despite objections, Cook was kept in shackles and manacles throughout the entire trial.

Cook could not read or write, signing his affidavit requesting a change of venue with an X. That didn't affect his imagination though. Two days prior to his execution he gave the following account of his life to a newspaper reporter revealing his advanced knowledge of geography:

> *My earliest recollections of life are of my being among the Indians—the Sioux. At that time the tribe had not been divided into the present existing factions, and roamed throughout the country known as the plains. I could never find out who my parents were but I am under the impression that they were captured and murdered by the Indians while traveling and I was taken a prisoner and adopted by the tribe. I remained with the Indians for sixteen years, and during that time was twice engaged in war against the whites. The Indians called me Laveris, which I have since found out to be a Spanish name. While with the Indians an Englishman, a Doctor Roach, who was hunting on the plains, came into our camp. No hostility prevailed against the whites at*

this time, but some of the warriors wanted to kill the doctor. They were overruled in this, and I was selected to guide the intruder out of our hunting grounds. The doctor took a fancy to me, and I concluded to accept his offer to accompany him in his travels as a body-servant and leave the Indians.

After journeying about six months in the United States we left for India, where for twenty months we remained tiger hunting in the jungles and sightseeing through the country. Tired of India, we left for Africa visiting all the prominent places and spending portions of our time in hunting, a pursuit the doctor was passionately fond of. We spent portions of the time in Abyssinia, the country surrounding the Red Sea, after which we crossed the great desert; thence to Alexandria, and after a short stay in Egypt we sailed for England. Remaining at the doctor's home for a short time, we left for Australia where I left the service of the doctor and started off on my book for America. I reached San Francisco all right, and after remaining there for some little while I followed the crowd then rushing to Nevada. I went to Virginia City, worked about there awhile, and then traveled through the state continuing my journey through Colorado and finally brought up in Texas where I was engaged as a stock driver. To this capacity I went to Arizona, and in 1865 found myself in Montana, from which place I returned to San Francisco. One morning I found myself on board the ship Yenisei. How I came there I could not comprehend at first, but shortly realized that I'd been shanghaied.

Captured by the crimps while drunk, and a long voyage before the mast was before me. We were bound for China, but never reached our destination. The ship ran on a reef, and myself and four others, were the only ones that escaped to the mainland after being in an open boat for nine days without food or water. After our rescue we tooted it through South Anam, and then on to Canton. We were then sent to Hong Kong, from which place I returned to San Francisco. I came to Oregon about sixteen months ago, and have lived in and about The Dalles during the time . . . . . I don't know what my name is. I took the name I now bear after leaving the Indians and going with Doctor Roach. I think I am about 45 years of age, but do not know of a certainty how old I am.[7]

This was just one of several versions Cook gave of his previous life, but it was certainly the most colorful. It's hard to know how much was true. The interviewer noted an English accent as Cook continually dropped the "h" in his words. One time he described himself as a murderous villain, and the next he pretended to be an innocent victim of circumstance.

On February 7 Cook ate a hearty breakfast and appeared almost eager to finally leave the jail for the scaffold. Ten armed men served as guards and surrounded the convict and his escort as they walked from his cell into the jail yard. Father Gauden, a local Catholic priest, arrived shortly before the scheduled execution and accompanied Cook up to the bench on the platform.

Sheriff Crossen read the warrant and asked Cook if he had anything to say. Cook replied, "I have nothing to say."[8]

Multnomah County Sheriff Ben Norden and Deputy Sheriff Haines were also on the trap with Cook. At precisely 1:17 p.m. the trap sprang open and the prisoner fell like a stone. The drop failed to break his neck, but the vertebrae were dislocated. It took seventeen minutes for his pulse to stop and five minutes later he was declared dead. Doctor Logan, Doctor Richardson and Doctor Morrison, formerly of Empire City of Coos Bay, were the attending physicians.[9]

Many people witnessed the spectacle including a dozen women. The twelve witnesses chosen to represent Wasco County at the hanging were: George Allen, J. A. Campbell, R. G. Closter, M. Finnigan, John J. Fitzgerald, J. W. French, H. H. Sausbury, John Moran, J. Michelbach, Charles H. Reed, J. A. Robbins, and John Y. Todd.[10]

The scaffold was erected in the jail yard and equipped with the newest modern invention—foot spring. The floor of the scaffold was covered with a carpet, which hid the foot spring connected to the trapdoor making the actual moment of the execution more discreet. James Cook died without ever revealing his name or background—an enigma until the end.

References

Coos Bay News (Marshfield, Oregon) February 19, 1879.

Daily Oregonian (Portland, Oregon) December 31, 1878, February 5, 1879, February 8, 1879.

Evening Telegram (Portland, Oregon) December 2, 1878, February 8, 1879.

McNeal, Wm. H. *History of Wasco County, Oregon*. The Dalles: 1953.

State of Oregon v. James Cook, Wasco County Circuit Court Case File #93A – 15, Box 25, Folder 90, Oregon State Archives, Salem, Oregon.

Chapter 18 notes

1 Wm. H. McNeal, *History of Wasco County, Oregon*, (The Dalles: 1953), p. 381.

2 *Daily Oregonian* (Portland, Oregon) February 5, 1879.

3 *Evening Telegram* (Portland, Oregon) December 2, 1878.

4 Wasco County Coroner's Report, George Craig, January 6, 1879, Oregon State Archives, Salem, Oregon.

5 State of Oregon v. James Cook, Wasco County Circuit Court Case File #93A – 15, Box 25, Folder 90, Oregon State Archives, Salem, Oregon.

6 State of Oregon v. James Cook.

7 *Daily Oregonian*, February 5, 1879. While the vocabulary attributed to Cook is not that of an illiterate and uneducated man, it is impossible to know how much was actually Cook's and how much belonged to the reporter interviewing him.

8 *Daily Oregonian*, February 8, 1879.

9 *Coos Bay News* (Marshfield, Oregon) February 19, 1879.

10 State of Oregon v. James Cook.

Chapter Nineteen
State of Oregon v. Archie Brown and James Johnson 1879

It isn't often a county sheriff had the responsibility of supervising a double hanging, so when Multnomah County Sheriff Ben Norden started to prepare for March 14, 1879, he did so with a great deal of careful thought. The case had begun seven months earlier.

About nine o'clock on the morning of August 20, 1878, three men entered the pawnshop owned by Walter O'Shea on First and Washington Streets in Portland.[1] O'Shea didn't notice it but the last man turned and locked the door behind him. They picked out some blankets and handed O'Shea some money. When the owner bent over to get change out of the safe, one of the men bashed him over the head with an iron bar and knocked him unconscious.

In a flash all three men began emptying the shop of everything valuable. Grabbing a valise (a leather bag) they scooped up twenty-three gold watches worth $1,100, fourteen silver watches worth $140, 200 fifty cent silver coins, and two gold watch chains worth $20.[2] Joseph Swords, the youngest of the group, noticed two little boys, Ed Miller and L. Backentos, watching through the front windows. Immediately the men smashed a back window, leaped into the alley, jumped over a fence, ran through the Levi and Strauss store, and exited into the street.

The little boys ran and fetched Constable Daniel Sprague who pursued the men onto Morrison and Third Street. Seeing Sprague running after them, all three drew revolvers, turned and faced the constable. According to witness T. A. Clark, the middle man was holding the valise with the loot, and the big man (Brown) fired his gun. The bullet struck the side of a tree Sprague was hiding behind, bounced off and killed a little boy, Louis Joseph, who in his curiosity was following the policeman.

The outlaws stole the Weeks and Morgan grocery wagon, whipped the horses and made their escape into trees on the edge of Portland. The outlaws were identified as Archie Brown, age 25, James Johnson, age 25, and Joseph Swords, age 18. A reward of $250 was offered for their capture.

On August 28, Portland Police Officer Gwyne arrested Joseph Swords near the Terminal Saloon. On September 3, Archie Brown (an alias for Eugene Avery) was arrested at a ranch eleven miles outside Portland. James Johnson (an alias for Frank Taylor) was recognized by a former fellow San Quentin convict and arrested October 14 in Los Angeles.[3]

Archie Brown's trial was held on November 18, 1878. Jurors were Charles Bartel, Thomas Burke, J. B. Carter, J. J. Domes, E. O. Doud, W. S. Keys, A. L. Kirk, J. D. Morris, James Morris, R. F. Murphy, George C. Sears, and B. E. Vestel. The defense attorneys were W. W. Page, Stott and Gearin.[4] J. F. Caples and M. F. Mulkey represented the prosecution. There wasn't much the attorneys could do about the assault and robbery charges since too many witnesses saw them holding the loot. However every effort was made to keep Brown off the scaffold and his lawyers pushed for a second-degree murder conviction. Part of their argument hinged on the definition of the word "robbery". The defense maintained that the robbery ended when the men left the store. The defense also maintained that the shot was fired—not to kill—but to prevent pursuit. If they could prove either point the defendant could get off with second-degree murder.

In 1878 Oregon law was explicit. In his address to the jury Judge C. B. Bellinger stated the case clearly:

Murder in the first degree is where one purposely, and of deliberate and premeditated malice kills another, or where one while in the commission of, or in the attempt to commit rape, arson, robbery or burglary, kills another . . . . . Under this indictment it is not necessary to prove expressly either a purpose to kill or deliberate and premeditated malice. The indictment having alleged the killing in the perpetration of a robbery, it is only required that the robbery and the killing, in the manner alleged, during the robbery, be proven to make out the case. In such a case and under such proof, the intent to kill and the deliberate and premeditated malice are incontrovertibly implied.

If there had been no interruption of delay in the removal, no putting down of the goods, no intervention of another act inconsistent with the carrying away; if the removal was continuous, uninterrupted and near in point of time and place to the act of violence; if there had been no opportunity to secrete or secure the fruits of the robbery, and while in such act of carrying, they shot and killed a person in the manner alleged, it is murder."[5]

Archie Brown was found guilty of first-degree murder and Judge Bellinger sentenced him to hang on Friday, February 7, 1879.[6]

Johnson's trial started on December 4, 1898. J. F. Caples, with M. F. Mulkey assisting, were the prosecuting district attorneys and C. B. Bellinger was again the circuit judge appointed to hear the case. C. A. Ball and William Evans were appointed James Johnson's defense lawyers. The twelve jurors were: E. O. Carsen, E. Carter, W. G. Carthey, A. T. Dunbar, D. S. Dunbar, Isaac Kay, Gilman Kelly, G. Linneman, H. C. Sattuck, J. C. Snover, D. Stimson, and Jacob Timmerman.[7]

The defense maintained that since Johnson didn't fire the bullet that killed the boy he wasn't guilty of first-degree murder. Again the question of when the robbery ended and if they intended to kill anyone became crucial. It was T. A. Clark, a witness at the shooting; who heard one of the robbers say, "Give it to him", and that set the scene for premeditated murder. He also testified that Johnson was still holding the valise with the loot at the time the little boy died. Since Constable Sprague was unarmed and no one was shooting at the robbers it was difficult to prove self-defense, although the lawyers certainly tried. The trial only lasted two days and the jury announced a verdict of guilty of first-degree murder on December 6, 1878. James Johnson was sentenced to hang with Brown on February 7, 1879.[8]

The 18-year-old, Joseph Swords, was convicted of second-degree murder and sentenced to the penitentiary for a life of hard labor. He arrived January 17, 1879 and died of consumption February 12, 1883. He had blue eyes, brown hair, a scar under his right jaw and several tattoos: two flags on the left arm, a ship on the back of his right hand, and on his right arm a sailor holding a sword with the letters J. S. underneath.[9]

Supreme Court Justices James H. Kelly, Reuben P. Boise, and P. P. Prim denied both requests for new trials on January 28, 1879.[10] The convicts were granted a short delay while Governor W. W. Thayer considered a citizen's petition to commute their death penalty to a sentence of life imprisonment.

Whereas, Archie Brown was on the 21st day of November, convicted, in the circuit court of the state of Oregon of the county of Multnomah, of the crime of murder in the first degree, and sentenced by the judge of said court to be hanged on Friday, Feb. 7, 1879; and

Whereas, Sufficient time has not elapsed since the decision of the Supreme Court rendered upon appeal from the judgment upon conviction of the said Archie Brown to enable him to make suitable preparations to meet the doom the law has pronounced against him.

Now, therefore I, W. W. Thayer, Governor of the State of Oregon, by virtue of the power in me vested, do hereby grant a reprieve of suspension of the sentence which He, the said, Archie Brown, is under for the murder of Louis Joseph, until the hour of 2 o'clock in the afternoon of Friday the 14th day of March A. D. 1879.

In testimony whereof, I have hereunto set my hand and caused the seal of state to be affixed, the day and date above written.

W. W. Thayer, Governor
R. P. Earhart, Secretary of State[11]

Johnson's reprieve was worded exactly the same except for the name, date of conviction and date sentence was passed. Executive clemency was finally denied and the convicted men were sentenced to hang together on March 14, 1879.[12]

It was at this time that public controversy over capital punishment began heating up. The Portland *Oregonian* published a lengthy and pertinent editorial on February 6, demanding Governor Thayer deny Brown and Johnson the life sentence they and their "weak, soft, and sappy" supporters so adamantly desired. A second editorial on February 7 covered both sides of the debate, but finished with the majority opinion that,

"there is no probability whatever that the criminals would be kept at penal servitude during the whole remainder of their lives. . . . Should they go to the penitentiary they could not make reparations for their wrong by contributing their labor to the common benefit, but would be kept as all other criminals are at an expense to the state far exceeding any profit to be derived from their labor, and in the comparatively short time would be released or make their escape.

Apparently the right to privacy was unknown in 1879 as the Portland *Oregonian* published Doctor Paul Brenan's psychological examination of both men. Eugene Avery (alias Archie Brown) was born in Wisconsin. He was 25 years old, 5' 10" tall, very stout, looking healthy and robust. Doctor Brenan measured his chest, and his head from various angles. He described Brown as not being too smart, lacking character, self-esteem, personal pride and impulse control. He drank too much and enjoyed the wild life everywhere he went. Brown had adequate language abilities and higher than average imagination and curiosity.[13]

Frank Taylor (alias James Johnson) refused to give his true name out of embarrassment and concern that his family back east would find out about his condition. In all other ways he talked freely with Doctor Brenan about his past. He was born in Belfast, Maine 25 years earlier. He was a handsome man, 5' 10" tall, with brown hair, hazel eyes, long features, and a good complexion. He was intelligent, witty and able to make friends easily. As a young man he failed to study and instead loved fast company. He lacked self-esteem, a sense of honor, and good moral principles. Both men were inclined to be lazy. Both would not work if they could get money in some other way and both felt that the world owed them a living. They expressed regret over their past actions now that they were caught, and stated, "Our lives should be a warning example to multitudes of young men who are on the downward road to crime and degradation, enticed by the flash and momentary excitement of wrongdoers."[14]

Dark clouds covered the sky the morning of the hangings but the rain held off until after the execution. The Emmett Guard, the City Rifles and the Washington Guard, all in full uniform, patrolled the area around the courthouse. The men carried loaded rifles and fixed bayonets. Cannons were set up on the corners of Main and Salmon Streets. Even though the sheriff had a 40-foot-high stockade erected around the gallows, half of Portland's 16,000 people were milling around on the streets waiting to witness the big event.[15] Some climbed trees to gain a view of the proceedings.

On March 14, 1879, the two men were marched to the gallows at 1:30 p.m. accompanied by Reverend W. C. Chattin, Multnomah County Sheriff Ben Norden, a jury of twelve official witnesses, numerous officials and reporters from all over the world.[16] The twelve assigned execution witnesses were Eugene D. White, George C. Sears, L. C. Potter, Leonard Stark, J. M. Gilman, L. Besser, P. Leonard, J. C. Stuart, William Showers, A. E. Bothwick, C. J. Graham and Charles B. Bartell.[17] At least thirty-one men sat on chairs arranged along the back stage of the scaffold.

Johnson didn't have much to say when asked if he had any comments except to say that he was the victim of judicial murder. Brown put on quite a show. He was stylishly dressed and admitted being the ringleader of a group of bank robbers in California.

Finally Sheriff Norden asked, "Brown, do you wish to recite every incident of your life? It is now a few minutes past two o'clock. Will you be through by half past two?"

Nodding calmly to Norden, Brown replied, "Yes, I guess so. I will simply say I am a noted highwayman, a great robber. I am guilty of every crime. I will say to the young men, listen to your mothers. If you do, you will not meet the doom I am to. I would like to sing a song."

Then he sang two songs; "John Rodgers", which began with the words, "Come all you kind-hearted Christians," and, "Trials by Jury". Johnson began getting impatient and pleaded with Brown to hurry up.

Finally Brown finished his oration and the main event got under way. Following the established routine, the officers strapped the men's legs together, tied their hands together in the back, and pulled a black cloth cap over their heads. After fitting the ropes snugly around their necks, Reverend W. C. Chattin said a brief prayer and the trap was pulled at exactly 2:22 p.m. Doctor R. G. Rex and Doctor W. H. Saylor declared the men dead about half an hour later.

Sheriff Norden accomplished his job without a hitch and both men died on schedule. Afterwards the bodies were put into their black wooden coffins and displayed on the sidewalk for ogling spectators.[18] By the end of the day they were covered with flowers and wreaths. Their bodies were delivered to Thomas Shortell at DeLin's Undertaking Establishment, and eventually to a cemetery in east Portland.

References

Century Edition of the American Digest, A complete digest of all reported American cases from the earliest times to 1896. Vol. 26, St. Paul: West Publishing, 1901. "Where the defendant committed a robbery, and, while carrying off the plunder, was pursued by a constable, whom he shot at, and in so doing, killed a boy standing near, held, that he was guilty of murder in the first degree", – State v. Brown, 7 Or. 186, p. 47.

Coos Bay News (Coos Bay, Oregon) March 19, 1879.

Daily Oregonian (Portland, Oregon) February 2, 1879, February 4, 1879, February 6, 1879, February 8, 1879, February 22, 1879, March 14, 1879, March 15, 1879, January 1, 1880.

Evening Telegram (Portland, Oregon) December 2, 1878, February 6, 1879, March 6, 1879.

Humbird, Jim. "When Hangings Were A Major Pastime." *Oregonian* (Portland, Oregon) September 3, 1939.

Olsen, Charles Oluf. "A Hangin' In Old Portland." *Oregon Journal* (Portland, Oregon) January 16, 1949.

Oregon State Penitentiary File No. 889, Joseph Swords, Oregon State Archives, Salem, Oregon.

Plaindealer (Roseburg, Oregon) November 19, 1878, December 28, 1878.

State of Oregon v. Brown A. etal, No. 1067, File No. 0970, Journal entry: Vol. 6, p. 356, Oregon Supreme Court Case Files, January 28, 1879.

State of Oregon v. Johnson J. etal, No. 1068, File No. 0972, Journal entry: Vol. 6, p. 357, Oregon Supreme Court Case Files, January 28, 1879.

Chapter 19 notes

1 Jim Humbird, "When Hangings Were A Major Pastime", *Oregonian* (Portland, Oregon) September 3, 1939.

2 State of Oregon v. Johnson J. etal, No. 1068, File No. 0972, Journal entry: Vol. 6, p. 357, Oregon Supreme Court Case Files, January 28, 1879, Oregon State Archives, Salem, Oregon.

3 Jim Humbird, *Oregonian*, September 3, 1939.

4 State of Oregon v. Brown A. etal, No. 1067, File No. 0970, Journal entry: Vol. 6, p. 356, Oregon Supreme Court Case Files, January 28, 1879, Oregon State Archives, Salem, Oregon.

5 Ibid.

6 *Plaindealer* (Roseburg, Oregon) December 28, 1878.

7 State of Oregon v. Johnson J. etal, No. 1068.

8 Ibid.

9 Oregon State Penitentiary Inmate Case File # 889 for Joseph Swords, Oregon State Archives, Salem, Oregon.

10 State of Oregon v. Brown A. etal, No. 1067.

11 *Daily Oregonian*, February 8, 1879.

12 *Daily Oregonian*, March 15, 1879.

13 *Daily Oregonian*, February 4, 1879.

14 Ibid.

15 Charles Olug Olsen, "A Hangin' In Old Portland", *Oregon Journal* (Portland, Oregon) January 16, 1949.

16 Ibid.

17 *Daily Oregonian* (Portland, Oregon) March 15, 1879.

18 Charles Olug Olsen, Oregon Journal, January 26, 1958.

Chapter Twenty
United States v. Kot-Ko-Wot 1879

In 1879, Portland was the site of the U.S. District court for the Territory of Alaska. On March 27 the *Daily Oregonian* printed an unusual grand jury indictment. Two Alaskan Chilikat Indians were accused of killing Thomas J. Brown, a white hotel keeper living in Hot Springs, about twelve miles from Sitka, Alaska on January 1, 1879.

On March 3, the British cutter, *Wolcott*, and the *Osprey* arrived in Sitka, Alaska to help protect the residents who were facing a difficult situation with the local Indians.[1] While the cutter was insufficient to protect the population it did help implement the following scheme until a government man-of-war could arrive.

The Indians were so afraid that within five minutes of the *Osprey's* arrival Brown's gun, ax, books and other possessions were turned over to the authorities. Ah-Na-Hontz and Stickeesh, two of the Sitka chiefs were arrested and their tribe given two hours to produce Anna, the wife of Brown's killer. At first the chiefs said that she was gone, but when they realized how serious their captors were, they quickly produced the woman.

She told the following story: Anna, Kot-Ko-Wot and his friend Okh-Kho-Not had arrived at Whale Bay on January 1, in their canoe. Kot-Ko-Wot left his wife and friend to watch the canoe, while he went up to Thomas Brown's house. While he was gone, the people on the beach heard two gunshots, and started running toward the house. On the way they met Kot-Ko-Wot and asked him what happened.

"I have killed Brown."

Anna asked, "But why? Where are you going? Do you want to leave us?"

"For the punishment from the soldiers while I was confined there. The soldiers wounded my brother and they did not pay anything for him. I asked Brown for some matches but he refused to give them to me so I shot him."

They all went into Brown's house and saw him lying on the floor with blood running out of his side. Kot-Ko-Wot was going to chop him up with the ax, but Anna pulled his hair and made him stop. After beating her for her interference, they dragged the body to a canoe, tied heavy rocks to it and dumped it overboard about three miles from Hot Springs in twenty fathoms of water.

Members of the Sitka tribe realized that Brown was missing and, in the usual manner, heard rumors that Kot-Ko-Wot and his friend, Okh-Kho-Not, were the parties responsible. A group got together, went to Kot-Ko-Wot's house and arrested the pair. Inside the house they found several items that belonged to Brown—an ax, a powder can, a rifle, two blankets, a handsaw and a piece of carpet. Wanting the authorities to release their chiefs they brought the two accused men to Sitka.

U. S. Marshal A. W. Waters arrived in Sitka on the steamer, *California*, and took charge of the prisoners. He also brought Anna, George Kastrametinoff, a Russian interpreter, and A-Ta-Chin, a Sitka Indian, back to Portland with him to testify at the trial.

The trial was held on April 16, 1879, in the U.S. Circuit Court building in Portland. Judge Matthew P. Deady presided. District Attorney Rufus Mallory served as prosecutor and Sydney Dell was appointed defense attorney. The twelve jurors were A. L. Alderman (from Yamhill County), J. A. Fisher (from Multnomah County), J. G. Brown, Absalom Byerly, Jason T. Fitzzel, Samuel P. Gibson, Paul Hellenbrand, Leonard Livermore, Albert Odell, Francis M. Smith, H. C. Sterling, and Sanford Watson (all from Polk County).[2] It took the jury an hour to reach a verdict.[3]

"We the jury in the case United State vs. Okh-Kho-Not, find the defendant **not** guilty as charged in the indictment."

"We the jury in the case United States vs. Kot-Ko-Wot, find the defendant guilty as charged in the indictment."

Okh-Kho-Not was released from custody and Kot-Ko-Wot was taken back to the county jail. Judge Deady sentenced him to hang on May 5, 1879. Judge Matthew P. Deady had served as a judge since 1853; yet this was his first time sentencing a man to death.[4] He also applied a portion of the law that up to now had rarely been used. He charged U. S. Marshal "after the due execution of this sentence, to deliver your (Kot-Ko-Wot) body to the medical school for dissection."[5]

This upset members of the jury and others in the community so much that Harvey Scott, editor of the *Oregonian,* rushed to defend his friend and political ally, Judge Deady.[6] . He printed the applicable section of the law in his newspaper on April 25, 1879.

> *The court before which any person is convicted of murder, may, in its discretion, add to the judgment of death, that the body of the offender be delivered to a surgeon for dissection; and the marshal who executes such judgment shall deliver the body after execution to such surgeon as the court may direct; and such surgeon, or some person by him appointed, shall receive and take away the body at the time of the execution.*
>
> Section 5340, Revised Statute of the
> United States, page 1043.

The same scaffold used to hang James Johnson and Archie Brown was used to hang Kot-Ko-Wot. Nearly everyone who wanted inside was admitted into the stockade, even though seventy-five engraved invitations were issued to keep unwelcome sightseers out.

The morning of May 5, Reverend W. C. Chattin came to Kot-Ko-Wot's cell and spoke with him. Reverend Chattin was one of the few people in Portland who spoke the prisoner's language.

Before he was escorted out of the jail, Kot-Ko-Wot told Reverend Chattin, "Annie and Okh-Kho-Not helped to kill Brown and were as guilty as myself, but I forgive them. I have put away all angry feeling. I feel as though you are the only friend I have, and I want you to be with me to the last and pray for me."

At 12:53 p.m. U.S. Marshal Waters, Deputy Marshal W. P. Burnes, Sheriff B. L. Norden, Constable M. B. Wallace and Reverend Chattin escorted Kot-Ko-Wot to the waiting scaffold. Kot-Ko-Wot was standing too close to the side of the trap when the pin was pulled and his body struck the side and bounced back and forth before he finally strangled to death.[7]

Judge Deady had the sad duty of consigning a second Alaskan Native to the gallows on March 11, 1882. Ka-ta-tah was found guilty of killing Maloney and Campini two years earlier in August 1880. Deady granted the convict's request to move up the date of the hanging three days to Tuesday, March 28, so his friends could see him hang before they returned to Alaska.[8]

Ka-ta-tah's body also was delivered to the medical school for dissection.

References
Daily Oregonian (Portland, Oregon) March 16, 1879, March 27, 1879, April 16, 1879, April 24, 1879, April 25, 1879, May 5, 1879, May 6, 1879.
Oregonian (Portland, Oregon) September 3, 1939.

Chapter 20 notes
1 *Daily Oregonian* (Portland, Oregon) March 16, 1879.
2 *Daily Oregonian* April 16, 1879.
3 Ibid.
4 Deady had been Creed Turner's defense attorney in 1851 and Adam Wimple' defense attorney in 1852. Judge Deady was a well-known defender of the civil rights of the Chinese living in Oregon. His career as a federal judge and his legal opinions were well respected across the United States.
5 *Daily Oregonian*, April 24, 1879.
6 Ruth B. Moynihan, *Rebel for Rights, Abigail Scott Duniway*, (Westford: Yale University, 1983) p. 45. "Among their (the Scott family) guests were Judge Matthew Deady, associate justice of the Territorial Supreme Court and a prominent Democratic politician."
7 *Daily Oregonian*, May 6, 1879.
8 Clark, Malcolm, Jr. Ed. *Pharisee Among the Philistines, The Diary of Judge Matthew P Deady 1871-1892*, Vol. 2, Portland Historical Society, 1975, pg 393-394.

Chapter Twenty-One

State of Oregon v. Ah Lee 1880

A h Lee was the first Asian American hanged in Oregon. He did-n't submit easily to Oregon justice. It took two trials and two appeals before his time finally ran out.

Oregon, Washington and California had the largest population of Chinese in the United States. Chinese men were imported to dig mines and build the railroads—jobs no one else wanted. When the railroads and mines no longer needed them, the Chinese migrated into the larger cities where they worked in domestic service and other menial jobs.[1] By 1880 there were 9,515 Chinese living on the west side of Portland and the city had become the second largest concentration of Chinese in the nation.[2]

On Wednesday evening, October 2, 1878, a young Chinese Christian, Chin Sue Ying, entered the Joss (God) House.[3] It was the general meeting place in Portland for all Chinese living in the area and the hall was being decorated in preparation for a religious cele-bration the next day. The place of worship was in a separate room con-taining various statues, flags, and significant icons. It was decorated with richly embroidered fabric, colorful feathers and beautiful furni-ture. Usually incense was kept burning and a large gong occupied one corner.[4] Before anyone could stop him, Chin Sue Ying walked in and dumped a bowl of thick, red, foul-smelling liquid on the floor dese-crating the room's holiness and insulting the Confucian, Buddhist and Taoist worshippers about to begin their holiday. Observers quickly tossed him out into the street.

The next afternoon, Chin Sue Ying, again walked into the Joss House camouflaged by a large group of men entering at the same time and joined nearly a hundred men already in the room. This time he had a large piece of raw meat hidden in his sleeve, which he planned to throw at the altar. Before he could get close enough, three men, prepared and waiting, spotted him and quietly surrounded him. One pulled a sharp hatchet out of his sleeve and struck Chin Sue Ying several times. Two others had pistols hidden in their sleeves and each shot Chin in the stomach.

The wounded man was taken into another room and laid on a table. Eventually, a doctor and the police were summoned. Bystanders recognized the men who had assaulted Chin and gave their names to the police.

The next day Ah Lee was arrested as he lay sleeping in his room. He denied striking Chin with the hatchet and declared that he had been home in bed the whole time. Charley Lee Quong also denied killing Chin. He admitted being in the Joss House all day but stated that he was in a back room singing out of the priest's book when Chin was killed. Lee Jong had disappeared from Portland and was never seen again. Ah Lee and Charley Lee Quong were brought to Chin Sue Ying's bedside where he identified them as his attackers. He managed to stay alive about thirty-six hours, dying about 2 a.m. on the morning of October 5, 1878.[5]

Ah Lee and Charley Lee Quong were indicted on October 25, 1878, and tried in court together. John F. Caples was the District Attorney. M. F. Mulkey was the defense attorney, and C. B. Bellinger was the judge. On December 28, 1878 both were found guilty of first-degree murder and sentenced to hang on February 7, 1879.[6] The defense lawyers issued an appeal to the Oregon State Supreme Court, and on May 20, 1879, the court granted the appeal for the following reason:

> *In a case of murder where the degree of the crime is not admitted by the prisoner, and there is any disagreement among the witnesses for the prosecution on the subject of premeditation, it is an error for the court to charge the jury that there is no evidence lending to reduce the degree of the crime from murder in the first degree and that the jury should either find the prisoner guilty as charged or acquit him.*
>
> *Where evidence is introduced in a criminal case to establish any proposition necessary to prove guilt, the evidence is sufficient to establish such proposition if it satisfies the jury of its truth beyond a reasonable doubt.*[7]

The judge had only given the jury two choices in his instructions – either the defendants were guilty of first-degree murder or they had to be acquitted. The Supreme Court disagreed with the instructions and felt that the jury should have been given the option of finding the defendants guilty of a lesser crime.

A second trial was scheduled for July 7, 1879. This time Ah Lee and Charley Lee Quong requested separate trials. Charley was tried first and was convicted of second-degree murder. He was sentenced to life in the penitentiary. Eventually he was pardoned and released on October 21, 1885.[8] Charley Quong was 34 years old when he finally walked away from the prison.

Ah Lee didn't get off so easily. This time the jury was determined to make someone hang for the murder of Chin Sue Ying. The unseen but highly influential rulers of Portland were anxious to set an example. "Most of the revenue which supported the city government was obtained by the high licensing of local saloons," opium dens and houses of prostitution.[9] They wanted to keep the activities producing income but needed a scapegoat or two to reassure the public of their safety.

Ah Lee was found guilty of first-degree murder and sentenced to hang on Tuesday, September 23, 1879. Mulkey and Whalley, his lawyers, filed another appeal to the Supreme Court, this time based on the fact the jury took a trip to the Joss House without the defendant or his attorney being present. The appeal was denied and for the second time Ah Lee stood in front of Judge Bellinger and was sentenced to die on April 20, 1880.

After being in jail for over a year and finally losing all hope, Ah Lee went into a terrible depression. The Chinese community had donated large amounts of money to Lee's lawyer and supported a petition to Oregon Governor Thayer. Eventually, the petition was denied and there was only the long wait for the execution,

Ah Lee's anxiety and intense fear of hanging affected everyone around him. Multnomah County Jailor Berry hired six men to guard the prisoner around the clock to prevent any attempt at suicide, escape or rescue. The jail authorities were determined to prevent another suicide from cheating the gallows. (In 1884 the authorities were not as careful, and Lee Sang committed suicide in the Multnomah County Jail by tearing his shirt into strips and hanging himself. He had been convicted of killing Wong Bin on August 5, 1884.)[10]

On his last morning Ah Lee put on a new silk Chinese blouse and black pantaloons. Jailor Berry helped him sort and arrange some long pieces of pasteboard on his body before he left the jail.

Outside in the stockade the crowd overflowed the space available, pushing and shoving each other, climbing the high fence, and crowding onto the balcony above the gallows. Hatred was so intense against

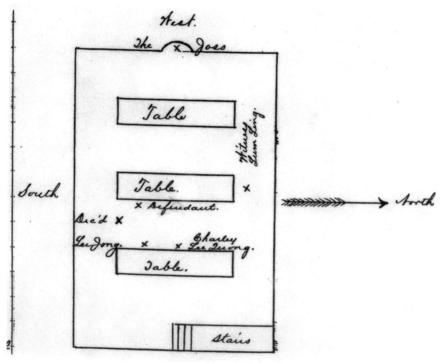

Trial record, State of Oregon v. Ah Lee
Floor plan of Portland joss house where Ah Lee murdered Chin Sue Ying.

the Chinese at that time that the authorities were concerned that the execution would incite a riot. A mob in Los Angeles had killed nineteen Chinese only nine years earlier. A few years later a riot in Rock Springs, Wyoming left twenty-eight Chinese dead. A mob burned down the Tacoma Chinatown and there were killings in Nevada and Colorado.[11] The most influential newspaper in the state, the Portland *Oregonian,* defended the Chinese rights; even after the Chinese exclusion acts were passed in 1880 and 1882.[12]

When Multnomah County Sheriff Ben Norden and his deputies led Ah Lee outside, the huge crowd shoved and jostled them. Printed invitations had been issued but the guards at the entrance of the stockade refused to intervene and the crowd rushed inside the small enclosure. Rude epitaphs and vulgar comments were hurled at the prisoner while his guards tried to push their way through the crowd. They finally reached the scaffold and took refuge on top. Above them the crowd was so thick on the balcony, the beams cracked and moaned.

99

At 11:22 a.m. Sheriff Norden pulled the black cap over Ah Lee's head and adjusted the rope. Ah Lee fell with a thump, but instead of dying quickly, he struggled and twisted for five minutes before finally taking his last breath.

> *The crowd that saw him hurled from earth was rough and boisterous. Sheriff Norden was held in no respect whatever. And why should he be? The mob had gone to see a sideshow, and they saw it in their own way, too, roughly, uncivilly and coarsely.* [13]

Ah Lee protested his innocence, over and over, right up to the moment of his death.

Considering the hatred against the Chinese on the West Coast, it's almost unbelievable that only two Chinese men were hanged in Oregon and both men executed for killing another Chinese. Twenty years later, in 1902, another Chinese, Lum You, was hanged in South Bend, Washington for murdering a white man.[14] Generally, the Chinese were the victims as white men harassed, beat, robbed, swindled and murdered them with little impunity. By 1870 nearly half the population of Grant County was Chinese.[15] In 1879 a law was passed forbidding Chinese men from marrying in the hope it would curb the population growth. It left 9,000 men without wives or families.[16] Anti-Chinese bigotry continued to increase, culminating in the 1887 murder of twelve Chinese miners in Hells Canyon on the Oregon/Idaho border.

References

Daily Oregonian (Portland, Oregon) February 4, 1879, April 29, 1879, May 21, 1879, October 19,1884.

Dicken, Samuel N. *The Making of Oregon: A Study of Historical Geography*. Portland: Oregon Historical Society, 1979.

Evening Telegram (Portland, Oregon) April 8, 1880, April 9, 1880, April 14, 1880, April 15, 1880, April 16, 1880, April 17, 1880, April 20, 1880, April 21, 1880.

Friedman, Lawrence. *Crime and Punishment in American History*. N.Y.: Basic Books, 1993.

Humbird, Jim, "When Hangings Were A Major Pastime." *Weekly Oregonian* (Portland, Oregon) September 3, 1939.

Maddux, Percy. *City On The Willamette: The Story of Portland, Oregon*. Portland: Binfords & Mort, 1952.

McLagan, Elizabeth. *A Peculiar Paradise.* Portland: Georgian Press Company, 1980.

Moynihan, Ruth B. *Rebel For Rights, Abigail Scott Duniway*. Boston: Yale University, 1983.

Oregon State Penitentiary Records located at the Oregon State Archives, Salem, Oregon. Inmate Register, Great Register, 1854-1946, Charley Lee Quong, #964, p. 33.

*Plaindeale*r (Roseburg, Oregon) December 6, 1879.

State of Oregon v. Ah Lee, No. 1213, File No. 01112, Journal entry: Vol. 6, p. 565, September 17, 1879, Oregon Supreme Court Appeals file, Oregon State Archives, Salem, Oregon.

Chapter 21 notes

1 Samuel N. Dicken, *The Making of Oregon: A Study in Historical Geography* (Portland: The Oregon Historical Society, 1979) p. 105.

2 Elizabeth McLagan, *A Peculiar Paradise* (Portland: Georgian Press Company, 1980), p. 89. Also see p. 193, #20.

3 Percy Maddux, *City On the Willamette* (Portland, Oregon: Binfords & Mort, 1952) p. 86. The first Chinese Baptist mission was established in Portland in 1874. Other Christian churches soon followed.

4 Ibid. pp. 86-87.

5 State of Oregon v. Ah Lee, No. 1213, File No. 01112, Journal entry: Vol. 6, p. 565, September 17, 1879, Oregon Supreme Court Appeals file, Oregon State Archives, Salem, Oregon.

6 State of Oregon v. Ah Lee.

7 *Daily Oregonian* (Portland, Oregon) May 21, 1879.

8 Oregon State Penitentiary Inmate Case File #964 for Charley Lee Quong, Oregon State Archives, Salem, Oregon.

9 Ruth B. Moynihan, *Rebel For Rights, Abigail Scott Duniway* (Boston: Yale University, 1983) p. 172.

10 *Daily Oregonian*, October 19, 1884.

11 Lawrence Friedman. *Crime and Punishment in American History* (N.Y.: Basic Books, 1993) p. 98.

12 Percy Maddux, pp. 80-81.

13 *Evening Telegram* (Portland, Oregon) April 20, 1880.

14 *Morning Oregonian*, January 31, 1902.

15 Daily Oregonian, March 3, 1879.

16 Ibid.

Chapter Twenty-Two

State of Oregon v. Arthur (Pat Edward) Murphy 1881

Sometimes the motive behind a murder is so murky, even the murderer has a hard time explaining why he did it. Such was the case when "Pat" Murphy killed Thomas D. French, age 42, in Heppner on June 10, 1880.

Pat Murphy, whose real name was Arthur, but was also known as Edward, was a 32-year-old Irishman herding sheep for S. S. Snyder. He emigrated from Ireland to Pennsylvania when still a small child with his siblings and widowed mother. Forced to leave school at age eleven to earn his living, he traveled to California in 1867 and fourteen years later came to Oregon. Some years earlier an accident had put his eye out and the scar marked his face, but otherwise he was described as a good-looking man with regular features, black hair, and a black beard, about 5' 8" tall and weighing 160 pounds.[1]

When sober Murphy was quiet, reserved and industrious. However, when he started drinking he was surly, vicious and unpredictable. In January of 1880 he lost his total life savings, $840, in a fire at Bridge Creek in Wasco County.[2] The loss of the money took away his hope and faith in the future. He started drinking heavily. On May 7 he came to Heppner and went on a three-day drinking spree. His employer, S. S. Snyder, retrieved his unconscious body and took it back to the sheep camp where he left him. Several days later T. D. French, who had a field of grain growing nearby, complained to Snyder that Murphy had neglected his sheep and was letting them graze in his grain field.

When Snyder sent a ranch hand, B. C. Henderson, to confront Murphy, the sheepherder replied, "I'll go down and shoot the s—of a b——!" He fetched his Remington revolver from his tent. Henderson was able to calm the excitable Irishman down and persuaded him to put the gun away.

Unfortunately, French rode into camp a little before dark and it became apparent the Irishman was still angry. Murphy again got his gun, stuck it in his pants and went to meet the visitor. As Henderson watched, the two men talked for a moment before Murphy pulled out his gun and shot French in the head. Henderson quickly rode the mile and a half into Heppner and returned to the sheep camp with a group of citizens. They found French unconscious, but alive until he died a few hours later.

Murphy ran away after the shooting but surrendered quietly three days later to A. J. Stevenson of Heppner when he was half dead from thirst and hunger. A mob tried to lynch him but Stevenson had planned ahead and Murphy was secretly taken to Pendleton where he remained in the Umatilla County Jail until his trial started on November 1, 1880.[3]

The community of Heppner raised money to hire G. W. Rea to help the Umatilla District Attorney prosecute the case. The firm of Conley and Leasure defended Murphy. Four days later the jury retired for a single hour before finding Murphy guilty of first-degree murder. His attorneys attempted to file an appeal, but were unable to complete it in time. Judge L. L. McArthur scheduled the hanging for January 5, 1881 in Pendleton.

Murphy was truly repentant and relied heavily on his Catholic faith to sustain him while he waited to die. He apologized publicly to the Widow French and her ten fatherless children. He didn't deny killing French but maintained it was done accidentally during a fight while he was drunk. He accused Henderson of lying about the circumstances involved. Exhibiting rare compassion, Umatilla County Sheriff William Martin let Murphy participate in a snowball fight in front of the jail just four days before the hanging.

On Wednesday, January 5, 1881, Murphy spent time with Father Conrardy, before dressing in a black broadcloth suit, a white shirt, a white silk tie, a large black slouch hat and embroidered slippers.[4] The gallows was surrounded with a high fence, which did little to keep the milling crowds out. Murphy had requested the drop be a clear six feet, which it was. At 3 p.m. the hanging party left the jail and entered the enclosure. L. B. Cox, editor of the *East Oregonian*, read Murphy's prepared farewell speech to the waiting audience.[5] In it he maintained the shooting was an accident and deeply regretted it. He accused S. S. Snyder, B. C. Henderson and A. J. Stevenson of lying about the incident. The rope was tightened around his neck and he shook hands with Sheriff Martin. His arms and feet were fastened together, the black cap was pulled over his face and he died a moment later of a broken neck.

Father Conrardy buried him in the Catholic Cemetery.

References

1880 Federal Census, Umatilla County, Oregon.

1865 and 1875 Oregon Census, Umatilla County, Oregon State Archives, Salem, Oregon.

Himes, George. Scrapbook #76, p. 86. Oregon Historical Society, Portland, Oregon.

The East Oregonian (Pendleton, Oregon) May 15, 1880, November 6, 1880, January 8, 1881.

Morning Oregonian (Portland, Oregon) January 7, 1881.

Chapter 22 notes

1 *Morning Oregonian* (Portland, Oregon) January 7, 1881.

2 *The East Oregonian* (Pendleton, Oregon) January 8, 1881.

3 Ibid. The circuit court records could not be found either in the Oregon State Archives nor the Umatilla County storage facility.

4 *Morning Oregonian*, January 7, 1881.

5 Ibid.

Chapter Twenty-Three

State of Oregon v. Alfred Andersen 1883

Since Cain murdered Abel, fratricide has been regarded as a heinous crime. Greed and jealousy caused that brother to murder his sibling, just as it did in 1882.

On Monday, October 9, 1882, Captain William H. Whitcomb was smoking a pipe and leaning against the rail of his steamboat, *Wonder*, as it steamed up the Columbia River. Across the water he watched two men disappear into the brush of Swan Island. About a half-mile later, as the boat continued up the river, he heard two shots close together and watched a single man, carrying two guns, come running out of the bushes. In his hurry the runner dropped one of the guns into the yellow mud, jamming dirt into the muzzle. Quickly he picked it up, jumped into a little rowboat that was tied to some bushes, and rowed away.

Captain Whitcomb didn't think too much about what he saw until two weeks later, on October 29, when the body of a man with half of his head shot off, was discovered on Swan Island. The coroner and several men rowed out to the island to look at the body where it was found, and declared it to be a homicide. Within a few days the body was identified as Charles Andersen, a Norwegian saloonkeeper, visiting from Chicago. Charles Andersen was 30 years old, 5' 6" tall, about 160 pounds, no beard, short hair and a long red mustache. He had arrived in Portland on September 27 on the *State of California* steamship with his girlfriend Bertha Nelson, and was met by his younger brother, Alfred, age 28. The authorities quickly began looking for Bertha and Alfred. Both brothers had been born in Christiania, Norway, while Bertha was from Sweden.

Portland Chief of Police J. H. Lappeus soon learned Alfred and Bertha had left Portland on October 11 in a steamer bound for Astoria. Portland Detective Hudson trailed the pair to Astoria, Kalama, New Tacoma, Victoria B.C., back to Tacoma, back to Victoria, and then to San Francisco.[1] Detective Hudson telegraphed the authorities in San Francisco, who were waiting when the steamer arrived. Alfred and Bertha's little vacation trip finally came to a stop on the evening of November 17 when they were both incarcerated in the Multnomah County Jail. Alfred was charged with his brother's murder and Bertha was jailed as a material witness.

There was a great deal of circumstantial evidence that led people to believe that Alfred had killed his brother Charles. Before the murder Alfred was well known by his friends and acquaintances to be broke and nearly destitute. After the murder he was seen gambling and losing hundreds of dollars in one night. He spent a great deal of money on hotels, boat tickets and meals. The only way he could have gotten the money was from his dead brother.

William Riley, a Portland salesman in the Hudson Store, remembered Charles and Alfred renting two shotguns on Monday, October 9. The next day Alfred, without Charles, brought the guns back. One of the guns had yellow mud smashed up into the barrel. William Riley was the last man to see Charles Andersen alive.

Besides money, Alfred also had his brother's clothes, a gold watch, a small revolver, and his mistress. Because they had no money to put up for bond, Bertha and another friend of Alfred's, Antoine Anderson, were stuck in jail until February 6, 1883, when the trial started.

Judge Raleigh Stott was in charge of the trial. W. M. Gregory and J. G. Chapman served as defense lawyers, while District Attorney John F. Caples and M. F. Mulkey were the prosecutors. The twelve jurors chosen were: L. H. D. Bondy, J. N. Bristol, C. A. Coursen, George Eckley, Adam Fisher, Plympton Kelly, E. Himmons, C. W. Lomler, L. C. Sharbo, John L. Smith, Aaron Vinson, and W. L. Higgins, foreman.[2] The jurors appeared to be intelligent and hard working. Most were family men, having lived in the area for a long time and were farmers and merchants.[3] For a week, fifty-six witnesses paraded before the Portland jury box. Everyone got up to tell their story; everyone except Alfred Andersen.

The day Bertha Nelson testified there was standing room only in the courtroom. Bertha had believed Andersen's explanation that his brother had returned to Chicago without her. While she had traveled with Charles from Chicago, she didn't live with him when they arrived in Portland. Their first night in Portland she had slept with the Sisters at the hospital, spent four nights at the Burton House and then rented a room on Fifth Street with Mrs. Brown. In court Bertha described a small silver plated pistol with a white handle belonging to Charles Andersen. She also identified a ring she'd given Charles that he wore on his little finger. Her testimony identified many other articles belonging to Charles that were found on Alfred when he was arrested in San Francisco.[4] After Charles disappeared Alfred Andersen proposed that they now travel together as his mistress just as she had traveled with his brother. In her naiveté she accepted his offer.

Oregon State Sheriffs Association

The trial took a week, which was a very long trial by 1883 standards. However, it only took about an hour for the jury to return a verdict of "guilty of first-degree murder." As Judge Stott read the sentence a hush settled over the large audience:

Multnomah County Sheriff George C. Sears was in charge of the hanging of Alfred Andersen.

> *The judgment of the courts, that you be taken from this place by the sheriff and kept in close confinement until the 13th day of April next, and on that day, between the hours of 9 and 2 o'clock, you will be taken to a place suitably prepared and there hanged by the neck until you are dead. And may the Lord have mercy upon your soul.*[5]

Alfred Andersen was sentenced to hang on April 13, 1883.

Defense Attorney Gregory prepared an appeal for a new trial to the Oregon Supreme Court, which was quickly denied. A new date was set for the hanging—July 20, 1883.

On the day of the hanging militia companies were stationed around the courtyard and around the jail. It was a wise precaution as they were the only reason the crowd didn't knock down the fence around the scaffold. About 300 spectators crowded into the enclosure, peered from the balcony and stared out the jail windows. The "death witnesses" were Wash. F. Allen, James Backenstos, William G. Beck, David Cole, John E. Courtney, Doctor L L. Hope, F. M. Hunson, L. B. Ind, F. B. Mason, J. M. Pittenger, Almon Smith, and Tim Stapleton.[6]

After Jailor Ned Dougherty, Sheriff George C. Sears and Deputy Witherell escorted the prisoner to the top of the scaffold, Andersen stepped to the edge and gave a lengthy speech while the deadly noose bounced against him.

> *There was no evidence to convict me, and I am convicted by circumstantial evidence alone. Every man of that jury who brought in a verdict of guilty against me, is guilty of murder in the first degree before the Lord . . . It's very well to go out and find a verdict against a man and if he has got money he can go free. I can go out on the street and take $100 and I can get five, ten, yes fifteen men to go on a jury and swear to whatever I tell them to. . . Who shall answer for my murder?*

Suddenly Andersen stopped and pointed directly at a man standing in the crowd, a man who served on the jury that found him guilty.

> *There is one. He will answer for it.*

He paused for a moment to catch his breath.

> *I die innocent, but I am satisfied to die innocent. I am glad to say I die innocent.*

His speech lasted one hour and twenty minutes.[7]

Apparently, Andersen believed if he stalled past the hour specified he could not be executed. If he believed that, certainly Sheriff Sears did not, as he quickly tied Anderson's hands and feet and pulled the black cap over the murderer's head.

After tightening the rope around Andersen's neck Sheriff Sears tripped the trap with his foot at exactly 2:09 p.m. Andersen fell through like a rock the full six feet and died with a broken neck. His body was taken down and put into a pauper's coffin, conveyed to the morgue and left on display for the curious to gawk and stare at as they filed by.

Bertha's incarceration in the county jail turned out to be quite beneficial. While there she struck up a deep friendship with Antoine Anderson, Alfred's friend and a witness against him at the trial. Shortly after the trial was over and they were released from jail, the couple was married in February 1883 and began living in Slabtown, a suburb of Portland.[8]

References

City Guard (Eugene, Oregon) February 24, 1883.

Daily Oregonian (Portland, Oregon) February 5, 1883, February 7, 1883, February 8, 1883, February 9, 1883, February 10, 1883, February 11, 1883, February 16, 1883, February 23, 1883, February 24, 1883, April 12, 1883.

Douglas Independent (Roseburg, Oregon) July 21, 1883.

Leeson, Fred. *Rose City Justice.* Portland: Oregon Historical Society Press, 1998.

Maddux, Percy. *City On The Willamette: The Story of Portland, Oregon.* Portland: Binfords and Mort, 1952.

The Northwest News (Portland, Oregon) February 23, 1883. February 24, 1883, April 12, 1883, April 14, 1883, July 20, 1883.

State of Oregon v. A. Anderson, No. 1475, File No. 01455, Journal Entry Vol. 7, p. 218, April 24, 1883, Oregon Supreme Court Appeals file, Oregon State Archives, Salem, Oregon.

Chapter 23 notes

1 *The Northwest News* (Portland, Oregon) July 20, 1883.

2 Plympton Kelley was a special object of the *Oregonian's* attention. Apparently he condemned newspapers as too sensational for his taste during his questioning and stated that they were of no more interest to him than a dogfight. The *Oregonian's* reply—"From his appearance it would seem that "dogfights" were about his size." February 7, 1883. Kelley also had a letter printed in the *Oregon Weekly Times* (Portland, Oregon) on May 8, 1852, proposing a mass convention of farmers to implement better markets for his wheat. His opinions seem reasonable and intelligent. Three of the names are spelled differently in *The Northwest News* of July 20, 1883: C. A. Corson, S. C. Shoms, L. C. Sharno, and John H. Smith

3 *Daily Oregonian* (Portland, Oregon) February 7, 1883. The *Oregonian* printed the examination of every juror and the testimony of each witness during the trial. At the end of each day's report the newspaper also printed a series of "Notes of the Trial". The "Notes" raised questions, made editorial comments and gave small anecdotes of personal information about the participants. My favorite note: "Alfred Andersen, the prisoner, is a confirmed tobacco chewer, and spits incessantly—many times a minute." 8 February 1883.

4 State of Oregon v. A. Anderson, No. 1475, File No. 01455, Journal Entry Vol. 7, p. 218, April 24, 1883, Oregon Supreme Court Appeals file, Oregon State Archives, Salem, Oregon. A complete transcript of the trial, including testimony of all witnesses is included in the case file. The court file spells the surname with an "O", while Andersen himself and all other references spell it with an "E".

5 *Daily Oregonian*, February 24, 1883.

6 *The Northwest News*, July 20, 1883. This article takes up nearly the entire page of the newspaper. It describes the crime, the last day of the convict, and the hanging in minute detail. Of interest is Andersen's complete 45-minute speech made from the top of the scaffold just before his death.

7 *The Northwest News*, July 20, 1883.

8 *The Northwest News*, February 24, 1883.

Chapter Twenty-Four

State of Oregon v. John W. Murray 1885

John Murray dressed carefully the evening of Saturday, January 5, 1884. Even though he was forty years old his hair and his mustache were still jet-black. By combing his hair up from the sides he was able to minimize the bald spot covering the top of his head. He was a medium sized man, about 165 lbs., with dark eyes and an arrogant manner.

With a last satisfied look Murray left his room in Mrs. Anderson's boarding house and sauntered down the street. Tonight was the Forester's Ball at the Masonic Hall.[1] Soon after he entered the hall, he saw his wife, Annie, enter the hall with her brother, Alfred Yenke. He and Annie had separated three weeks earlier after a stormy four years of marriage. She and their 3-year-old daughter had moved in with her parents after Murray's cruelty and jealousy drove her away. He was a house painter and wood worker and had arrived in Portland from Massachusetts six years earlier.

Smoothing his hair back he approached his wife. "Would you like to dance?" he asked pleasantly.

"No thank you. As we have decided to separate I do not think we should be seen together. I would prefer not to associate with you any longer."

Furious, Murray replied, "I'm going to watch you. If you go home with anyone I'll have you both arrested."

Calmly she turned away and left him standing alone, embarrassed and angry. He left about midnight, not speaking to her again.

His landlady, Mrs. Fannie Anderson, and her daughter, Clara Dougherty, were also at the dance, but returned home about 11 p.m.

Murray arrived shortly afterward, dashed into his room and returned with an old shotgun which he slammed onto the floor.

"Here is the old gun. Do you see it? Do you hear it? I've got two shells in it and six or seven more in my pocket. I'm going to shoot any damned man that goes home with Annie. I don't care who he is, and then I'm going to shoot her."[2]

"Please don't!" Mrs. Anderson demanded. "Put the gun up and go to bed. Tomorrow you will feel differently. You have a good wife and a perfect lady. Why do you want to kill her away from your beautiful little girl?"

Murray acted ashamed, but muttered obstinately, "Well, I'll see about it." Picking up the gun he left the boarding house and ran toward First Street.

Meanwhile Annie, May Reeder and George Herrall, Jr. left the dance. They met Alfred Yenke, Annie's 20-year-old brother, on the corner of First and Hooker. They visited for several minutes before separating; May and George going one way and Annie and Alfred going another.

A few minutes later, just as Annie and Alfred came to the corner of Second and Clay Streets Murray yelled, "Now I've got you", and fired two shotgun blasts. Fifty-two shot pellets hit Alfred in the chest and knocked him off the plank sidewalk into the muddy street. Annie screamed and ran down the dark street.

The noise woke several families in nearby houses. When witnesses arrived they found Alfred dead.

Portland Police Detective S. Simmons arrested John Murray at his boarding house about 5 a.m. His trial was set for February 13, 1884.

Alfred Yenke, born 1864 in Germany, was buried January 7 in the Lone Fir Cemetery.[3] The members of the Turn Verein, a German fellowship, conducted the funeral at their hall in Portland. A band playing mournful melodies preceded the wagon carrying the coffin and the long procession of carriages to the cemetery.

R. D. Coy was Murray's defense attorney while Multnomah District Attorney John F. Caples served as the prosecution. Circuit Court Judge Seneca Smith supervised the trial. The first day of the trial, fifty men were summoned for jury duty. By the end of the day only eleven men had been chosen to serve. Those chosen were J. B. Carter, F. M. Coleman, Fred Daly, Daniel Dunbar, J. R. Nelson, J. F. Niles, William Simmons, B. Snover, F. Storr, D. G. Webster, and J. R. Wilkinson.[4] The next day "C. E. T. Cooper, a colored barber", was chosen as the twelfth juror.[5] Oregon law governing jury selection had only been changed for two years. From 1843 to October 24, 1882, jury selection was limited to "a *white* male inhabitant of the county in which he is returned and who has been an inhabitant thereof for the year next preceding the time he is drawn or called".[6]

Caples provided a capable and thorough prosecution. Fannie Anderson, and her two daughters, were a devastating witness against Murray as they described their conversations with him just minutes before he left her house and shot young Yenke. Of particular interest were Murray's instructions to 13 year-old Jennie Dougherty. He wanted her to keep his beloved dog inside the night of the murder when normally he took the dog everywhere with him.

Aaron F. Elkeles saw Murray at the Masonic Hall the night of the murder. He heard Murray say, "I'll get even with the . . . . tonight. I'll show you how the work is done."

Elkeles warned some people about the threat because he was afraid there would be trouble and Murray might kill somebody.

D. J. Halpruner saw Yenke at the dance at the Portland Clubhouse the night before the ball. Murray pointed Yenke out to Halpruner by saying, "I would rather see a rattlesnake there than that boy."

The defense did its best to persuade the jury that John Murray was insane at the time of the shooting. More than fifty co-workers (J. H. Lyon, John L. Smith, J. H. Eagan, John Linn, etc.) and friends (W. J. Hewitt, H. P. McGuire, etc.) testified to Murray's erratic behavior, incoherence, and insanity during the months preceding the murder. E. Atkinson, a schoolmate of Murray's in Poplar Grove, Boone County, Illinois, testified that Murray's father had been an inmate of the Illinois State insane asylum. The testimony was so boring and repetitious even the most determined members of the audience left the courtroom. Annie Murray was not allowed to testify at the trial. The defense recalled many witnesses who testified that Murray also drank heavily, sometimes as much as twenty-five to thirty glasses of beer a day.

On February 21, Assistant District Attorney M. F. Mulkey gave his summation speech. Mulkey claimed that when a man commits a crime and attempts to deny and conceal it the fact is proof that he was not insane and that he knew what he was doing. "The planning and carrying out of the murder was inconsistent with the theory of insanity, and that before the plea of insanity could be allowed it must be shown that the disease of mind must be such that the defendant did not know right from wrong."[7]

The jury retired to decide its verdict at 8 p.m. on February 22, 1884. At 11:20 the jurors sent word they had reached a verdict. The next morning, the verdict was read: "We the jury in the above entitled action, find the defendant guilty of murder in the first degree. F. M. Coleman, foreman." Murray was sentenced to hang on May 9, 1844.

Murray's attorney immediately filed an appeal to the Oregon Supreme Court, which automatically postponed the execution. By November 24, John M. Gearin was the new district attorney and he wrote and filed the opposition to the appeal.

For the next seven months the prisoner languished in the Multnomah County Jail, playing cards with the staff, visiting with friends and eventually finding religion. A rumor that Murray had another family in Amsterdam, New York was confirmed by the *Evening Telegram*, "He was known there as Amsterdam Jack, and he fled that part of the country about eight years ago leaving a wife and two children. She is working for the support of herself and children in one of the knitting mills at that place, and had heard that her husband was in Oregon, where he had married a German girl. He was in the painting business in Amsterdam, and the news of his arrest here on the charge of murder, had created a sensation in Murray's former home."[8] John Murray was not only a murderer; he was also a bigamist.

Finally the Supreme Court heard the appeal but rejected the request for a new trial. Judge Seneca Smith resentenced Murray to hang on February 13, 1885, a little over a year from the time he killed Yenke.

Local militia companies under the direction of Captain H. Cooke were stationed around the courthouse and jail yard. Nearly 1,000 curious citizens gathered on the sidewalks around the courthouse and the streets nearby.[9] Only thirty people were invited to view the event. They gathered in the courthouse until 1 p.m. when Sheriff George Sears invited them to go into the enclosure surrounding the scaffold. A light rain was falling giving a sad and dreary aspect to the proceedings. Episcopal minister Nathan Pearcy and Charles Kaffenden preceded Sheriff Sears and Deputy Sheriff Witherell. The neatly dressed prisoner marched slowly between them leaning on the arm of D. C. Lounsberry and Jailer Dougherty until he stood on the center of the trap. Sheriff Sears read the judgment decree and at the end asked Murray if he had anything to say about why the sentence of the court should not be executed.

"Well, I don't know as I can say a great deal; I can't help it, I suppose that is all there is about it." He paused for a few minutes and then continued. "Well, I don't see what I can say; I have got to go I suppose; I must die."

Mr. Pearcy gave a little speech concerning Murray's acceptance of the Episcopal faith and read the church burial service. Jailer

Dougherty handcuffed the prisoner's wrists behind his back and attached the cuffs to a leather strap that was secured around his waist. His ankles were strapped together in a similar manner. Deputy Sheriff Witherell placed the black cap over Murray's head and carefully tightened the noose around his neck. "A few seconds later, pressure on the button which opened the electric circuit, sprung the trap, Murray was suspended in mid air, and had paid the penalty of the law for his crime."[10] This was Oregon's first use of electricity during an execution.

The body was cut down fourteen minutes later, placed in a coffin and carried to the coroner's office. Since Murray was a Union veteran of the Civil War, members of the Grand Army of the Republic paid for a decent funeral. By 9 p.m. more than 1,500 people had filed through the coroner's office to view the body, including sixty or seventy respectable looking women.[11] Alfred Yenke's killer joined him at last.

References

Eugene City Guard (Eugene, Oregon) July 14, 1888.

Morning Oregonian (Portland, Oregon) February 3, 1884, February 4, 1884, February 5, 1884, February 6, 1884, February 13, 1884, February 14, 1884, February 15, 1884, February 16, 1884, February 17, 1884, February 19, 1884, February 20, 1884, February 21, 1884, February 22, 1884, February 23, 1884, May 3, 1884, May 5, 1884, May 8, 1884, May 28, 1884, February 14, 1885.

State of Oregon v. J. W. Murray, No. 1598, File No. 01517, Journal entry: Vol. 7, p. 422, June 29, 1884, Oregon Supreme Court Appeals file, Oregon State Archives, Salem, Oregon.

Chapter 24 notes

1 State of Oregon v. J. W. Murray, No. 1595, File No. 01517, Journal entry: Vol. 7, p. 422, June 29, 1884, Oregon Supreme Court Appeals file, Oregon State Archives, Salem, Oregon.

2 State of Oregon v. J. W. Murray, testimony of witnesses also reproduced in Portland area newspapers: *The Standard, Evening Telegram, Northwest News* and *Morning Oregonian*.

3 State of Oregon v. J. W. Murray, newspaper clipping from the *Evening Telegram* used to support a change of venue request.

4 *Morning Oregonian* (Portland, Oregon) February 13, 1884.

5 *Morning Oregonian*, February 14, 1884.

6 Judge Matthew Deady, *The Organic and Other General Laws of Oregon* (Salem: 1874) p. 291

7 *Morning Oregonian*, February 21, 1884.

8 The article was included as part of the evidence presented in the change of venue request. No date is mentioned.

9 *Morning Oregonian*, February 14, 1884. The authorities feared the crowd could become violent and used the hometown militia for protection.

10 Ibid.

11 Ibid.

Chapter Twenty-Five

State of Oregon v. Joe Drake 1884

Although Jacksonville was traditionally known to be Oregon's center of Southern sympathy and antipathy to African American people, Marion County was the first county to hang a black man.

In April 1884, Joseph Drake, a 25-year-old black man, was living in Marion County a few miles south of Salem. He worked hard, earning his living cutting wood and selling it to farmers and businessmen in the area. He boarded with the Henry family whose home was about a mile from their nearest neighbor, David Swarts. Swarts had filed for divorce from his wife, Mary, on April 1, 1884, naming Drake as Mary's lover, and causing problems for everyone in the neighborhood. In retaliation, Mary called Drake as a witness in charges that David abused his youngest son.

David and Mary Swarts were married on April 12, 1866, in Benton County and were the parents of three children: George, age 16, Charles, age 13, and Lulu, age 11. In the suit, David charged Mary with rendering "his life burdensome during the month of March 1884 by her bad conduct in leaving his house and home at various and divers times in the daytime and remaining absent from home during the daytime a portion of the night and that during such absence to associate with a negroe and Indians of bad character" (meaning Drake and the Henry family) and women of ill fame, Rose Burns and Kate Jones.[1] Swarts accused Mary of committing adultery with Joseph Drake on March 21, 1884. His lawyer was W. G. Piper. On April 3, 1884 David Swarts was granted custody of all three minor children.

Drake boarded with William and Emma Henry about two miles from the Swarts farm. The Henry family was good friends with Mary Swarts, but they all despised her husband. David was one of eight children born to 1853 immigrants, Simon and Polly Swarts. David was also a bully and kept a feud going between the neighbors. He constantly complained about Henry's pigs getting into his pasture and threatened to shoot the pigs and their owner. He insulted Emma Henry by calling her a squaw, or a prostitute, and accused her of running with the Indians and having two illegitimate children. Swarts accused Will of breaking his hay reaper and tried to make him pay for it. Even among his brothers and sisters David Swarts helped fuel a family feud after their parents died.[2]

Joe didn't know it but the decision to board with the Henry family was the worst mistake of his life. The version of events on Saturday, May 3, 1884 vary widely depending on who was testifying—the Henry family or Joe Drake. If you believe the Henrys, than Drake was a cold-blooded killer. If you believe Drake, than he was totally innocent and was a patsy set up by Mary Swarts and the Henry family.

On Saturday, May 3, Emma and William Henry went into Salem for the day. Joe and Delinda Henry (William's mother) stayed home. Joe worked on his wagon doing repairs and repainting it. About 5 p.m. the Henry family got home and, while the women cooked dinner, Will Henry went to fetch the cow. Joe went along to do some hunting. Soon they separated, Joe to shoot a grouse and Will to fetch the cow out of Swarts' pasture. While they were separated, Will met Mary Swarts who told him her husband had gone to Bass's Mill with the wagon for lumber and wouldn't be home until later.

When the men got back to the cabin, Mary Swarts was there with her son George and they ate dinner together. That's about all the two parties agree on. From this time on no one seemed to agree on anything.

Joe stated that after dinner he went outside to smoke his pipe. While outside Mary Swarts sent George to fetch him, as she waited about fifty yards away. She wanted him to take some eggs into town on Monday. They parted, and he went to bed for the night.

According to Delinda Henry, after dinner Joe and Mary had an intimate conversation in the parlor, and Joe walked with Mary to her home. She told the court that Joe and Mary were having an affair, and Joe threatened to shoot David Swarts earlier that day. She varied her story from one testimony to another. At the preliminary hearing she said that Emma was sick that night and she got up several times to take care of her. At the trial she said she went to bed after dinner and didn't wake up until morning. In any case she claimed not to know anything about a murder until the next morning when she heard Joe bragging about killing Swarts.

Emma Henry testified that after dinner Joe left with Mary, and Will Henry saddled two horses, got the gun from her and left the house. She went to bed, slept through the night and didn't hear a thing until morning. She testified that Joe and Mary were having an affair. She didn't know a thing about the killing until the next day.

It was William Henry's testimony that really nailed Joe. William Henry was a 37-year-old farmer from Iowa, standing about 5' 8" tall, with light brown hair and gray eyes.[3] Will admitted being an accomplice to the killing. After dinner he met Joe coming back from the Swarts cabin and the men rode two miles up the road where they hid the horses and waited for their target to ride by. Joe shot Swarts while Will ran out to stop the horses. When Swarts tried to get up off the ground, "Joe Drake ran to me and grabbed my pistol out of my hand and ran up to Swarts and shot him in the neck with the pistol."[4]

The Marion County Grand Jury handed down a joint indictment for first-degree murder on June 12, 1884, against Joseph Drake and Mary Swarts. Marion County District Attorney W. H. Holmes and W. G. Piper headed the prosecution team. (Perhaps Piper had some animosity toward Mary and Joe as he had represented David Swarts in his divorce petition.) Tilmon Ford and William M. Kaiser defended Drake, and N. B. Knight represented Mary. On June 14, she was granted a petition for a separate trial.[5] On May 16, Alfred Stanton filed foreclosure notice against the Swarts family home on an 1874 promissory note of $500. Apparently, Swarts had refused to pay anything against the mortgage for the previous year.

Drake's trial started on June 17 with Judge R. P. Boise officiating. Subpoenas were issued to George W. Swarts, Charles A. Swarts, Lulu Swarts, Jack Kays, James Coffey, George Anderson, Warren Cranston, William Brown, E. A. Downing, Jesse Macy, Doctor W. C. Warriuer, Ben Foruster, Johnny Veatch, James. R. Herren, Mrs. W. J. Henry, Delinda Henry, Charley Barker, A. L. Swarts, William Brown, Martin Rowley, J. P. Veatch, R. L. Swarts, and Alonzo Swarts. (Alonzo was sentenced to life in prison for second-degree murder on June 22, 1895. He served nine years until Governor George Chamberlain pardoned him on June 8, 1904).

Drake testified in his own behalf. He admitted carrying one or more pistols with him all the time, but denied having an affair with Mary Swarts or having anything to do with the shooting.[6]

During the summation, prosecutor Piper reviled Drake for carrying guns with him all the time because, "no good citizen will be found in the habit of carrying a pistol upon his person in this community."

Piper continued, "I do not ask you to convict this defendant on account of his color, but that can be no excuse or protection for him when he violates the law." This was a legitimate point. The 1883 Oregon Legislature had just passed a new law making it illegal to carry concealed guns or knives.[7]

In 1845 the Provisional Legislature passed an exclusion clause prohibiting black citizens—free or slave—from living in Oregon. Supposedly, two or three black men had been involved in a brawl with some Indians, which resulted in two white men dying. The law provided a punishment of flogging every six months and arrest until they remained outside Oregon's borders.[8] The exclusion law wasn't removed until 1926.

Piper also brought up the recent Cincinnati Riot as an example of what happens when a guilty man is turned loose and clearly threatened the jury that the same thing could happen in Salem.

Mary Swarts was not allowed to testify on Drake's behalf since she was indicted jointly with him. However, the judge allowed William Henry to testify against Drake even though a week earlier the grand jury had returned an indictment against him charging him with the same crime.

The jury believed the Henry's testimony and Joe Drake was found guilty of first-degree murder. On June 26, he stood in front of the judge and was sentenced to hang on August 13, 1884, between 10 a.m. and 3 p.m.[9]

The Oregon Supreme Court heard the appeal on Tuesday, October 28, 1884. A new trial was denied and Drake was again sentenced to hang on March 27, 1885. In the meantime, Mary Swarts was tried and acquitted and William Henry was sentenced to life imprisonment at the Oregon State Penitentiary. Henry served from June 26, 1884, to January 14, 1893, when Governor Pennoyer pardoned him at the recommendation of the Marion County district attorney.[10]

A scaffold was constructed on the east side of the Marion County Courthouse with a high board fence enclosing it. By now most of the community firmly believed that Drake didn't deserve to hang. That belief didn't stop the hundreds of people from crowding outside the fence in the hope of hearing a dying man's confession. County workers, their family and friends crowded into the courthouse to watch the execution from the courthouse windows overlooking the scaffold. The crowd was orderly, but the "necktie party" atmosphere was apparent.

Drake spent a restless last night, finally falling asleep about midnight and waking up at 7 a.m. on March 27, 1885. Reverend M. C. Wire of the Methodist Church arrived shortly after breakfast and spent the rest of the day with the condemned man. Sheriff John Minto escorted the prisoner to the scaffold. Reverend Wire walked on one side of Drake, while deputies Ed Croisan, S. R. Foster and W. J. Bennett followed behind.

Drake denied the killing in his final speech:

> *I am going to be hanged for the company I keep and not for the crime I committed. I have not much to say. I am going to be executed for a crime I know nothing about. I am about to die for a deed committed by other hands. Neither do I know anything about the crime. I lived with William Henry some time and did not think him a very bad man. Henry surely did the work if he knew anything about it. I think it is pretty hard that I have to lay down my life like this. I can't say who did the work for I was not there. I know I have been rudely dealt with. I thank the people who have tried to help me for their kindness. I would like to announce to the people that I am thankful for. Mr. Minto's folks have done a good part by me and I thank them for it. They treated me kindly and given me all the privileges possible under the circumstances.*[11]

Witnesses at the execution were Sheriff John Groves of Polk County, Sheriff William Knight of Clackamas County, Marshal Harbord of Salem, Doctors H. R. Holman, W. H. Byrd, and H. Parks of Salem; Policemen James Mead, Gaines Fisher, Mr. Burphy, and W. A. McPherson; newspapermen F. M. Salisbury, stenographer, and A. D. Cridge, reporter for the *Vidette*, Frank Cornoyer, reporter for the *Talk*, a representative of the *Statesman* and the jury that convicted Drake—Charles Benson. George Morris, T. H. Hubbard, Henry Hall, C. L. Keller, Adam Omart, T. H. Denham, John McIntyre, Sam Adolph, James Volney, Jesse Massey, and E. C. Cross.[12] About 500 people were outside, on the sidewalk and standing around the grounds, waiting to hear the fatal plop of a man's death. Fifteen execution witnesses signed the death warrant: R. C. Ramsley, J. W. McIntosh, Jesse Macy, C. L. Keller, James P. Valby, Gaines Fisher, Charles Benson, G. W. Morris, R. S. Denham, Adam Ohmart, William Knight, Samuel Adolph, T. H. Hubbard, R. J. Hendricks, and F. P. Talkington.[13]

At 1:48 p.m. the sheriff touched the pin with his foot and the execution went off without a hitch, ending Marion County's hanging history on a particularly tragic note.

Joseph Drake had no family in Oregon to claim his body, so he was buried in the Waldo Cemetery, a private cemetery where George Beale, another murderer, was buried in 1865.

References

Benton County Marriages, Oregon State Archives, Salem, Oregon.

David Swarts v. Mary E. Swarts, Marion County Circuit Court Case File #3775, April 1, 1884. Oregon State Archives, Salem, Oregon.

Lavender, David. *Land of Giants*. Garden City: Doubleday, 1956.

McKanna, Clare V. *Homicide, Race and Justice in The American West, 1880–1920*. Phoenix: The University of Arizona Press, 1997.

McLagan, Elizabeth. *A Peculiar Paradise*. Portland: Georgian Press Company, 1980.

Marion County Court Documents 1880–1884, Simon Swarts, David Swarts, Alonzo Swarts, Levi Swarts vs. F. A. Wanless, Henrietta A. Wanless, Hannah Butler, Jane Bolenbaugh, Melisie Scholds, A. C. Swarts, Clarissa Fetter, John Fetter and Isaac Fetter. In the matter of the estate of Polly Swarts. Oregon State Archives, Salem, Oregon.

Maxwell, Ben. "Frontier Hangings Were Gala Occasions in Salem." *Capital Journal* (Salem, Oregon) January 30, 1952.

Morning Oregonian (Portland, Oregon) May 1, 1884, May 6, 1884, May 7, 1884.

Oregon State Penitentiary Records located at the Oregon State Archives, Salem, Oregon. Inmate Register, Great Register 1854-1946, W. J. Henry, #1541, p. 122. And Alonzo Swarts, #3445.

Stanton, Alfred v. Mary E. Swarts, et. al., Marion County Circuit Court Case File #3769, Oregon State Archives, Salem, Oregon.

State of Oregon v. Alonzo Swarts, Marion County Circuit Court Register and Fee Book, 1849–1890, Book 3, p. 583, Oregon State Archives, Salem, Oregon.

State of Oregon v. Joseph Drake and Mary E. Swarts, Marion County Circuit Court Case File #3771, Oregon State Archives, Salem, Oregon.

State of Oregon v. Joseph Drake, No. 1592, File No. 01506, Journal entry: Vol. 7, p. 410, Oct. 6, 1884, Oregon Supreme Court Appeals file, Oregon State Archives, Salem, Oregon.

Statesman (Salem, Oregon) March 30, 1885.

Chapter 25 notes

1 David Swarts v. Mary Swarts, Marion County Circuit Court Case File #3775, Oregon State Archives, Salem, Oregon.

2 See Swarts, etal. v. Wanless, etal. Marion County Court Documents 1880- 1884, Oregon State Archives, Salem, Oregon.

3 Oregon State Penitentiary Inmate Case File #1541 for W. J. Henry, Oregon State Archives, Salem, Oregon.

4 State of Oregon v. Joseph Drake, No. 1392, File No. 01506, Journal entry: Vol. 7, p. 410, October 6, 1884, Oregon Supreme Court Appeals file, Oregon State Archives, Salem, Oregon.

5 State of Oregon v. Joseph Drake.

6 Clare V. McKanna. *Homicide, Race, and Justice in the American West, 1880–1920* (Phoenix: University of Arizona Press, 1997) p. 61 and 156. McKanna's study emphasizes the normality of young Black males carrying weapons to defend themselves. Drake's guns were a necessary and common habit in his perception.

7 *Register Guard* (Eugene, Oregon) November 11, 1882.

8 David Lavender,. *Land of Giants* (Garden City, N.Y.: Doubleday, 1956) p. 244.

9 State of Oregon v. Joseph Drake.

10 Oregon State Penitentiary Inmate Case File #1541 for W. J. Henry.

11 *Statesman* (Salem, Oregon) March 30, 1885.

12 Ibid.

13 State of Oregon v. Joseph Drake and Mary E. Swarts, Marion County Circuit Court Case File #3771, Oregon State Archives, Salem, Oregon.

Chapter Twenty-Six
State of Oregon v. Lewis O'Neil 1886

L ewis McDaniel was walking home after closing up his grocery store on Thursday, November 20, 1884.[1] At 7:30 p.m., it was pitch dark and raining. About seventy yards from his front door, as he turned the corner of Church Street in Ashland, a bright flash flared from behind him. By the time the sound followed the flash McDaniel was falling to the ground, the top and left side of his head blown away in a shower of metal slugs. When a neighbor came to investigate, McDaniel, age 48, was taking his last breath.[2] His hands were still in his coat pockets. He never knew who shot him.

Ashland night watchman, Charles H. Miller identified the body and took Eugene Walrad with him to McDaniel's home. After ringing the doorbell six or eight times and getting no answer the men went across the street to the Rockfellow's house. No one there knew where Amanda, Lewis McDaniel's wife, might be. The men went back to McDaniel's house, tried the doorknob and finding it open, went inside. Several other men had joined the pair and Miller lit a candle sitting on the fireplace mantle so they could see better. Suddenly Amanda McDaniel opened the door from a small bedroom off the living room and acted surprised to find her living room crowded full of people.

Justice of the Peace M. Purdin had married Sarah Amanda Henry to Lewis McDaniel on October 5, 1881.[3] When McDaniel died four years later, the 35 year-old widow was his only heir.[4] Her son Wilson T. Henry was only ten at the time of the murder.[5]

Amanda seemed strangely unconcerned when the men told her that her husband had been shot. Miller left about twenty minutes later and joined Ashland Marshal Taylor at the murder site. About 10 p.m. they found Lewis O'Neil sitting in High and Taylor's Saloon and arrested him on suspicion of murder. A sordid story of conspiracy, jealousy and murder was soon splashed all over Jackson County's newspapers.

Lewis O'Neil was a 48 year-old carpenter from Colusa County, California. In 1882 he had left a wife and six children in Colusa and slowly worked his way north along the railroad route. He arrived in Ashland about August 1884, rented a room at the Pioneer Hotel on September 10 and stayed for two weeks. On September 10 he took a little vacation and visited his brother who was prospecting a claim on Grave Creek about sixty miles from Ashland. George W. O'Neil, age 72, seemed to welcome this visit from a brother he hadn't seen for fifteen years. When Lewis left he took a fancy shotgun with him that George had been trying to sell. The muzzle-loading double-barreled shotgun had a distinctive carving of an alligator's head on the stock.[6] As O'Neil walked back to Ashland he met several travelers and spent the night at Edward Penning's house. Everyone noted the peculiar gun he was carrying. O'Neil returned to Ashland on October 2, stayed for five days and left to work on a building in Talent where he boarded with P. K. Hendrickson. On November 2 he returned to Ashland and the Pioneer Hotel where he stayed until arrested for McDaniel's murder.

The morning he left Penning's house was the last time anyone saw the gun until it turned up Sunday, November 23, in Ashland scattered in pieces around the lot at Cooledge's Nursery. The area had been thoroughly searched the previous two days and O'Neil was still in jail so someone else had to be in cahoots with him. Amanda McDaniel was the obvious suspect.

Boot tracks were followed south from the body to Granite Street, through several vacant lots, over fences, across Ashland Creek, into and through a hog pen, and above the Ashland Flour Mill. O'Neil's boots were compared to the track and matched exactly. Cooledge's Nursery was in the opposite direction, 100 yards north of the body.

It's hard to keep a secret in a small town and even harder when it's a secret about sex. Every gossip in Ashland knew what was happening when O'Neil and Sarah Amanda McDaniel started having an affair. She had been separated from her husband for several months, and only returned to his house shortly before the murder. Lewis McDaniel had forbidden O'Neil to visit his home based on his knowledge of the "crooked relations" and intimacy with his wife.[7] Several people had seen O'Neil loitering around McDaniel's house in the weeks before the murder.

A coroner's jury was held on Saturday, November 22 and the prisoner was questioned intensely. He steadfastly denied shooting McDaniel or ever having any gun. Later he maintained that he had sold his brother's gun to a stranger he met along the road to Ashland.

Lewis McDaniel's funeral was held the same day. More people attended the hearing than attended the funeral of the victim. John McDaniel arrived from Little Butte, Oregon and when interviewed by the reporter from the *Ashland Tidings*, expressed his determination to find his brother's killer.

O'Neil was incarcerated in the Jackson County Jail to wait for the trial to begin. His was the first murder trial to be held in the brand new brick Jackson County Courthouse.

The trial began on February 27, 1885, with Judge Lionel G. Webster presiding. Webster, a resident of Jacksonville, had been appointed judge after Judge H. K. Hanna retired and was then elected for a subsequent term of six years. Jackson County District Attorney T. B. Kent and retired judge H. K. Hanna prosecuted the case. Two of the best attorneys in the state, C. Wesley Kahler and James K. Neil were appointed to defend O'Neil.[8] It took several days and two special venires before twelve jurors were finally selected: W. H. Bailey, Jacob Bowman, Benjamin Carter, Levi Gartman, J. H. Griffis, Thomas Martin, James McDonough, George Megerle, J. S. Morgan, J. D. Neathamer, John E. Pelton, and E. S. Trimble.[9]

The judge, the attorneys and the jury traveled to Ashland and visited the crime scene. Everyone trekked around Ashland following the boot tracks, scrutinizing the ground where the gun was found and wondering why Amanda McDaniel didn't hear the loud pounding on her front door. Two weeks later, an unusually long time for a trial, the attorneys finished questioning two-dozen witnesses, summarized their cases and the jury retired to their deliberations. The prosecution must have done a good job because the jury only took an hour to reach a verdict and on March 12, 1885, the defendant was found guilty of first-degree murder. O'Neil was sentenced to hang on May 21, 1885.

Meanwhile, Sarah Amanda McDaniel, while staying with her sister at Eagle Point, Oregon, was arrested on May 15, 1885, and charged with being an accessory before the fact in the murder of her husband. While O'Neil was in jail he confessed to another inmate that Amanda was also implicated in the murder of her husband. The following day, her brother-in-law, J. J. Fryer, was also charged with suppressing evidence (possibly trying to intimidate or payoff probable witnesses). He was released the same day for lack of evidence.

Amanda's trial started on Tuesday, November 17, 1885, with the firm of James R. Neil, J. T. Bowditch and C. Wesley Kahler (the same lawyers that defended Lewis O'Neil) serving as her defense counsel. The jury included Rufus Cox of Little Butte, Ralph F. Dean of Willow Springs, G. W. Howard of Medford, T. J. Keaton of Poorman's Creek, J. T. Layton of Applegate, William Mayfield of the Meadows, B. F. Miller of Rock Point, William M. Miller of Applegate, Frank Parker of Rock Point, J. W. Plymire of Manzanita, H. C. Turpin of Little Butte, and George S. Walton of Medford, foreman.[10]

The prosecutor, District Attorney T. B. Kent, charged that Amanda was the instigator of the plot and O'Neil simply carried out her instructions. The return to her husband's house had been a ploy to turn suspicion away from them both. Nineteen witnesses were subpoenaed to testify, including Thomas E. Nichols, Joseph H. Hyzer, Eugene and Nora Walrad, J. D. Gray, James Pease, Phillip Mullen, Mrs. M. J. Goodyear, C. D. Morgan, H. Farlow, Mrs. A. S. Jacoby, N. R. and R. J. S. Parsons, S. D. Taylor, John A. and Louisa Gridley, and Jesse. N. Banks.[11] Convict Levi Grigsby was O'Neil's new friend from the jail and testified against her. Only seven sheets of paper remain in the Jackson County Case file, so it's unknown what each witness said at the trial. The jury retired to deliberate on the verdict at 11 a.m. on November 23. They didn't return with an acquittal until 8:30 the next morning.

Amanda McDaniel left Ashland the night before O'Neil's hanging and later operated a small café in Talent, Oregon. She was named administrator and liquidated her husband's estate by July 8, 1885, after she was acquitted for his murder. After paying the taxes and the outstanding bills she only netted about $2,000.[12]

By January 1886, O'Neil was becoming desperate. Unable to read or write, he dictated all correspondence to a guard in the county jail. The guard kept copies of the letters because four were later printed in the *Oregon Sentinel*. One was addressed to Mandy McDaniel, another to Mr. Egerton, a lawyer in San Francisco, another to his sister, Elizabeth Fouts, and the last to a friend named Johns. All dealt with various plots to have someone else take the blame for the murder and get him out of jail. The letter to Amanda McDaniel was dated January 1886 and was the most incriminating. Since she had been cleared of all charges, he wanted her to now confess to the killing and clear him. He would then sue the state for a great sum of money, split the money with her or give her all of it. "I hope you will not delay as I know you can save my life and the disgrace will be no worse on you than it is now."[13]

Apparently Amanda had second thoughts about the wisdom of O'Neil's plan, because she didn't do as he asked. His last letter was addressed to George W. O'Neil, his brother in Grave Creek, begging

Southern Oregon Historical Society #7329
Lewis O'Neil, center, listens as Sheriff A. J. Jacobs,
right, reads the execution warrant

him to confess to the murder, because "the most trying feature is in leaving my six children to the mercy of a world without protection and the disgrace of their father being hanged. According to my age I might live long enough to raise my children up so they could take care of themselves. As for you, you have lived to be a very old man, and in the natural course of events you can expect to live but a very few years more and are liable to drop off at any time. If you had one hour to live it would be a hard request to ask you to come and state that you done the killing and that I had not any hand, act or part in it or any knowledge of it. That would clear me, and spare me to my children, and only on their account I could ever think of making such a request of you."14

This ironic request was made by a man who had abandoned his family four years earlier and had an affair with a married woman. Unknown to O'Neil his brother had died of typhoid fever just two weeks before the hanging.

O'Neil's evil nature even extended into the psychic realm. The *Democratic Times* of Jacksonville noted the jail cell visit of a ghostly apparition, which closely resembled Tong the Chinaman, who had hanged himself in the jail in 1877. The supposed ghost made noises and moved things around until O'Neil was executed and then disappeared back to its unearthly abode.

O'Neil's attorneys appealed to the Oregon Supreme Court for a new trial. The appeal was denied, and he was again sentenced to hang on Friday, March 12, 1886.[15] Several weeks before the appointed day, carpenters arrived to build the stockade and gallows. A sixteen-foot high fence formed a courtyard forty by sixty feet, enclosing the area between the courthouse and jail. County Sheriff Abraham S. Jacobs issued invitations to the hanging and asked the twenty-seven members of the Jacksonville Fire Department armed with real rifles to serve as guards.[16] Sandbags were used to stretch the rope and test the drop the day before the hanging.

A. S. Moon, O'Neil's nephew by marriage, arrived from Colusa, California where O'Neil's wife and six children lived, to visit the condemned man. Moon traveled to Salem and appealed to Oregon Governor Moody for a reprieve, but the governor refused to intervene. O'Neil's only other visitors were the nuns from the Catholic Sisters of Mercy and Father Blanchet.[17] Father Francois Norbert Blanchet and Father Modeste Demers had arrived in Oregon in 1838 at the urging of John McLoughlin of the Hudson's Bay Company.[18]

On March 12, 1886, at 2:10 p.m. Sheriff Jacobs and Deputy Sheriff Steadman escorted Lewis O'Neil out of the courthouse, through the stockade gate, and up the gallows steps. About 120 people, including several women and two or three children were waiting inside the enclosure erected in front of the county jail.[19] Twelve official witnesses signed the death warrant, but only eleven signatures can be read on the document: Jesse N. Banks, A. J. Barlow, William Bybee, R. J. Cameron, J. H. Cook, B. W. Dean, Heaten Fox (a member of the Coroner's jury that indicted O'Neil) John A. Hanley, Joseph H. Hyzer, and H. T. Severance.[20] When Sheriff Jacobs asked O'Neil if he had anything to say, Father Blanchet spoke up for him and answered with a quick, "No".

The execution was quite successful as the rope snapped O'Neil's neck and he died without a struggle. Doctors Aiken, Robinson, Lembert and DeBar pronounced him dead at 2:30 p.m. He was buried in the pauper section of Jacksonville Cemetery.[21]

The new manila rope, one inch in diameter, was cut into small pieces and retained by the audience as mementos of the occasion. A few days later the gallows, the fence and any other evidence of the hanging was torn down and removed. The total cost to Jackson County for O'Neil's trial and incarceration was $5,900.

References

Jackson County Marriages, 1853-1896, Vol. 1, Oregon State Archives, Salem, Oregon.

Ashland Tidings (Ashland, Oregon) November 28, 1884, December 19, 1884, March 6, 1885, March 13, 1885, March 20, 1885, March 27, 1885, April 13, 1885, May 8, 1885, November 18, 1885, November 27, 1885, February 19, 1886, March 5, 1886, March 19, 1886.

Derry, Larry. "On Trial for Murder", a term paper presented to Doctor Frank Haines, December 1961, Southern Oregon Historical Society, Medford, Oregon.

Hegne, Barbara. *Settling the Rogue Valley–The Tough Time, The Forgotten People*. Medford, The Southern Oregon Historical Society, 1995.

Jackson County Probate file for Lewis McDaniel, #0834, January 13, 1885, Oregon State Archives, Salem, Oregon.

Lavender, David. *Land of Giants*. Garden City: Doubleday, 1956.

Maddux, Percy. *City on the Willamette: The Story of Portland, Oregon*. Portland: Binfords & Mort, 1952.

Oregon Sentinel (Jacksonville, Oregon) March 14, 1884, November 22, 1884, November 29, 1884, January 2, 1885, January 16, 1885, March 7, 1885, April 11, 1885, May 16, 1885, January 30, 1886, February 27, 1886, March 6, 1886, March 12, 1886, March 13, 1886.

State of Oregon v. Sarah A. McDaniel, Jackson County Circuit Court Criminal Case File #State 6, File 27, November 18, 1886, Oregon State Archives, Salem, Oregon.

State of Oregon v. Lewis O'Neil, No. 1700 1/2, File No. 01637, Journal entry: Vol. 7, p. 658, June 22, 1885, Oregon Supreme Court Appeals file, Oregon State Archives, Salem, Oregon.

State of Oregon v. Lewis O'Neil, Jackson County Circuit Court Criminal Case File #State 6, File 41, February 24, 1885, Oregon State Archives, Salem, Oregon.

Webber, Bert and Margie. Jacksonville, Oregon: The Making of a National Historic Landmark. Fairfield: YeGalleon, 1982.

Chapter 26 notes

1 Bert and Margie Webber, *Jacksonville, Oregon: The Making of a National Historic Landmark* (Fairfield: YeGalleon, 1982), pp. 134-5.

2 *Oregon Sentinel* (Jacksonville, Oregon) November 22, 1884.

3 Jackson County Marriages, 1853-1896, Vol. 1, Oregon State Archives, Salem, Oregon.

4 Jackson County Probate File of Lewis McDaniel, #0834, January 13, 1885, Oregon State Archives, Salem, Oregon.

5 *Ashland Tidings* (Ashland, Oregon) November 28, 1884.

6 Ibid.

7 Ibid.

8 Bert and Margie Webber, p. 134, "two of the best lawyers in the valley."

9 State of Oregon v. Lewis O'Neil, No. 1700 1/2, File No. 01637, Journal entry: Vol. 7, p. 658, June 22, 1885, Oregon Supreme Court Appeals File, Oregon State Archives, Salem, Oregon.

10 *Ashland Tidings*, November 18, 1885.

11 State of Oregon v. Sarah Amanda McDaniel, Jackson County Circuit Court Criminal Case File #State 6, File 27, November 18, 1885, Oregon State Archives, Salem, Oregon.

12 Jackson County Probate file for Lewis McDaniel, #0834, January 13, 1885, Oregon State Archives, Salem, Oregon.

13 *Oregon Sentinel*, March 13, 1886.

14 *Ashland Tidings*, March 19, 1886.

15 *Oregon Sentinel*, January 30, 1886.

16 Bert and Margie Webber, pp. 134-135.

17 David Lavender, *Land of Giants* (Garden City, N.Y.: Doubleday, 1956), p. 190. Other sources spell the name Father Demaris. Lavender points out that by bringing Catholic priests to Oregon the retiring personnel of the Hudson Bay Company, primarily French Canadians, more readily stayed in Oregon. They married, raised families and were supportive of the company's policies.

18 Percy Maddux, *City On The Willamette,* (Portland, Oregon: Binfords and Mort, 1952) p. 7.

19 *Oregon Sentinel* March 13, 1886. The *Ashland Tidings* March 19, 1886, says that 200 people were inside the enclosure.

20 State of Oregon v. Lewis O'Neil, Jackson County Circuit Court Criminal Case File #State 6, File 41, February 24, 1885, Oregon State Archives, Salem, Oregon.

21 *Oregon Sentinel*, March 13, 1886. Barbara Hegne, *Settling the Rogue Valley–The Tough Times: The Forgotten People,* (Medford: The Southern Oregon Historical Society, 1995) p. 88.

Chapter Twenty-Seven
State of Oregon v. Richard Marple 1887

It was Friday, November 11, 1887, in the small town of Lafayette. The prisoner was angry, bitter and defiant as he stood on the hangman's trap. He was determined to hide any weakness from these people he hated. As his wrists were strapped together with a leather belt and his legs were tied with rope, he glared at the crowd gathered below him. He had defied them all for so long not even his eminent death could change how he acted.

The black cap was pulled down over his head and he exclaimed, "Murder! May God judge you all!"

The noose tightened around his neck and he struggled slightly, protesting, "No need to be so brutal, don't choke me with the rope."

Yamhill County Sheriff Thomas J. Harris stepped back and an awful stillness prevailed for the space of a few seconds, and at 12:48 p.m. the trap was sprung, dropping the prisoner six feet closer to earth. Unfortunately, in those last few seconds, the man turned his head and the knot in the rope slipped under his chin. Instead of a swift death from a broken neck he strangled slowly and painfully. He struggled and twitched at the end of the rope until the medical examiner pronounced him dead eighteen minutes later.

The case began over a year earlier on November 1, 1886, when David I. Corker, a 56-year-old carpenter and storekeeper from New York, was discovered dead in his bed.[1] The man had been brutally beaten, chopped about the head and face with an ax and left to slowly die from blood loss.

Corker was a single man, solitary in nature. Even though he'd lived in Yamhill County for six years he didn't have many friends or any family that anyone knew about. However, he was well liked and respected, considered to be a hard worker, and his murder was a shock to the whole community. Lafayette had been the county seat and was the first city established in Yamhill County. It was a growing town and Corker had grown with it. In 1880, he was living in a boarding house in Amity and identified himself as a carpenter.[2] Six years later he had his own store with cozy living quarters off the back and a steady clientele for his general merchandise business.

Lafayette, incorporated on October 17, 1878, was a bustling town in late 1886.[3] It had three dry goods and grocery stores, two drug stores, two millinery stores, two hardware stores, two livery stables, two doctors, a saloon, a flourmill, a furniture store and a Chinese laundry.[4] It also had several public buildings, including a town hall, three lodge halls and, of course, the county jail. As in any growing western town, there was the rowdy element, but Sheriff Thomas J. Harris and Deputy William Nelson kept a pretty tight grip on things.

The oldest Masonic Lodge in Oregon was in Lafayette and some of the most prominent men in the state were members.[5] With a population of more than 600, the little town fully expected to continue growing. Trouble was on the horizon, however, and the papers of 1887[6] detailed the growing influence of nearby McMinnville and its eventual success in wresting the county seat away from Lafayette.[7] However, Corker had put his lot in with the hardy pioneers of Lafayette and seemed happy there.

The night of November 1, 1886, about 10 p.m., two young men were walking by Corker's store and heard what sounded like someone yelling for help. Gideon Ely, age 17, and Thadeus Dunn, age 18, immediately ran to get Sheriff Harris. When the sheriff got to the store, he found the back window pried open. Inside he made a grisly discovery. David I. Corker was dead, covered in blood, and laying naked on his bed. Beside the bed lay bloody clothes and a bloody ax. The back window had been forced open from the outside. Later it was discovered that money had been stolen.

A small crowd came to see what all the commotion was about and eagerly watched from outside the store. In the crowd was 27-year-old Richard Marple. He and his family had moved to Lafayette from Corvallis a year earlier. Marple refused to work at an honest job for any length of time and Sheriff Harris suspected he was involved in a series of robberies occurring in the area. Several months earlier Marple had arrogantly mocked Corker and noted how easy it would be to rob him because of his deafness. Marple didn't seem to care who heard him say it either.

The next day Lafayette Detective Singleton and the sheriff went to the Marple home. The family, which included Anna, Richard's mother, Julia, his wife, and their children, lived in a two-room shack on the outskirts of town. There was little food in the house and Julia Marple was sick in bed. Before they arrested him, they noticed blood on Marple's coat and made him take it off. Searching his clothes they found a piece of bloody paper in his pants pocket, and in his coat pocket they found a small black diary Marple kept. Also in the house was a box of chisels and other tools, useful for breaking and entering. Anna, his mother, was also arrested as a suspected accomplice.

At the subsequent coroner's inquest, Marple was questioned about the murder. In his usual cocky manner he denied killing Corker and then made nasty comments about the dead man, which infuriated the listeners. He accused Detective Singleton of taking his coat over to Corker's store and dipping it in Corker's blood to frame him. Anna and Julia both testified that the blood on Marple's clothes came from a child's injury. Marple testified that the blood came from a hog head he had carried home to feed his family. No one in the jury believed Marple, and they quickly decided to arrest Anna and Richard Marple for the murder of David Corker. Mother and son were locked up together in the Yamhill County Jail and waited for the grand jury to convene.

During the next term of the circuit court on April 18, 1886, the grand jury returned three indictments against Marple. One for the murder of Corker, one for assaulting Sam Lee a month earlier, and one for a burglary of a warehouse in Polk County.

Anna Eliza Marple, Marple's mother, was also indicted for the burglary.[8] However, there was no evidence directly linking her to the murder or burglary, so the charges were eventually dropped after she had been in the county jail for several weeks. Because of the seriousness of the murder charge against Marple, the last two indictments, for assault and burglary, were set aside until after the murder charge was resolved.

Richard Marple's trial for first-degree murder started on Wednesday, April 2, 1887, in Yamhill County Circuit Court in front of Judge Reuben Boise.[9]

There was a great deal of interest in the case and the courthouse in Lafayette was crowded. At 9 a.m. Sheriff Harris brought Marple, accompanied by his father, Ezekiel Marple, into court. The accused was dressed in a dingy, well-worn suit and a collarless, coarsely woven, striped shirt. According to the newspapers, he was pale after being locked up so long and his blotched, retreating forehead, prominent nose and continual self-satisfied smirk gave him a rather sinister air.

While his court appointed defense counsel, H. Y. Thompson, was examining the prospective jurors, Marple watched the proceedings intently, smiling when any of them said they were prejudiced or had already formed an opinion in the case. He gave a broad grin when anyone was excused because they were prejudiced against him. At 11 a.m. on April 3, twelve jurors were finally sworn in. They included J. W. Briedwell, Wilson Carl (named jury foreman), Jobe J. Cary (a farmer), Joseph L. Davis (a day laborer in Lafayette), F. H. Harpool, H. L. Jones, A. J. Killen, George W. Olds, S. Root, J. B. Stillwell (a Dayton farmer), S. W. Wilson, and William W. Wright (a McMinnville farmer).[10]

George W. Belt, the district attorney, who was assisted in the prosecution by James McCain and H. Hurley, made the opening statement for the state. He explained that no one, except the murderer, had witnessed the deed, and the evidence was circumstantial, yet he believed he could convince the jury that Marple committed the murder. He described the tools found in Marple's house, which were probably used to break into Corker's store, and promised to prove that Marple didn't even have the coat when he carried home the dead hog and couldn't possibly have gotten blood on it from that. Belt also said that he would prove the defendant had lied at the coroner's inquest, had asked different people whether Corker slept in his store, and told others it would be easy to get rid of the old man.

H. Y. Thompson, the defense attorney, tried to explain that the prisoner's nasty comments made him an angry, not a guilty, man.

At noon, an officer of the court escorted the jury from the courthouse to the Corker's store to inspect the murder site. During the afternoon and evening, a dozen witnesses came forward and testified for the prosecution. All agreed that Marple was a bad man with an even worse reputation. Many recalled remarks he had made about possibly robbing and killing Corker.

Sheriff Harris gave the most damaging testimony against Marple.[11] He was present when Corker's body was discovered and took charge of the bloody clothing found at the scene of the murder. He first saw Marple after the murder about 11 p.m. outside the store. He showed the jury Marple's diary, bloody coat and papers taken from the accused the next day. He also explained how the chisels could be used to break into a building.

The sheriff had allowed Marple to visit the murder site twice while waiting for trial on the pretext of looking for evidence to clear himself.

The crime scene had been closed to the public until the murder could be resolved. During the first visit Marple took a tape measure and measured the rooms. The second time he kicked over some rubbish and the sheriff noticed a pair of gold sleeve buttons, which were missing from Corker's shirt when his body was dressed for burial. Marple picked up a reamer (crowbar) and two pieces of wire, which he thought looked like someone else's burglar tools.

On Thursday, April 3, the trial resumed at 9 a.m. The courtroom was even more crowded than the day before. The prosecution continued presenting witnesses until noon. After lunch the defense presented its case until 4 p.m. The principal witnesses for the defense were Julia Marple, his wife, and Anna Marple, his mother.[12]

District Attorney Belt made a half hour summation, while the defense attorney, H. Y. Thompson, talked until 6 p.m. Everyone thought he did a masterly job, and his contempt for the purely circumstantial evidence very clear. After Judge Boise ordered a short recess, Thompson finished at 9 p.m.

The next morning Prosecutor Hurley made his closing argument, and the judge dismissed the jury to their deliberations at 10 p.m.

It was a tense afternoon as many in the crowd waited near the courthouse for the jury to reappear. The town saloons were busy places as speculation varied whether the jury would find Marple guilty. When nothing had happened by suppertime, many went home thinking to return the next day. Every hotel and boarding house was full with out-of-town reporters and other interested observers staying with families making a bit of money by renting out spare beds.

At 9 p.m. the jurors announced they had reached a verdict and Marple was marched back into the courtroom.[13] At the request of the court, the prisoner stood up while the verdict was read. He displayed no emotion as the foreman read the verdict, "guilty as charged in the indictment."

On Saturday, April 9, at 11 a.m. Marple returned to the courtroom to hear his sentence. He walked quietly between Sheriff Harris and his deputy and took his seat before the judge. He appeared to be just as cool and collected as the previous evening, when he had heard the verdict. When the judge asked if he had anything to say, he stood up, faced the audience and started on a long rambling speech. He declared that he was innocent, but knew who really committed the murder, although he didn't say who that was. He admitted shooting at the man from China, Sam Lee, a year earlier and everyone laughed with him when he said, "My gracious, I had to shoot. There was no getting around it, I had to shoot."[14]

At that point Judge Boise got disgusted and asked Marple to stop. Marple turned back to the judge and told him that he was about to sentence an innocent man and that someday he would regret it. The prisoner then defiantly folded his arms and waited.

The judge had no option in the matter, the jury had found him guilty and it was his sad duty to pronounce the sentence. Oregon law at that time was very precise—a conviction of first-degree murder was always a sentence to hang. Outside of a successful appeal to the state supreme court, the governor was the only person who could change such a sentence.

Judge Reuben Boise was respected in 1887 by the state bar and the public for his painstaking manner when he considered cases. He was usually patient and meticulous with the different cases in his court-room. Judge Boise had watched eight men die after he'd passed sentence. He'd earned a solid reputation by displaying intelligence and legal insight in the past. However, this case was not his best showing.

Judge Boise pronounced the verdict:

> *It is the sentence of this court that you be taken from hence, and confined in the county jail until the 29th day of May, 1887 and upon said day between the hours of 10:00 a.m. and 2:00 p.m., you be taken from said jail to the place of execution and in accordance with this judgment, you be hanged by the neck until dead, and may God have mercy upon your soul.* [15]

Unfortunately, May 29, 1887, fell on a Sunday and it was illegal in Oregon at that time to have a hanging on a Sunday. A member of the court staff told the judge about the error after Marple had been taken back to his cell. The judge had the prisoner immediately returned to the courtroom. Not admitting that he had made a mistake the judge then changed the appointed date of the hanging to June 29, 1887. After the second sentencing the judge dismissed the court for the term. [16]

An appeal was sent to the Oregon Supreme Court and heard on May 27, 1887. It found that there was no error alleged sufficient to authorize a new trial—but the court found that the judgment of the lower court was not in conformity of the law, and that said judgment ought to be modified, because June 29 was eight-one days from April 9 and Section 218, Chapter 21 of the 1887 criminal code of Oregon read:

> *When judgment of death is pronounced the warrant signed by the judge of the court and attested by the clerk, with the seal of the county affixed, must be drawn and delivered to the sheriff*

*of the county; the warrant shall state the conviction and judg-
ment, and appoint a day on which the judgment is to be executed, which must not be less than thirty or more than sixty days
from the sentence of judgment."*[17]

Judge Boise reconvened the court on October 1, 1887, at the beginning of the next term of the circuit court, and set November 11, 1887,
as the new date for the hanging.[18]

The day before the execution, Marple observed sarcastically that
all the hammering and sawing on the outside of the jail was for the
construction of a new sheep corral. Marple's father held the forlorn
hope that the governor might pardon his son clear up to the very last
minute. The hanging day dawned bright and cold. Again the town of
Lafayette was full of bystanders wanting to catch a glimpse of the
infamous murderer or to hear stories about his last days.

The hanging was scheduled for 1 p.m. There were about thirty witnesses inside the scaffold consisting mostly of court officers, jury
members and reporters. Marion County Sheriff John Minto was down
from Salem and assisted Sheriff Harris. Witnesses named as the
twelve bona fide electors at the execution were; E. Carpenter, N. M.
Daniels, Z. Davis, Jesse Dixon (the Lafayette jailor), A. P. Fletcher, G.
W. Goucher, T. N. Graves, Sterling F. Harding, Joel J. Hembre
(Lafayette justice of the peace), Ben F. Houston, J. A. Houston, and
Thomas B. Nelson (owner of the Lafayette livery stable).[19]

E. B. Collard and Mr. Rudder built the execution stockade and
scaffold of undressed lumber. The platform was seven by eleven feet
with a trap door three feet square in the middle. The rope was
attached to a beam fifteen feet above the ground, and the platform
itself was about seven feet above the ground. A flight of steps ran from
the window in the old sheriff's office directly to the scaffold. A lever
controlled two iron points, which held the trap door up. Throwing the
lever back released the points and opened the trap door under the
prisoner.[20]

Marple had spent the last week drinking whiskey laced with opi-
ates and today was no different. He was offered a bottle, which he
gratefully accepted but refused to dress himself when the time came.
When his execution clothes were brought in the sheriff had to do the
disagreeable duty.

When finally dressed Marple commented, "This is the best suit of
clothes I have had on for ten years."

At 12:30 p.m., Marple marched from his cell to the scaffold passing
the waiting coffin and mounting the scaffold steps. His arms were
already tied so Sheriff Harris held up a flask of whiskey while Marple

drank several big gulps. The small audience of thirty men waited patiently as it took several minutes before he could talk. If anyone thought they were going to hear a confession they were disappointed. Instead Marple continued to maintain his innocence just as he had in the past. He believed that Corker's death was part of a conspiracy and now he was going to suffer the consequences. He said five men were in the conspiracy and that two of them were watching inside the enclosure. The ringleader of the conspiracy was Sheriff Harris and his (Marple's) defense lawyer, with the assistance of Almond Fletcher, Ransom Clark and Warren Eastman. He accused Sheriff Harris of abusing him while he was in jail. Finally he finished and E. B. Collard read the death warrant to the crowd.

Upon hearing the words, "R. E. Marple murdered D. I. Corker," Marple interrupted, "false as hell."[21]

Father White of the Catholic Church prayed with the condemned man for a few minutes just before Sheriff Harris gave the signal to spring the trap door.

As he was hanged, his mother, a suspected gypsy, shouted curses from outside the enclosure and threatened to burn down the city. Whether it was the result of her curse or not, eventually three fires did occur, the last in 1904, burning the whole business district of Lafayette down.

People thought that was the end of Marple's story, so it was a great surprise when a few days later a new story appeared in the local newspaper. William Henry Hess had been locked in the Lafayette jail along with Richard Marple for four weeks prior to the execution. On November 18, 1887, the day after Marple's execution, Hess came forward and told the following horrific story, causing many to bolt their doors and most to shake their heads at such depravity.[22]

Marple had maintained the same defense, that three of the most prominent Yamhill businessmen, Ransom Clark, Almond Fletcher and Warren Eastman, together with the Masons, had committed the murder. On the day before the hanging, Hess said to him that he didn't believe Marple's accusations that others had murdered Corker. After hesitating a few moments Marple made a deal with him. He would tell Hess the truth only if he promised to keep it a secret in the event the governor granted him a reprieve.

While they were talking, Marple and Hess were alone in the north corridor and the other prisoners were in the south corridor of the jail. Their conversation was occasionally interrupted by the comings and goings of various officers and prisoners. They had to talk in low voices so they couldn't be overheard.

Marple admitted making up the story about the Masons and other rich people in Lafayette killing Corker. He had written out his story and memorized it so that he could tell it alike every time. The community thought he was a fool but they were wrong about that. He had an extraordinary memory. He accused Sheriff Harris because he hated him and wanted to ruin the sheriff's reputation.

Marple told Hess he desperately needed money and knowing that Corker was rich, conspired with Anna, his mother, and Julia, his wife, to rob the man. Marple thought he was knowledgeable in the use of drugs and proposed to drug the poor victim. Anna Marple was sleeping with Corker and had visited him privately in the back of his store many times. On the night of the murder Anna was in Corker's bedroom and she administered a sleeping drug to Corker in a drink she made up for him.

After waiting long enough for the drug to take effect, Marple tried to enter the store's backdoor, but discovered that his mother had forgotten to unlock it. He went around the side of the building and got in through an open window. He found Corker in an uneasy stupor and his mother waiting for him when he finally got into the bedroom. At that point it finally dawned on Anna that she would be the prime suspect after the robbery, so Marple suggested killing Corker and setting the building on fire to hide their crime. His mother found an ax in the store and struck Corker a glancing blow on his forehead with the pole, or back, of the ax, which only served to wake Corker out of his stupor and struggle up into a sitting position. Quickly Marple grabbed the ax out of the old lady's hands and started chopping the wounded man with the sharp edge. Because poor Corker lay in an awkward position for a left-handed man such as Marple to get a blow it was a few minutes before Marple got a satisfactory swipe at him. Finally, after many missed attempts, he gave him a center blow that killed the bloody man. The mother and son stole $203.75, which Anna took with her. Mrs. Marple "acted a hog" (refused to share the money) and didn't give her daughter-in-law half the money like she was supposed to do.

After Corker was dead, they straightened him out in a ritualistic position to make it look as though someone in the Masonic order had committed the murder. Hearing sounds outside the store, Marple helped his mother out the window before he scrambled after her and she returned home while Marple waited in the crowd to see what happened. The murder was committed between 9 and 10 p.m. They had intended to leave town the next night after the murder, waiting the extra day to throw suspicion off them, but his wife, Julia, was so sick he didn't think it safe to leave her. Instead, they were arrested and held in the Yamhill County Jail. His mother would have given the whole thing away if she had been kept in jail even a week longer. It was a relief to him when they let her go.

Hess told Marple that he thought it was horrible to chop up a man like that just for money. Marple thought it was no harder to kill a man than to kill a hog. In 1879 he helped kill an old lady named Hager in Oregon City. After two men were tried and acquitted, James W. King, age 22, was convicted in October 1879 of the murder. The governor subsequently commuted King's sentence and he was released on January 28, 1887, after serving eight years for a crime he didn't commit.[23] Mrs. Hagar was a perfect tiger and had put up a desperate fight. She got the best of his partner, the first man who tackled her. Marple caught the hatchet and struck her before she pushed him back and dropped the hatchet. The third man caught it, hit her a fatal blow and finished her off. One of the men lost his shirt collar in the struggle and they didn't get much money. Marple showed Hess a ring he was wearing that he stole from Mrs. Hager after she was dead. They had heard she'd received a check for a considerable amount of money but they couldn't find it.

Marple also told about killing a French woman in Portland and had gotten quite a lot of money from her. He and his friends killed her by chopping her to death. There were four of them connected with that murder—three inside that did the work and one outside watching.

Only Ezekiel Marple, the old Indian fighter, seemed to mourn his dead son. He died March 18, 1898, on his homestead near Corvallis.[24] The rest of the family went their individual ways. Julia Marple didn't waste much time mourning her husband or finding a new one. She married Iredell Pillman June 27, 1888, in Benton County.[25] Anna Eliza Marple died in poverty on March 11, 1916, in Jackson County.[26] If the dates she entered on the Indian War Pension Application are correct, she was 94 years old when she died. She was never arrested or charged with Corker's murder, as the only witness against her was dead.

References

1880 and 1890 Federal Census, Yamhill County, Oregon.

Benton County Marriage Index, Oregon State Archives, Salem, Oregon.

Bryan, Elizabeth. "Lafayette." *Old Yamhill*. Lafayette: Yamhill Historical Society, 1967.

Daily Journal (Salem, Oregon) November 6, 1900.

Indian War Pension Application #750, of Anna Eliza Marple, November 13, 1899, Oregon Historical Society, Portland, Oregon.

Letter from W. M. Stone, Attorney at Law, to J. W. Lewis, O.S.P. Warden, 30 January 1934.

Oregon Death Index, Oregon State Archives, Salem, Oregon.

Oregon Donation Land Claims, Vol. III, 2nd Edition, DLC #335, Ezekiel Marple, Portland: Genealogical Forum of Oregon, 1987.

Oregon Register (Lafayette, Oregon) August 12, 1887, September 9, 1887, November 18, 1887.

State of Oregon v. Ann Eliza Marple, Judgment #2101, Reg. #79, April 2, 1887, Yamhill County Circuit Court, Oregon State Archives, Salem, Oregon.

State of Oregon v. R. E. Marple, No.1998, File No. 01867, Journal entry: Vol. 8, p. 222, May 14, 1887, Oregon Supreme Court Appeals file, Oregon State Archives, Salem, Oregon

State of Oregon v. R. E. Marple, Judgment #2208, Reg. #68, March 31, 1888, Yamhill County Circuit Court, Oregon State Archives, Salem, Oregon.

State of Oregon v. R. E. Marple, Judgment #2207, Reg. #67, April 8, 1887, Yamhill County Circuit Court, Oregon State Archives, Salem, Oregon.

West Side Telephone (Lafayette, Oregon) April 2, 1887, April 11, 1887, April 30, 1887, November 2, 1887, November 12, 1887, November 13, 1887, November 18, 1887.

Chapter 27 notes

1 1880 Federal Census, Yamhill County, Oregon.

2 Ibid.

3 Elizabeth Bryan, "Lafayette", *Old Yamhill*, (Lafayette: Yamhill Historical Society, 1967), p. 40.

4 Ibid.

5 Marple's hatred of the Masons was nearly pathological. Perhaps he or his father were rejected for membership at one time. The Masons were a secret, semi-religious organization and members were voted into the club by secret ballot. There are still active chapters in Oregon.

6 *Oregon Register* (Yamhill, Oregon) August 12, 1887.

7 *Oregon Register*, September 9, 1887.

8 State of Oregon v. Anna Eliza Marple, Yamhill County Circuit Court, Judgment #2102, Reg. #79, April 2, 1887, Oregon State Archives, Salem, Oregon.

9 State of Oregon v. R. E. Marple, No. 1998. File No. 01867, Journal entry: Vol. 8, p. 222, May 14, 1887, Oregon Supreme Court Appeals file, Oregon Sate Archives, Salem, Oregon.

10 *West Side Telephone* (Lafayette, Oregon) April 2, 1887 and April 30, 1887.

11 *West Side Telephone*, April 2, 1887.

12 State of Oregon v. R. E. Marple, No. 1998.

13 *West Side Telephone*, April 11, 1887.

14 Ibid. For a more detailed discussion about discrimination against the Chinese see Case #24, State of Oregon v. Ah Lee.

15 State of Oregon v. R. E. Marple, No. 1998.

16 Ibid.

17 Ibid.

18 Ibid.

19 Ibid.

20 *West Side Telephone*, November 12, 1887.

21 ilbid.

22 *Oregon Register*, November 18, 1887.

23 Letter from W. M. Stone to J. W. Lewis. Barbara Hagar was killed in her house near Oregon City on February 21, 1879. Her head and neck had been split open—probably with an ax. Joseph Broeder was arrested on February 28, 1879 and eventually acquitted. In April 1879 Louis Graichen, a German, was arrested, tried and acquitted of the murder. Later James King was convicted of murder in the second degree and sent to the penitentiary for life.

24 Indian War Pension Application #750, of Anna Eliza Marple, November 13, 1899, Oregon Historical Society, Portland, Oregon. Ezekial Marple and Anna Eliza Rizeor were married in Benton County on May 30, 1858 according to the Benton County marriage records. However, her statement on the pension application states they were married on May 13, 1858. She was 36 years old (born July 7, 1822) and he was 28 (born October 26, 1830).

25 Benton County Marriage Index, Oregon State Archives, Salem, Oregon.

Chapter Twenty-Eight

State of Oregon v. William Landreth 1888

The motives that propel men to commit murder are often vague and unacknowledged by the perpetrator. While the fact that they killed someone isn't in doubt, to themselves or to others, why they did it may be clouded and murky. When a man kills his young stepdaughter the instant assumption is that he must have been sexually intimate with her and wanted to cover up the crime. However, that isn't always the only reason.

On May 12, 1888, Dallas was bursting with visitors. William Landreth's trial had started and besides the trial witnesses, many people were there just to watch and be part of this historic occasion. Promptly at 8 a.m., Polk County Sheriff Ira S. Smith escorted the defendant into the courtroom, with District Attorney George W. Belt following.[1] Circuit Court Judge Reuben P. Boise was officiating. Subpoenas were issued for nine prosecution witnesses: T. J. Lee, O. D. Butler, W. W. Williams, J. S. Bohannon, Miriam and Wilbur Miller, J. G. Brown, Lizzie Landreth (the defendant's wife), all from Independence, and Louis Frieze, Lizzie Landreth's brother, from Portland. Miriam E. Landreth, William Landreth Jr., and Willis (also known as Wilburn) Landreth, children of William and Lizzie, had testified in front of the grand jury, but they weren't called to testify at the trial.

Elizabeth (Lizzie) Frieze had married William Landreth in Lane County on April 5, 1872—fifteen years earlier.[2] Landreth's first wife, Jane, had died leaving him to raise four daughters: Mary, Ellen, Sarah, and Catherine.[3]

Only a year earlier, on July 7, Oscar Kelty had been abducted from the Polk County jail and lynched after killing his wife, Clara. Because of that experience, Sheriff Smith moved Landreth to Salem to be locked safely in the Marion County Jail until the day of the trial.

The witnesses told the story of a young girl being butchered. Early on the Sunday morning of January 29, at about eight o'clock, the Landreth family of Independence was wakened by horrendous screams. The oldest son, William Landreth Jr., age 19 and Wilburn, aged 13, rushed into Simmie Landreth's bedroom and found their father stabbing her with a 14" butcher knife. Before they could stop him he stabbed his 18 year-old stepdaughter fourteen times in the head and chest.[4]

The father ran from the home and jumped into the slough north of the house in a futile attempt to drown himself. William Jr. chased his father as he ran up the hill and across the bridge toward old Independence. T. J. Hartman heard the boy's cries for help and tackled Landreth before he could escape. After being locked in the city jail Landreth made several more suicide attempts and acted in an irrational manner.

A preliminary exam was held the next day. The girl's mother, Lizzie Landreth, testified against her husband. She'd heard her daughter screaming and running into her room saw her husband holding her with his left arm and stabbing her with the knife in his right hand. After the boys helped her pull him off Simmie, she had tried to stop the bleeding but Simmie died a short time later. Lizzie knew that Landreth had been sexually intimate with his stepdaughter and he was furious with Simmie for telling people about it. Lately Landreth's temper had been particularly severe and he'd accused Simmie of having sex with other men. She thought her husband had been abusing the girl since she was a small child. The other children supported her testimony.

In contrast to Landreth's later confession, the Corvallis *Gazette* maintained that Simmie was well respected by all who knew her and was popular with her neighbors and friends.

On May 24, Landreth produced a four-page letter he had written while sitting in jail. It was rather incoherent, with poor spelling, punctuation and capitalization. In it Landreth referred to five letters he had written to his brother-in-law Louis Frieze that explained the predicament the family had with Simmie. He accused Simmie of being simple-minded, behaving inappropriately, and refusing to abide by the family rules.

The letter said that he and maw had "suspision on the girl after wee moved to the new house when the girl wood go out at nite and stay out till after midnight. Maw noes in the presents of god that she has had the same suspision on the girl that I had."

Landreth threatened to disgrace others living in Independence that may have been sexually involved with Simmie for the past year. Near the end, he admitted killing Simmie but claimed it was a spur of the moment act and not premeditated. "I wood have pled giltey to that inditement if it had bin wirded different. I could not plead giltey to premeditated murder which is not true all tho I never have denied doing the crime . . .

He totally denied the accusations of incest against himself and Simmie.

> *I say these acusations that is made against me & that girl is fals it is not trew as I have put the girl out of the wirld god puts it in my harte to speak in behalf of the girl I doo say positively in the presence of god that wee never did have connection. Donte disgrace her being she is gon if I have ever had that benneyfit I wood plead gilty and go to god with that disgrace rather that go to him with a ly in my harte & mouth . . . I doo say she is free uv doing that with me.*[5]

He killed her, he said, because she was telling others he'd forced her to have sex with him and her accusations disgraced him in the community. In the rural counties of Oregon a man's honor was an extremely valuable commodity. Landreth was not alone in his respect for the code of moral persuasion wielded by the local community. In 1902 Elias Boggs killed a neighbor and his wife. When he heard that a posse was coming to arrest him he committed suicide before they arrived.[6]

On May 26, the foreman of the jury, J. D. Kelty, father of Oscar Kelty, the man lynched in 1887, stood in front of a bursting courtroom and announced that the jury had found the 66-year-old farmer, William Landreth, guilty of first-degree murder. They believed that on January 8, 1888, he had stabbed to death Simmie Alice (Antle) Landreth, his 18-year-old stepdaughter. Judge Boise sentenced Landreth to hang on July 6, 1888.[7] No appeal to the Oregon Supreme Court or request for executive clemency was filed.[8] Sheriff Ira Smith escorted the doomed man back to Salem to wait for his execution.

On July 6, at 10 a.m. Landreth arrived from Salem escorted by ex-Polk County Sheriff John F. Groves and Marion County Sheriff Edward M. Croisan. The hanging rope, used to hang Richard Marple on November 11, 1887 and Joe Drake on March 26, 1885 was decidedly experienced and needed little stretching to make sure it was ready to use. When it came time to dress for the ceremony Landreth began bawling like a baby and laid on his jail cot unable to stand. Sheriff Croisan gave him a glass of whiskey to calm him down and soon he was ready to eat a little. Landreth was offered a last meal, but only ate some of the cake and pie.

He visited with Mr. Crow, from Independence, and gave him his Bible to carry to his wife. A letter inside marked Matt. 11:28-30. "Come unto me all ye that labor and heavy laden and I will give you rest. Take my yoke upon you, and learn of me, for I am meek and lowly of heart, and ye shall find rest unto your souls; for my yoke is easy and my burden is light." The letter was addressed to the citizens of Independence and signed William Landreth. It begged them not to "cast any reflections upon the name of his family as he alone was to blame, that this was the truth and was his last writings and contained his dying words."[9]

At 11:50 the reporters, lawmen and execution witnesses walked out of the jail. The scaffold was waiting on the north side of the jail. The fence surrounding the stockade was twenty-two feet high and the area measured sixteen by twenty feet across.[10] The sheriff had roped off an area directly in front of the scaffold to keep the crowd back. About 12:20 p.m. Landreth exited the jail still escorted by John F. Groves, ex-sheriff of Polk County and Marion County Sheriff Edward Croisan. The execution witnesses were W. W. Brooks, C. C. Doughty, J. D. Ellis, Charles R. Farley, T. J. Graves, P. W. Haley, George E. Houck, I. T. Mason, D. J. Riley, Cass Sargeant, J. A. Smith, and W. W. Williams.[11]

As Landreth waited to climb the steps of the scaffold, reporters asked him again why he had murdered his daughter.

"Because she has ruined me," he replied.

Sheriff Smith, Sheriff Croisan and John Groves accompanied Landreth to the top of the scaffold. While Landreth sat on a chair Sheriff Smith read the death warrant aloud to the witnesses and the waiting crowd. The prisoner was brought forward, his hands were tied, the rope was put around his neck, and the black cap was pulled over his face. At 12:30 p.m., Sheriff Smith pulled the lever and the trap was sprung.

The *Morning Daily Herald* of Albany described the last minutes of Landreth's life:

> *After the fall the body hung motionless, and not a visible tremor shook the frame. Two minutes after the drop his pulse was 75, four minutes, and it had quickened to 120, six minutes, and it was 140. At seven minutes it was so rapid that it could not*

be counted, at eight minutes, it was very slow beating about once in ten seconds, and then grew fainter as his life ebbed away.[12]

Ten minutes later doctors L. N. Woods and T. J. Lee pronounced Landreth dead. His neck was broken instantly and he died very quickly. His body was placed in a coffin and put on display for spectators (including women and children) to gawk at the corpse.[13] He was buried in Potter's Field, the old graveyard south of Dallas, beside Tarr, a man who killed a Dallas woman seven years earlier and then committed suicide.

In the end, Landreth didn't feel nearly as stigmatized admitting to Simmie's murder, as he was being accused of sexually violating her. Incest was perceived as the grossest violation of the social order.[14] He knew that and when caught, chose to destroy his accuser.

References

1860 Federal Census, Marion County, Oregon.

Bellesiles, Michael A. *Lethal Imagination: Violence and Brutality in American History*. N.Y: New York University Press, 1999. "Cultural Representations and Social Contexts of Rape in the Early Twentieth Century" by Mary E. Odem.

City Guard (Eugene, Oregon) July 1, 1888, July 14, 1888.

Daily Democrat (Albany, Oregon) May 12, 1888, May 17, 1888, July 6, 1888, July 7, 1888.

Gazette (Corvallis, Oregon) February 3, 1888, July 13, 1888.

Herald Disseminator (Albany, Oregon) May 18, 1888, June 15, 1888, July 27, 1888.

"Historically Speaking", Vol. III, Polk County Historical Society, Dallas, Oregon.

Laythe, Joseph W. "Bandits and Badgers: Crime and Punishment in Oregon, 1875–1915." Ph.D. diss., University of Oregon, 1996.

McArthur, Scott. "Greed and Sex Lead to Six Hangings in County." *Great Events II*, Special Edition of Polk County History by Sun-Enterprise Newspaper, Monmouth Oregon, Craig Lockwood, Editor. Article located at the Polk County Museum, Rickreall, Oregon.

Morning Daily Herald (Albany, Oregon) July 7, 1888.

Oregon State Journal (Eugene, Oregon) April 13, 1872.

Polk County Observer (Monmouth, Oregon) May 19, 1888, July 7, 1888.

State of Oregon v. William Landreth, Polk County Circuit Court Case File #1661, Oregon State Archives, Salem, Oregon.

Chapter 28 notes

1 George W. Belt was the prosecutor at the Marple and the Landreth trial.

2 *Oregon State Journal* (Eugene, Oregon) April 13, 1872.

3 1860 Federal Census, Marion County, Oregon. "L. B. Landreth, age 25, laborer, b. North Carolina. listed as head of household. Also living with him: "William Landreth, age 33, farmer, b. North Carolina, wife, Jane, age 29, Mary, age 10, Ellen, age 6, Sarah, age 3, and Catharine, age 1month."

4 *Gazette* (Corvallis, Oregon) February 3, 1888.

5 State of Oregon v. William Landreth, Polk County Circuit Court Case File #1661, Oregon State Archives, Salem, Oregon.

6 Joseph W. Laythe, "Bandits and Badges: Crime and Punishment in Oregon, 1875 – 1915" (Ph.D. diss., University of Oregon, 1996) p. 88.

7 State of Oregon v. William Landreth

8 *Daily Democrat* (Albany, Oregon) July 6, 1888.

9 *City Guard* (Eugene, Oregon) July 14, 1888.

10 *Polk County Observer* (Monmouth, Oregon) July 7, 1888.

11 State of Oregon v. William Landreth.

12 *Polk County Observer*, July 7, 1888.

13 Ibid.

14 Michael A. Bellesiles. *Lethal Imagination: Violence and Brutality in American History,* (N.Y: New York University Press, 1999). "Cultural Representations and Social Contexts of Rape in the Early Twentieth Century" by Mary E. Odem, p. 362.

Chapter Twenty-Nine

State of Oregon v. Chee Gong 1888

By the late 1800's Portland had the second largest Chinese population in the United States. By 1886 prejudice against the Chinese also peaked when mobs ransacked homes and forced groups of Chinese to leave town. The murder of young Lee Yik didn't help stop Portland's violent discrimination tactics.

In 1887 Lee Yik, age 20, attended the Chinese Mission School of the United Brethren Church and worked as the second cook in the Saddle Rock Restaurant on First Street in Portland. The first cook was Chee Gong's cousin. When Lee Yik had a fight with Chee Gong's cousin he left the Saddle Rock Restaurant and went to work at the St. Charles Hotel. Later Chee Gong saw the owner talking to Lee Yik. This made his family and him angry and they all stopped working for the Saddle Rock. The owner, Berger, hired Lee Yik back as first cook. This squabble between two men started the feud that eventually led to one man dying, another being hanged and two more being sent to the penitentiary.

The Chinese brought their culture to the United States just as the early settlers brought theirs. One of the social institutions they imported with them was the "highbinder societies". The "highbinders" were fraternal organizations that provided support, protection and a sense of family loyalty to their members. Nearly three-quarters of the Chinese living in North America belonged to one of the societies.[1] As time went on these organizations (also called "tongs") became more powerful and in most cases they also became involved in illegal activities such as gambling, prostitution, and opium smuggling. In Portland there were at least six highbinder groups—Hip Sing, Hup

Sing, Suey Sing, Hoo Leong, Hung Sing, and Luen Yu.[2] Lee Yik was a member of the Luen Yu Tong while Chee Gong was a member of a rival tong.[3] Feeling that he had been treated unfairly Chee Gong's friends got together and prepared to exact revenge. Their method was deadly.

On the evening of November 6, 1887, a large crowd of Chinese were attending the Chinese Theater owned by Lee Toy located on the corner of Second and Alder in Portland. Toy, after serving seven years in the San Quentin Penitentiary, had built the theater in 1879 and was a very powerful man in Chinatown.[4] Just before midnight five men leaped off the stage, surrounded Lee Yik and started beating him. One of the men brandished a large knife and slashed Lee Yik on the head with it.

The assault was so unexpected that very few actually saw what happened or who did it. The police were called and refused to let anyone leave until everyone could be searched and questioned. They found a bloody knife lying on the stairs of the theater. Lee Yik was able to name two of his assailants, Fong Long Dick and Chee Gong.

Lee Yik was taken to Good Samaritan Hospital where he died eleven days later. Police Officer Hoxie and Officer Meyers arrested Fong Long Dick hiding on the roof of a low shed behind his boarding house and Chee Gong in the boarding house where he lived

Five men were named in the indictment by the Multnomah Grand Jury for the murder of Lee Yik: Chee Gong, Fong Long Dick, Ching Ling, Yee Long and Chee Son. On December 13, 1887, three of them, Chee Gong, Fong Long Dick, and Chung Ling, stood in front of Judge Loyal B. Stearns ready to be tried for first degree murder. Ching Ling demanded a separate trial and two of the indicted men (Chee Son and Yee Long) were never found.

Two days later, Chee Gong and Fong Long Dick had their trial. A jury of their "peers" was chosen to hear the case: C. F. Gilbert, C. A. Schaeffer, E. E. Purdin, C. G. Staples, E. S. Edwards, A. McKinnie, H. J. Morrison, J. T. Hembree, William Harris, E. Kahn, F. H. Page, and R. Weeks, jury foreman.[5] The Multnomah County District Attorney Henry E. McGinn, N. D. Simon, Rufus Mallory, and ex-Governor George L. Woods prosecuted the case. M. F. Mulkey and John Caples defended the pair.

During the trial, a note was intercepted as it was smuggled past the guards out of the jail. Deputy Sheriff Witherell saw a man outside the jail take it as it was handed to him through a window. The deputy confiscated the note. It was written in Chinese and, according to an interpreter, it read: "Young Show and Woo Sine. Both kind friends: Again tell Low Hong be my witness. Be sure testify that I and Low

Hung lived in same room two months. Not say longer. Tell that we are acquaintances. Tell at that time I came back to my room at half past seven or eight o'clock. Be sure and answer. Signed by Found Deg."[6] Who wrote the note was never identified. The prosecutor believed it was a plea from Chee Gong to two of his friends to perjure themselves and provide support for his alibi.

Many Chinese witnesses testified against the accused. Most testified because they were in the theater audience when the murder occurred, but a few testified about the animosity between Chee Gong and Lee Yik. The witnesses identifying Chee Gong and Fong Long Dick all had a peculiar feature—their stories were identical. Defense witnesses testified that Chee Gong and Fong Long Dick were not in the theater at the time of the killing.

On Thursday, December 15, 1887, the jury returned a verdict of guilty of murder in the first degree after conferring for only forty minutes. Chee Gong and Fong Long Dick were sentenced to hang on Friday, February 17, 1888.[7] On December 24 Ching Ling was also found guilty of first-degree murder.[8]

Violence plagued the Chinese community during these years and undoubtedly influenced the jury's feelings. In late November 1887 Wong Dock and Lung (also Leong) Ging had a fight in the same Chinese Theater. A witness, Ah Sin, was charged with perjury for telling the grand jury that Lung Ging didn't have a gun. On December 20 the newspapers described the assassination attempt. Lung Ging had tried to kill Wong Dock and was allowed to plead guilty to simple assault.[9] On December 14 custom inspectors arrested three Chinese men for smuggling opium into Portland.

A year later, on December 2, 1888, three men from the Chinese Hup Sing Tong shot Mah Bing as he sat on an outside bench on a sidewalk in Portland. Within moments the rival gang of Hoo Leong arrived and a regular riot ensued. Six men died of their wounds.[10] These kind of events before Chee Gong and Fong Long Dick's two trials most definitely influenced the juries hearing the murder trials.

The defense attorneys hurriedly filed papers to postpone the hanging and appeal the sentence to the Oregon Supreme Court. Almost a year later, on November 13, 1888, the Supreme Court granted the appeal. Now the district attorney had to decide whether to hold another trial or let the men go. It didn't take them long to decide.

A second trial was scheduled for January 1889. This time Chee Gong and Fong Long Dick were tried separately. Fong Long Dick was convicted of second-degree murder and sentenced to life imprisonment on February 21, 1889. Governor Lord pardoned him nine years later on December 6, 1898, just after Fong's thirty-first birthday.[11]

Hopefully, he was able to return to China and reunite with his wife who remained there.

Ching Ling was tried a second time and this time he was found not guilty.

Jurors for Chee Gong were chosen for his second trial. The twelve men were W. Jacques, J. Kronenberg, George Faulkner, C. Schuman, Joseph Delay, E. Himmons, D. M. Roberts, Clark Hay, J. S. Royal, Almon Smith, William Coburn, and O. T. Short.

Chee Gong was not so lucky. He was convicted of first-degree murder and sentenced to hang again. The defense team filed another appeal with the Oregon Supreme Court, but on June 20, 1889, the court denied his appeal and he was sentenced to hang on August 9, 1889.

Construction of the scaffold began on August 7. Instead of building a high fence around the gallows, the scaffold was built at the north end and inside the sixteen by twenty-foot woodshed behind the jail. Sheriff Kelly issued about forty invitations, mostly to fellow lawmen around the state. No Chinese were allowed to witness the execution. Instead of using a rope to drop the trap door, an electrical connection was installed to "trip the trap". The trap door opened in the middle and had two hinges on each side. Underneath, in the center, was a spring and lever attached to the side of the platform. An iron pin with a 50-pound iron block hanging from it was connected to the spring. The electrical wire linked the block to a battery and a push button. Just the slightest pressure on the button released the trap door.[12]

A. Rosenthal, a Chinese scholar from San Francisco, visited Chee Gong in jail and petitioned Governor Pennoyer on Chee Gong's behalf. There wasn't much chance Pennoyer would intercede in any Chinese conviction, as the governor was avidly anti-Chinese.[13] Judge Stearns had already conferred with Pennoyer and discussed the issue of unreliable Chinese testimony. There were many affidavits from witnesses at the trial who swore they were forced by the highbinder tongs to testify against Chee Gong. There also were affidavits from prominent Chinese opposing the hanging. The two officials both agreed that two juries had convicted Chee Gong and while it was within the Governor's power to intervene, it was best to support the juries' decisions. An editorial in the *Oregonian* noted, "the assassins rather than the mere spectators of assassination generally seek concealment."[14] Using that logic Chee Gong was the only man who shouldn't be convicted, as he was the only one not hiding from the police when arrested.

On Friday morning, August 9, just before the execution, Chee Gong became hysterical and started raving that he didn't want to be executed inside the woodshed. Reverend John Gordan of the First Baptist Church and Yueng Chuen[15], a Baptist missionary, joined Reverend Nathan Pearcy and Chee Gong in his cell. Quoting Bible verses with gentle persuasion, the men were able to calm the condemned man.

At 12:25 p.m. Chee Gong was led from the rear door of the jail through a high board fence and into the woodshed. When Sheriff Penumbra Kelly asked Chee Gong if he had anything to say, the little Chinese stepped forward and gave a well-received speech. He denied killing Lee Yik and maintained that he was accused of killing Le Yik because the real killer was a member of his "family". Since the real killer had disappeared Chee Gong was sacrificed in his place.

Standing in front of the crowd just below the gallows were the twelve execution witnesses chosen by Sheriff Kelly. They included M. Marcuse, J. K. Tighe, J. D. Coleman, S. Simon, E. J. Ladd, D. L. Povey, W. Harris, W. A Richardson, William Coburn, J H Kessler, A. Bergman and A. Maudens.

After the execution the body was removed, placed in a coffin and taken to the morgue. A noisy group of boys clamored aboard the wagon carrying the body, peaked under the lid of the coffin, and followed the wagon down the street. A Christian funeral was held three hours later at DeLin & Holman's Mortuary. Before the funeral the body was available for all the hundreds of men, women and children to view. Seid Back, a well-known merchant in Portland, paid to bury the body in Lone Fir Cemetery.[16]

The last hanging of a Chinese National was on January 8, 1892, in Grant County, when Ming How was executed in Canyon City.[17] Ming How stabbed Ah Foo to death on September 26, 1891. All the witnesses were Chinese—Lung On, Ming Sing, Kang Yok, Ah Mow, and Han Fue. County Sheriff Oliver P. Cressap officiated at the final event.

References

The Evening Telegram (Portland, Oregon) November 8, 1887, December 12, 1887, December 14, 1887, December 15, 1887, December 16, 1887, December 17, 1887, December 20, 1887, December 21, 1887, December 23, 1887, December 24, 1887, December 29, 1887, August 7, 1889, August 8, 1889, August 9, 1889, August 10, 1889, August 11, 1889.

Laythe, Joseph W. "Bandits and Badgers: Crime and Punishment in Oregon, 1875–1915." Ph.D. diss., University of Oregon, 1996.

Maddux, Percy. *City on The Willamette: The Story of Portland, Oregon*. Portland: Binfords & Mort, 1952.

Morning Oregonian (Portland, Oregon) November 7,1887, November 11, 1887, February 3, 1889, February 22, 1889, February 26, 1889, August 10, 1889, August 11, 1889.

Oregon State Penitentiary Inmate Case File #2166 for Fong Long Dick,
Oregon State Archives, Salem, Oregon.
Peterson del Mar, David. *Beaten Down: A History of Interpersonal Violence in The West.* Seattle: University of Washington Press, 2002.
State of Oregon v. Gee Gong, etal., No. 3099, File No. 02043, Journal Entry
Vol. 8, p. 589, March 6, 1888, Oregon Supreme Court Appeals file,
Oregon State Archives, Salem, Oregon.
State of Oregon v. Chee Gong, etal., No. 4061, File No. 02163, Journal Entry
Vol. 9, p. 726, May 7, 1889, Oregon Supreme Court Appeals file, Oregon
State Archives, Salem, Oregon.

Chapter 29 notes

1 David Peterson del Mar, *Beaten Down: A History of Interpersonal Violence in the West* (Seattle: University of Washington Press, 2002) p. 100.
2 Percy Maddux, *City on the Willamette: The Story of Portland, Oregon* (Portland: Metropolitan Press, 1952), pp. 91-2. Maddux lists the first five and Laythe lists the sixth. Joseph W. Laythe, "Bandits and Badges: Crime and Punishment in Oregon, 1875–1915" (Ph.D. diss., University of Oregon, 1996) p. 57.
3 Laythe, p. 56.
4 *Evening Telegram* (Portland, Oregon) December 23, 1887.
5 State of Oregon v. Gee Gong, etal., No. 3099, File No. 02043, Journal Entry Vol. 8, p. 589, March 6, 1888, Oregon Supreme Court Appeals file, Oregon State Archives, Salem, Oregon.
6 State of Oregon v. Gee Gong, etal., No. 3099.
7 State of Oregon v. Gee Gong, etal. No. 3099.
8 *Evening Telegram*December 24, 1887.
9 *Evening Telegram*, December 20, 1887, December 21, 1887.
10 Maddux, pp. 92-93.
11 Oregon State Penitentiary Inmate Case File #2166 for Fong Long Dick, Oregon State Archives, Salem, Oregon.
12 *Evening Telegram*, August 8, 1889.
13 Laythe, p. 57. Laythe states that Chee Gong was hanged on August 10, 1889. However the case files and local newspapers state that he was hanged on August 9.
14 *Morning Oregonian*, August 10, 1889.
15 Also identified as "Gee Yueng Chuen, a gray-haired Chinese missionary" in the *Evening Telegram* of August 9, 1889 and "Foon Chuen" in the *Oregonian* of August 10, 1889. The legal papers and newspapers had a terrible time with the Chinese names. The spellings varied wildly.
16 *Morning Oregonian*, August 11, 1889.
17. State of Oregon v. Ming How.

Chapter Thirty
State of Oregon v. John F. Gilman 1889

C hildren were rarely in danger from strangers or neighbors during Oregon's early years. Accidents, disease and natural events took far too many children on the Oregon frontier as it was. So when Chris Eationhover found the body of his 5-year-old son under that of his murdered wife, the community of Coquille City, in Coos County was up in arms ready to decorate a cottonwood (lynch) with the culprit. He wasn't hard to find.

Eationhover had been working away from home at Heuckendorff's farm during the week and was ready to return home Saturday evening. Chris, Elizabeth, his wife, and William, his young son, had moved to Coos County from Wasco County a year earlier and rented a farm from Mr. and Mrs. John Gilman. The young German couple had built a modest house on it. When Eationhover reached the river he hollered for Gilman to come over with a boat and take him home, which Gilman did.

Once they reached the other side, the 60-year-old Gilman followed Eationhover up the narrow path to the house and into the corral. Suddenly Gilman smashed a broken oar over Eationhover's head and started stabbing him with a knife. In his excitement he pulled the knife with a broken blade from his pocket instead of the knife with the good blade. That probably saved Eationhover's life. The men fought, both falling down a ravine, until Mrs. Gilman arrived and pulled her husband off the younger man. Eationhover managed to escape, stumbled back to the boat and alerted neighbors across the river.

When the neighbors arrived at the house they found Gilman in his house sound asleep in bed, still wearing his bloodstained clothes. He denied knowing anything about the location of Elizabeth or William Eationhover. Inside the Eationhover home the table was set for breakfast and the little boy's plate still had food on it. It wasn't until the afternoon of the next day that the searchers found a shallow grave hidden in a gulch with the mother and child buried in it. Both had been strangled to death. Just above their grave an open pit waited for the father.

Acting Coroner J. A. Simons quickly assembled six men for an inquest jury. The jurors included Amos L. Nosler, E. B. Miller, Henry Lorenz, John S. Lawrence (Larense), Samuel D. Howell, and Robert J. Dean, Jr. Their verdict on July 15, 1889, stated that both Elizabeth and William Eationhover had been murdered.[1]

Mr. and Mrs. Gilman were both arrested and taken to Coquille. Later they were taken to the county jail in Empire City to stand trial for murder. (It wasn't until 1897 that the county seat was moved to Coquille.)[2]

While Gilman was in jail over the next three months, he confessed to murdering the Eationhover family. It seems that there were some minor disagreements between the owners and the new tenants. The Gilmans regretted renting their farm and wanted the Eationhover family to leave. The family still had four years to go on their lease and didn't want to leave. They were unaware that in an effort to make them leave, Gilman had previously poisoned some bread they had left out. Only the quick use of sweet oil saved their lives.[3]

Finally on July 12, 1889, Gilman decided to kill the family. Gilman went to the Eationhover house where he attacked Elizabeth with a hoe. Her body showed a bad cut and blunt trauma to the back of the head below the left ear. Her nose was broken, both arms and her left hip were bruised. Her right arm had fingerprints on it and there was a bad bruise on the right hip. She was beaten and left alive long enough for the body to show bruising before Gilman strangled her. William tried to run away, but Gilman caught him, wrapped a rope around his throat and choked him to death. To make sure the little one couldn't tell anyone what had happened, he laid William's head across his knee and broke the child's neck.

The Coos County grand jury met and on October 9 returned a first-degree murder indictment against John F. Gilman for the death of Elizabeth Irene Eationhover and her son, William Wiat Eationhover. Forty witnesses gave testimony at the hearing.

Coos County District Attorney J. W. Hamilton decided to try Gilman for the boy's death first. The trial began in Empire City on Tuesday, October 17, 1889. John F. Hall, David L. Watson and A. M. Crawford assisted District Attorney Hamilton. Gilman's defense team consisted of J. M. Siglin (also editor of the *Coos Bay News*) and T. G. Owen. Forty-seven men were questioned before twelve were chosen for the jury. The jurors were B. A. Adams, T. A. Armfield, William Barkis, E. W. Guptill, S. J. Hulbert, Henry W. Holverstott, C. E. Houser, N. U. Martinson, James Masters, G. W. Skaggs, George M. Sealy, and Benjamin F. Ross, jury foreman.[4] Gilman's lawyer applied for a continuance based on the testimony of Doctor V. R. Vance (Gilman's former physician then living in Woodland, California), William P. Skelly (Gilman's son-in-law who was working at a California navy yard) and Laura E. Lawrence (age 16, who was raised by the Gilmans and lived in Portland) that the prisoner was insane.[5] Gilman was trying to prove he was hit on the head by a falling tree and "that the said injury seriously affected his mind. That he became moody and abstracted at times with a vacant look in his eyes and rambling in his conversation."[6] Judge R. S. Bean overruled the motion and the trial continued.

By overruling the motion Judge Bean was not denying the possibility that Gilman was insane, only denying Gilman extra time to gather witnesses he thought necessary to prove it. It was up to the jury to decide whether he was incapable of knowing right from wrong or merely suffering from an outburst of violent rage.

Ten more people testified: H. B Tucker, a neighbor across the river; Mrs. M. Willard, another neighbor; Mrs. Jane Morgan, the last person to see the victims alive on Thursday, July 11 about 4 p.m.; Joseph Johnson, Coquille City Marshal who led the posse that discovered the bodies; Sam P. C. Johnson, a brother of Joseph and another member of the posse; John L. Baker, another member of the posse; David Hutcheson, who helped Coos County Sheriff Harlocker and Doctor Cook escort Gilman from Coquille to Marshfield and who heard Gilman's first confession; Richard Haughton (Hauten), who saw Gilman leaving the area where the bodies were found; Andrew Jackson and Captain Hill who heard Gillman's confession while he was in jail; and Mrs. Copley, who helped to shroud (prepare for burial) Elizabeth Eationhover's body. Witnesses subpoenaed by the state were: J. J. Baker, Mrs. L. Bantell, Tom (William) and Belle Copley, S. B. Cathcart, J. N. Cecil, John Clinton, J. G. Cook, J. A. Dean, Thomas Drew, H. W. Dunham, E. M. Gallier, (Stephen Gallier was elected sheriff 1902-1906) John Jenkins, Mrs. L. Harper, James Hill, David H. Hutcheson, Andrew Jackson, Fred Kronenburg, Doctor J. T. McCormack, Mr. and Mrs. John Morgan, Frank Randall, J. L. Roy, J. A. Simon, Thomas Sponogle, H. B. Tucker, Charles Wickham, and Matilda Willard.[7]

Attorney Siglin strenuously objected to Justice of the Peace J. M. Simon's actions at the trial. Hamilton asked him if any clothing was left in his possession after the inquest. Simon answered that some clothing and a hat were left with him. At that point Simon pulled out of a satchel a woman's bloodstained dress, a man's bloodstained shirt and jumper, a hat and a rough wooden club about two feet long and two inches in diameter. Simon identified the hat, the shirt and the jumper as being given to him by Constable Sam Johnson at the inquest. No one asked about or mentioned the bloody dress or club lying on the floor in full view of the jurors. It was only later that Simon told Siglin that the club was not originally in the satchel. Jury members assumed that the club and the dress were part of the evidence even though no one specifically referred to them. They could only have been part of the evidence against Gilman in relation to Elizabeth Eationhover's death not William's. Siglin tried to use Simon's actions as grounds for a mistrial but Judge Bean dismissed the motion.

On October 16, 1889, the jury was only out twenty minutes before finding Gilman guilty of killing five year-old William Wiet Eationhover.[8]

The execution was scheduled for Friday, December 13, 1889 in Empire City. Sheriff I. Lintner Harlocker made the arrangements and several hundred people came to witness the event. When reporters interviewed Gilman the morning before the hanging, they asked him if he had anything to say about the murders.

"I was wild at spells; my wife often told me things I had done that I did not know of." Soon he broke down sobbing and crying in despair. "If I had my rights and justice, in the way I was, I wouldn't hang."

Many people thought Gilman had also killed George Morras (son of William and Elizabeth Morras) who had been murdered a year earlier. At one point Gilman confessed to that murder too, but later recanted the confession.

At 1 p.m., everyone was on the scaffold ready for the final moments in John Gilman's life. Several hundred people waited below ready to witness the death of a child killer.[9] Sheriff Harlocker named the following as witnesses: ex-Coos County Sheriff Andrew G. Aiken, Simon B. Cathcart, Doctor J. G. Cook, J. A. Doale, Doctor J. P. Easter, Charles E. Edwards (retired County Commissioner), John Flanagan, Thomas Hirst, David. H. Hutcheson, Thomas Remie, Abrum Rose, Doctor Samuel. L. Leneve and G. B. Self.[10] Gilman was calm and composed as he stood on the scaffold with his arms tied behind him. According to witnesses his missing upper teeth made him appear to be smiling at the crowd. A few minutes later Sheriff Harlocker sprang the trap and Gilman plunged to his death. He was buried soon after.

Fidelia Gilman was also arrested and charged with "aiding another who had committed a felony, with knowledge that he had committed such felony, with intent that said person might escape arrest, trial and conviction therefor."[11] She was tried and acquitted five months later in May 1890.

Besides the murder conviction, Gilman was also assessed $849.45 by the court for trial expenses. The order to seize all of Gilman's personal property was received October 15, 1895, by Coos County Sheriff William W. Gage. The sheriff did his best to find anything of value but finally gave up on February 20, 1896, stating that "I have been unable to find any personal property belonging to . . . John F. Gilman, and that all the real property . . . is heavily mortgaged and that said mortgages are prior to that date of the judgment within set forth".[12]

The tragedy didn't end there. Chris Eationhover never recovered from his family's death. On October 21, 1892, nearly two years after Gilman was executed, Eationhover committed suicide at the home of E. S. Spurgeon in Coquille City.[13] He was buried next to his family.

References

Coos Bay News (Marshfield, Oregon) July 17, 1889, July 24, 1889, October 16, 1889, October 23, 1889, December 18, 1889.

Coquille City Herald (Myrtle Point, Oregon) October 8, 1889, October 22, 1889, November 5, 1889, December 10, 1889.

Dodge, Orville. *Pioneer History of Coos and Curry Counties*. Salem: Capital Printing Company, 1898.

Eugene City Guard (Eugene, Oregon) December 21, 1889.

State of Oregon v. John F. Gilman, Coos County Circuit Court Case Files, Coos County Courthouse, Coquille, Oregon.

Wasco County Naturalization Document, Chris Eationhover, October 25, 1880, Oregon State Archives, Salem, Oregon.

Chapter 30 notes

1 State of Oregon v. John F. Gilman, Coroner's Inquest, Coos County Circuit Court Case Files, Coquille, Oregon.

2 Orville Dodge, *Pioneer History of Coos and Curry Counties* (Salem: Capital Printing Company, 1898) p. 243.

3 Orville Dodge, p. 242.

4 *Coquille City Herald* (Myrtle Point, Oregon) October 22, 1889.

4 State of Oregon v. John F. Gilman, Motion and Affidavits for Continuance, October 11, 1889, Coos County Circuit Court Case Files, Coos County Courthouse, Coquille, Oregon,

6 State of Oregon v. John Gilman, Coos County Circuit Court Case Files, Coos County Courthouse, Coquille, Oregon.

7 Ibid.

8 Ibid.

9 *Coos Bay News* (Marshfield, Oregon) December 18, 1889.

10 Ibid.

11 *Coos Bay News*, October 23, 1889.

12 State of Oregon v. John F. Gilman, Writ of Execution, Coos County Circuit Court Case Files, Coquille, Oregon.

13 Orville Dodge, p. 242.

Chapter Thirty-One

State of Oregon v. John Reiter 1893

On August 4, 1892, Otto Johansen of Olney, Oregon, was ready to send his employee, John W. "Victor" Snellman, an honest and reliable young man about 25 years old, to Astoria with $22 in gold to buy supplies for the farm and boarding house. That same evening another young man, John Reiter, showed up at the boarding house looking for work. Johansen didn't have any work for him but let him spend the night and gave him some dinner.

The next morning Johansen and another boarder, Gustaf Adolph, left early to put in hay at James P. Fox's house. They left Snellman and Reiter eating breakfast. It was the last time anyone saw Victor Snellman alive.

When Snellman didn't return to Johansen's ranch by August 12, he sent word to the Clatsop County Sheriff in Astoria. Sheriff H. A. Smith immediately rounded up a search party. Two men, Jonathan Duncan and Louis Brazee, smelled the decomposing body on August 19 as they rode their horses on Green Mountain near the Military Road, an isolated spot a few miles from Olney. Victor Snellman had been hit on the right side of the head at least three times and slashed with a knife three times in the abdomen letting several inches of intestines fall out. Coroner William Pohl estimated that he had been killed August 4, the same day he left Johansen's ranch.

Suspicion focused on the young stranger, John R. Reiter, as the last person to see Snellman. The area was a German farming community where neighbors knew each other and strangers were recognized at once.

Sheriff Smith set up a reward fund of $200 for Reiter's capture and telegraphed a description all over the state:

> *Age about 25, height about 5' 8", weight about 150, fair complexion, light hair, pompadour cut, blue eyes, small lump on bridge of nose close to forehead, small light moustache on August 3, last, spare features, tattooed blue ring on third finger of left hand, covered by silver ring, small tattooed anchor on back part of left hand near thumb, soft hands inside, wore at that time, laced shoes, striped pants, black and white running up and down, blue sack coat, white shirt, no vest, turned down collar, white four-in-hand necktie, with the picture of a dog for scarf-pin, and white straw hat with black band.*[1]

On August 23 the *Daily Astorian* announced that Sheriff Smith had arrested John Reiter for the murder of John Victor Snellman. Smith had traced Reiter from Astoria to Portland. Deputy Sheriff Dell Mooer and William Kohler (who could identify Reiter) were dispatched to Portland aboard the steamer *The Telephone*. They met Portland Detective Henry Griffin and arrested Reiter where he was washing dishes at the Terminus Restaurant on Everett and Third Streets. The lawmen also traced a watch Reiter had pawned that had once belonged to Snellman.

On August 23, while in the Astoria jail, Reiter confessed. At first he said that they had met a shipmate who killed and robbed Snellman. Later he amended the statement and wrote out the following confession:

> *The other statement I made was true, except where I said that my shipmate done the killing. (T)hat was not true. I knocked Snellman over the head with a stone and cut him afterwards and took all his money. I cut him with this knife, with the small blade. I was afraid that after I took his money and he was not dead that he would have me arrested for taking his money. I and Snellman were sober at the time.*
>
> *John Reiter, Signed in the presence of H. A. Smith and Chas. M. Celler, Astoria, (O)r Augt 25/93* [2]

A preliminary hearing was held in Astoria on August 27, 1893, just twenty-three days after the murder. Judge Cleveland presided and Assistant District Attorney Curtis questioned the various witnesses. Reiter was held without bond to be questioned again by the grand jury on September 21, 1893. The fourteen witnesses questioned by the grand jury were A. A. Cleveland, Portland Detective H. D. Griffin, Albert Friend, Doctor A. C. Fulton, Coroner William Pohl, Celiettie

(Laura) Snodgrass, Otto Johanson, Gustaf Adolph (also identified as August Dolphin), James Fox, James Turk, B. M. Lichtenstein, William Koehler, H. A. Smith, and Charles M. Celler.[3]

The trial was held September 3 in Liberty Hall because the circuit court room was too small to hold the curious crowd. Circuit Court Judge Thomas A. McBride presided.[4] District Attorney W. N. Barrett prosecuted and was assisted by F. D. Winton. Ex-judge Frank J. Taylor and Frank Spittle were appointed to defend Reiter.[5] Ten of the twelve men appointed to the jury were J. N. Coffey, C. H. Gribble, J. F. Kindred, J. Lewis, Dennis Lucy, J. McGuire, Thomas Norman, Charles H. Stockton (foreman), P. Trullinger, and O. P. Williams.[6]

Even though it took most of the morning to pick the jury, the questioning of the witnesses ended late in the afternoon of the same day. In addition to the witnesses who appeared in front of the grand jury, Jonathan Duncan and Louis Brazee of Astoria, and Frank Turk of Portland also testified.[7] The audience listened raptly when Miss Laura Snodgrass, a dancer at the local dance house, *The Ivy*, testified. She had met Reiter on Tuesday and Wednesday (August 1 and 2) and again Friday afternoon (August 4). She said Reiter didn't have any money when he left Wednesday but showed her $15 on Friday. She also testified that he had no watch when he left but had one when he returned. Later Reiter accused Laura of stealing his money on Wednesday, August 2, and blamed her for everything that happened after that. It only took the jury twenty-five minutes to reach a guilty verdict. Reiter was sentenced to hang the same day as another convicted murderer—John Hansen—Friday, December 1, 1893.[8]

Reiter was born in Creishau, West Prussia, Germany on February 1, 1872, twenty-one years earlier.[9] His farmer father was dead and his mother was quite ill. He was one of five sons and three daughters born to the family. He was a sailor who had deserted off the British ship *Cabull* from Antwerp when it arrived in Portland the previous May.

Sheriff Smith bought Reiter a new black suit and began preparations for the big event. The scaffold was built to accommodate both convicted murderers with the trap door a full sixty-nine inches off the ground, but Hanson's execution was delayed until May 18, 1894. The invitations to Reiter's execution listed both men. At 11:10 a.m. the doors to the enclosure were opened and "the crowd merged to the front as if they were going on a visit to Barnum's circus."[10]

At 11:52 Sheriff Smith led the prisoner out the jail door and up the scaffold steps. Reiter's arms were tied behind him and his feet were tied together and heavy weights attached. A few seconds after the black cap was pulled over his head the sheriff tapped twice with his foot on the specially built electric trapdoor switch and the murderer

Clatsop County Sheriff's Department
Hanging in Clatsop County of either John Reiter or John Hansen.

died almost instantly. His neck was dislocated and stretched two inches. Another foot and he would have been decapitated. Coroner Pohl took the body and had it buried in the old Warrenton pauper cemetery. Offical witnesses included George A. Colmann, John Fox, S. E. Harris, J. W. Hume, Adolph Johnson, L. Lebark, Hugh McCormick, H. G. Smith, S. G. Trullinger, Jas. W. Welch, G. Wingate, and C. S. Wright. [11] It cost Clatsop County $2,284.35 to try and convict John R. Reiter.[12]

John Hansen, a convicted murderer waiting in the jail for the Supreme Court's decision on his appeal heard the distinct thump of Reiter's death and said to his guard, "There he goes. I only wish it was myself instead."[13]

In a strange turn of events, Sheriff H. A. Smith became a wanted man two years later when he stole the county tax receipts and disappeared in Belgium.[14] He had been elected sheriff in 1888 after working as a fisherman for several years and emigrating from Cape of Good Hope, South Africa.[15]

Reiter wasn't the only person hanged in 1893. Grant County had been dealing with the murder of A. W. Shaw. In a dramatic trial, F. W. Gallin and Lina Shaw (A. W. Shaw's wife) were tried together for murder. Lina was acquitted and Gallin was found guilty. He was hanged in Canyon City by Grant County Sheriff Joseph D. Combs on July 14, 1893.[16]

164

References

Daily Astorian (Astoria, Oregon) August 20, 1893, August 22, 1893, August 23, 1893, August 24, 1893, August 25, 1893, August 26, 1893, August 27, 1893, September 3, 1893, October 3, 1893, December 8, 1893.

"Death Among the Raspberries." *Cumtex*, Clatsop County Historical Society Quarterly, Vol. 17, No. 4, Fall 1997.

Friedman, Lawrence. *Crime and Punishment in American History*. N.Y.: Basic Books, 1993.

McCarthy, Linda. *A History of the Oregon Sheriffs, 1841-1991*. Portland: Oregon State Sheriff's Association, 1992.

Morning Oregonian (Portland, Oregon) August 23, 1893, September 30, 1893, December 2, 1893.

"Murder on Olney Road." *Cumtex*, Clatsop County Historical Society Quarterly, Vol. 17, No. 4, Fall 1997.

State of Oregon v. John Reiter, Clatsop County Case File, Clatsop County Courthouse, Astoria, Oregon.

Chapter 31 notes

1 *Daily Astorian* (Astoria, Oregon) August 22, 1893.
2 State of Oregon v. John Reiter, Clatsop County Circuit Court Case File, Clatsop County Courthouse, Astoria, Oregon.
3 Ibid.
4 Thomas McBride became judge of the circuit court of the fifth district in 1892. He remained there for seventeen years until appointed to the state supreme court in 1909.
5 *Daily Astorian*, 3 September 1893.
6 Ibid. For some unknown reason only ten names are listed in the newspaper article and the names are not listed in the court records.
7 State of Oregon v. John Reiter.
8 *Daily Astorian*, October 3, 1893.
9 "Murder On Olney Road," *Cumtex* (Clatsop County Historical Society Quarterly, Vol. 17, No. 4 – Fall 1997) p. 30.
10 "Murder on Olney Road", p. 32.
11 State of Oregon v. John Reiter
12 *Daily Astorian*, December 8, 1893.
13 "Death Among the Raspberries," *Cumtex*, (Clatsop County Historical Society Quarterly, Vol. 17, No. 4, Fall 1997) p. 39.
14 "Murder On Olney Road", p. 33.
15 Linda McCarthy, *A History of the Oregon Sheriffs, 1841-1991* (Portland: Oregon State Sheriff's Association, 1992) p. 25.
16. State of Oregon v. F. W. Gammin, Grant County Circuit Court Case File #1694, Oregon State Archives, Salem, Oregon.

Chapter Thirty-Two

State of Oregon v. John Hansen 1894

When a husband kills his wife it is usually because she has decided to leave him or because he's jealous of her attentions toward another man. John Hansen killed his wife of thirty years because she wanted him to help with the farm work and refused to give him any of her hard earned money to buy whiskey.

John Hansen was an alcoholic and would go on long drunken binges. He and his wife lived about twelve miles from Astoria and the only way to reach their home was by boat. For nearly two weeks he was gone from home and was found drunk and passed out in his boat tied to a wharf in Astoria. On Sunday, July 23, 1893, Caroline Hansen finally persuaded a neighbor to go to Astoria to find Hansen and bring him home. He stayed home all day Monday, but went fishing in the evening. Early in the morning on Tuesday, July 24 he stopped at the home of Martin Hansen (no relative), but was so sick from alcohol cravings he couldn't even eat breakfast. He was able to drink some whiskey. About 9 a.m. he returned home and met his wife returning from Peter and Henrietta Svensen's house.

Three days later Hansen described what supposedly happened next. After getting home he lay down on the sofa to take a nap. Caroline announced sarcastically, "If you don't go to work, I will kill you".

"I have been out fishing all night and I now want to rest." He got up and went upstairs to sleep until about 3:15 p.m. When he woke up he was craving alcohol again and in a vile mood. He went outside to see what his wife was doing.

The two of them got into an argument when she asked him to help her pick the raspberries. When he refused she told him to leave and he told her that he didn't want to leave. Then she threw a rock at him but missed. A few minutes later, when she had her back to him he smashed her over the head with a three-foot-long stick. She lay face down in the dirt and the blood, her head crushed and broken by the man she'd lived with for more than thirty years.

An hour later Hansen found John Nyland, who was fixing a break in the dyke along the river and told him Caroline was dead. Nyland rowed to Astoria and notified

Astoria Daily Budget, May 18, 1894
John Hansen murdered his wife.

Coroner Pohl. The victim's son, 29 year-old Victor Hansen, and a jury of six men (E. H. Coe, A. H. Church, D. W. Burnside, W. R. Grimes, G. W. Cole and E. Erickson) hurried to the site of the crime.

The coroner's jury, knowing Hansen's drinking habits, immediately suspected the husband and arrested him. A few days before her death Mrs. Hansen told her niece she believed her husband would kill her.[1] Caroline Hansen's body was taken to Astoria with her husband. At the morgue hundreds of people filed in to pay their respects and look at the body. Still pretending to be the sorrowful husband, Hansen kissed his dead wife's forehead just before they lowered her into the grave. She was buried July 28, 1893, in the Greenwood Cemetery.

John Hansen was born in Jakobstad, Pietasaari, Finland almost 56 years earlier. He had married Caroline Gustafson on May 17, 1861, thirty-one years before he killed her. They immigrated to Astoria with their son, Victor, in 1882. Caroline Gustafson was fifty years old.[2] Hansen was a stocky man about 5' 8" inches tall with blue eyes and a long reddish beard. When he wasn't drinking or carousing in town, he earned a living by fishing in the nearby Columbia River. Hansen signed legal papers requesting Victor Hansen be named administrator of his wife's estate. After paying $116 for a casket and a plot in the Greenwood Cemetery Victor eventually inherited $1,389.[3]

Three days later, while being held in the Clatsop County Jail, Hansen confessed to killing his wife and signed a written confession. Besides admitting that he killed her, he told how he stood over her until he was sure she was dead, stole a key out of her pocket, unlocked a bureau drawer and drank a bottle of kummel (a liquor flavored with caraway seeds, anise, or cumin) that was locked in it. That evening he chopped up the board he used to kill her, put it in the wood box and burned it in the stove.

Two weeks later, during a conversation with Peter Svensen, he described what happened that day. Svensen reported what Hansen told him.

There was a club lying there that was to change the calf in the pasture and he took up that club to change the calf and all of a sudden he had an impulse and took the club and hit his wife in the head. He said she was standing there picking berries at the time. I asked him if he had any cause for it, and he said he had no cause whatever, and he didn't know at that minute what he done it for, but he said he done it, and he didn't hardly know how it happened himself at the time.[4]

At the trial John Nyland, a boarder and hired hand of Hansen's, testified that on Monday morning when Hansen returned from town he complained to Nyland that all his money was gone. Yet Thursday morning, after Caroline Hansen's death, Sheriff H. A. Smith found $52.25 in Hansen's pockets. Caroline had been furious that her husband had spent all his money on liquor instead of paying bills. Nyland had previously left some money with Caroline and after Hansen said Caroline was dead Nyland checked the bureau drawer for his money, found it unlocked and all the money gone. Nyland immediately asked Hansen about it and was told, "Your money is alright. You won't lose a nickel".

Later when Nyland checked, his money was back in the drawer. Victor Hansen testified that he found $5 in cash and certificates of deposit worth $1,200 in his mother's bureau drawer. This was the same locked drawer Hansen unlocked after he killed his wife.

The trail began Wednesday, September 27, 1893. The twelve men chosen for the jury were J. L. Carlson, John Chitwood, W. T. Chutter, W. L. Gillett, E. B. Kunzler, Hugh McCormick, Alfred Olsen, Thomas Ryrie, P. A. Stokes, D. P. Williams, Andrew Young, and H. G. Mallett, foreman.[5] The Clatsop County circuit courtroom was considered unsafe to hold the expected crowd so Sheriff Smith rented the Liberty Hall.[6] The audience was unusually rowdy until Judge Thomas A. McBride started sentencing the louder members to jail for contempt of court. Jack Adams not only clapped his hands, but also stamped his feet loudly after the district attorney's opening remarks.[7] After the judge sentenced him to five days imprisonment, the audience was considerably more restrained.

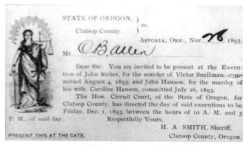

Clatsop County Sheriff's Department
Invitation to John Hansen's hanging.

The defendant pleaded not guilty by reason of temporary insanity brought on by chronic alcoholism. A plea of insanity due to alcoholism was a difficult defense to prove. Even blind drunk Casterlin couldn't prove it in 1860. In this case Hansen hadn't had much alcohol to drink since Sunday—three days before the killing. If Hansen could have proven that he was ordinarily a kindly, industrious and virtuous man, perhaps the citizens of Astoria could have accepted the temporary insanity plea. However, according to the strict interpretation of the law—getting drunk was no excuse for killing someone.[8] The fact that Hansen searched his wife's possessions for money right after the killing seemed to indicate premeditation and malice.

Both local physicians, Doctor Jay Tuttle and Doctor W. D. Baker testified that Hansen was not insane, although Victor Hansen and various neighbors testified to Hansen's history of erratic behavior. Defense attorney Charles Fulton subpoenaed eleven witnesses to testify for the defense: George Larsen, Peter Broche, A. E. Muriard, Jacob Baker, Mrs. Morie Show, Leonder Lebeck, Earnest Lawson, George Leeland Ward, Olaf Peterson (a.k.a. Fong Olof), Gust Hildebrand and Joseph Surwott. W. N. Barrett, district attorney for the Fifth Judicial District, called fourteen witnesses to testify for the prosecution: H. A. Smith, Mrs. R. D. Church, Mrs. H. C. Svensen, Alex Johnson, Andrew Fransen, Martin Hansen, Charles Lind, Emil Holm, F. J. Dunbar, William C. Pohl, Doctor Walter C. Belt, V. H. Coffey, Elmer A. Coe, and John Nyland.

On the stand Victor tried to help his father's case:

Whenever he would come to town and get whiskey, he was always drunk, and after that it never failed once yet, when he could get whiskey; and after that when he got home he never slept, and he was restless, and two or three days afterwards, he would try to work, and he went to work and started in early in the morning, and quit and started on something else, and kept

on for maybe eight or ten days of this. He used to talk to himself.
He would go by himself and talk, and sit in the boat and talk,
and would imagine there was somebody else in the boat, and
when it came time to pick up the net, he would imagine there was
a little man to help him pick up the net. Sometimes he would
laugh when he was out of his mind, then he was sitting crying,
and then he was dancing, and there was an old accordion he
would play and play dancing tunes on it, and then he would cry.
I had to tie him outside once. I tied him outside of the house in
the cold air, he was out of his head.[9]

At the end of the trial Judge McBride included the following in the jury's instructions, "The law presumed every man sane and sober until he proved otherwise without a reasonable doubt. The burden of proof lay with him, and if the jury were not certain whether Hansen had been insane or not at the time of the crime, the benefit of the doubt should be given to the state."[10] This seemed in contradiction to the precept of "innocent until proven guilty".

The jury retired to its deliberations at 10:30 p.m. and returned with its verdict of "guilty as charged in the indictment" just before midnight.

Judge McBride sentenced Hansen to hang on December 1, 1893, the same day as John Reiter, the murderer of Victor Snellman. However, Charles Fulton, Hansen's lawyer, filed an appeal to the Oregon Supreme Court, an action that automatically postponed Hansen's execution. The lower court's decision was upheld on February 19, 1894, and the state charged Hansen a fine of $358. The county paid F. D. Winton $500 to assist District Attorney W. N. Barrett during the trial and to prepare the Supreme Court papers. A final accounting filed April 13, 1894, showed that, including the Supreme Court fee, it cost Clatsop County $1,999.50 to prosecute John Hansen.[11]

Judge McBride sentenced the convicted murderer to hang on May 18, 1894. The same scaffold, borrowed from Multnomah County, was used to hang Hansen as was used to hang John Reiter on December 1, 1893.

The morning of the hanging Hansen ate a hearty breakfast of coffee, five eggs, bread, and a nice juicy steak. Reverend Short and son, Victor, visited the prisoner until the time came to leave the jail. Outside there were nearly 1,000 people standing on the hills, climbing in trees, and peering through knot holes around the jail trying to see inside the stockade. Thad Trullinger tested the electrical drop the day before to make sure it worked.[12] Astoria had the newest invention —

an electric plant. It provided electricity for streetlights and other conveniences. Where ropes were used before, now electricity was used to release the pin opening the trap door on the floor of the scaffold. This was the third time in Oregon's history electricity was used in a hanging.

The enclosure was so small that the fifty people inside were sweaty and hot by the time the prisoner was escorted outside. The witnesses chosen to watch the execution were A. Andersen, Peter Brach, W. E. Clinton, F. Cook, S. Danziger, E. C. Hughes, Jas. F. Kearney, J. T. Leasy, A. Montgomery, M. Olsen, F. Quinn, and A. M. Twombly.[13]

Hansen's arms and legs were tied, the black cap slipped over his head and the noose placed in position. Just as the whistle started announcing the noon hour, there was a quick motion of the sheriff's hand and the trap fell open.

No one paid much attention to the last bystander. Andrew Oster of Bear Creek, Caroline Hansen's brother, came over and gazed at the body of his brother-in-law as it lay in the coffin.[14] Then he slipped away, making no comment about the proceedings.

References

Daily Astorian (Astoria, Oregon) August 31, 1893, September 24, 1893, September 28, 1893, September 29, 1893, October 3, 1893.

Clatsop County Probate File #H-026, Caroline Hansen, 1893, Oregon State Archives, Salem, Oregon.

Clatsop County Probate File, #2057, Victor Hansen, 1929, Oregon State Archives, Salem, Oregon.

"Death Among the Raspberries." *Cumtex*, Vol. 17, No. 4, Fall 1997.

East Oregon Herald (Burns, Oregon) August 2, 1893.

Friedman, Lawrence. *Crime and Punishment in American History*. N.Y.: Basic Books, 1993.

Morning Oregonian (Portland, Oregon) September 29, 1893.

State of Oregon v. John Hansen, Clatsop County Circuit Court Case File No.2651, October 17, 1893, Clatsop County Courthouse, Astoria, Oregon.

State of Oregon v. John Hansen, No. 4606, File No. 02705, Journal entry: Vol. 10, p. 404, Dec. 4, 1893, Oregon Supreme Court Appeals file, Oregon State Archives, Salem, Oregon.

Chapter 32 notes

1 *East Oregon Herald* (Burns, Oregon) August 2, 1893.

2 "Death Among the Raspberries," *Cumtex* (Clatsop County Historical Society Quarterly, Vol. 17, No. 4, Fall 1997) pp. 34–39.

3 Clatsop County Probate File #H-026, Caroline Hansen, 1893, Oregon State Archives, Salem, Oregon.

4 State of Oregon v. John Hansen, No. 4606, File No. 02705, Journal entry: Vol. 10, p. 404, December 4, 1893, Oregon Supreme Court Appeals File, Oregon State Archives, Salem, Oregon.

5 *Daily Astorian* (Astoria, Oregon) September 28, 1893.

6 *Daily Astorian*, September 24, 1893.

7 *Daily Astorian*, September 29, 1893.

8 Lawrence Friedman, *Crime and Punishment in American History*, N.Y.: (Basic Books, 1993) p. 147. Friedman discusses this concept in Chapter 6. If the drinking made it impossible to form intent to murder, or if the murder was committed in a moment of insane passion, the accused could be sentenced for second-degree murder.

9 State of Oregon v. John Hansen. Per signatures at the bottom of the warrant.

10 *Daily Astorian*, September 29, 1893.

11 State of Oregon v. John Hansen, Clatsop County Circuit Court, Bill of Costs and Disbursements, April 13, 1894, Clatsop County Courthouse, Astoria, Oregon.

12 "Death Among the Raspberries", p. 35.

13 State of Oregon v. John Hansen.

14 "Death Among the Raspberries", pp. 36-7.

Sensational Journalism
Takes Control,
1896–1905

Chapter Thirty-Three

State of Oregon v. Loyal (Lloyd) Montgomery 1896

It was a glorious sunny day Tuesday, November 19, 1895, in Brownsville, Oregon where John Montgomery and Elizabeth Moran Montgomery, well respected owners of a large farming family, were relaxing in their home just outside town. They had finished delivering their successful hop crop to buyer, Fred Gilkey, earlier in the week and were feeling much relieved. Hops were a difficult crop to produce. In the fall it took a large number of workers to come and pick the prickly vines of their bitter berries in order to send them off to be processed into beer mash. They had moved to Oregon from Howard County, Missouri some years back and were happy living in this little western valley.

About 4:30 p.m. Gilkey drove up in his buckboard, stopped and yelled at the house.[1] The oldest son, Lloyd Montgomery, who had just turned 18 in August, came around the house from the back and stared at him for a moment. Lloyd was a heavy set, stout young man with a swarthy complexion, looking older than his age.

"Hi Lloyd, is your father home?"

"Sure is. Want me to get him?" Lloyd went into the house and fetched his father who came out to visit with Gilkey.

While they were talking, Daniel B. McKercher, owner of the Crawfordsville flourmill, came by on his horse and stopped to chat with the group. After a pleasant conversation, Gilkey left and continued on his way to Brownsville past Robert Templeton's farm next door. Templeton was Elizabeth Montgomery's brother and the families were very close. McKercher stayed and the Montgomery couple continued visiting in the yard. While they were standing there, Lloyd came out to join the group.

Frowning, his father asked, "Where have you been since yesterday? You haven't done any of your chores and your brother Orville has been working all day."

"I went hunting. What does it matter to you?" Lloyd muttered sullenly and refused to look his father in the eye.

Angrily John Montgomery slapped his son and started yelling at him to go cut some wood for his mother.

"Sorry, Daniel. My son needs a lot of discipline at times," Montgomery apologized as he turned away from his son.

"I understand. Discipline is a good thing for children." McKercher agreed with Montgomery and turned to Lloyd. "You should be grateful to your parents. They deserve your obedience and respect."

Abruptly, Lloyd left and stomped into the house. He was a full-grown man being treated like a small child. Inside the house he went to his parent's bedroom, fetched his father's 40/82 caliber Winchester hunting rifle and stood in the kitchen door watching his father and McKercher talking by the fence.

He was angry and excited but his aim was right on and all those hours spent hunting instead of doing farm work had made him a deadly shot. Deliberately he raised the rifle, aimed and shot his father through the left side of the head. In that second, looking at his father's brains splattered all over the white picket fence, his destiny was decided.

Swinging around he fired again, but McKercher was faster than he was and had already started running behind the house. Lloyd jumped off the porch and ran around the house. McKercher was just going through the front door when Lloyd raised the rifle and fired again, shooting McKercher in the back of the head where he fell dead into the sitting room. Lizzie Montgomery, screaming and crying for mercy, tried to escape out the back door, but only got as far as the dining room. Lloyd raised his rifle again firing twice. He hit his mother once in the middle of the back and once in the back of the head. Then there was silence. The smell of gunpowder and blood sat like a pall in the heavy autumn air.

Carefully Lloyd laid the rifle beside McKercher's body and left the house. Thinking to establish an alibi before anyone saw him; he headed to the field where his brother, Orville, was plowing. He didn't quite make it because on his way he met his sister, Eva, age 12, little brothers, Robert and Clarence, and cousin, Clyde Templeton, age 13, coming home from school.[2] Unfortunately, Robert, age 11, had heard the shots and asked Lloyd about them. Lloyd denied hearing anything.

176

Robert, running ahead to ask his parents about the shots he had heard, was the first person to reach the house and went in the front door. Lloyd followed with the other children and was waiting outside when Robert Montgomery came back out screaming that there was a dead body in the sitting room. Never going into the house, Lloyd began yelling and jumped on McKercher's white horse, which was tied to the fence. He rode to his Uncle Robert Templeton's house through the hop yard where several people were working. He met William Piper, a blacksmith in Brownsville, and thinking to preserve his quick alibi, told him to come quick,

Lebanon Express, November 21, 1895
Lloyd Montgomery

that his parents and another man were dead. Piper immediately ran to the house and found the bodies. Lloyd also fetched his aunt, and Doctor J. F. Henry. Mrs. Templeton had just left the Montgomery house about 4 p.m. with her mother. She had missed being murdered herself by only thirty minutes.

Lloyd was instantly suspected of the deed. It didn't take much intellect or investigation to figure out that the only person in the vicinity probably did the deed and Lloyd's story was pretty thin. Even before the murders, Lloyd Montgomery had a bad reputation in his hometown. It was well documented that he had made repeated threats against his parents, and most of his neighbors and family immediately suspected him when they heard of the killings.

After the deputy sheriff arrested Lloyd, his grandmother told the officer, "Be sure and have a strong guard over him, or he will be back and murder a lot more of the family."

The major evidence against Lloyd was his advance knowledge of his parent's death when according to his brothers and cousin he never saw their bodies until after Piper got there.

A coroner's jury was held on November 20 in Brownsville and Lloyd Montgomery was the primary suspect. The threat of a lynching in Brownsville was so high that Deputy Sheriff J. A. Wilson immediately escorted Lloyd by train back to Albany.[3]

Over the next several days Lloyd gave several different fictional accounts of the events leading up to the murders. In the beginning, he denied knowing anything, saying he was in the field with his brother when the shots were fired. Then he made a partial confession, saying that Daniel McKercher had killed his parents after a quarrel over some money and Lloyd had killed him in self-defense. No one believed that for a minute. Just the halfhearted accusation against McKercher made people furious. McKercher was a highly esteemed businessman in the community. He was past district deputy in the International Order of Odd Fellows, a past master workman in the Associated Order of United Workmen and was liked by all who knew him.

Eventually, ten days later, Lloyd made a full confession while talking to J. S. Van Winkle, a newspaper reporter. He broke down and sobbed wildly, "I don't know what made me do it. I just got to shooting and kept on until I shot them all. I had no idea of killing them until I got so mad and then I didn't know what I was doing until it was all over. After putting the gun down beside McKercher, my first thought was to get away. I ran out into the field a short distance, but saw the other children nearby coming home from school and came back with them."

"How had your father abused you? Had he flogged you?"

"No, but I had worked hard all my life and he always treated me mean and verbally abused me."

"Had they accused you of committing any crimes, or did you have any other trouble in the neighborhood?"

Lloyd liked to whine and snivel and this was no different. "No, not to amount to anything. I did sign my uncle's name to a money order, or check, from William Scott for $5.00, but I had worked for him and he owed me that much, and I thought it would be all right." Lloyd had run away when the forgery was discovered. His father had to pay the money back to William Scott and had reluctantly paid train fare to fetch Lloyd back.

Haltingly with frequent outbursts of crying Lloyd confessed, "I have a violent temper and am easily angered. When my father slapped me, it made me so angry I didn't know what I was doing."

The Linn County Grand Jury brought in an indictment for first-degree murder against Lloyd Montgomery on December 5, 1895. Members of the grand jury were C. W. Richardson, foreman; I. Fox; Charles Bogart; E. C. Russell; Jason Carothers; Frank McKnight and W. H. Kirk.[4]

After a great deal of consultation Montgomery's lawyers, J. J. Whitney and N. M. Newport, decided to enter a plea of not guilty by reason of insanity.

The Montgomery trial was held Tuesday, December 17, 1895.[5] While there was no direct witness to the murders, and Lloyd Montgomery rescinded his confession of November 29, the trial went smoothly and the jury had no problem finding Montgomery quite sane and guilty of "murder in the first degree." James McCain and Captain N. B. Humphrey represented the state and Judge George Burnett was the presiding circuit court judge. In an unusual turn of events, five members of the jury, A. Croft, T. N. Umphrey, J. H. Caldwell, E. C. Roberts and Frank Trites, also served on the jury in the Emma Hannah murder trial. Lloyd killed his parents exactly forty-one days after Emma Hannah was convicted of murdering Lottie Hiatt.[6]

The execution date was set for January 31, 1896, less than two months from the time Montgomery killed his parents and Daniel McKercher.[7]

Immediately after the sentencing, Lloyd announced that his confession was a mistake and a fabrication. He now maintained that he was totally innocent and a victim of a justice system gone awry. Again he tried to blame McKercher for the deaths of his parents. He told the press that while he admitted killing McKercher, it was done only in an attempt to save his own life after McKercher had killed his parents.

Between the time of the conviction and the final sentence was carried out the Montgomery case was almost continually in the newspapers. Coming as it did on the tail end of the Hannah case this new murder caused a great deal of comment in most of Oregon's newspapers. All the area's local newspapers had opinions they wanted to express about Montgomery's guilt, motives and probable execution. Lloyd's unusual behavior and antics over the next few months only served to increase the drama. For the first time in Oregon history, the defendant and his lawyers used publicity to try to gain sympathy for their cause.

Reverend B. J. Kelley, of the United Evangelical church in Brownsville gave a sermon on December 5 to a large audience based on the saying in Proverbs, "Spare the rod and spoil the child." Reverend Kelley, among other things, told of an incident in the life of young Montgomery that illustrated his irreverence for his parents. When Lloyd was only ten years old he found a fifty-cent piece. He went to Brownsville one day when his father was ill and offered to bet it with the boys of the town that his father would die before morning.[8]

In the same issue of the paper, it was reported that Lloyd was "becoming crazy". He was in a very distressed condition of mind and had become violent, bitten his hands and arms and continually cried out in despair.

"Take them away. Don't let them hang me," he cried piteously to his visitors and jailers, disturbing the entire building.

Two doctors came and administered medicine to calm his nerves. Several men had to pacify him until he quieted down. It was thought that if he wasn't already insane, the memory and guilty feelings of his crime were enough to make him that way. There was some concern he would try to commit suicide. Several ministers visited the young man and tried to prepare him for his upcoming death. For a time the murderer seemed to take a deep interest in religion. He read the Bible industriously for a day or two but then lost interest. Lloyd's attention span remained short at best.

After the verdict, with great bravado, Lloyd declared that he didn't want a new trial. He bragged to Sheriff James A. McFeron that he was unconcerned about his death and would spring the trap himself if allowed. However, when his lawyers, Judge J. J. Whitney and N. M. Newport, came to his cell and proposed to give up the appeal process, he relented and begged them to do their best in the Supreme Court appeal to procure him a new trial. His macho self-interest dwindled quickly when faced with the actual probability of death.

Montgomery's actions played to the public's interest in him. He became an instant celebrity. On January 3, 1896, the *Oregonian* printed a letter Montgomery had received from a Mrs. Judd in Turner, and his reply to her. In part he stated, "You spoke of your three sons, and I wish to tell them that if they are in any way inclined to walk through this life in a crooked and thorny path, to stop and think before it is too late, that they may be delivered from darkness into light." He knew what to say, if not what to do.

Sheriff James A. McFeron of Linn County was the first county officer in nearly twenty years given the duty of planning an execution. He was 37 years old and had come to Brownsville from Missouri with his parents when he was fifteen. His behavior throughout the investigation, trial, custody and execution of Lloyd Montgomery was commendable. He performed his duty without flinching, giving the sheriff's office dignity and respect.

Up to this time there had been only three executions in Linn County history. Andrew Pate was hanged on May 27, 1862. Thomas Smith was hanged on May 10, 1866, for the murders of his brother, Sidney, and sister-in-law, Barbara Presley Smith, and W. Kay Neil was hanged on January 26, 1877. Lloyd Montgomery was the fourth murderer convicted and sentenced to hang since the first Linn County courthouse was built in 1853.[9]

Near the end of December 1895, three burglars, Poole and the two Fox brothers, were arrested near the murderer's home and imprisoned in a cell next to Lloyd Montgomery. Lloyd was delighted to have his old friends and companions for company. On New Year's Eve, he and Poole blackened their faces with charcoal and with some red blankets from their beds, and began dancing, singing and yelling like wild Indians. The Fox boys beat a stick on the steel bars, using them for a drum, while the condemned murderer and his companion yelled and danced. A crowd was attracted by the din, which forced the sheriff to quiet them down.[10]

Lloyd didn't seem bothered much about his upcoming death. The newspapers note that he ate and slept well, happily entertaining visitor and jailors alike with his violin and harmonica. His basic intent was to have as good a time as possible before he was hanged. The sheriff thought he was behaving this way to keep from thinking about the murder and his coming execution. Others thought he just didn't care about his parent's death.

The governor's power to indiscriminately pardon convicted criminals was thoroughly debated in the state newspapers—some arguing for it and others against it. The newspapers printed stories about several cases where convicted murderers were sent to the penitentiary for life and within a few years the convict was pardoned and set free by the governor. Governor William Paine Lord was terribly disturbed by a deluge of letters from women in various parts of Oregon and as far off as California begging him to interfere and spare the life of young Montgomery. The governor had a tender heart, especially for a woman's appeal. However, he ruled in favor of common sense and refused to grant the feminine petition for mercy.

The press' influence was felt all over Oregon. Another young man living near Beaver Creek in Benton County resided with his father, two sisters and a brother-in-law. After reading the accounts of Lloyd Montgomery's murders he told everyone that he agreed with Montgomery's actions and thought it was a great thing Lloyd had done. One day there was some trouble in the family and the youth jumped up from the dinner table, seized a Winchester rifle and threatened to kill the whole family. "I will make another Lloyd Montgomery affair!" he shouted with such emphasis that a stranger who happened to be in the house at the time became frightened and left.[11]

The Albany *State Rights Democrat* of December 20, 1895 wrote the following editorial discussing the current and most popular theory of what it meant to be insane in the modern era of 1895.

The doings of Lloyd Montgomery suggest an inquiry into what insanity is. There may be a technical definition but for practical purposes a practical definition is needed: . . . Whenever that is reached he will be found to be dethroned of reason, and entirely irresponsible for his act; but because a man is weak in the upper story, or peculiar, or cranky, or irritable, or quick tempered, he should not be considered insane. Insanity is absolute irresponsibility . . . So a man of animal nature, once started, may keep shooting, regardless of the ones before his bullet. This is not insanity.[12]

The Oregon Supreme Court upheld Montgomery's conviction and sentence. The morning of his execution Lloyd was talking with his friend and Brownsville neighbor, Joseph Hume. Hume urged Lloyd not to go to his maker with a lie upon his lips, but to tell the truth.

Lloyd was very impressed with his neighbor's plea. Acknowledging Hume's fatherly request the doomed man burst out crying and said he would confess.

"I am guilty," he said. "I killed them all. I will write it out."

He then wrote out the following statement:

I did it, I am guilty. Oh, God! Have mercy on me. Take me, as I am, a poor sinner. I am sorry for what I have done. God, do have mercy on my poor soul; for my sake do and forgive all my sins, each and every one of them, and forgive those who sin against me. Oh God, help the precious souls to see the way of life for my sake. Do help them and guide them through this life.[13]

Hume and Reverend J. E. Snyder of the Brownsville First Presbyterian Church prayed with Montgomery there in his cell shortly before Sheriff McFeron came to escort him to the scaffold.

A panel of twelve witnesses was drawn from the official list of Linn County's qualified voters. Besides the twelve appointed witnesses, Sheriff McFeron issued engraved invitations to fifty people—mostly newspaper reporters, physicians, sheriffs of other counties, and ministers of the gospel.[14] The execution was performed with marked precision and perfect order. Every precaution was taken to prevent any accident, which might make the unhappy event any worse than it already was.

The duly appointed witnesses included Montgomery's neighbor, Joseph Hume, John Clelan of Albany, W. C. Cooley of Brownsville, J. W. Glass of Crawfordsville, William Faber of Albany, J. D. Irvin of Brownsville, A. J. Johnson of Scio, Charles McDowell of Brownsville, M. M. Perry of Scio, J. H. Scott of Tangent, Jerry Shea of Foster and

R. L. White of Harrisburg.[15] The hangman's rope and noose with its terrible history was given to John McKercher, brother of Daniel McKercher.

The evening prior to the execution Montgomery wrote a letter to his brothers and sister and asked that it be published and a copy sent to them. In it he says, "This life seems to me like a dream, in fact life is nothing but a dream."[16]

Loyal Bryson Montgomery was executed in the Linn County courthouse jail yard as required by law on Friday, January 31, 1896, at 7:00 a.m.[17] Sheriff McFeron pressed the scaffold trigger and the body shot down six feet. Montgomery didn't struggle, but died quietly. Under the black cap his head bent forward and to one side. As soon as the twitching ceased the appointed physicians approached the body and recorded the final heartbeats.

After the execution the body was cut down and displayed for the crowds for several hours. It was then turned over to nine physicians interested in doing the autopsy. Physicians who participated in the autopsy were Doctors Wallace, Ellis, Davis, Beers, Maston, Hill and Irvine of Albany, Doctor Cusick of Salem, and Doctor Starr of Brownsville.[18] The body was removed to the jail after the autopsy, where the funeral took place at 10 a.m. on Saturday.

The physicians found nothing unusual at the autopsy. Montgomery had been a strong and healthy young man and had died when the fourth cervical vertebra was dislocated. Medical opinion at that time believed that deep convolutions on the brain's surface indicated mental intelligence. Montgomery's brain lacked such convolutions.[19] The dead man's brain weighed 49 1/8 ounces. At first a few doctors thought the left side of the brain had some scarring, perhaps from some infection, but nothing else showed any abnormalities and eventually they all agreed that the brain was normal. The doctors retained the brain for future examination, and floating in its solution of preservative, it made an excellent paperweight for many years to come.[20]

References

1880 Federal Census, Linn County, Oregon.

1900 Federal Soundex, M532 Montgomery, Oregon Census.

Hainline, Pat. "An 1895 Triple Murder." *Northwest Passages.* Vol. 10, No. 4, Brownsville: Calapooia Publications, March/April 1995.

Herald Disseminator (Albany, Oregon) November 23, 1895, November 28, 1895, January 2, 1896, January 9, 1896, January 16, 1896, January 23, 1896, January 30, 1896, February 6, 1896.

Lebanon Express (Lebanon, Oregon) November 21, 1895.

Oregonian (Portland, Oregon) January 3, 1896, February 6, 1896.

State of Oregon v. Emma Hannah, Linn County Circuit Court Case, Vol. 17, #6599, October 30, 1895, State Archives, Salem, Oregon.

State of Oregon v. Loyal Montgomery, Linn County Circuit Court Case, Vol. 17, #6600, December 17, 1895, Oregon State Archives, Salem, Oregon.

States Rights Democrat (Albany, Oregon) November 29, 1895, December 6, 1895, December 20, 1895.

Weekly Herald (Albany, Oregon) January 6, 1896.

Chapter 33 notes

1 *States Rights Democrat* (Albany, Oregon) November 29, 1895.
2 Ibid.
3 *Herald Disseminator* (Albany, Oregon) November 23, 1865. Brownsville was and still is a very small community where many families are related. Montgomery's callous indifference to the pain his extended family suffered angered nearly everyone in the local area.
4 *State Rights Democrat*, November 29, 1895.
5 State of Oregon v. Loyal Montgomery, Linn County Circuit Court Case File #6600, December 17, 1895, Oregon State Archives, Salem, Oregon.
6 State of Oregon v. Emma Hannah, Linn County Circuit Court Case Vol. 17, #6599, October 30, 1895, State Archives, Salem, Oregon.
7 State of Oregon v. Loyal Montgomery.
8 *States Rights Democrat*, December 6, 1895.
9 *Herald Disseminator,* February 6, 1896.
10 *Herald Disseminator*, January 2, 1896.
11 *Herald Disseminator,* January 16, 1896.
12 *States Rights Democrat*, December 20, 1995.
13 *Herald Disseminator*, February 6, 1896.
14 Ibid.
15 Ibid.
16 Ibid.
17 Ibid.
18 Ibid. This is the first time autopsy results were printed in the paper. It's unknown if earlier autopsies were performed.
19 *Oregonian* (Portland, Oregon) February 6, 1896.
20 *Herald Disseminator*, February 6, 1896.

Chapter Thirty-Four

State of Oregon v. Lemuel Melson 1897

Lemuel W. Melson abided by his wife's wishes right up until his execution. While standing on the scaffold, the Josephine County sheriff asked if Melson had anything to say. He gazed out at the hundreds of witnesses making a party of his death and slowly lowered his head. To everyone's shock he spoke in a barely audible voice:

"I am guilty of killing Perry, and am sorry for it. May God have mercy on my guilty soul."[1]

It was only then that the true story of this man's crime was finally revealed to the world.

Charles Perry, age 50, and Lemuel W. Melson, age 42, were good friends.[2] They enjoyed talking about their families, playing cards and fantasizing about setting up their own mining company. Neither enjoyed working for someone else or making small time wages. Perry was a mining engineer from Connecticut.[3] For the past two years he had been working at the Waldo copper mine in the hills outside Grants Pass. His wife and seven children remained in Connecticut while he worked in Oregon. Melson's wife, Mary, and three two children, Alta, Edna and Virgil, had lived in Clatsop County with him in 1895 but moved to Del Norte, California, shortly after he went to work at Waldo.[iv]

In March 1896 Perry and Melson announced that they were going on a trip to Crescent City, California. For several months Melson had been regaling Perry with stories about a fine mining opportunity south in the Siskiyou Mountains. Perry, having considerable more money than Melson, financed the trip by buying supplies and horses for the trip.

A few days later Melson showed up in Crescent City without Perry.

"Where's your buddy?" Friends asked curiously.

"Oh, he went back to Waldo. We didn't get along and decided to part company during our trip."

Back in Waldo, people became concerned when Perry didn't return to work. A couple months went by and the mine owners received a letter from Perry's family asking why they hadn't heard from him. His coworkers knew him to be responsible, sober and industrious, certainly not a person to disappear without cause.

Four months later, on August 25, 1896, a search party from Crescent City was organized. After two days travel into the Siskiyou Mountains, the party discovered a body in an old well near a deserted mining claim called Bain's Station.[5] The claim fell right on the boundary line between Josephine and Curry counties and was only a short distance from the Oregon/California border. The smell wafting from the shaft was enough to half kill anyone in the vicinity. The searchers pulled the body out and realized they had finally found Charles Perry. He had a bullet wound in his right side, below his heart. A shell from a 41-caliber Colt revolver was on the ground near the well and it proved to be a match to the bullet taken from the corpse's wound. Wrapping the body in an oilskin cloth the party headed back to Crescent City.

About this time, remembering that Lemuel Melson had been the last person to see Perry, the Josephine County sheriff contacted the sheriff in Crescent City. It wasn't much of a surprise to discover that Melson had been spending money freely, though no one knew where he had gotten it. A shopkeeper volunteered information that last July he had purchased a 41-caliber Colt revolver from Melson. Searchers also found a watch in his pocket with Perry's initials carved on it.

Although Melson was arrested in Crescent City, he was hauled back to Grants Pass, Oregon for trial since it was believed the murder took place in Josephine County. William Crawford was appointed to defend him while District Attorney J. A. Jeffery, and associate counsel G. W. White represented the state. The trial started Saturday, May 8, 1897, in Grants Pass.

The twelve-jury members were S. D. Bristow, I. S. Curdy (named foreman), J. H. Hickox, S. E. Isham, Walter Jordan, J. M. Mansfield, Fred Miller, R. M. Robinson, R. W. Rogers, W. E. Stockbridge, W. C. Wilson and W. B. York.[6] After Fred Jassman was appointed special bailiff, the court was dismissed until 8 a.m. on Monday. Over the next two days testimony and evidence showed that Perry was shot in the back and Melson did it. The defense tried to prove Melson's good character, but it was a hard case to make and the jury didn't believe it. By late Tuesday the jury brought in a verdict of "guilty".

On May 14, 1897 Melson was convicted of first-degree murder and sentenced to hang by Judge H. K. Hanna.[7] During his entire incarceration and trial Melson maintained his innocence, never once admitting to the murder.

The day before the scheduled hanging Melson was granted his wish to attend the local Episcopal Church and be baptized by Reverend Isaac Dawson. Tears rolled down

Oregonian, July 5, 1897
Lemuel Melson and his victim,
Charles Perry

Melson's face as he listened to the church ceremony and the congregation's singing. He spent the rest of the day reading and writing letters. His wife had refused to visit him during his incarceration although she wrote frequently. She did hire attorney George B. Hart to write an affidavit to the Oregon Supreme Court for a certificate of probable cause for stay of execution which was rejected.[8] Governor Lord refused to grant a respite postponing the execution. Mrs. Melson wasn't surprised by the jury's decision, and she had very little sympathy for her husband. Her only request was that he not confess to the crime so that his children could maintain the fiction of his innocence. Up to this time he had honored her wish.

Friday, July 5, 1897, was the date chosen for the big event. Sheriff Joseph G. Hiatt issued 100 engraved and printed invitations to various dignitaries to watch the execution from inside the enclosure. Nearly 500 people had arrived in town to watch the activity from outside the board fence.[9] The scaffold was built so that observers outside the enclosed area also had an easy view. The scaffold had originally been constructed to accommodate convicted murderer Charles Fiester. Melson got to use it first. Fiester must have had a good view of the proceedings from inside his jail cell.

Melson slept well his last night and ate a substantial breakfast at 8:45 Friday morning. Reverend Dawson spent the last few minutes with Melson. During the visit, Melson broke down and made a full confession to the minister. Evidently, the guilt was just too much for him to carry any longer.

At 10 a.m. Melson calmly mounted the scaffold steps and Sheriff Hiatt read the death warrant to the assembled observers. About fifty invited guests watched from inside the enclosure, while 500 watched from outside.[10] To make it easier for those outside to see, boards were removed from the stockade fence. The company bowed their heads as Reverend Dawson gave a short prayer. When asked if he had anything to say, Melson made his startling confession of guilt to the audience and at 10:13 a.m. he said good-bye. The black cap was pulled over his head, the rope was tightened around his neck and the floor fell out from underneath him. Death was nearly instantaneous.

He was buried in a pauper's grave outside Grants Pass at the expense of the county.[11] In the end he failed his promise, his family, and his community.

References

1895 Oregon Census, Multnomah County, Oregon State Archives, Salem, Oregon.

Lewis, Raymond. "The First Judicial Hanging in Josephine County." *The Table Rock Sentinel*, Vol. VI, No. 4, June 1986.

Oregon Union (Corvallis, Oregon) July 9, 1897.

Oregonian (Portland, Oregon) July 1, 1897, July 3, 1897.

State of Oregon v. Lemuel Melson, Josephine County Circuit Court Journal, May 8, 1897, May 10, 1897, May 11, 1897, May 12, 1897, Josephine County Law Library, Grants Pass, Oregon.

Chapter 34 notes

1 *Oregon Union* (Corvallis, Oregon) July 9, 1897.

2 *Oregonian* (Portland, Oregon) July 3, 1897.

3 *Oregon Union*, July 9, 1897.

4 1895 Oregon Census, Multnomah County, Oregon State Archives, Salem, Oregon.

5 Raymond Lewis, "The First Judicial Hanging In Josephine County", *The Table Rock Sentinel*, Vol. VI, No 4, June 1986, pp. 9-14.

6 State of Oregon v. Lemuel Melson, Josephine County Circuit Court Journal, May 8, 1897, Josephine County Law Library, Grants Pass, Oregon.

7 *Oregon Union*, July 9, 1897. This was probably not a water well, but a deep hole in the ground used for rubbish and trash. Water would have covered the body and made finding it almost impossible.

8 *Oregonian*, July 1, 1897.

9 *Oregon Union*, July 9, 1897.

10 *Oregonian*, July 3, 1897.

11 *Oregon Union*, July 9, 1897.

Chapter Thirty-Five

State of Oregon v. Kelsey Porter 1897

E ven in the late 1890s solitary and unsociable men were regarded with suspicion and curiosity. Kelsey Porter was a shy and
very private man living alone in Pine Valley, an area surrounded by brown rocky hills in the most isolated part of Union
County. He lived in harmony with his neighbors until the Joseph B.
Mache family moved onto the property next door in the fall of 1896.

Unfortunately, the most convenient road to the Mache's new farm
crossed Porter's land only a few feet from Porter's barn, and Joseph,
Mary, and Ben (their 17 year-old son) Mache, didn't seem to care if it
bothered Kelsey Porter. When Porter nailed a fence across the route,
the Mache family just pulled it down. About Christmas time, after
Porter complained to Justice of the Peace Compton, Ben Mache and a
friend, ex-con "Six-Shooter Bill" Rockwood, decided to get even. They
fired shots at Porter as he worked in his field and, when he hid in his
cabin, they stole some equipment from his barn. Compton had advised
Porter to ignore the hoodlums, because there wasn't anything the law
could do to help him. Believing that the law wasn't going to help him,
Porter decided to protect himself, and borrowed a Winchester repeating rifle.

On the morning of January 1, 1896, Joseph and Mary Mache were
returning to their home in a sleigh pulled by two horses. Son Ben was
riding a horse behind them. According to Porter, he was shoveling
snow off the roof of a shed next to the barn and when he saw the couple ride by he yelled at them, "Put the fence back up and keep off my
land!"

Joseph stopped the sleigh and yelled back at him, "You lie! This is a public highway. If you fence it up again, we'll kill you!"

Young Ben Mache rode his horse closer and started shooting. One slug barely missed Porter's head. This time Kelsey Porter had the Winchester for defense and quickly dashed into his house. He came back out with the rifle—shooting like crazy. A lucky shot hit the boy and dropped him to the ground. Two more bullets killed Joseph and Mary Mache. Meanwhile. the horses pulling the sleigh bolted. One of the horses had been hit by a bullet and dropped dead at the edge of the creek sending the man's body flying into the water. Mary Mache's body stayed in the sleigh. Porter fired at least sixteen shots at the family. Mache died with a fractured skull and two bullets in him.[1]

Porter rode to Pine and confessed killing the Mache family to Justice Compton. Several neighbors and Compton accompanied Porter back to the valley and waited for Union County Sheriff J. F. Phy to arrive from Union City. Instead he sent Deputy Sheriff J. H. McLachlin and the county coroner, Doctor E. R. Lang.

People in the valley were sad about the killing, but no one really blamed Porter. Most people thought the Mache family was trouble-makers and young Ben had a bad reputation as a gun slinging hot head. They felt Porter had a right to protect his land and his life.

Deputy McLachlin and Coroner Lang must have felt differently because they ordered Porter arrested and held for a preliminary hearing. On February 4 the Union County grand jury returned three indictments against Kelsey Porter for first-degree murder. His Pine Valley neighbors staunchly supported Porter and raised $100 to hire defense attorneys J. M. Carroll and Charles E. Cochran.[2] Neighbors found it hard to believe that Kelsey Porter could kill anyone. The 47-year-old bachelor was born in Quiney, Owen County, Indiana, and was a well-liked and respected farmer in Union County for many years.[3]

Little was known about the Mache family except that they had lived in Telocaset, Washington, twelve to fourteen years earlier and kept a hotel there.

What Porter and his supporters didn't realize was that a new day was dawning in Union County. The mines were played out and the wild frontier days were coming to an end. The county needed to present a more respectable and "lawful" face to attract families to settle in the area. There had been many murders committed in the same locale and the perpetrators were let off scott free. This time the community leaders weren't prepared to turn away and forget the whole thing. The time had come to make someone pay.

The grand jury returned three indictments for first-degree murder against Porter and District Attorney John L. Rand decided to try him on the death of Joseph Mache first.[4] After being postponed a day because some of the witnesses hadn't yet arrived, the trial began on Wednesday, February 12 with Judge Robert Eakin presiding, and District Attorney John L. Rand prosecuting, and T. H. Crawford assisting. Originally, Judge Lowell was going to hear the case as Eakin was busy with some cases in Pendleton, but Eakin managed to get to Union in time to supervise the trial. It took all day and a special venire but twelve jurors were finally chosen.

Oregonian, November 10, 1897
Kelsey Porter

They included Gus Benglesdorff, Ed Boswell, J. C. Christiansen, F. C. Crandall, B. W. Grandy, C. D. Huffman, Jesse Imbler, G. G. Gray, W. E. Martin, W. H. Stafford, J. N. Rinehart, and P. L. Kelly, foreman.[5]

Porter's brother from Scranton, Iowa, arrived to provide support.[6] Ben Mache's brother from Canada and Reverend G. L. Marvin, a nephew of Mary Mache from Glendale, Montana, had arrived in the little town of Union to represent the victims.[7] Porter's neighbors donated money and hired C. E. Cochran, C. F. Hyde, and J. M. Carroll to defend him.

It soon became apparent that the prosecution team had information the newspapers and the public didn't have. District Attorney Rand ordered the bodies exhumed and reexamined. Joseph B. Mache did not die from a bullet like Porter said; instead he died from having his head bashed in. That presented a whole new scenario.

Rand built his case carefully. Witnesses testified that only a small portion of the shed roof was cleared and marks in the snow gave the impression Porter had laid in wait for the Mache family and shot the boy as the family came by. His body was found about 310 feet from Porter's barn. With the boy dead Porter followed the parents as they tried to escape in the horse drawn sleigh. A bullet killed Mary Mache and another killed one of the horses sending the sleigh off the road into the water. Porter caught up with the parents and hit Joseph on the head with the butt of the gun, reloaded his rifle and shot the dead

191

man two or three times. The sled came to rest about 400 feet from the barn.

The defense called a witness named Hunsacker, who had spent the night before the murders at the Mache's house. Mache was complaining about Porter. He boasted that Porter couldn't stop him from knocking the fences down and letting the cows out. He asked Hunsacker if he wanted to stay the next day as they were all going to Porter's and have a "touch of high life". Hunsacker declined the offer.[8]

A few weeks prior to the murders Ben Mache had asked Thomas Ludiker to help him build a road around Porter's property. Until the new road was built Mache was determined to continue using Porter's road, and promised to give Porter "any gunplay" if that's what he wanted.

Dan Tarter testified hearing Ben Mache, Jr. and his friend, William Rockwood, promise to "do him up" for accusing them of taking some harness.[9]

Kelsey Porter testified in his own behalf basically giving the same story he'd confessed to when he was arrested.

The jury retired to deliberate the verdict at 10 p.m. on Saturday night. On Sunday morning the jury requested instructions from the judge to avoid a deadlock. Expecting another long day everyone was surprised when the jury returned at 9:30 a.m. The evidence was too much to overcome and they pronounced Kelsey Porter guilty of first-degree murder. Judge Eakin sentenced him to hang on April 10, 1896.[10]

Porter and his brother had a tearful farewell, knowing they were never going to see each other again.

Attorney Charles Cochran hurriedly drew up papers asking for the Oregon Supreme Court to grant a new trial. The appeal was denied.

Porter's friends in Pine Valley wrote letters and circulated petitions requesting Governor Lord's intervention by gathering 500 signatures. There was some hope the governor would grant the request. However he had been on the state supreme court for twelve years and didn't respond to emotional appeals.[11] After due consideration he refused.

There were allegations that Porter's mother was insane and that Porter had spent time in the Salem Insane Asylum. However, a few days before the scheduled execution, three Union County physicians examined Porter in his cell and testified that he was of sound mind.

The hanging was rescheduled for 6 a.m. Friday, November 19, 1897.[12] About seventy-five men witnessed the hanging inside the stockade of the Union County jail yard.[13] Porter refused to give any interviews before his death and kept his silence as he stood on the gallows. His arms were handcuffed and his legs were tied together. Sheriff Phy placed a black cloth bag over his head and adjusted the rope around his neck. Twelve minutes later Kelsey Porter was dead.

Porter was buried in an unmarked grave in the Union Cemetery. Just before his death he gave Reverend Shields, a Presbyterian minister, a letter that was printed in the newspaper the next day. It ended with a request: "This is my last request on earth. The real cause of my trouble is the way children are raised to try and live too easy, regardless of the law of justice and right. Parents, please raise your children with a principle that will defend their character."[14] His last words on earth blamed the parents of Ben Mache for their own death.

References

Cassel, Ann and Jeff Hall. "The day they cut ol' Kelsey down." *Observer* (La Grande, Oregon) December 6, 1976.

Oregonian (Portland, Oregon) January 5, 1896, January 6, 1896, January 7, 1896, February 3, 1896, February 6, 1896, February 11, 1896, February 13, 1896, February 14, 1896, February 16, 1896, February 17, 1896, February 19, 1896, November 19, 1897, November 20, 1897.

Recorder (Elgin, Oregon) June 23, 1905.

State of Oregon v. Kelsey Porter, Drawer and File No. P. 244, July 3, 1896, Union County, Oregon Supreme Court Appeal file from Pendleton District, Oregon State Archives, Salem, Oregon.

Warren, Larry. "Fence Cutting and Murder." *Frontier Times*, December – January 1976.

The Weekly Eastern Oregon Republican (Union, Oregon) February 15, 1896, February 22, 1896, April 11, 1896, April 18, 1896, April 25, 1896, June 6, 1896, June 27, 1896.

Chapter 35 notes

1 *Oregonian* (Portland, Oregon) February 3, 1896.

2 *Oregonian,* January 6, 1896.

3 *Oregonian,* January 7, 1896.

4 In 1885 John L. Rand was elected district attorney of the sixth judicial district, which included seven counties. In 1921 he was appointed to the state supreme court.

5 State of Oregon v. Kelsey Porter, Drawer and File No. P. 244, July 3, 1896, Union County, Oregon Supreme Court Appeal file from Pendleton District, Oregon State Archives, Salem, Oregon (note name spelled with an "e" in legal documents and an "a" in newspapers and later articles).

6 *Oregonian,* February 11, 1896.

7 *Oregonian,* February 3, 1896.

8 *Weekly Eastern Oregon Republican* (Union, Oregon) February 15, 1896.

9 Ibid.

10 State of Oregon v. Kelsey Porter.

11 *Oregonian,* November 19, 1897.

12 *Oregonian,* November 20, 1897.

13 Larry Warren, "Fence Cutting and Murder," *Frontier Times,* December–January 1976. He says the hanging was on November 20, 1897, pg. 53.

14 *Oregonian,* November 20, 1897.

Chapter Thirty-Six

State of Oregon v. Charles Fiester 1898

C harles and Nancy Fiester had long-standing problems causing their marriage to fail and Nancy to leave her husband. Charles Fiester stood outside his wife's house in Grants Pass and gazed casually around the neighborhood before walking up to the door. Pausing only a few seconds, he opened the door and walked in. He was 52 years old with a scraggly beard on a long narrow face and thinning gray hair. His large brown eyes bugged out slightly, giving him a perpetually surprised look. Before moving to Merlin he had been a member of the Salem police force.[1]

Two hours later Charles and Nancy Fiester came out of the house together. Sunday, May 19, 1895, had dawned rainy and cool but by noon the sun had come out and warmed the air considerably.

"Come on children. Hurry up!" Two boys, around ten and eight, came running outside, clearly excited about their excursion.

"Okay Charlie. Let's talk as we go. I don't want to argue while we visit the older children in Merlin."

The couple had been married thirty years and this separation was difficult for the entire family.[2] Charles and Nancy had lived in the Kerby area for twenty years before moving to Merlin. Their seven older children were Edward, 28, William, 26, Mary, 24, Jessie or Jet, 22, Dolly, 19, John, 17, and Josie, 16, who lived with their father in Merlin.[3] Three younger children, Samuel, 12, George, 10, and Margaret, 6, moved with their mother to Grants Pass.

Fiester's stooped posture gave the impression to bystanders that he was a quiet peaceful man. But that was untrue. Nancy had left him because she was fed up with his violent bursts of temper. For the first time in thirty years she was free of bruises and no longer living in fear for her life. The two younger boys were doing well in school and all three children seemed happier in Grants Pass.

"I want to see the letters you been receiving," Fiester demanded about five miles outside town as they walked along the Southern Pacific railroad tracks. "Jet said you been seeing another man." Only wagons and horses made their way on the muddy road. The railroad tracks made an excellent sidewalk keeping dress hems and boots out of the sticky clay mud.

Oregonian, June 11, 1898
Charles Fiester

"Well, that's none of your business anymore and I don't appreciate our daughter telling you tales on me. I can write or see who ever I want and it isn't any of your interest." Nancy straightened her back and glared defiantly at her husband. She was 42 years old and the mother of ten children. Years of hard work had scarred her body but not her spirit. "I like Mr. Mudd and he likes me. When this divorce is done we plan to be together."

By now the three children had noticed the angry voices and had stopped to stare at their parents.

"It ain't right you leaving me and the children. You're my wife and you shouldn't be doing this. I want you to come back and stay at Merlin." Fiester's voice trailed off as he muttered to himself, his fists opening and closing spasmodically. "It ain't right. It just ain't right."

Nancy stopped. "If this is all you got to say, then I'm going back." She turned around and glared at Fiester, hurling a nasty barb back at him, "Mr. Mudd has spent more enjoyable nights with me than you have this past year."

Fire seemed to kindle behind Fiester's eyes and quick as a snake he seized Nancy's arm, twisting it behind her back. She tried to defend herself with her parasol but Fiester roughly swept it aside. As they struggled he smashed it with his boots into the spring mud.

The early morning showers had left standing water along the railway. Holding on to her hair Fiester dragged Nancy screaming and crying off the rail line and across the ground to a nearby pool. "It ain't right you being a tramp. It just ain't right. You come back to Merlin. Okay?" He held her head underwater, pushing her down with all his strength. The children stared pop-eyed as their father tried to drown their mother.

At first Nancy kicked and struggled but within a few minutes she relaxed and lay quietly in her husband's arms. The quiet seemed to wake Fiester out of his trance and he let her go. It was obvious by then that she was dead.

The children stood in stunned shock watching their father as he sat in the mud with their mother dead beside him. Bright pink fabric torn from the parasol ribs lay churned into the mud.

"You children better run on to Merlin and get your brothers." Samuel grabbed George and Margaret's little hands and pulled them along the tracks. Big tears rolled down his face and they ran away as fast as they could.

Fiester stayed with his wife's body until a crowd came from Merlin to investigate the story told by the three children. Two of the men accompanied Fiester to Grants Pass to make sure he turned himself over to Josephine County Sheriff Joseph G. Hiatt.

Josephine County Coroner Creamer went at once to the scene, and the corpse was taken to Merlin where an inquest was held the next day. Nancy Fiester's family held a small funeral a few days later.

The grand jury issued an indictment charging Fiester with first-degree murder on Tuesday, September 24, 1895.[4] Robert G. Smith, Fiester's lawyer, attempted to squash the charges against his client but District Attorney Henry L. Benson protested and the motion was denied. The trial began on Monday, September 30, 1895, and lasted four days.[5] The twelve jurors chosen to hear the case were Columbus Bennett, John J. Brown, George Cronk, Samuel Davidson, W. A. Leonard, M. Powell, Nicholas Sauer, Joseph Skeeters, J. F. Stith, J. S. Warthen, Calvin Wells, and Isaac Wiley.[6]

The defendant pled innocent by reason of insanity.[7] Insanity was a very difficult defense to prove unless the defendant already had a long history of irrational behavior. That didn't apply to Charles Fiester. Prior to the tragedy he had always been regarded as a good citizen and a hard worker. Neighbors testified about the couple's fights and the many times Nancy had been beaten. Finally on Friday, October 5, the attorneys finished their summation and let the jury retire to their deliberations.

The jury only took forty minutes before coming back with a verdict. George Cronk, the jury foreman, read the verdict, "Guilty as charged". On October 30, 1895, Fiester faced circuit court Judge H. K. Hanna and was sentenced to hang on November 29, 1895, the day after Thanksgiving.[8] G. W. Colvig, assistant counsel to Fiester's attorney, was allowed the sum of $50 for his services.[9]

Fiester seemed sure that the Oregon Supreme Court would grant his appeal and he would get a new trial, which would result in either a successful plea of insanity or a term in the penitentiary. Sheriff Hiatt wasn't so sure and went ahead with plans for the execution. Workers built the scaffold and a tall stockade alongside the jailhouse. Invitations were printed and ready to hand out.

A few days before the execution date, Fiester's attorney succeeded in securing a stay pending an appeal to the Supreme Court. About this time Fiester began acting "crazy." A physician was called. After an extensive examination he pronounced the convict insane. Since it was illegal to execute an insane person, the execution was put off indefinitely. Fiester lay on his bed in the jail, neither talking nor responding in any way to the people around him. The sheriff's deputies had to feed him and help him with personal needs. It seemed to be a hopeless situation.

The citizens of Josephine County accepted Fiester's condition, as it wasn't unusual for violence against women to be regarded as a kind of insanity during the late 1800s. Some men willingly admitted that beating their wives was the result of an inability to control their tempers and occurred only when a man was not in his right mind.[10]

However, by May 10, 1897, when William, Fiester's 26-year-old son, was arrested and convicted of larceny in a warehouse, everyone was ready for a change.[11] William was sentenced by Judge Hanna to serve two years at the Oregon State Penitentiary in Salem. While he was in the jail cell next to his father, other inmates overheard the two talking and whispering in the middle of the night. They reported it to the sheriff.

The next morning Deputy Fallen brought a breakfast tray into the cell, set it down and told Fiester, "You can eat that or let it alone. I will never feed you again." Fallen left the cell and when he returned Fiester had eaten his breakfast.[12]

Looking at the empty dishes Deputy Fallen glared at the convict, "Old man, you have played your game well."

"Yes, but it has been hard," Fiester replied.

He had played his crazy act for a year and a half. It took incredible mental and physical discipline to spend 515 days acting catatonic to avoid the death penalty. Not many people could have done it. Besides the mental toll, the physical discomfort must have been difficult.

Part of the local grand jury's responsibility was inspecting the county jail. Their report of September 30, 1895, reads as follows: "We have inspected the county jail and find it well kept, but we are of the opinion that it is not a safe place in which to confine men charged with crime and totally inadequate for the purposes of its construction."[13]

Meanwhile his case had languished in the Supreme Court.[14] None of the available records adequately explain why Fiester wasn't transferred from Grants Pass to the Oregon Insane Asylum during that time. Normally a man in Fiester's condition would have been sent to the Salem asylum. One explanation involved the pending Supreme Court decision. In securing a stay of execution, Fiester's lawyer also placed the case in a state of limbo waiting for a decision. The Writ of Probable Cause filed November 23, 1895, stated: "The death sentence will be stayed pending the hearing of said appeal and until the further order of this court and that the defendant Charles Fiester be safely kept by the Sheriff of Josephine County, Oregon, pending such appeal".[15]

The sheriff did try to get rid of Fiester. "Josephine County Court has also sent in a perplexing request. That body has declared the wife murderer, Charles Fiester insane and has requested the governor to commit him to the asylum. This is a matter requiring considerable thought and the governor has taken it under advisement."[16]

After his crazy act was exposed, the verdict of the lower court was finally considered and sustained.

On Thursday, April 21, 1898, Judge Hanna pronounced the death sentence upon Charles Fiester and fixed Friday, June 10 as the date of execution.[17] Before pronouncing sentence, the judge asked Fiester if he had anything to say as to why sentence shouldn't be pronounced. Fiester turned toward his attorney, Robert G. Smith, with a piteously appealing look on his face.

Smith's only answer was a negative shake of his head, whereupon Fiester whispered, "No."

Judge Hanna stated, "I am required to perform a painful but important duty. You have been tried and convicted by a jury of your peers of the crime of murder in the first degree. An appeal was taken to the Supreme Court. The Supreme Court sustained the verdict as found by the jury. There is nothing left but to carry out the mandate of the court. This I do with great sorrow and regret."

The judge then pronounced sentence and said, "May God have mercy on your soul." Fiester wept like a child.

Fiester's attorney tried his best to prevail upon Oregon Governor Lord to intercede, but nothing could be done. The prisoner collapsed the morning appointed for his execution and lay like a dead man upon his cot. At first Sheriff Hiatt thought Fiester had taken poison and that he would die before the hour set for his execution. The court-appointed physicians finally decided that Fiester had simply collapsed. His eyes rolled back in his head and he seemed to have so much trouble breathing that when 10 a.m., the time of the execution arrived, Sheriff Hiatt decided to wait until 1 p.m. hoping that by then Fiester would already be dead. When nothing had changed, Sheriff-elect Edward Lister and Constable Colby strapped Fiester to a board and carried him to the scaffold.[18] He didn't seem to be conscious of what was going on. Sheriff Hiatt drew the black cap over his face, tightened the noose and stepped back. On June 10, 1898, at 1:10 p.m. the trap was sprung and Charles Fiester's neck was broken.[19]

It was the same gallows originally built for his hanging in November 1895. It took three years, but in the end, justice prevailed.

References

1850 Federal Census, Clackamas County, Oregon.

1865 State Census, Marion County, Oregon.

1880 and 1900 Federal Census, Josephine County, Oregon.

1900 Federal Soundex, F236 Fiester, Josephine County, Oregon

Ashland Tidings (Ashland, Oregon) April 25, 1898, June 16, 1898.

Michael A. Belleisles, ed. *Lethal Imagination: Violence and Brutality in American History.* NY: New York University Press, 1999. "Seduced, Betrayed, and Revenged" by Lee Chambers-Schiller.

Herald Disseminator (Albany, Oregon) January 23, 1896.

Lebanon Express (Lebanon, Oregon) October 4, 1895, October 11, 1895, November 1, 1895, May 24, 1896.

Morning Oregonian (Portland, Oregon) June 10, 1898, June 11, 1898.

Oregon Observer (Grants Pass, Oregon) October 5, 1895, October 12, 1895, May 25, 1896, September 28, 1896, April 30, 1898, June 14, 1898.

Roseburg Plaindealer (Roseburg, Oregon) June 16, 1898.

State of Oregon v. W. B. Fiester, Josephine County Circuit Court Journal, May 10, 1897, Grants Pass, Oregon.

State of Oregon v. Charles Fiester, Josephine County Circuit Court Journal, September 24, 1895, Grants Pass, Oregon

State of Oregon v. C. Fiester, No. 5033, File No. 03096, Journal entry: Vol. 12, p. 78, December 17, 1895, Oregon Supreme Court Appeals file, Oregon State Archives, Salem, Oregon.

Peterson Del Mar, David. *What Trouble I Have Seen—A History of Violence Against Wives.* Cambridge: Harvard University Press, 1996.

Chapter 36 notes

1 *Oregon Observer* (Salem, Oregon) September 28, 1895.

2 Ibid.

3 1880 and 1900 Federal Census, Josephine County, Oregon.

4 State of Oregon v. Charles Fiester, Josephine County Circuit Court Journal, September 24, 1895, Grants Pass, Oregon.

5 *Morning Oregonian* (Portland, Oregon) June 11, 1898.

6 State of Oregon v. Charles Fiester, Josephine County Circuit Court Journal, October 2, 1895, Grants Pass, Oregon.

7 Michael A. Bellesiles, ed. *Lethal Imagination: Violence and Brutality in American History* (N.Y.: New York University Press, 1999) p. 189. "Seduced, Betrayed, and Revenged. By Lee Chambers-Schiller. " . . . insanity was defined . . . as a state of mind in which the defendant could not differentiate between right and wrong nor understand the consequences of his or her actions."

8 *Oregon Observer*, October 12, 1895.

9 State of Oregon v. Charles Fiester, Josephine County Circuit Court Journal, October 4, 1895, Grants Pass, Oregon.

10 David Peterson Del Mar, *What Trouble I Have Seen–A History of Violence Against Wives,* (Cambridge: First Harvard University Press, 1996) p. 55. By 1890 Oregonians were beginning to frown on men who beat their wives. "Men more often attributed their violence to a lack of self-control than a well-entrenched right." In addition, "violence occurred only when a man was not in his right mind and that it was therefore an unnatural and inappropriate act."

11 State of Oregon v. W. B. Fiester, Josephine County Circuit Court Journal, May 10, 1897, Grants Pass, Oregon.

12 *Morning Oregonian*, June 11, 1898.

13 State of Oregon v. Charles Fiester, Josephine County Circuit Court Journal, September 30, 1895, p. 162.

14 State of Oregon v. C. Fiester, No. 5033, File No. 03096, Journal entry: Vol. 12, p. 78, December 17, 1895, Oregon Supreme Court Appeals file, Oregon State Archives, Salem, Oregon.

15 Ibid.

16 *Herald Disseminator* (Albany, Oregon) January 23, 1896.

17 *Oregon Observer*, June 14, 1898. This was the last man Judge Hanna sentenced to death, who actually climbed the scaffold. He was always regarded as an unusually compassionate individual.

18 *Roseburg Plaindealer* (Roseburg, Oregon) June 16, 1898.

19 *Oregon Observer*, June 24, 1898.

Chapter Thirty-Seven

State of Oregon v. Claude Branton 1899

The fire was noisy and huge—at least twelve feet wide and six feet tall. Orange and yellow flames and sparks leaped forty feet high into the starry night. The two men had worked long and hard hauling wood and brush for the bonfire, stacking it against a tall fir tree. If someone was around to watch, they might have wondered why anyone would need such a big fire so far from civilization. The flame cast a ghostly glow on the men's faces and only then was it possible to see that they wore bandannas wrapped around their noses and mouths against the ungodly stench rising with the smoke. Suddenly, the burning branches in the center collapsed, sizzling and popping.

Soon the flames burned down to red-hot coals and the men were able to remove the bandannas as the smoke and the smell receded. Resting on a nearby log one man played a rousing melody on his harmonica. The other took up the melody and sang along in a lusty baritone. Their hound dog pointed his snout heavenward and joined the melody with eerie howls.

Their celebration continued for most of the night. The deed was done. No one could catch them now. Instead of three there were only two. Their secret was safe.

Courtland Green was 22 years old on March 14, 1898, when he went to Condon in Gilliam County to work for Pat Skelly. During the next three months he met and visited with a friend of his, Claude Branton, also age 22, who lived in Condon with his mother. Both young men were in love and wanted to get married to McKenzie River girls. Branton had a plan and persuaded Green to join him. The plan centered on stealing some horses from a local rancher, John Linn. The young men believed Linn carried at least $1,000 on him at all times. They wanted to persuade Linn to bring his horses to the desert in Crook County where they would dispose of Linn and steal his property. Branton had previous business dealings with Linn and now had a partnership for shares in the horses.

The three men, Branton, Green and Linn, drove the herd of horses 100 miles from Gilliam County down into Crook County to graze. On June 11, they decided to leave Crook County because the two conspirators found that there were too many possible witnesses if they robbed and killed Linn there. Instead the partners persuaded Linn to take the horses over the mountains to the McKenzie River Valley near Eugene and sell them there. They left John Cobb's place in Crook County with about seventy head of horses on June 14 after Clarence, Claude's older brother from Grass Valley in Sherman County, met them. He was on his way back to Condon. It was a long hard drive through the dusty dry desert that day. The men traveled on, eating in the saddle and stopping only at night for supper and rest.

Clarence Branton was aware of the scheme but wanted no part of the planned murder. He said good-bye to the group at Cold Springs and continued on to Condon. When he left them, Clarence gave a sly grin to his brother and wished him luck. This left the three men— Branton, Green and Linn—alone. Again the three men, with the herd of horses, crossed the summit of the mountain, arrived at Isham's Corral (later called Alder Springs) and set up camp, eating dinner about 9 p.m.[1]

After Linn retired, Branton and Green went off to the side and whispered together. "Do you feel very stout? Don't you want to do this?" Branton asked.

"No," Green replied and sat down to take off his boots and dry his feet.

Branton mimed shooting at various trees and bushes with the American Bulldog revolver he had hidden in his saddlebags. The two partners argued quietly as the fire burned down. Suddenly Branton got up, walked over to where Linn was sleeping on the ground and, to Green's astonishment, shot the old man twice in the chest.

Now, Linn was dead and they were committed. Branton was furious when all he found in Linn's pockets were three $20 gold pieces, one $5 gold piece, forty cents in small silver coins, a jack knife, a pocket watch, a Woodmen's receipt, and an IOU note against a Mr. Monroe for $800.[2] Apparently Linn had decided to lend Monroe money shortly before the trip and the cash was gone. The partners dragged Linn's remains over to the fire and piled wood on the body in the fire all night. About 1 a.m. they smashed the larger bones with an ax and threw some back on the coals, hoping it would look like the remains of a successful hunting party. Other bones they buried in a hole under a rock about 300 feet from the corral. Branton took the money, Linn's saddle, branding iron, and the IOU.

At daylight, they hurriedly moved the horses to John Wyckoff's place where they rested for a few hours before continuing on through the mountains with the herd. About five miles down the trail they met S. L. Henderson from Corvallis. Henderson rode up beside them and inquired where they had camped last night.

Branton was curt and unfriendly. "At the summit," he said and rode on.

Henderson looked off toward the sunrise and saw smoke rising into the sky. About a mile further, R. B. Dixon from Roseburg saw the herd of horses and waved as the partners passed by. He was concerned about a possible forest fire when he saw smoke coming from Isham's corral but as it gradually faded away he forgot all about it.

Now the partners were frightened and all their greed turned to thoughts of how to conceal their crime. Branton's hasty action without regard for the consequences now became all too clear. Gradually they realized too many people knew they were the last to see Linn alive and it was only sensible that suspicion would fall on them. During their ride they came up with a plan. They would use the money they had stolen and the horses they were driving to bribe a witness to testify that Linn was still with them after they came off the mountain. All they needed to do was find someone willing to take a bribe. With their new plan solving their immediate worries, they set up camp and bedded down for the night.

On the morning of June 16, they ate breakfast at James Belknap's IXL ranch near McKenzie Bridge. The Belknap family had a large homestead they had settled in 1869 when hardly anyone lived in the mountains beyond Walterville. Branton told Artie (Arthur) Belknap, age 16, that he had camped with his herd of horses at Alder Springs and showed him the three gold pieces he had in a leather purse. Artie thought it strange that Green paid the bill when Branton had so much money. Otis Finn, Ella Belknap's brother, walked out to the porch after breakfast and chatted about the horses Courtland Green and Claude Branton were driving. Again Branton couldn't resist showing Finn his leather purse with so much gold in it. After arousing the suspicion of everyone living at the ranch, the partners left and headed down the valley herding their horses with them.

At a rest stop Green had a bad bout of remorse and threatened to commit suicide with the pistol. Gradually Branton talked him out of it and he calmed down. They agreed to throw Linn's watch, eyeglasses and knife into a nearby stream. Then they continued on their quest to find a witness to swear that John Linn had been seen alive on this side of the mountains.

They stopped briefly at James and Emma (Finn) Wyckoff's place near Blue River about 4 p.m. The Wycoff family had constructed a couple lean-to sheds for travelers to use on the old McKenzie Toll Road. Even though the county had taken over upkeep on the road in 1895 visitors still occasionally used the sheds for shelter. Green was still sullen and depressed, not talking much to anyone. James Wykoff saw Linn's branding iron accidentally fall out of Branton's saddlebags before he mounted his house. Finally, on June 17, the two men arrived in Walterville where Branton's family lived and where he had grown up. While the horses grazed and rested, they immediately started trying to find someone to help them with their scheme. It seemed to have escaped their notice that up to this point at least eight people had already seen them without Linn.

First they approached Lawrence Millican who had known Branton all his life and Courtland Green for the last six years. The Millican family was a founding family of Walterville and had experience running cattle and horses between central Oregon and the valley. After telling Lawrence that Linn was back in the mountain catching strays, Branton spun a yarn about some imaginary problem and offered him the pick of the herd if Lawrence would say they had seen Linn with them. Lawrence thought their story was pretty fishy and he wanted nothing to do with such an obviously shady scheme. Shaking his head in disbelief he watched the two young partners walk back to their camp.

The next day the partners continued to wander around Walterville trying to find someone to help them with their alibi. They talked with Ben Dearing. They offered a horse to David Fountain. Claude told him he had got into trouble over the horses and would give David a horse if he would help him out by swearing he got the horse off a certain man whom he would describe. A little later they saw Walter, David's brother, and tried to enlist him in their scheme. He described Linn as a small man, with auburn hair, a red complexion, wearing a blue jumper, and about 45-60 years of age. He slyly admitted that Linn was nowhere to be found and that he would probably never show up. Displaying more intelligence than Claude and Courtland, the men of Walterville refused to join their scheme and tried to send the boys on their way. Being totally obtuse to the not so subtle hints, Claude and Courtland continued trying to convince people to join their plan.

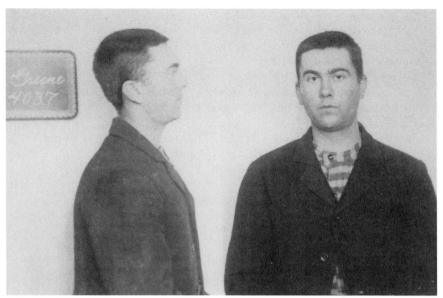

Oregon State Archives
Courtland Green was sentenced to life in the Oregon State Penitentiary.

That day they ate dinner and supper at Lizzie and Myron Thomas's place with their son Mike, age 23, a sheepherder, and George Ward of Lost Creek. They hired William Price, age 38 and a farmer in Walterville, to guard the horses. Claude told them that they were waiting for John Linn to come up and that Linn was back gathering up some stray horses. Courtland was in a bad way, being unable to eat or sleep since the deed was done.

On the morning of June 19, Claude rode down to Hayden Bridge, about eight miles east of Eugene to Will Seavey's place. He contracted with Seavey to pasture the herd of horses for the next week. During the day he tried to talk James Allen, and the Trotter boys (sons of Abel Trotter) into helping him out by swearing they saw John Linn.

"For God's sake don't say anything or it will cost me my head," he warned Walter and Waldon Trotter, twins, age 17.

Later that evening Ora Anderson Gilbert, age 24, a farmer in Camp Creek, saw Branton and Green at Mike Thomas's place. Gilbert had known Linn in Condon and wanted to know where he was.

Branton admitted being in trouble with Linn. "I want you for a witness," he said. "You will make the best one I can get. If you help me you can have the pick of the horses if you want one."

"A witness to what?" Gilbert asked.

"A witness to say that you saw Linn with us. You see we want to go up the road a little while as I expect Linn to come along later. I only have two ways to get out of this trouble. One is to run away and the other is to clear it up at court."

Gilbert thought Branton was pretty confused and Green rather sullen as he refused to talk to anyone. He left after refusing to help them in their scheme but not knowing that something deadly had happened to Linn.

At 9 p.m., near dusk, the duo left Thomas' farm with William Price and the herd of horses heading down to Seavey's pasture. Before arriving at Seavy's, Branton made a set of false whiskers from a horse's tail and wore them as his Linn disguise along with a white hat and black coat. It was dark and Seavey was asleep when they arrived so he couldn't see them very well. Using the night to help disguise himself Branton identified himself as John Linn and said he was going to Eugene and would probably be down in the valley for a week or more. Seavey recognized Branton's voice from the night before. Green wanted to put Linn's horse in the barn but Seavey refused. He did let them leave Linn's saddle and bridle in the barn.

Over the next few days the boys tried to sell Linn's horses. Because they didn't have any sales slips or proofs of ownership, buyers were suspicious and they didn't have any luck.

The partners decided to split up. Branton headed for eastern Oregon, where he sold his horse and took the train to Little Rock, Arkansas where he enlisted in Company I, 2nd Regiment, U.S. Volunteers. After he passed the examination, he apparently had a change of mind and refused to sign the induction papers. By July 5,1898, he was in Kansas.

Meanwhile Green's conscience was making it impossible for him to go on with his life. On July 3, after a long night of drinking he confessed the murder to a friend, Henry Day, Deputy Sheriff of Lane County. Even though it was nearly 3 a.m., Day accompanied Green to the home of Assistant District Attorney Lawrence T. Harris. Harris was supposed to make a speech later that day at the July 4 celebrations, but this startling news changed his plans. It also became the biggest news item to hit Eugene since the city was established. The testimony and trial was front page news for the next eight months.

Lane County Sheriff William W. Withers rounded up supplies and a small party of men headed into the mountains. Besides Harris, Doctor W. L. Cheshire, Horace Offut and A. S. Powers also accompanied Green to the killing site. It took a hard day's travel to reach McKenzie Bridge that night. The next morning the team reached Isham's Corral just west of Sisters.

Withers proceeded to display the skills that had given him the reputation of being a "super-human bloodhound."[3] He raked the ashes of Linn's funeral pyre and found some suspender buttons, which were later traced to Linn.

Going back to Eugene, Withers arrested Green and started proceedings to convene a grand jury. Charles Wintermiere, justice of the peace, and acting magistrate in Lane County, bound over Courtland for trial. Figuring that Branton might write letters to his girl friend in McKenzie Bridge, Withers talked to the postmaster and asked him to waylay any letters arriving for her. It didn't take long before they were steaming open a letter from Branton in Kansas City.[4] Withers believed the letter implied that Branton was heading home. Running out of funds Branton arrived back in Eugene on July 19. Orie Finn, a friend, confided to him that Green had confessed and been arrested on July 10 and there was a $250 reward offered by the Commissioner's Court for Branton's arrest. Finn wanted to collect the reward, but Branton declined to give himself up for Orie's benefit.

Word quickly circulated that Branton was back and the next day at 2:30 p.m. Deputy Sheriff Day arrested Claude Branton on a charge of murder. He stuck with his made up story and immediately asked if John Linn had sworn out a complaint against him. He said that he had last seen Linn a few minutes after he placed the horses in Seavey's pasture. Claude had about $40 on him in a leather purse and said that he had just returned from Topeka, Kansas. Sheriff Withers later traced the distinctive leather purse back to John Linn.

In jail where they occupied adjoining cells, Green apologized to Branton when he'd told the sheriff that Branton had done the shooting. "I have confessed and told a lie. I am sorry for it. If I had not done that, I would tell the straight of it now. The reason I said it, was that I thought you was never coming back. It wouldn't hurt you is the reason I told it, to protect myself."

The *Eugene Guard* plastered the murder tale all over the front page off and on for the next year. So many people were reading the story in the paper that when the time came to pick a jury the sheriff had to call in sixty men before they could agree on the final twelve. *The Guard* was so pleased by this it ran an advertisement on the front pages of the October 31 and November 3 editions stating,

With ONLY ONE exception the jurors under examination as to their fitness to serve on the jury, stated the accounts they had read of the murder of Linn were published in the EUGENE GUARD.[5]

The grand jury finally returned an indictment of "murder in the first degree" against Claude Branton and Courtland Green. The arraignment was held October 31 in Eugene at the Lane County Courthouse. There were so many people trying to get a seat the sheriff had to institute a "first come first seat order" just to keep the peace. The young ladies of Eugene were all in a dither after the local newspaper published pictures of the two handsome young men and many were steadfast attendees of the trial, hanging on to every word of the testimony.

At the arraignment Branton's two lawyers, L. Bilyeau, and H. D. Norton, asked for a continuance until the next term of court in order to subpoena the following witnesses based on the following statement by Branton:

> *William Witt of Sisters in Crook county, Mr. Thompson of Squaw Creek, James and David McMullin, living 15 miles from Condon, Mrs. Wassom, John Knox, George Stevens and H. R. Hendricks of Gilliam county; that they each were well acquainted with John A. Linn long and prior to June 15, 1898, that said Linn was of a sullen, treacherous and uncertain disposition and that I owned an interest in a certain band of horses in said Linn's possession and that said Linn was indebted to me just prior to June 15, 1898. That I was then and for a long time had been desirous and anxious to separate myself and my property from him but that he refused to settle with me or to permit me so to do, and thereby compelled me to remain with him against my will. That just prior to June 14, 1898, I made every effort to avoid crossing the Cascade mountains with said Linn, but that he would not permit me so to do, and that when I started across the Cascade mountains, just prior to June 15, 1898, it was without my consent and against my best judgment. That said Linn was and had been abusing me and had on previous occasions endangered my life by his vicious acts.*[6]

Judge Hamilton overruled the motion. He told the defense lawyers that the defendant had been indicted on October 26 and waiting until the evening of October 29 to ask for a continuance wasn't proper.

By the end of the day on Monday, October 31, twelve jurors had been chosen: James Beebe, age 65, from Springfield; Henry (Charles) Calloway, 50, from Coyote precinct; John Cruzan, 43, from Pleasant Hill; George Gross, 38, from Irving; James Inman, 31, from Spencer precinct; Preston McPherson, 51, from south Eugene; C. B. Morgan from Florence; William W. Neely, 36, from Mapleton; John W. Stone, 49, from Creswell; Melville Taylor from Coburg; David Thompson, 63, from north Eugene; and Silas M. Yoran, 65, from south Eugene.[7] All were farmers, except David Thompson who was a teamster, and Silas Yoran, a merchant, who was voted foreman.

In the courtroom next door, Courtland Green was arraigned separately. His lawyers were George A. Dorris and L. L. Stevens. The indictment for first-degree in the killing of John A. Linn was read Tuesday, November 1, at 8:30 a.m. Head held high, Green slowly stood up and faced the judge.[8]

"How do you plead?" Judge Hamilton asked.

Firmly, and looking intently at the court, he calmly uttered the word, "Guilty," as everyone in the room gasped in surprise.[9]

Daily Eugene Guard, May 12, 1899
Claude Branton.

The Oregon Criminal Code of 1898 provided as follows when a person pleads guilty under the above circumstances: "Sec. 1728 (520). If upon an indictment for murder the defendant be convicted upon his own confession in open court, the court shall hear the proof and determine the degree of murder and give judgment accordingly."[10] His sentencing was set aside until after Branton's trial.

On Tuesday, November 1, at 7 a.m., Branton's trial started with District Attorney George M. Brown making his opening statement. The defense attorney declined to make a statement, saying that they were not ready to give their defense away at this time.

The first witness was the Lane county coroner, Doctor W. L. Cheshire. He told about the inquest that was held on July 7 at Isham's corral fourteen miles east of McKenzie Bridge. The remains of the fire were still there and showed where a large fir log had been burned. The audience was shocked as he related finding human bones still in the coals, in particular articles of clothing, teeth, buckles and buttons. At this point the witness dramatically produced the bones, spreading them out on a table so the judge and audience could see.

I made an examination of the bones found at Isham's corral. I've made a long study of the human anatomy and this is a small piece of bone of the lower jaw. This bone is a piece of the head. This bone is a piece of the collarbone. This bone is from the foot. This is a part of the temple. This bone I hold in my hand is a part of the jawbone. These small bones are the terminals of the toes and fingers. I have several teeth here. This is a small bone of the hand. This is the little bone of the wrist.[11]

The doctor said he was pretty sure these were all human remains. Other bones he wasn't so sure about, were probably from the vertebrae, skull, arm, hand, and kneecap. Besides the bones, he produced various pieces of clothing, buttons, buckles, and some underclothing with pieces of bone still attached. All were introduced into evidence.

Courtland Green's testimony impressed the jury and the audience. His manner and his story seemed believable, even though his confession made Branton out to be a cold-blooded killer and Green a rather pliable assistant. He freely admitted helping burn Linn's body and hide the evidence. He denied that the sheriff had offered him immunity if he testified against Claude, saying only that, "his conscience smote him to tell the truth."

During Green's testimony Branton broke down, wept and raved aloud. At times it was nearly impossible to hear the witness. His family tried unsuccessfully to comfort him. It was a painful time for court officers, attorneys, jurors and auditors. During the whole commotion the audience displayed a keen interest in Branton's misery.

A. S. Powers testified that he was present at the inquest when buttons, buckles and remnants of garments were taken from the Isham corral fire. He found a pan about forty feet from the corral, which was produced and introduced into evidence.

Other witnesses called by the prosecution and testifying about seeing Branton and Green with the horses included S. L. Henderson, R. B. Dixon, Arthur Belknap, Otis Finn, Lawrence Millican, David Fountain, Walter Millican, Mike Thomas, George Ward, William Price, James Allen, Walter and Waldon Trotter, Ora Anderson Gilbert, Will Seavey, Frank Payne, and John Cobb.[12]

John Isham of McKenzie Bridge testified about a conversation he had with Branton while Claude was in jail. He admitted he was in a close box (the evidence was heavy against him) but maintained that the evidence heard at the coroner's inquest wasn't true.

Branton explained his actions to Isham:

> *Linn insisted on coming over the mountains with us. I didn't want him to accompany us and offered to pay a man's wages to help us with the horses if he would stay behind. I shot Linn and watched the blood ooze out. I intended to come to Eugene to tell about it, but Courtland said that that wouldn't do. He thought*

it better to burn the body and we did. We came down with the horses to the pasture and I took the train to Arkansas and signed my name to volunteer in the army but when examination day came around I disappeared and concluded to return to Oregon and face the music.

P. H. Stevenson, 32, a merchant from Condon, was a member of the Woodmen of the World lodge in Condon. Stevenson said he had written a receipt for $1.50 to J. A. Linn on April 6, 1898, for dues. He knew John Linn and described him as a short heavyset man with a full dark brown and gray beard, sandy complexion and grayish hair.

Horace Offut of Eugene testified that he found a Woodsmen's receipt made out to John Linn about forty feet from Isham's corral on July 7. This was the same receipt signed by Stevenson. It helped place Linn at the scene of the fire and was introduced into evidence.

Deputy Sheriff John Day said that Green came to his house and voluntarily confessed early on the morning of July 4. A. J. Johnson, Lane County sheriff on July 4, 1898, was also present at Green's confession. Deputy Sheriff Day testified that he arrested Claude Branton at 2:30 p.m. on July 20. He said that Claude had a leather purse with $40 in it and that he had just returned from Topeka, Kansas.[13] (In a stunning turn of events, John Day disappeared a year later on November 3, 1899 with $2,110.49 of the county's tax money.[14])

At that time the court adjourned until Wednesday morning at 8:30 a.m.

The next morning at 7 a.m. a crowd of men and women gathered in front of the courthouse to gain admission. When the doors were opened at 8 a.m., the rush resembled a band of cattle stampeding to the best seats in the courtroom.

The first witness called was Lane County Sheriff, William W. Withers, 39. The sheriff revealed his investigation to the audience and produced a saddle, bridle and spurs Claude had left with Mr. Seavey, a harness received from Claude's father on July 17, and a trunk he had found in the Davis place on July 26.[15]

John A. Palmer, C. N. Wilson, and David B. Trimble, farmers and residents of Condon, testified that they had known John Linn and that the various articles of evidence, including the saddle, bridle, harness, trunk and leather purse, belonged to Linn.

George Croner, 39, the night watchman of Eugene told how he went with Courtland Green to see Sheriff Johnson (the sheriff before Sheriff Withers took office) at 1 a.m. the morning of July 4 when Green turned himself in and confessed to the murder.

C. E. Lind traveled from Central City, Nebraska, to testify. He was John Linn's brother (last name spelled differently) but hadn't seen him for nearly twenty-six years.[16] He described his brother as a hard working cattleman. The prosecution rested their case about noon and the court adjourned for lunch.

At 1 p.m. the defense attorney called Claude Branton to the stand, who testified on his own behalf. The crowded courtroom was hushed as they waited to hear what he had to say. Branton's story was similar to Green's, except that Branton maintained that Green had shot Linn three times while Branton was off getting water. He said that after the fire he helped put the large bones in a pan and gunnysack. He carried them to a rock where Green mashed them up with the ax and placed them under a rock.[17]

Mrs. Lee (E. M.) Bailey of Eugene testified that Claude Branton was her brother. She said that his friends could easily persuade him to do nearly anything. He was easily influenced and his mind at times was very weak. She didn't think he knew right from wrong at times. Her uncle was an inmate in the asylum at Salem and Claude took after him in many ways.[18]

Mrs. Caroline Branton, mother of the defendant, testified about her insane brother. She maintained that Claude's mind was deficient at times.[19] She didn't clarify her relationship with Linn but other witnesses testified that Claude met Linn through her. Linn was helping her get a divorce from her husband. Linn's anger at Caroline for not continuing on the trip may have precipitated the dispute with Claude later described in a letter Branton wrote.

Doctor R. B. Russell, a practicing physician of Thurston, testified that he had known the defendant for fourteen years and that his mind was weak.

Clarence Branton, 23, an older brother of the defendant, testified that an uncle and a cousin were insane and that Claude was very weak minded and easily influenced by friends. Clarence blamed Green for the murder and felt that Courtland was very obvious in his hostility toward Linn during the trail ride, saying, "He intended to live hereafter without work. Linn's horses would be something big to him. He had no sympathy for Linn since he had treated Claude so badly. Courtland told him that no one could smell Linn's decaying body out on the desert."[20]

The court was adjourned until 8:30 Thursday morning.

On the morning of November 3, Lawrence T. Harris, a young deputy district attorney, addressed the court. Great credit was accorded Harris and Sheriff Withers for collating and collecting the mass of evidence introduced at the trial. He spoke in a calm, considerate and pleasant manner for one hour and fifty minutes. Newspaper reporters felt that he gave a fair and accurate review of the testimony.

H. D. Norton, attorney for the defense, gave a careful review of applicable law and instructions to the jury. He also pointed out the slight discrepancy in Courtland Green's two confessions—one maintained that he had put the handle on the ax and the other that Branton had put the handle on the ax used to cut up the body and smash the bones. As Green was the main witness against Branton, it was important that his testimony be discredited. Norton felt that public opinion and the jury had been unduly influenced by the newspaper reports. Norton reviewed Green's other testimony, as the defendant, Mr. and Mrs. Branton, his parents, and Mrs. Bailey, his sister, were weeping. He spoke three hours and made a good plea.

The second defense attorney, Larx Bilyeau, 46, of Eugene, spoke next for two hours. He presented the argument that Branton was due an acquittal since Green had already confessed to the murder so Branton couldn't be guilty of murdering the same man. Bilyeau was a good speaker, impressing his audience with his style and eloquence. According to the reporter of the *Eugene Guard* no better plea was made in any court.

At 5:10 p.m. Lane County District Attorney George M. Brown commenced addressing the court. He gave a strong speech for an hour and thirty-five minutes.

Court resumed November 4 at 9 a.m. Friday morning when Judge J. W. Hamilton gave his instructions to the jury. Judge Hamilton gave a lengthy explanation about the legal precepts involved in the case. In particular he explained the law as it applied to Green's confession and accusation against Branton: "That a conviction cannot be had upon the testimony of an accomplice, unless he be corroborated by such other evidence as tends to connect the defendant with the commission of the crime."[21]

Court was adjourned as the jury left to begin deliberations. Barely an hour later word came from the bailiff that the jury had reached a decision.[22]

Branton stood and faced the jury as the foreman, Silas Yoran, carefully read the guilty verdict. While his mother and sister cried, Branton listened stoically to the judgment.

Four days later on Tuesday, November 8, Claude Branton faced the court to hear his sentence.

The court has a painful duty here to perform. The sentence for the crime of which you are convicted is that on Friday, the 23 day of December 1898, at the hour of 10:00 a.m., that you be taken to the jail yard, where you are now enclosed in the jail, and then in the presence of twelve bona fide electors of Lane county, Oregon, that you be hanged by the neck until you are dead, and God have mercy on your soul.[23]

Judge Hamilton seemed more affected by the death sentence than Branton did. Around the courtroom many observers had tears rolling down their cheeks. This was the first time in Lane County history anyone had been sentenced to hang.

The convicted murderer was held in the Lane County jail until the day of his hanging. Most people assumed this would be the end of Claude's story until the day of the execution. However, Claude hadn't given up. He may not have been too smart, but he was persistent.

"Murderer Branton Fiendishly Attacks Deputy Sheriff Day". The Eugene newspaper had two front-page headlines Friday, November 4 —one detailing the murder conviction and the other describing an attempted jailbreak.

Branton's attempted escape was viewed as another symptom of his evil character. While Deputy Day was searching Branton's cell, the Sheriff and Branton waited in the corridor. They had just returned from hearing the verdict read in open court.

After the handcuffs were removed, Branton made a dash toward Deputy Day who was on his hands and knees with a candle cleaning an iron ventilator. Branton jumped on Day's back, choked him with one hand and tried to get the revolver with the other.[24] The deputy's hand got his revolver almost the same instant that Branton's did and gripping the murderer by the wrist the deputy twisted his arms around out of danger.

Sheriff Withers immediately rushed to help, placing both thumbs on Branton's windpipe quickly choking him into submission. Adrenalin gave the well-muscled convict superhuman strength and it took the efforts of both lawmen to subdue Branton. Branton later admitted that if he could have gotten the revolver he would have escaped even if he had to kill everyone to do it. Sheriff Withers decided to hire a "deathwatch" whose only job was to watch Branton until he was executed. Robert Pratt was hired to do the night duty and William Andrews to guard during the daytime.

During Courtland Green's trial for murder, the prosecution introduced into evidence a sensational letter written by Claude Branton to an unidentified party.[25] In it he reminds Courtland what really happened at Isham's Corral and justifies killing Linn as an act of self-defense. It sounds as though he wanted to protect Courtland. The letter was written during Branton's trip to Kansas.

July the 5th, 1898

On Rescue race I have made a very poor race and lost my money up the chance. It is good that nobody from Eastern Oregon has done anything yet. So I will ask of you another chance for us and a hopeful one - that is - to see Courtland and tell him to bear in mind that we must not forget what happened on that trip, and how Linn and I got into difficulty disputing over them horses. He said that he would rather kill every one than to let me have a single one because I would not splice with him, and I wanted a settlement so we began to dispute and he picked up the ax and said that he would not only kill the horses but he would kill me too. And he started at me, him being on the south side of me about 20 feet or more only reached within about 6 or 8 feet of me.

And two shots were fired; instantly the victim fell backwards and I instantly grappled him and piled him in the midst of the burning flames of a big log heap fully 6 or 7 feet high and 12 or 15 feet long which we had prepared on that stormy night while Courty was getting out some dried pears on the north of myself. After Linn said he would kill me I never said a word back but felt for my gun, which was in my hip pocket. Courtland wants to bear in mind that it was led on by me not going in with him when that was not the trade we made. I took them on shares. And he was to pay me, which he had not done and wanted me to take him and nothing for all summers work and breeding and because mother did not stay he was mad. Courtland wants to memorize this and not have much to say and not tell this until the last thing. Hang on and stick to it. This will only save him. He never touched him and I never took a thing. I am writing on the train and it is going. This is the last time for a while. Good-bye, Claude.[26]

Courtland Green, the first man to plead guilty to murder in Lane County, was found guilty of second-degree murder on November 7, and received a sentence of life imprisonment in the state penitentiary. On Friday, November 10, 1898, Sheriff Withers took Green to Salem where he was turned over to Superintendent Gilbert of the Oregon State Penitentiary to begin serving his sentence. Ten years later he received a conditional pardon from Governor Chamberlain and was released on January 25, 1909.[27]

On December 19, 1898, Supreme Court Justice, F. A. Moore, signed a certificate of probable cause that suspended Branton's execution pending an appeal of the state supreme court.[28]

Branton was again in the news, when the *Eugene Daily Guard* reported the baptism and confession of his sins. Reverend Patterson of the Eugene Divinity School, Reverend W. L. Matlock, supply pastor of the First Baptist church and Reverend M. L. Rose, pastor of the First Christian Church, baptized Branton in the jail bathtub at 2:15 p.m. on February 6.[29] While still dripping water Branton said that he had repented his sins and hoped he would be forgiven. He hoped his example would persuade others to avoid bad company and criminal activities. Sheriff Withers kept close watch on his captive just in case the new convert would repeat his previous actions. The sheriff and ministers even left their pocketknives outside before entering the cell.

On February 12, 1899, the state Supreme Court heard Branton's appeal. Justice F. A. Moore delivered the Court's decision on February 27 while Chief Justice Charles E. Wolverton, Associate Justice Robert S. Bean, and J. J. Murphy, clerk, were on hand. The decision of the lower court was affirmed and Claude's execution would now have to be rescheduled.

On March 1, Claude proved that his baptism didn't mean he was willing to go down without a fight. At 8 a.m. Sheriff Withers had a strange experience after he sent John Pratt, the deathwatch, out for breakfast. He let Claude out of his cell and into the corridor between the steel cells to exercise and wash. While the Sheriff was reading his mail, Claude exclaimed, "You are a Christian, ain't you Mr. Withers?"

"Yes."

"If you were in here wouldn't you get out if it was possible?"

The sheriff, good naturedly, replied, "Yes," hardly looking up.

Then Claude stepped back into the corridor, where it was a little dark and holding in his hand what resembled a navy six-shooter, said loudly, "Throw up your hands."

Sheriff Withers was amazed and thought Claude had by some means procured a gun, but kept his cool and said, "Oh, come off."

In a few seconds Claude decided that his trick had been discovered and laughed, claiming that he meant nothing by it. He confessed that he had planned to make the sheriff throw up his hands, so that he could reach through and get his revolver. This would have been impossible as the sheriff was too far back from the iron grating. In his desperation to escape he had to try anything.

The alleged pistol was an ingenious model of a navy revolver. It was made out of a roasted potato for a barrel and a piece of tin from one of his suspenders for a sight. The chamber was made from another piece of boiled potato and the leaden messengers were pieces of burnt bones. The device was covered with silver foil.[30]

216

Oregon State Historical Society, OrHi 23665
Claude Branton standing on the gallows in Eugene.

District court was convened April 5 at 1 p.m. Sheriff Withers, followed by Deputy Day and deathwatches, William Anders and John Holland, Marshal Stiles and Policeman Croner, led the prisoner into the courtroom. Branton begged the sheriff to remove his handcuffs before being escorted into court. The sheriff explained to Judge Hamilton that Claude was a desperate criminal and had threatened to jump out a courtroom window if he had the chance.[31] The judge understood and the handcuffs stayed on.

Judge Hamilton declared," Said Claude Branton will be kept in close confinement until Friday, the 12th day of May, 1899, and upon said day, between the hours of 10 a.m. and 2 p.m. thereof the said Claude Branton be hanged by the neck until dead."[32]

May 12 dawned bright and sunny. While some still hoped Governor Greer would commute Branton's sentence, most didn't believe there was much chance. Branton spent his last few hours writing letters, reading his Bible and saying good-bye to his family.

Claude's parents, Mr. and Mrs. S. C. Branton, his sister Lee Bailey, his brother Clarence, and other relatives were very subdued when they made their last visit to the condemned man's cell at 9:25 a.m. They only remained about twenty minutes.[33] In the months before the execution they had circulated an unsuccessful petition asking the governor to commute Branton's sentence to life imprisonment.

There was an undercurrent of suppressed excitement throughout the city. In the jail yard all the advance preparations were finished. Lumber for the enclosure and scaffold was ordered, prepared and set in place. The Griffin Hardware Company provided the rope.[34] It was a three-quarter inch grass hemp rope, fifty feet in length, and had been thoroughly stretched and tested with weights before it was put to official use.

The prisoner walked out of the jail only to find himself still separated from the free world by a twelve-foot high board wall, which formed a passage leading to an enclosure containing the gallows. With only the blue sky visible, the first murderer to be hanged in Lane County walked slowly from the jail to the gallows. Special deputies were stationed at various places to keep everyone out of the jail yard while they guarded the stockade.

The jailhouse square attracted quite a crowd by 8 a.m. Those holding engraved invitations filed into the enclosure at 10 a.m. About fifty people witnessed the execution. Among those present were members of the jury convicting Branton, seven newspapermen, twelve physicians, the undertakers and other officials. The twelve citizens selected by Sheriff Withers to officially certify to the execution included Jerry Atkinson, J. A. Ebbert, Daniel Elliott, G. W. Griffin, J. A. Fugate, C. Marx, William Mayer, Will Seavey, M. Sommerville, John Stewart, G. W. Whitsett and J. B. Young.[35] A woman later admitted witnessing the execution from the window of the courthouse clock tower by standing on a box.

Some of the law officers from around the state attending the execution were sheriffs Peter Rickard of Benton; William Blakely of Umatilla; Alfred H. Huntington of Baker; D. Y. K. Deering of Union; J. A. Munkers of Linn; Joseph G. Van Orsdel of Polk; Robert L. Stephens of Douglas; John J. Cooke of Clackamas county; Marshals F. W. Dillard of Roseburg and J. Frank Curtis of Junction.[36]

Reverend E. M Patterson and Reverend Jno. Handsaker mounted the scaffold with the prisoner. At 10:05 a.m. Sheriff Withers read the death warrant to Branton, who remained composed throughout the trying proceedings. He wore a black suit, low collar and blue tie, with a bouquet of pansies on the lapel of his coat. After marching to the scaffold, he was placed on the trap and straps were placed around his body; one around his arms and waist, one around his legs just above the knees and one around his ankles.[37] Only once did Branton become emotional and that was when the straps were being put around his arms and he took his final farewell. With tears in his eyes, he thanked Sheriff Withers, Deputy Day, and Guard Andrews for their kind treatment. Branton assisted officers in tying his hands and was very cooperative.

After a short prayer Branton made his final statement, "I haven't much to say. I hope for God's sake no one will try to run my folks down on account of this. They are innocent. I hope people will learn a lesson from this and tread the right path. I hope to meet you all in the other world. I ask this for Jesus sake. Amen."

The noose was placed over Branton's head, the black cap adjusted and at 10:45 a.m. Sheriff Withers jerked the lever. The body dropped straight down a distance of seven feet and his neck broke instantly. Doctors T. W. Harris and L. D. Scarborough came forward, felt for a pulse and sixteen minutes later pronounced Claude Branton dead.[38]

The body was cut down, prepared by undertakers R. M. Day and Harry Graham and turned over to relatives. A tombstone marks Branton's grave in the Camp Creek Cemetery.[39]

After the execution, Branton's diary was given to his family. The last entry read, "Three can keep a secret only when two are dead."[40]

References

1880 and 1900 Federal Census, Gilliam County, Oregon.

1880 and 1900 Federal Census, Lane County, Oregon.

Bohemia Nugget (Cottage Grove, Oregon) May 19, 1899, June 9, 1899, November 3, 1899.

Century Edition of the American Digest, A complete digest of all reported American cases from the earliest times to 1896, Vol. 26, West Publishing, St. Paul, 1901. A confessed accomplice testified that he and defendant had planned to kill the deceased and that, while the three were in camp together, defendant did the killing. Defendant testified that the accomplice had told him that he was going to kill deceased for his property and that he advised against it: that the two of them induced deceased to go with them to the pace of the killing, and, while defendant was away from camp, the alleged accomplice did the killing; that, in order to shield his companion, defendant assisted in disposing of the body and personated deceased. Several witnesses testified that defendant told them he was in trouble which might cost him his life, and endeavored to persuade them to testify that they had seen a person answering to the description of deceased since the murder. Held sufficient to go to the jury on the question whether defendant did the killing.–State v. Branton, 56 P. 267, 33 Or. 533.

Daily Eugene Guard (Eugene, Oregon) October 27, 1898, October 29, 1898, October 31, 1898, November 1, 1898, November 2, 1898, November 3, 1898, November 4, 1898, November 5, 1898, November 7, 1898, November 10, 1898, November 14, 1898, December 17, 1898, December 19, 1898, December 20, 1898, December 31, 1898, December 23, 1898, January 21, 1899, February 2, 1899, February 7, 1899, February 11, 1899, February 21, 1899, February 27, 1899, March 1, 1899, March 28, 1899, April 3, 1899, April 5, 1899, May 11, 1899, May 12, 1899.

Inman, Leroy B. *Beautiful McKenzie*. Roseburg: South Fork Press, 1996.

McArthur, Lewis. "Oregon Geographic Names: Sixth Supplement." *Oregon Historical Quarterly*, Vol. 45, Portland: Oregon Historical Society, 1945.

Oregon State Penitentiary Inmate Case File #4037 for Courtland Green, Oregon State Archives, Salem, Oregon.

State of Oregon v. C. Branton, No. 5224, File No. 03303, Journal entry: Vol. 513, p. 151, Oregon Supreme Court Case Files. December 19, 1898, Oregon State Archives, Salem, Oregon.

Tugman, Peter N. "hand for hand, foot for foot, Deuteronomy." *Oregonian* (Portland, Oregon) March 27, 1966.

Tugman, Peter. "Recalls First Hanging." *Eugene Register Guard* (Eugene, Oregon) May 27, 1953.

Chapter 37 notes

1 Lewis McArthur, "Oregon Geographic Names: Sixth Supplement", *Oregon Historical Quarterly*, Vol. 45 (Portland: Oregon Historical Society, 1945) pp. 42-43.

2 *Daily Eugene Guard* (Eugene, Oregon) November 3, 1898. Branton's testimony at his trial.

3 Peter Tugman, "Recalls First Hanging", *Eugene Register Guard*, May 27, 1953. This article provides a speech given by Lawrence T. Harris at a Lane County Bar Association meeting detailing the murder trial of Claude Branton fifty-five years earlier when Harris was a young deputy district attorney.

4 Ibid.

5 *Daily Eugene Guard*, November 3, 1898.

6 State of Oregon v. C. Branton, No. 5224, File No. 03303, Journal entry: Vol. 13, p. 151, Oregon Supreme Court Case Files, December 19, 1898, Oregon State Archives, Salem, Oregon.

7 *Daily Eugene Guard*, November 1, 1898.

8 *Daily Eugene Guard*, November 7, 1898.

9 *Daily Eugene Guard*, November 1, 1898.

10 Ibid.

11 Ibid.

12 *Daily Eugene Guard*, November 2, 1898.

13 Ibid. The prosecution presents its case and witnesses testify.

14 *Bohemia Nugget* (Cottage Grove, Oregon) November 3, 1899.

15 *Daily Eugene Guard*, November 2, 1898.

16 Ibid.

17 *Daily Eugene Guard*, November 2, 1898.

18 *Daily Eugene Guard*, November 3, 1898. Details all the defense witnesses' testimony, including Branton.

19 Ibid.

20 Ibid.

21 *Daily Eugene Guard*, November 4, 1898. Gives a detailed account of the defense attorney's summation, the prosecutor's summation, the judge's instructions and jury's verdict. In another article Branton's attempt to escape the jail is described and a floor plan of the jail is provided.

22 Ibid.

23 *Daily Eugene Guard*, November 8, 1898.

24 *Daily Eugene Guard*, November 4, 1898.

25 *Daily Eugene Guard*, November 7, 1898. Courtland Green's attorneys make a plea for second-degree murder. Green receives a life sentence and a sensational letter is introduced. The letter, in Branton's own handwriting, proves that Branton did the killing and Green was an accessory. In the *Eugene Register Guard* of May 27, 1953, featuring Lawrence T. Harris, the judge mentions a letter sent by Branton to his girlfriend that is intercepted by the local postmaster and read by Sheriff Withers. This may be the mysterious letter revealed at Green's hearing.

26 Ibid.

27 Oregon State Penitentiary Inmate Case File #4037 for Courtland Green, Oregon State Archives, Salem, Oregon.

28 *Daily Eugene Guard*, December 31, 1898.

29 *Daily Eugene Guard*, February 7, 1899.

30 *Daily Eugene Guard*, March 1, 1899.

31 *Daily Eugene Guard*, April 5, 1899.

32 State of Oregon v. C. Branton.

33 Ibid.

34 *Daily Eugene Guard*, December 17, 1898.

35 *Daily Eugene Guard*, May 12, 1899. The execution story covers the entire front page with pictures of the murderers, the victim, the location of his death, a drawing of the gallows, stockade, and floor plan of the jail.

36 Ibid.

37 Ibid.

38 *Bohemia Nugget*, May 19, 1899. This was a supplement printed the day before Branton died. It was printed in very small print and seven columns wide. The article contained Branton's autobiography and confession of killing Linn.

39 Ibid.

40 Peter Tugman, "Recalls First Hanging".

Chapter Thirty-Eight

State of Oregon v. William Magers 1900

T he hammering pounded in his head. For two days William Magers could hear nothing but the hammers—throbbing and thumping—over and over. Today the wall surrounding the Polk County jail and courthouse was nearly up to its full height. As the prisoner watched from his cell, the last of the boards blotted out the sun and black shadows fell across his face. They were done. A thirty-foot wall surrounded the hanging gallows—high enough to keep out not only the curious crowds but the sun too. Even a pouring rain wouldn't stop the work nor delay the upcoming event. Tomorrow was the day.

He mumbled under his breath, the same phrase again and again, "Tomorrow they hang an innocent man."

The tense atmosphere in Dallas, Oregon on December 7, 1898, made the men drinking in the saloons anxious, and shoppers lingered in small gossipy groups on the wooden sidewalks. Finally E. Hayter, the Polk County clerk, and Samuel L. Hayden, the district attorney, came out and stood on the courthouse steps. After a small crowd gathered, Hayden cleared his throat, and solemnly read aloud the following announcement:

> W. G. Magers is accused by the Grand Jury of the County of Polk by this indictment of the crime of Murder in the first degree committed as follows: The said W. G. Magers on the 13th day of September, A. D. 1898 in the County of Polk, and the State of Oregon, then and there being did then and there unlawfully, feloniously, purposely and of deliberate and premeditated mal-

ice kill Andrew Raymond Sink, by then and there purposely,
unlawfully and feloniously and of deliberate and premeditated
malice striking him and the said Andrew Raymond Sink with
an instrument the name and nature of said instrument is to the
Grand Jury unknown . . .[1]

So began what up to that time was one of the most expensive and notorious murder trials in Oregon.

William Magers was a very handsome but spoiled young man. He was 4 years old when his father, James, died in 1878. Nancy Magers, born 1845 in Illinois, had given birth to eight children.[2] Three still lived nearby—Emma, who was born in 1869 and married to Eugene Manning in Gervais; Linest D. a younger son who was born in 1875 and was living in Portland; and her favorite, William, who was born June 24, 1873, in Gervais.[3] William was named after his uncle who was a physician in Marion County. His widowed mother doted on him as he grew up, making sure he had well-tailored clothes, fast horses and plenty of money to spend. She ignored his gambling and wild ways, focusing instead on his handsome face with its dimpled chin and his charming manners.

Magers' conduct finally caught up with him on December 10, 1896, when he was 23 years old. He was convicted of breaking into a neighbor's farmhouse and stealing money. Samuel Hayden was Polk County district attorney at the time and pressured Judge George K. Burnett to impose the harshest punishment possible on Magers. Burnett sentenced the young man to eighteen months in the state penitentiary and fined him $373.[4]

On December 11 Magers arrived in Salem where they shaved off his hair, dressed him in prison stripes and he began his sentence. Records show that Magers served the full time plus six days extra for some undefined misbehavior.[5] He was released on November 28, 1897.

Magers had difficulty finding work suited to his abilities in Polk or Marion County, so seven months later he left for Sherman County to work for Raymond Sink, a rich rancher owning about 600 acres. While Magers was there, Sink began to regard the young man as a friend. Sink confided that he wanted to buy a commercial property in the valley and move there when he got married. Magers was excited about Sink moving to the Salem area and thought he knew someone in Gervais that might have a place to sell. Late in July the two men visited the Willamette Valley, staying in Gervais at the home of Mager's sister, Emma, and her husband, Eugene Manning. Renting a horse and buggy, the two friends drove to the little town of Woods, Oregon, in Tillamook County for a little vacation. After a relaxing week on the coast they returned to Sink's ranch.

A month later Sink decided to revisit Gervais. Before leaving, Sink pocketed $125 expense money for the trip. Sink considered buying a livery stable that was for sale by Sylvester Manning (Eugene Manning's brother). Manning was asking $3,400 for the establishment but Sink only wanted to pay $2,400 cash. After much dickering the men were unable to reach an agreement on the price. Sink decided to make a trip to Salem and let the matter rest. Magers went with him.

On the morning of September 13, Magers and Sink bid farewell to the Manning family. Before they left Raymond Sink told Emma Manning, "Good-by. Next time you see me I will be married and bring my wife with me."

After renting a buggy and team of horses from the livery stable in Gervais, they drove about twelve miles and arrived in Salem about 10 a.m. They left the buggy, the gray and the bay horses at Keeler's Livery Stable. The stable was near the Willamette River Bridge in downtown Salem. The men went about their business, eating dinner at Strong's Restaurant and renting a room in Captain Down's Rooming House. They took short naps and returned to the stable about 7:30 p.m. Magers paid fifty cents, only part of their bill, and assured the owner, D. D. Keeler, that they would return shortly. Hitching up the horses they left the stable with Magers driving. The men nodded politely to W. Edmunson, who was walking by. Later Edmunson testified in court that he watched the buggy cross the Willamette Bridge all the way into Polk County.

A few minutes after sundown, a young farmer, John Spar, saw two men, later identified as Magers and Sink, drive by him in their buggy as he was loading wood into a wagon. Spar observed the buggy speed by going north on the Lincoln highway near the river. Curious, he continued watching it for some time as it went back and forth along the river roads. The buggy drove down a lane leading to the home of E. E. Harritt, before it turned out of sight. A few minutes later it came back out of the lane and continued north and turned off into another road. This road dead-ended in a lonely stretch of wasteland covered with brush and cut up by watery sloughs. Spar heard a dog barking. It must have frightened the men in the buggy because a few minutes later it returned to the main road. It turned south toward Salem and into Harritt's lane, turned around again and drove out to the main road. After loosing sight of it, Spar finished loading his wood and left. The confused antics of the buggy and the men driving it left an indelible imprint on his mind.

224

Later that night, at about 11 p.m., Magers returned to Salem alone, leaving the horses and buggy for half an hour at the Fashion Stables. He returned to Captain Down's lodging house, picked up Sink's grip (suitcase) and went back to the stables. From there Magers drove to Gervais to the home of his sister and brother-in-law. He arrived about 1 a.m., meeting two young girls and another young man, Tom Chalfone, in a tent at the hop yard. Using his ample charm and showing them a wad of money, he persuaded the girls to be ready to leave with him.

The next morning he left for Portland, taking the girls with him, and rented rooms for them at the Depot Hotel. Waving

Oregon State Archives
William Magers, prisoner 3759, served 18 months in prison for larceny.

money around, he generously paid for and registered one girl as his wife and the other as his niece. Over the next several days they had a wonderful time in the big city as he paid for their meals, tickets to the theater and various musical entertainments.

Meanwhile back in Salem things were not going well. September 20, 1898 was a good day for fishing when L. Hamilton and a friend launched their skiff into the Willamette River. They didn't find any fish but they did catch a man's bloated body floating about 100 feet from the Polk County shore near the steel bridge. Coroner L. N. Woods of Polk County was notified and arrived to hold an inquest. The man's forehead had been bashed in, the right carotid artery of his throat cut, his mouth bruised and several teeth knocked out. His arms and legs were tied together with rope and iron weights attached to them in such a way as to make the body float in a standing position from the bottom of the river.

F. F. Toeves noticed that both pockets were turned inside out and all identification had disappeared. Only a rusty watch remained on the body. The watch was filled with water and the time stopped at 7:10. The authorities thought it might have stopped at the time the man was killed. However, after being rewound it ran for a considerable amount of time, so apparently the water had nothing to do with the time it had stopped. E. E. Harritt, a Polk County farmer, identified the iron weights as those stolen off his gate about a week earlier. John Spar heard about the body and went to the Marion County morgue. He identified the body as one of the men he had seen riding back and forth in the erratic buggy when he was loading wood on September 13.

Meanwhile Raymond Sink's brother was quite concerned about his brother's disappearance. He knew Sink had been with Magers until they arrived in Salem. He notified the Marion County authorities of his brother's disappearance and traveled to the valley to look for his brother. Finally he tracked Magers to Portland where he confronted Magers and demanded to know where his brother was.

"Why he went to Newberg with a lady friend. You are not uneasy about him are you?" Other than that Magers claimed ignorance and refused to help Mr. Sink.

Sink was unable to get any more information about the disappearance until E. Niece, a farmer from Sherman County, identified the body in the Marion County morgue as Raymond Sink. Niece happened to be visiting Salem on business and knowing that Raymond Sink was missing decided to check the morgue. Sink's family was immediately notified.

Portland Police Detective John Cordano confronted Magers at the Depot Hotel on September 21 where he was still staying with his girlfriends. In his pocket they found $58.60. This was much more money than he could possibly have earned from honest employment. Money they figured he stole from Raymond Sink.

He didn't seem surprised to be arrested. But he didn't seem frightened either. Before they took him away he hugged his pretend wife. "Go home," he ordered, "they are going to take me to jail and it may be some time before we can meet again."

Portland Chief of Police Dan McLaughlin and Detective Cordano questioned the suspect extensively before his lawyer could arrive. After many evasive and contradictory answers Magers finally settled on one story. He maintained that Raymond Sink had met an old school friend about 7 p.m. the evening of September 13, 1898 and drove to Newberg in the rented buggy with the friend. Magers said he had seen Sink in Portland a few days earlier and he thought a friend named Stephen Hilbauch had talked with Sink in the last day or two.

The last two statements surprised the police since Sink's body had been recovered from the river the day before, and the police knew Sink had been dead at least a week. It wasn't until later that the prisoner found out Sink's body had been found. The last lie about seeing Sink in Portland was Magers' undoing. He could never explain that story away and it haunted him for the rest of his short life.

County Sheriff Joseph G. Van Orsdel escorted Magers back to Dallas and into the Polk County Jail where he waited for nearly two months until the grand jury could convene. They heard testimony from twenty-four witnesses over three days before they returned an indictment on December 7 against W. G. Magers for the crime of murder in the first degree. The trial started the next day.

It took two days, but on December 9, 1898, the court was finally able to impanel twelve impartial jurors. Chosen as jurors were Wilson Ayres, Thomas W. Brunk, 41, a Dallas farmer; Ezra Conner, Harry S. Butz, 37, a Dallas farmer; M. L. Dorris, Ebenezer C. Keyt, Jr., 29, a Dallas farmer; William Kraber, 33, a Dallas farmer; D. Webb Lewis, 29, a Spring Valley farmer; Holt McDaniel, 32, a Rickreall farmer; William M. Muscott, 40, a day laborer from Dallas; William Riddell, 53, a Monmouth farmer and Andrew W. Teats, 54, a Dallas farmer, who was named jury foreman.[6] The jurors were representative of their community in ages and occupation. If residents weren't directly employed by the Pendleton Woolen Mills, the farmers and laborers provided support for those who did work in the mills.

The defendant's mother hired the defense team of W. H. Holmes of Salem and John J. Daly of Dallas to defend her son. He faced District Attorney Samuel L. Hayden, who had a long and illustrious career in Dallas. He was experienced and tenacious—a bad sign for Magers. J. E. Sibley of Dallas and United States District Attorney John H. Hall of Portland were hired by the Sink family to assist the prosecution.

The trial started on Wednesday and lasted five days. The prosecution's most damaging testimony came from Portland Police Chief Dan McLaughlin. His testimony that Magers pretended to see Sink in Portland and talked to Hillbaugh was particularly damaging. Defense attorney Holmes tried to get McLaughlin's testimony suppressed based on the fact Magers had not been warned of his right to be silent and not incriminate himself. The judge overruled Holmes. It would be many years before the law changed and the Miranda warning became a legal right.

Magers took the stand and testified in his own defense. His charm and self-confidence was evident. He wore a well-tailored suit, a high white collar and a precise black tie. The young women of Dallas flocked to the trial. Mager's testimony was a little different from what he had told McLaughlin. This time he said that after leaving Keeler's stable they met a friend of Sink's whose name he couldn't remember. Sink and the new friend took the buggy while Magers stayed in Salem. Later that evening he found the team they had rented from

Gervais standing hitched near the river. Recognizing it as the team he had hired, he took the team and proceeded on his way.

When asked why he didn't look for Sink, he replied, "I thought he had left with his friend."

Examination revealed bloodstains on the floor and back curtain of the buggy. Prosecution expert, Doctor W. A. Cusick testified that the blood was exactly the same as human blood, and that human blood differed from that of fish or fowl.[7] It looked to him like someone had tried to scrub the floor of the buggy.[8] The lap robe ordinarily left in the buggy was never recovered. Shoes were removed from the horses Magers and Sink had rented and were used to match the prints left in Harritt's barnyard.

The defense brought in their experts, Doctor W. H. Byrd and J. B. Tuttle, to testify that it was impossible to identify what kind of blood, if any, was in the buggy. B. B. Herrick, a surveyor, used an intricate drawing of the Willamette River currents to show that Sink died on the Marion County side of the river and floated to where he was found. Guy M. Powers, an agent of the O.R. & N. Railroad Company, testified that the steamboats going up and down the river would tend to push the body away from the Marion County side toward the Polk County side. If Sink had been killed in Marion County the trial in Polk County would be invalid.

Linest D. Magers and George Ritchey Jr. testified that the money Magers had on him was consistent with what they saw him have several days prior to the murder. F. Obermuller testified that the tracks found in E. E. Herritt's barnyard were made by newly shod horses and the horses rented by Sink and Magers were not shod with corks or toes and were much more worn.

The jury didn't think much of the defense. They brought back a guilty verdict on Sunday morning, December 11, 1898, after deliberating only twelve hours. At 4 p.m. on Wednesday, December 14, Judge George Burnett sentenced William G. Magers to hang by the neck until dead. The execution date was set for Friday, February 3, 1899.[9] Magers' lawyers immediately filed an appeal to the state supreme court. On April 24, 1899, the Oregon Supreme Court agreed that there was an error in the trial proceedings as alleged by the defendant for two reasons. The court erred:

1. In refusing to declare to the jury the time when the sun set September 13, 1898, the day when an alleged homicide is supposed to have been committed, the fact in question being material in the case;

2. That, assuming, as the counsel on both sides admitted in the argument, that all the testimony in the case in reference to intent with which the killing is inferred to have been done is contained in the bill of exceptions, an instruction to the jury that they might have found defendant guilty of manslaughter would have been proper and should have been given. The judgment is therefore reversed and the cause will be remanded for a new trial.[10]

Polk County Observer, February 2, 1900
William Magers, as he he appeared at his execution.

The question about the time the sun had set was an important one. Mr. Keeler and two other men had testified that Magers and Sink left the stable at 7:30 p.m., and he knew that for sure because the outdoor electric lights had only been burning for ten minutes. Later in the trial John Spar testified that he saw two men who resembled Magers and Sink driving a buggy two miles from the stable about "fifteen minutes after sundown." That raised a real dilemma for the prosecution as the official sunset time was at 6:15 p.m. So how could Sharp see the men an hour before they actually left the livery stable? The contradiction was never resolved during the trial and it became a valid reason to grant an appeal.[11]

Magers and his family expected him to be released when the appeal was granted, but District Attorney Hayden immediately filed a second indictment keeping the accused in jail until another trial and jury could be convened.

The unexpected setback must have hit Magers hard because he began planning his escape. On May 1, 1899, he and Harry Leonard, another prisoner, put their plan into effect. Sheriff Joseph Van Orsdel brought the prisoners their evening meal as usual and then left to go out front and pump fresh water. When he came back Magers and Leonard jumped him. Van Orsdel fought back. He hit Leonard hard on the head with the heavy padlock he was still carrying in his hand

and cut the prisoner's cheek. But two against one put the sheriff in a bad way. Magers got both hands around the sheriff's neck and strangled him into submission. Even as he blacked out he struggled to make as much noise as possible in the hope someone passing by would hear and come to investigate.

The prisoners gagged Van Orsdel with a towel and tied his hands and feet with strips of mattress ticking they had torn up. Luckily the sheriff was not wearing his sidearm so the men did not gain a weapon.

As Magers got ready to make his escape several loud voices greeted him, "Magers, if you come out that door we'll kill you dead. Give it up now."

The noise of the struggle had alerted a woman walking by the jail and she spread the alarm to three men working in the livery stable next door. Thinking that a mob was waiting outside the would-be escapees reluctantly untied the sheriff and begged him to protect them. After that the 46 year-old sheriff was much more security conscious. The episode also dispelled all doubts he had about Mager's guilt.

On May 12, 1899, Judge Burnett sentenced Harry Leonard, age 34, a stationary engineer, to seven years in the state penitentiary as a result of his attack on Van Orsdel.[12]

Magers' second trial began on Monday, May 23. It took three days and 105 men to finally impanel twelve jurors. The men chosen were: Jackson Baker, a Falls City farmer; P. Bartholomew, a farmer from Ballston; Alexander Burkhalter, a Dallas farmer; Harry Coad, a Douglas farmer; D. G. Henry, a Spring Valley farmer chosen foreman; L. R. Kimes, a farmer from Falls City; D. Riley Hubbard, a Dallas farmer; C. Lorence, a Monmouth farmer; Tracy McTimmonds, a farmer from Lewisville; James Mitchell, a tanner from Dallas and James Olmstead and C. D. Purvine, both farmers from Rickreall.[13] The defense used eleven of their twelve peremptory challenges and the state used five of its six challenges. The other possible jurors were dismissed for admitted bias. ninety-five percent of the jurors had read accounts of the murder in *The Oregonian* even though the court made a determined effort to draw men from the rural areas of Polk County.

District Attorney Samuel Hayden and Assistant J. E. Sibley were still the prosecutors, while Holmes and Daly remained Magers' defense team. Sink's relatives again hired United States District Attorney John Hall from Portland and J. H. Townsend to assist the prosecution. This time Spar testified that he saw Magers and Sink in the buggy "sometime after sunset" instead of the more specific "fifteen minutes after sundown." William Magers did not testify in his own behalf. The last arguments and statements finished at 2:15 p.m. on

Saturday, May 27, 1899. To no one's surprise the jury returned their verdict at 3:50 p.m.—guilty.[14] The defense attorneys asked the jury to be polled. When Judge Burnett asked, "Is this your verdict?" One by one all the jurors replied, "It is."

William G. Magers was sentenced to hang on July 21, 1899.[15]

W. H. Holmes filed two interesting affidavits on May 27, 1899, immediately after the jury returned its verdict. The affidavits requested a mistrial based on the purported bias of juror, James Mitchell. During the trial a friend of Mitchell, J. S. Macomber, stated in the presence of William Grant, J. J. Wiseman and others, "If those lawyers knew what I know,

Oregon State Sheriffs' Association
Polk County Sheriff J. G. VanOrsdel

they wouldn't have Jim Mitchell on the jury. He told me if ever a dammed son-of-a-b——h needed hanging, Magers is the man."

The second affidavit maintained that Mrs. Jim Mitchell had a dream before the trial, that Magers was hanged and that her husband participated in the hanging. She asked her husband if he would do such a thing and he replied, "He did not want to be a juror, but if he was, that was just what he would do."

Mrs. Mitchell relayed the story to Lula and Mary Macintosh who disclosed the conversation to the defense.

A hearing was held on June 2, 1899, to consider the defense attorney's request for subpoenas to question some very reluctant witnesses. Judge Burnett refused to issue the orders.

A third pair of affidavits signed by John Savage Jr. and his son G. L. Savage, maintained that their small skiff had been stolen from its fastening place on the Salem side of the river shortly before Sink's body was found. Blood found in the boat could have been from the murder. If Sink was murdered on the Salem side and the body dumped in the river, not only would Polk County have no jurisdiction,

231

but also the testimony against Magers would be diminished and a mistrial would be necessary.

Judge Burnett dismissed this set of affidavits also.

Magers' lawyers filed a second appeal to the state supreme court, which automatically put the execution on hold. This time the Supreme Court dismissed the defendant's arguments and upheld the conviction. On November 13, 1899, the court denied the appeal.[16]

A hearing held on December 13, 1899 in front of Judge George Burnett set February 2, 1900 as the date for Magers' hanging—the fifth public execution to be held in Polk County.[17] The last previous hanging was of William Landreth on July 6, 1888 for the murder of his stepdaughter.

The day before the hanging, Nancy Magers visited her son for the last time. With tears dripping down her face she begged William to tell the whole truth concerning the events surrounding Sink's murder. He replied that he was innocent and had nothing to confess.

That evening Elizabeth Van Orsdel, the sheriff's wife, made fried chicken and chocolate cake with nut-filled frosting for Magers' final dinner. Nancy Magers, his mother, spent the morning of February 2 waiting and grieving with Elizabeth until Linest Magers came to take her home.

February 2, 1900, dawned cold and very wet.[18] Sheriff Van Orsdel had sent 200 engraved invitations to various public officials, including the final twelve jurymen who found Magers guilty.[19] A thirty-foot-high fence was built around the scaffold and jail yard. Despite the heavy rain the streets were full of hundreds of people who had come to see whatever they could from outside the enclosure. Sheriffs from surrounding counties were present including William Holder of Sherman County; William Blakely of Umatilla; D. Y. K. Deering of Union; A. L. Alderman of Tillamook; J. A. Munkers of Linn; Frank W. Durbin of Marion; and Deputy Walter G. Henderson of Yamhill.[20] Raymond Sink's two brothers, Edward and T. O. Sink were present, as was Eugene Manning.[21] The rope was the same used in Lane County to hang Claude Branton on May 12 1899. Four newspaper reporters—F. F. Toevs, 36, the editor of the Salem *Daily Oregon Statesman* and a witness at the trial; Davenport of the *Examiner*; Hayter of the *Polk County Observer*; and Fiske of the *Polk County Itemizer*—were also present inside the enclosure.

Twelve esteemed gentlemen were chosen from the Polk County voting list as execution witnesses. Their signatures mark the end of Mager's short life: I. M. Butler, David Cosper, S. C. Denny, John F. Groves, L. M. Hall, Hardy Holman, H. B. Plummer, William

Ridgeway, I. M. Simpson, I. S. Smith, W. L. Wells, and J. J. Williams.[22]

Magers' lawyer, brother and brother-in-law spent the previous evening with Oregon Governor Geer begging him to commute the death sentence to life imprisonment. Despite the desperate appeal the governor declined to intervene. The men returned to Dallas and met with Magers just after 7 a.m. when Magers finished his breakfast.

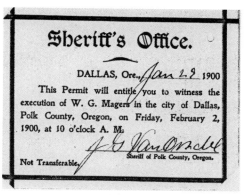

Sheriff's Office.

DALLAS, Ore., *Jan 29* 1900

This Permit will entitle you to witness the execution of W. G. Magers in the city of Dallas, Polk County, Oregon, on Friday, February 2, 1900, at 10 o'clock A. M.

J. G. Van Orsdel
Sheriff of Polk County, Oregon.

Not Transferable.

Polk County Historical Society
Invitation to the hanging
of William Magers.

Up to this time the convicted man had some hope of delaying his death sentence.

After calling the jurymen into the jail, Sheriff Van Orsdel again polled the men and confirmed that they all voted Magers guilty.

At 10 a.m. the sheriff entered Magers' cell and read aloud the death warrant. The prisoner became furious and in his frustration destroyed every piece of furniture in the cell. Ten minutes later he was calmer and seemed better prepared to go to his death. Elder Barton Riggs of the Christian church led the way with Deputy Sheriffs John T. Ford, 52, and W. E. Williams on either side of him. Charles McDermitt, the 60 year-old nightwatch, followed. Elder Riggs offered a prayer.

Magers then gave his final statement in a quivering voice, "Gentlemen, you are looking upon an innocent man. I pray that those who testified against me will be forgiven and that I will meet them in heaven. I forgive those who have done me wrong."[23]

As soon as he finished, the sheriff secured Magers' arms and legs, tugged the black cap over his head and immediately pulled the lever springing the death trap. The body fell like a stone and broke the man's neck instantly. Doctor R. E. L Steiner of Dallas and Doctor Otis D. Butler of Independence pronounced the time of death as 10:18 a.m. The body was turned over to Eugene Manning and buried in the Old Dallas Cemetery.[24] William Magers was 27 years old.

After the execution, Linest Magers gave attorney W. H. Holmes the following letter from his brother. Holmes gave it to the Salem *Journal* and they published it on February 2, 1900, in the *Polk County Observer*.

I told the truth when I was arrested, and no one would listen to me. Then I told it again at the trial–the whole thing, absolutely, without so much as a word added. I set it all out truly, so help me God.

I told the truth when and where I saw Ray Sink last, and all that I had said and done, just as it occurred the last time I saw my friend, and what did I get for it? Convicted of murder.

I am as innocent of it as any man who sat upon the jury that tried me. I am not going to argue to make out a case for myself, but I beg the kind readers to bear all the facts in their minds and ask themselves whether a man could get a fair trial. When a man with a previous conviction, and when once the black mark is against his name, you know that he cannot get justice, or really a fair trial. They will convict him on general principles and public sentiment.

I will tell you, before my God, I had nothing to do with it, and that I am innocent of the crime I am charged with. I pray to God that those who convicted me by false swearing that there may no night pass that they are not haunted by the thought of the man they sent to the gallows by their notoriously lying tongues.

I have very much to tell you, and I shall do it the best way I can, but as all friends know that my pen is unaccustomed to public writing, I crave special indulgence for all shortcomings. May God's hand strike me down if I go one inch over the truth.

We will discuss the money matter first, because I want your readers to know that I know that Ray Sink did not or could not have money as John Hall and Sam Hayden sanctioned the report that Sink was a man of great wealth. It is not true, for he told me himself that his place was mortgaged for a large sum. He (Ray Sink) said with good crops by January 1, 1899, that he could get out of debt, and he would mortgage his place again and get the money and come down to the valley and buy a livery stable. And Mr. Sink told D. Manning of Gervais, in my presence, September 10, 1898, that he would have to go home first and make arrangements before he could buy the stable. I am giving you these facts so you can honestly judge and see for yourself that I know Ray Sink did not have money when he was down here last, as he had not harvested his crop yet, and could not have had money.

The people were sharpened against me and poisoned by incredible stories, which sprung up from somewhere and spread like wildfire, and were eagerly accepted and implicitly believed. It bore no marks of authorship; it was accompanied by no proof.

234

Oregon State Sheriff's Association
A 30-foot stockade was built around the gallows at the Polk County Jail.

Yet intelligent people drank it in and loaded their tongues with falsehood, and spread it to everybody that they could get to listen to them with their heart's content.

I honestly believe that the murderer of Ray Sink will come to light some day and my name shall be clear of the false charges that have been placed against me. My heart aches for those people who have wronged me falsely, and I ask them in the name of God to go on their knees and ask God to forgive them of their sins. You can have my sympathy, and I forgive you, but God can only help you, and not mankind. God have mercy on your poor souls. You stand in a worse place today than I do. I can die with a clear conscience, and I am ready to meet my God, but you false witnesses are not. You are murderers in the sight of God and justice. I can easily forgive you, but I beg of you to make your peace with God.

Was he truly innocent as he stated throughout the entire ordeal? Did the state make a terrible mistake? Today we would be able to use many advanced forensic tests to get more accurate evidence. Certainly Magers was right about one thing, once he got a black mark against his name, being in the wrong place at the wrong time made him a perfect candidate for the hangman's noose. In 1900 a single lie and a man's bad reputation could kill him.

References
1900 Federal Census, Marion and Polk County, Oregon.

Century Edition of the American Digest, A complete digest of all reported American cases from the earliest times to 1906, Vol. 26, West Publishing, St. Paul, 1901, p. 174. "In a prosecution for murder, on an issue as to whether accused had obtained money by committing the crime, evidence of specific expenditures in the line of riotous living after the homicide is not inadmissible where it is offered in connection with evidence that he had no money prior to the homicide. - State v. Magers, 58 P. 892, 36 Or. 38.

Historically Speaking, Vol. III, and VIII, Polk Co. Historical Society, PO. Box 67, Monmouth, Oregon, August 1974 and 1988.

Morning Oregonian (Portland, Oregon) May 2, 1899, May 6, 1899, May 22, 1899, May 24, 1899, February 2, 1900, February 3, 1900.

Oregon State Penitentiary Case File #3759, William Magers, Oregon State Archives, Salem, Oregon.

Polk County Circuit Court Journal File Vol. No. 11, pp. 118, 122, 131, 172, 177, 178, Oregon State Archives, Salem, Oregon.

Polk County Itemizer (Dallas, Oregon) February 2, 1900.

Polk County Observer (Dallas, Oregon) December 10, 1898, December 12, 1898, December 16, 1898, May 5, 1899, May 26, 1899, June 2, 1899, February 2, 1900.

State of Oregon v. W. G. Magers, Polk County Circuit Court Case Files #2815 and #3073, Oregon State Archives, Salem, Oregon.

State of Oregon v. W. G. Magers, No. 5271, File No. 03409, Journal entry: Vol. 13, p. 282, January 23, 1899. Oregon Supreme Court Appeals file, Oregon State Archives, Salem, Oregon

State of Oregon v. W. G. Magers, No. 5346, File No. 03469, Journal entry: Vol. 13, p. 482, July 12, 1899. Oregon Supreme Court Appeals file, Oregon State Archives, Salem, Oregon

Telephone Register (McMinnville, Oregon) May 18, 1899.

Wade, Daraleen Phillips. *Genealogical Abstracts of the first 2500 Probate Records in Marion County*. Salem: Willamette Valley Genealogical Society, 1985.

Chapter 38 notes

1 State of Oregon v. W. G. Magers, No. 5271, File No. 03409, Journal entry: Vol. 13, p. 282, January . 23, 1899, Oregon Supreme Court Appeals file, Oregon State Archives, Salem, Oregon.
2 1900 Federal Census, Marion County, Oregon.
3 *Morning Oregonian* (Portland, Oregon) February 3, 1900.
4 Oregon State Penitentiary Case File #3759, William Magers, Oregon State Archives, Salem, Oregon.
5 Ibid.
6 State of Oregon v. W. G. Magers, No. 5271.
7 W. A. Cusick was a physician in Gervais from about 1870 to 1882 when he moved to Salem. Most likely he would have known the Magers family. He was elected to the state legislature in 1884 and was active in local politics.
8 State of Oregon v. W. G. Magers, No. 5271.
9 Ibid.

10 State of Oregon v. W. G. Magers, No. 5271.

11 *Morning Oregonian*, May 2, 1899.

12 *Telephone Register* (McMinnville, Oregon) May 18, 1899.

13 *Polk County Observer* (Dallas, Oregon) May 26, 1899.

14 *Polk County Observer*, June 2, 1899.

15 State of Oregon v. W. G. Magers, No. 5346, File No. 03469, Journal entry: Vol. 13, p. 482, July 12, 1899, Oregon Supreme Court Appeals file, Oregon State Archives, Salem, Oregon.

16 Ibid.

17 Ibid.

18 *Polk County Itemizer*, February 2, 1900.

19 *Polk County Itemizer,* February 2, 1900.

20 Ibid. Alderman was a juror at the trial of Kot-Ko-Wot in 1880.

21 Ibid.

22 State of Oregon v. W. G. Magers, No. 5346. Holman was a Polk County Justice of Peace.

23 Morning Oregonian, February 3, 1900.

24 Ibid.

Chapter Thirty-Nine

State of Oregon v. Coalman Gillespie 1900

On Tuesday, September 19, 1899, Joseph Hare, a 52-year-old mail carrier, rode around the bend in the trail and suddenly pulled his horse to an abrupt halt. He had been smelling smoke drifting on the wind for the last mile and now he knew why. The cabin was burned to the ground.

Only a few smoking beams remained. Joseph immediately searched for any possible survivors in the nearby barn and woods, but found no one. The county sheriff was notified and a group of neighbors arrived. Pushing aside the debris they came upon a grisly scene. The 77-year-old owner of the cabin, Christina Geisel Edson, was dead. Her charred remains were lying across the bedsprings in her bedroom. She obviously had died before the fire began, as she'd made no effort to escape. On the floor beside the springs was an empty can of coal oil with a knife slit in it. It certainly looked as though someone had helped the fire along.

It was the end of a long and tragic life. Christina Bruck was born in Prussia, Germany in 1823. She married John Geisel in 1843 and with their children moved to Curry County in 1854.[1] They did a little gold prospecting, farming and managed a small hotel near Gold Beach. They were making a new life for themselves and their children until Christina was 27 years old. Their new life changed on the evening of February 22, 1856. Christina was recovering from the birth of her fifth child, Annie, only two weeks old. Mary, age 13, John Jr., age 9, Henry, age 7, and Andrew, age 5, were asleep when someone knocked on the door.[2]

"Who is it?" John Geisel asked cautiously. Rumors about violent

Indians had been flying around the settlement for a month. Just last week the Indian agent had stopped by and reassured the family that they were safe.

A guttural voice replied, "It's me, Joe. Let me in." Joe was a friendly Indian John had hired to help on the farm.

Raising his eyebrows at Christina, he sighed, shook his head and unbarred the cabin door. The door crashed open and five Indians rushed into the cabin brandishing guns and knives. John tried to defend his family but was quickly overpowered. While trying to help her husband Christina nearly had a finger severed.

The horror that followed next is described in an affidavit Christina made thirty years later.

> My oldest daughter, then but thirteen years old, was dragged out of her bed, and she and I were securely bound. My little boys were then one by one brought out and brutally murdered in my presence. I being compelled to witness the awful deed and my daughter and I were then removed from the house in our night clothes, and securely tied till the Indians searched the house and removed every thing of value there and took away with them all our money and gold dust and the clothing of our family. They then set fire to the house, not permitting my husband and sons being removed from the burning house.

Ben Wright, the Indian agent, and twenty-three other people were killed that night and sixty homes burned. It was the worst Indian uprising in Oregon's history. Christina, Mary, and baby Annie were captives for fourteen days before the settlers at the Rogue River Fort ransomed them.

Chief John and his followers were defeated on May 28, 1856, at the Battle of Big Bend near the junction of the Illinois and Rogue Rivers.[3] The settlers wanted vengeance. Fourteen unarmed and nameless Indian captives were later lynched when they camped near the Geisel homestead. The Indian that betrayed the Geisels was captured, lynched and buried in Ellensburg (Gold Beach). Enos, the Canadian Indian leader of the renegades, was captured in Washington state and returned to Port Orford. Christina was unavailable to testify and it looked like he would be released for lack of evidence. A mob intervened and he was lynched just outside Port Orford. On July 3, 1856, 710 Indians were transported to the Grande Ronde and Siletz reservations.[4]

In 1878 a tombstone, enclosed by a white picket fence, was established to mark the death of the Geisel family, just five miles north of the mouth of the Rogue River and a quarter mile from the Pacific

Ocean. The engraving reads: "Sacred to the memory of John Geisel, also his three sons John, Henry and Andrew who were massacred by the Indians, Feb. 22d, 1856. Aged 45-9-7-5 years respectfully."[5]

Over the next forty-three years Christina married three more times. In 1870 she married James Pate. By 1880 she was living with her third husband, Avery J. Edson and they owned a general store. He died in 1893 leaving $1 to his son Thomas and the remainder of his estate to his beloved wife, Christina. Five pages listed the various items in the store netting her a total of $171.82.[6] After his death she settled into a new home near Gold Beach. She never had any more children. Twice she petitioned the U.S. government for compensation for the loss of her family. Eventually, she was awarded a $25 a month pension under a congressional act that authorized payments for Indian "depredations" during the Indian wars. Her first check of $75 arrived Monday, September 18, 1899, the day before she died. Everyone suspected that someone wanting to steal her money had killed her.

There were few leads in the murder and Curry County advertised a $450 reward for information leading to the killer. Finally a government check made out to Christina Edson was turned in at a Roseburg bank. Coalman Gillespie, a 21-year-old neighbor of Christina, had sold the check to C. O. White of Myrtle Creek. Gillespie was recognized and arrested by Constable Warren McFarland in Cottage Grove a few days later.[7] McFarland escorted Gillespie to Roseburg, the seat of Douglas County, and notified the Curry County authorities to come get him.

Curry County District Attorney, George M. Brown immediately made arrangements to travel over the coastal mountains and question the suspect. Jesse Turner, the county sheriff, and Deputy Alf Miller went along. They met Coos County Sheriff William W. Gage and two guards who were just returning from escorting three prisoners to the penitentiary in Salem.

They arrived in Roseburg on October 1 to find a defiant Gillespie waiting in jail for them. At first he tried to stick to a story about buying the Edson check from a man he met along the road between Charles Zumwalt's farm on the Sixes River and the little town of Denmark. Brown's skillful questioning soon got Gillespie so confused that he gave up and confessed to being part of the duo that killed Christina Edson.

After taking custody of Gillespie the group left Roseburg and traveled to the nearest Justice of the Peace in Langlois District of Curry County, who remanded Gillespie to Sheriff Gage's custody. Considering the danger of mob violence if Gillespie were taken to Gold

Beach, he was escorted to Coquille's jail to wait until the circuit court could convene ten months later.

Coalman Gillespie lived with his mother and sister, Mrs. Louis Marsters, in what used to be the old Masonic Hall near the courthouse in Gold Beach. Mrs. Gillespie was a good friend of Christina Edson. Two years earlier Gillespie had been indicted by the Curry County grand jury on September 24, 1897, for larceny and served a term in the county jail.[8] He was convicted of stealing a silver watch, a watch chain, a revolver, and two finger rings from S. E. Marsters (later county sheriff from 1902-1908) a year earlier. He was well known in the community as a wild and reckless young fellow who liked to hang out in the bars and gambling halls. Occasionally, he did manual labor for various farmers and ranchers.

Gillespie was escorted to Coquille where he made a written confession. His six-page handwritten confession detailed the planning and execution of the murder and named Charles Strahan as his partner.[9] Strahan, a 28-year-old salmon fisherman, was the son of Henry and Mary Strahan, early Curry County settlers. He lived with his wife, Hilda, age 20, and one-year-old daughter, Rita, in Gold Beach.[10] Strahan was never indicted for the Edson murder as he disappeared before he could be arrested. Some people think he drowned in the Rogue River while trying to escape. Others claimed he fled to Port Orford and drowned with two others in a fishing accident.

Gillespie's attorney, W. C. Chase, tried hard to suppress the written confession and various statements Gillespie made while he was in the Roseburg jail but the judge overruled. Sheriff Jesse Turner later testified Gillespie confessed to choking Mrs. Edson, pouring coal oil on her and setting fire to the house, although that was not included in the written confession.

According to Gillespie,

> *Chas Strahan . . . was the one that did the planning . . . he said he would not hurt her when he went in but he grabed her and the first thing she said was yess yess I will give you all I got so she got the check for him and he said $11.75. . . . Chas S. said when he came to let me out of the barn that he was sure of $75 for she had got her check so he was eather at the Po Office that night or someone told him about it.*[11]

Gillespie was lodged in the Coos County Jail, because Curry County was in the process of building their first courthouse and jail. Gillespie waited there for a year until the judicial wheels started turning and the courthouse was finally finished. Instead of convening a grand jury, George Brown, the Curry County District Attorney, filed a first-degree murder charge against Gillespie and the trial began on August 21, 1900, in front of judge J. W. Hamilton. Riol Davidson, Joseph White, John McGuhen, A. A. Lawrenceson, and J. F. Lowery were the first five chosen as jurors. George Fitzhugh, 55, a Port Orford teacher, was voted jury foreman. Francis Hughes, 24, Robert Jordan, 55, John McKenzie, 35, William Miller, 45, Albert Smith, 41, and Frank A. Stewart, 53, were the last six chosen.[12] Most of the jurors represented families that had lived in Curry County for many years and knew both the victim and the defendant.

Seventeen witnesses testified. There were tears in many eyes when Mary Blake and Annie Doyle, Christina's daughters, told of seeing their mother the day before she died. They had begged her to come live with them but Christina declined.

Joseph Hare described finding the burning house. Jesse Turner, now the former county sheriff, and I. B. Riddle testified to the authenticity of Gillespie's confession. C. O. White confronted Gillespie about selling Christina's government check. Other witnesses called were: C. E. Bogue, F. W. Dillard, W. W. Gagnon, Jeremiah Huntly, Mrs. Marsha E. Huntly, Bert Sheffer, J. R. Thornton, Charles S. Winsor, William W. Wren, and Delos Woodruff. The last reluctant witness was Mrs. Louis Marsters, Gillespie's sister.[13]

The next day the jury returned a guilty verdict after less than an hour's deliberation. On August 23, Judge J. W. Hamilton sentenced Coalman Gillespie to be hanged on October 5, 1900, in Gold Beach.[14]

The judge expressed the same opinion felt by many of the county citizens. Christina Edson had seen her husband and sons tortured and burned by the Indians. The savages could be excused because they were fighting for their rights to the land they once owned. Gillespie's crime was even more horrifying because it was in cold blood for a few dollars. Even if he didn't do the actual deed he participated willingly in the planning and execution.

On October 4, 1900, the day before his death, Coalman Gillespie wrote another confession and accusation against Charles Strahan:

> In September 1899 between the first and fifteenth Charles Strahn made the proposed to me to help robb the old lady Edson . . .when I went past the door of her bed room I saw Chas and her standing there but I went on in to the kitchen and ate something and while I was in there eating he came in and said come on lets get out of this in a hurrey.[15]

Curry County was not as populated as other Oregon counties so between the jury, the trial witnesses, and the hanging witnesses, most of the male population was involved in the Gillespie case. The

Curry County Historical Society
The execution of Coalman Gillespie, October 5, 1900.

twelve men chosen as official hanging witnesses were: William E. Burrows, 65, a farmer from Ophir; Joseph Crockett, 46, a farmer from Jerry's Flat; John Jensen, 43, a blacksmith from Flores Creek; William C. Lake, 41, a farmer from Chetco; Nathaniel B. Moore, 22, a farmer from Chetco; William R. Miller, 45, a farmer from Quarten; John R. Miller, 36, a businessman from Port Orford; Thomas Smith, 61, a farmer from Jerry's Flat; Frank A. Stewart, 53, a farmer from Ophir; Charles S. Winsor, 35, a businessman from North Bend; Delos Woodruff, 65, a farmer from Ophir; and William H. Crook, 33, a farmer from Pistol River. William Miller and Frank Stewart were jurors at the trial.[16]

Later in life William Crook told his grandson that, although legally convicted of murder, Gillespie was not responsible for the killing. Crook was the son of Asa Crook, an ex-Curry County sheriff and joint Coos/Curry state representative. He believed that Gillespie was retarded and used by another fellow who was the real perpetrator.[17]

Gillespie's family members begged the governor to intercede and commute his sentence to life imprisonment, but he refused. Sheriff James G. Walker escorted Gillespie to the gallows at Gold Beach on October 5, 1900, at 3 p.m. He died the hard way, by strangulation rather than a broken neck after dropping six feet.[18]

It was the first, last and only legal public hanging in the county.

References

1880 Federal Census, Coos County, Oregon.

1880 and 1900 Federal Census, Curry County, Oregon.

Coos Bay News (Coos Bay, Oregon) October 3, 1899 and October 9, 1900.

Coos Bay News (Marshfield, Oregon) January 16, 1878.

Coquille City Herald (Coquille, Oregon) October 3, 1899, October 9, 1899, October 10, 1899, October 17, 1899, October 24, 1899, October 9, 1900.

Crook, William. 6000 Arch Rock Butte, 101 South, Pistol River, Oregon. Interview.

Curry County Probate File #68, A. J. Edson, May 22, 1893, Oregon State Archives, Salem, Oregon.

Herald (Crescent City, California) February 1856.

Oregon Sentinel (Jacksonville, Oregon) October 6, 1899, October 31, 1899.

Peterson, Emil R. and Alfred Powers. *A Century of Coos and Curry*. Portland, Binfords and Mort, 1952.

Scrapbook #269, p. 11. Photo of the Giesal Monument, Oregon Historical Society, Portland, Oregon.

State of Oregon v. Coalman Gillespie, Curry County Circuit Court, September 24, 1897, Oregon State Archives, Salem, Oregon.

State of Oregon v. Coalman Gillespie, Curry County Circuit Court Case Files, 1872-1939, Case No. A–345, Oregon State Archives, Salem, Oregon.

Wimmer, Vernon J. "Christina Geisel: A Story of Kidnapping and Tragic Deaths." Curry County Museum, Gold Beach, Oregon.

Chapter 39 notes

1 Emil R. Peterson and Alfred Powers, *A Century of Coos and Curry,* (Portland: Binfords and Mort, 1952) p. 535.

2 Vernon J. Wimmer, "Christina Geisel: A Story of Kidnapping and Tragic Deaths", Curry County Historical Society, Gold Beach, Oregon.

3 Emil R. Peterson and Alfred Powers, p. 91

4 Ibid, p. 92.

5 *Coos Bay News* (Marshfield, Oregon) January 16, 1878.

6 Curry County Probate File #68, A. J. Edson, May 22, 1893, Oregon State Archives, Salem, Oregon

7 *Oregon Sentinel* (Jacksonville, Oregon), October 6, 1899.

8 State of Oregon v. Coalman Gillespie, Curry County Circuit Court, September 24, 1897 Oregon State Archives, Salem, Oregon. The records spell Gillespie's first name in many ways, but he signed it "Coalman" at the bottom of both confessions.

9 State of Oregon v. Coalmam Gillespie, Curry County Circuit Court Case Files, Case File No. A-345, Oregon State Archives, Salem, Oregon.

10 1900 Federal Census, Curry County, Oregon.

11 State of Oregon v. Coalman Gillespie, Case File No. A-345.

12 Ibid.

13 Ibid.

14 Ibid.

15 Ibid.

16 Ibid.

17 Crook, William. 6000 Arch Rock Butte, 101 South, Pistol River, Oregon. Interview. Grandson of William Crook, witness and juror.

18 Coos Bay News, October 9, 1900.

Chapter Forty

State of Oregon v. John Wade and B. H. Dalton 1902

For the first time in more than twenty years, two men again stood on the gallows together. Partners in crime, they now faced their execution. It was the last time the public would see such a spectacle and just about everyone who received one of the 400 invitations packed themselves into the jail yard enclosure the morning of January 31, 1902.[1] Oregon's justice was fast—only seventy-one days from murder to execution.

It all began a little after midnight on Thursday, November 21, 1901. John (also called Jack) Wade and William Dalton left a saloon on Portland's Hawthorne Avenue, walked two blocks and around the corner when they met James Barkley Morrow, a young bartender on his way home after visiting his fiancé, Leah Hildge.[2]

"I know him," Dalton said. "He's a gambler." He drew his 44-caliber Colt revolver and thrust all 16 inches of blue steel in Morrow's face. "Put your hands up."

"All right, fellows. That's all right," the poor man said and fumbling in his jacket tried to get his wallet for the thieves. Just as Wade reached out to assist him, the gun went off, killing Morrow instantly.

Mrs. W. T. Whitlock, the owner of a boarding house at 181 First Street in Portland, rented a room to Dalton and two confederates, Charles Smith and William H. Martin. She grew suspicious of her boarders on Saturday when they rummaged through her belongings and stole $60 worth of clothes and jewelry.[3] She also became suspicious of the men after hearing about Morrow's killing. By Saturday she had made up her mind to report her worries.

Bravely she confronted Martin, Smith, and Dalton when they returned to her house that afternoon. After the confrontation she left the men and telephoned her lawyer, Alexander Sweek, and asked him what she should do next. He advised her to call District Attorney Chamberlain. Unable to contact Chamberlain because the line was busy, she finally called the police station and asked to have a policeman come immediately as she had been robbed. When no one had arrived by 10 p.m. that evening she called Chamberlain at home.[4]

"Who's there?" he asked, rather cranky that someone was calling so late in the evening as the family was going to bed.

"Never mind. I want you to come to 181 First Street at once. Something important has happened."

"Can't you come to my office, during business hours? Won't it do tomorrow?"

"If you knew what I wanted you for, you'd step over here quickly. You are working on that murder across the river, are you not? Well, it's about that. Now you understand. Ask for Mrs. Whitlock."

Chamberlain telephoned Detective Day and they agreed to meet at Third and Morrison. From there they went to Mrs. Whitlock's home and interviewed her two boarders. Neither man knew anything about the murder. Just then Dalton arrived and with very little encouragement confessed to the murder—only now he insisted that Wade had done the shooting.

Dalton was arrested and they all trooped around to various saloons looking for Wade. About 2 a.m. Wade was arrested in his room at the La Fayette lodging house.

The next day James Nevine, superintendent of Pinkerton's Detective Agency, District Attorney Chamberlain, and Chief of Police Dan McLaughlin interrogated the suspects. Wade and Dalton both confessed to the killing—each naming the other as the shooter.

Wade, whose real name was Joseph T. Ewing, was 23 years old, born in Pittsburgh, Pennsylvania, with a bulldog countenance and an air of supreme self-confidence.[5] His father was Thomas Ewing of Wampum, Pennsylvania. He accused his sister and brother of turning him in to the local authorities at a young age. "They sent me to reform school," he said, "and there I learned all my bad tricks. I was turned out in the world without a cent, I knew nothing and I had to eat and the easiest way to get grub was over the transom."[6]

B. H. Dalton, whose real name was William H. Strickland, born in Augusta, Georgia twenty-one years earlier, was a much smaller man, nervous and soft-spoken.[7] He had been adopted at age 9 by George Willis from Aiken, South Carolina. It wasn't a happy family and four years later, at age 13, he ran away. Dalton swore that Wade had served time in the Montana penitentiary and had killed twenty-five other men in the past.[8] John Wade, also known as Kid McFadden, swore that Dalton was part of a group of hobo highwaymen living off the spoils of multiple robberies.

The prisoners were initially taken to the city jail but the crowd outside became so unruly that officials began to fear a lynching. So one-by-one, they were spirited away to separate jails outside the city of Portland. Dalton was housed in Oregon City before being taken back to the Multnomah County jail.[9]

Jack Wade, alias Kid McFadden, principal.

William H. Dalton, accomplice.

Morning Oregonian, January 31, 1902
Jack Wade and William Dalton were hanged on January 31, 1902..

The men were arraigned in circuit court in front of Judge Arthur L. Frazer on November 25. John F. Logan was appointed to represent John Wade and Clarence Veazie was appointed to represent William Dalton.[10] Wade pleaded guilty and threw himself on the mercy of the court, all the while maintaining that Dalton fired the gun. According to Oregon law, it didn't matter who fired the fatal shot. Both were guilty of murder in the first degree, being joint participants in the conspiracy and its consequences.[11] Dalton pleaded not guilty, but just ten days later he was tried and convicted of first-degree murder in front of Judge Cleland. Both men were sentenced to hang on January 31, 1902. Shortly before the execution Wade finally confessed that he was holding the gun when it "accidentally" fired, killing Morrow instantly.

The week before the hanging Dalton became feverish and ill, his throat swelling to the point he could hardly swallow. Physicians called to the jail relieved the congestion and by January 30 he was feeling better and eating again.[12]

On the day of the hanging, the prisoners finished their breakfast of chicken, eggs and ham, just as it started raining.[13] George and Frederick Marshall met with the condemned men and held a simple ceremony and sang several hymns. One brother was a clerk and the other a carpenter. Both were associated with a local Christian mission in Portland.

Sheriff Frazier issued nearly 400 invitations even though the enclosure could only hold 250.[14] At 7:41 a.m. the men were released from their cells and headed for the gallows. A twenty-foot tall fence and a gallows platform had been built in the courtyard of the Multnomah County Courthouse. Two ropes with nooses dangling at the end were hung eight feet apart.[15]

Charles Smith, the young man that was arrested with Dalton at Mrs. Whitlock's boarding house was one of the first to enter the area, ready to watch his friends die. Five deputy sheriffs escorted the two men up the stairs and on to the scaffold with its double trap doors. The twelve men chosen as official witnesses were Doctor C. W. Cornelius, John P. Sharkey, Dave Raffety, Doctor James C. Zan, G. Orlo Jefferson, Roscoe R. Merrill, F. S. Smith, William McLean, C. B. Bartel, Herbert W. Cardwell, John B. Bridges and J. B. Slemmons.[16] Doctors H. R. Littlefield and Harry McKay were attendant physicians.[17]

While the people were well behaved inside the enclosure, the crowd standing outside in the snow was quite different. It was estimated 1,000 spectators crammed Salmon, Taylor and Fifth Streets behind guarded and roped off barriers.[18] Telephone poles, roofs, and surrounding windows were crammed with bodies trying to get a peek at the execution. At times the mob surged uncomfortably close to the wooden wall threatening to push it flat to the ground before the police could get in control again. Even though it was so early in the morning there was much drinking, joking, laughing and a general party atmosphere.

After everyone climbed the steps and maneuvered into position, the men were asked if they had anything to say. Wade replied that he had nothing to add to his published confession. But Dalton couldn't resist the final word. Like a preacher at a revival Dalton held the audience spellbound with exhortations to shun evil and do good. After repeating his confession he concluded, "Though I received salvation behind the bars, I glorify the name of the Heavenly Father forever and forever."[19]

As Dalton paused, Wade couldn't resist the opportunity and pulled a cigar and a handkerchief from his pocket and tossed them into the crowd. Next he grabbed the noose swinging beside his head, brought it to his nose, sniffed audibly and winked. "It's tough," he laughed. His comical antics amused the crowd and clearly irritated the more serious-minded Dalton.

Wade finally stepped forward, his eyes glistening with tears, and gave his final performance, "Don't any of you follow in the tracks of Jack. Now don't you do it. You may think I am happy here. I am not. I'm here because I can't do any better in this world. What would a life in Salem be to me?"

Straps were tied around the men's arms and legs and black caps pulled over their heads. At 7:58 a.m. Sheriff William Frazier raised his hand as a signal to three unseen and unidentified men who pulled the three ropes, one of which released both trap doors at the same instant. Two of the ropes were blind pulls. Dalton fell 5' 6" and Wade fell a little over six feet.[20] Their bodies twisted slowly from the gallows for at least fifteen minutes before being cut down.

Special guests to the entertainment included Marion County Sheriff Frank Durbin, Baker County Sheriff Alfred H. Huntington, Yamhill County Sheriff Frank Sitton, Clackamas County Sheriff John J. Cooke, Clatsop County Sheriff Thomas Linville, Morrow County Sheriff James Matlock, Polk County Sheriff Joseph Van Orsdel, Linn County Sheriff G. W. McHargne, Wallowa County Sheriff Hiram Cramer, Grant County Sheriff Elijah Laurance, Lincoln County Sheriff James Ross, J. D. Lee, superintendent of the State Penitentiary, and a variety of other city and county officials.[21] Besides the invited guests, nearly a dozen women watched the event from the roof of a nearby building.

Wade and Dalton's bodies were put in coffins and taken to the county morgue where special guards were posted as the public was allowed to file past. Later an autopsy on both men revealed that Dalton's neck was broken and Wade was strangled to death. Inside the scaffold enclosure the crowd swarmed over the gallows, cut down the ropes and passed out small pieces as souvenirs.

The most learned professors on the west coast scientifically examined the dead men's brains. They believed that the development of the gray matter rather than its gross weight indicated the amount of intellectual ability. Dalton's brain weighed 46 ounces and Wade's brain weighed 53-3/4 ounces.[22] The doctors explained that while Wades's brain was a few ounces over the average and Dalton's was considerable less, that did not mean that Wade was more intelligent. Both men were buried in the Multnomah County Poor Farm Cemetery.

After paying the $500 reward to Mrs. Whitlock for information leading to the arrest of Wade and Dalton, it cost Multnomah County

$1,400 to convict and execute the murderers of James Morrow. Each of the three men pulling the ropes that released the trap received $25.[23]

Multnomah County District Attorney George Chamberlain was not as impressed by the spectacle on January 31, 1902. After he was elected governor in 1903, he proposed a new law requiring future executions to be conducted at the state penitentiary, "out of hearing and out of sight of all except officials".[24]

J. D. Lee, Superintendent of the state penitentiary, did not agree with Chamberlain's new law and he let his opinions be known. He warned that executions would anger the prison population making riots and other forms of resistance more likely. His opinions concerning where and how men should be executed were slightly different from the governor's:

I believe in executions without publicity, and also believe it would be a good thing perhaps to have a central prison, where such executions should be conducted. Such a prison should be located in Portland, the electric chair should supplant the gallows and no date for executions should be fixed. It would be better for the public not to know anything of executions until after they are over.[25]

References

Bedau, Hugo. "Capital Punishment in Oregon, 1903-1964." *Oregon Law Review, Vol. 45*, 1965.

City of Portland Death Index, 1881–1905. City of Portland Record of Deaths for January 1902, Oregon State Archives, Salem, Oregon

Evening Telegram (Portland, Oregon) January 30, 1902, January 31, 1902.

Humbird, Jim. "When Hangings Were A Major Pastime." *Oregonian* (Portland, Oregon) September 3, 1939.

"Law Enforcement-Executions", Vertical Files, Oregon Historical Society, Portland, Oregon. Letter from Martha Gaddis, February 1, 1962. Letters from Francis Lambert, Sheriff of Multnomah County, February 9, 1962, and November 27, 1973.

Long, William. *A Tortured History: The Story of Capital Punishment in Oregon*. Eugene: The Oregon Criminal Defense Lawyers Association, 2002.

Morning Oregonian (Portland, Oregon) November 25, 1901, November 26, 1901, November 27, 1901, November 28, 1901, December 2, 1901, January 2, 1902, January 4, 1902, January 31, 1902, February 1, 1902, February 2, 1902.

State of Oregon v. John Wade, Multnomah Circuit Court Case File, Reg. 1434B, Judgment #29165, Portland, Oregon.

Chapter 40 notes

1 *Evening Telegram* (Portland, Oregon) January 31, 1902.
2 Ibid.
3 *Morning Oregonian* (Portland, Oregon) November 25, 1901.
4 Ibid.
5 City of Portland Death Index, 1881–1905, Oregon State Archives, Salem, Oregon. Ages for both men are listed. Only Wade's birth state is given.
6 *Morning Oregonian,* January 31, 1902.
7 *Morning Oregonian,* February 1, 1902. The 1895 Marion County Oregon Census lists William L. Dalton living with Edna and H. C. Dalton. William Dalton is listed as being between the ages of 21 and 18. Is it possible William Strickland knew this Dalton and adopted his name?
8 *Morning Oregonian,* November 25, 1901.
9 *Morning Oregonian,* November 26, 1901
10 *Morning Oregonian,* November 28, 1901.
11 *Morning Oregonian,* November 26, 1901.
12 *Evening Telegram,* January 30, 1902.
13 Some newspapers reported snow falling and snow drifts on the city streets.
14 *Evening Telegram,* January 30, 1902.
15 William R. Long, *A Tortured History* (Eugene: The Oregon Criminal Defense Lawyers Association, 2002) p. 25. Long describes the execution of Wade and Dalton in detail.
16 *Evening Telegram,* January 31, 1902.
17 *Morning Oregonian,* February 1, 1902.
18 *Evening Telegram,* January 31, 1902.
19 *Morning Oregonian,* February 1, 1902.
20 Ibid.
21 Ibid.
22 *Morning Oregonian,* February 2, 1902.
23 Ibid.
24 Hugo Bedau, "Capital Punishment in Oregon, 1903-1964" Oregon Law Review Vol. 45, (1965) p. 5.
25 *Evening Telegram,* January 31, 1902.

Chapter Forty-One

State of Oregon v. August Schieve 1902

Joseph Schulkowski, a 27-year-old Polish immigrant, had a good life planned ahead of him. In August 1901 he had been released from the army, after serving in the Philippine War. He had deposited his pay, all $275, in a local St. Helen's bank and settled on a homestead near Yankton among other Polish farmers. The day after Christmas he had breakfast with the Schieve family, whom he boarded with, put on his jacket and started walking to his homestead on the Bunker Hill Road. It was the last time anyone saw him alive.

The next day James K. McKay and O. D. Garrison, miners at the Bunker Hill Coal Mine, were walking to work on the Bunker Hill Road when they noticed tracks with blood in them.[1] Following the grisly trail, they found a man's body sitting on the ground leaning against a tree. The upper torso was covered with a jacket and the legs crossed over one another. According to a letter tucked in the jacket pocket, it was Joseph Schulkowski. He had been shot once in the back and once through the mouth. His money belt—thought to contain $150 in gold—and his gold watch were gone.

Suspicion immediately focused on the Schieve family, as they were the last to see Schulkowski alive. August Schieve was a friend of Joseph's, and the same age. He was well known in the area and had worked as the mail carrier between Houlton and Vernonia and as a teamster in St. Helens.[2] The newspapers emphasized the fact that his mother was an inmate of the Oregon State Insane Asylum.[3]

August Schieve was arrested on December 28 and charged with the murder of Joseph Schulkowski. On January 4, Columbia County Sheriff R. S. Hattan took the road of caution and transferred Schieve to Portland where he was confined in the Multnomah County jail until his trial started on May 14 in St. Helens.

The Columbia County Grand Jury was convened and witnesses were called to testify. Witnesses included Sheriff R. S. Hattan, Julius Floeter, E. T. Gore, Mrs. Frank Gliniecki, A. King, James Spense, C. H. Briggs, Gus Sandberg, W. W. Blakeley, Frank George, Gus Bus, E. C. Dalton, Fred Watkins, H. P. Ford, A. F. Leonard, J. L. Lamberson, August G. Spexarth, Doctor H. R. Cliff, J. B. Godfrey, W. A. Wood, and Joseph Nitch.

James McKay and O. D. Garrison testified about finding the body,

Morning Astorian, July 3, 1902
August Schieve

while a neighbor, Joseph Sobieski testified that Schulkowski visited the Schieve family that Christmas. Doctor Edwin Ross was called to testify about a letter addressed to him that was found in Schulkowski's coat pocket. The young man had just returned from fighting in the Philippine War and the letter requested an exam to qualify him for a pension. He must have been permanently injured in some way.

It took three days and nearly 100 candidates to select the jury. The twelve chosen were Homer Bennett, O. J. Bryant, W. B. Colvin, G. C. Daywatt, C. M. Graham, William Horsapple, W. C. Lee, T. J. Popham, W. H. Smith, J. M. Van, Jared Wilson, and Henry Kratz, foreman.[4] Thomas McBride was the judge and W. T. Vaughn of Portland was Schieve's lawyer. Harrison Allen was the Columbia County District Attorney.

Brothers of the defendant, Adam and Adolph, both testified that August left the house riding a white horse and carrying his Winchester rifle shortly after Schulkowski left, but returned for dinner at 12:30 p.m. An affidavit signed by his sister, Eva Zeller, was introduced into evidence on the tenth day. In her grand jury testimony she had put her X on the affidavit saying her brother had returned home later than that. However, when she was cross-examined by Defense Attorney Vaughn, she denied ever signing the paper. She testified that she had been "plied with liquor before making the affidavit and that she might have been forced to make her mark and sign it."[5]

Joseph was the only one in the family who could read or write. The family spoke very little English, and instead spoke their native Polish language at home.

Twenty-two witnesses testified. August Schieve appeared on his own behalf. He denied killing Schulkowski and maintained that it was impossible for him to have done so as the crime was committed four miles from his home and he couldn't have returned in time to eat dinner at 12:30.

The prosecution didn't have to work very hard to create confusion and distrust about the Schieve family's testimony. The Winchester rifle belonging to Schieve was identified as the weapon that killed Schulkowski.

Sheriff Hattan's testimony was very damaging. "I found an empty 32-20 Winchester shell about eighteen feet from where the body lay. I believe the defendant had ridden ahead of the deceased and tied his house in the brush near the road. He then concealed himself behind a thick screen of cedar boughs and waited for his victim. Schulkowski was shot first in the left side, the shell extracted from the gun, and the second shot fired after Schulkowski had fallen."[6]

Fifth District Attorney Harrison Allen was also able to connect white horse hairs and the size of the hoof prints found at the death site to a horse Schieve frequently rode. The newspapers compared him to Sherlock Holmes as he followed the circumstantial evidence from the crime site to the accused murderer. From one witness to the next he tracked Schieve from his home to the murder and back again. Pages from a book, *Reveries of a Bachelor* were found in both the victim's and the defendant's pockets. After the defense testimony was finished the jury traveled out to Bunker Hill Road and visited the place Schulkowski was murdered.

Fifteen days into the trial, the jury retired to a small room to decide its verdict. Fourteen hours later, on Sunday, May 25, the jurors returned with a verdict of "guilty of murder in the first degree." On Saturday, May 31 the parties convened in the courtroom and Judge Thomas A. McBride sentenced August Schieve to hang on Wednesday, July 2, 1902.[7]

Many county residents, including Sheriff Hattan, signed a petition requesting Shieve's sentence be commuted to life imprisonment. Governor Geer refused to interfere.[8] Two local carpenters, A. H. George and William Wellington built the 16-foot-tall stockade wall next to the county jail.[9] The hanging scaffold, built directly in front of the little fir tree between the courthouse and the jail, was ready by July 2 for the 23-year-old convict.

The morning of the hanging, Schieve ate a hearty meal of fried chicken. Reverend Lew Davies of the Scappoose Methodist Episcopal Church had baptized Schieve a few days before the hanging and accompanied the condemned up the steps.[10] Reverend C. A. Priessing and Reverend. F. H. Lange, pastors of the Portland German Methodist Episcopal Church, also accompanied the condemned.

Carl Schieve, the young man's uncle, stayed by his side as he climbed the scaffold steps and waited beside him throughout the event. Even though it was raining, over 250 people witnessed the execution, including the condemned man's father and brother who watched from the jail window.[11] Only men presenting engraved invitations were allowed into the stockade enclosure. The twelve witnesses chosen to observe the execution for the state were A. B. Dillard, W. A. Miles, George A. Hall, Martin White (elected sheriff from 1904-1911), J. B. Godfrey, also a witness at the trial, L. W. VanDyke, Washington Mudele, E. Seffert, F. M. Thorp, H. Mirgus, John Gilmore, and R. H. Mitchell.[12]

Before they brought Schieve out of his jail cell, Sheriff Hattan climbed the scaffold and addressed the crowd. He told the crowd that he believed Schieve was guilty but was not mentally responsible for his actions.[13]

The night before the hanging Schieve promised Sheriff Hattan that he would make a "clean breast of it" before his death. Apparently he changed his mind because in broken English he swore he was innocent of the crime. He was prepared to die and expected to go to a better world. He urged his listeners to live better lives and hoped to meet them in the next world. He had no ill will against anyone and bid good-bye to his friends. Then he handed a white silk handkerchief to his Uncle before they strapped his hands. At 12:05 the young man's arms and legs were tied and he spoke his last words. As the sheriff tightened the noose around his neck he begged him "have that knot hard."[14] The black cap was pulled over his head and at 12:16 p.m. he was pronounced dead by Doctors W. K. Haviland of Portland, R. J. Pilkington of Astoria, A. P. McLaren of Rainier, and H. R. Cliff of St. Helens.[15] His was the first, last and only hanging in Columbia County.

After the execution, the wood used to build the board fence was torn down and used to build a new woodshed behind the courthouse.[16] In a shocking turn of events, on his deathbed August Schieve's father confessed to the killing of Joseph Schulkowski.[17]

References

City of Portland Death Index, 1881-1905, Oregon State Archives, Salem, Oregon.

Columbia County History, Vol. 4, 1965, p. 48.

"Major Crimes Committed in Columbia County." *Columbia County History*, Vol. 2, 1962.

Morning Astorian (Astoria, Oregon) July 3, 1902, July 4, 1902,

Morning Oregonian (Portland, Oregon) December 29, 1901, December 31, 1901, May 18, 1902, May 23, 1902, May 24, 1902, July 2, 1902, July 3, 1902.

Oregon Death Index, 1903-98, Oregon State Archives, Salem, Oregon.

Oregon Mist (St. Helens, Oregon) May 30, 1902, June 6, 1902, June 27, 1902, July 3, 1902, July 4, 1902.

Oregon State Board of Health, Certificate of Death for Adolffene Schieve, #806, Oregon State Archives, Salem, Oregon.

State of Oregon v. August Schieve, Columbia County Circuit Court Case File, July 10, 1902, Columbia County Courthouse, St. Helens, Oregon.

Chapter 41 notes

1 *Morning Oregonian* (Portland, Oregon) May 18, 1902.
2 Ibid.
3 *Morning Oregonian*, 3 July 1902. I am unable to verify this. There is no record of any Schieve being admitted to the Oregon Insane Asylum. The July 2 *Oregonian* says that his mother had been in the Oregon Insane Asylum since he was a little boy. The December 31, 1901, *Oregonian* says that his mother was sent to the Insane Asylum several months earlier.
4 *Morning Oregonian*, May 18, 1902.
5 *Morning Oregonian*, May 24, 1902.
6 *Morning Oregonian*, May 23, 1902.
7 *Oregon Mist* (St. Helens, Oregon) June 6, 1902.
8 *Morning Astorian* (Astoria, Oregon) July 4, 1902.
9 *Oregon Mist*, June 27, 1902.
10 Ibid.
11 *Morning Astorian*, July 3, 1902.
12 State of Oregon v. August Schieve, Columbia County Circuit Court Case File, July 10, 1902, Columbia County Courthouse, St. Helens, Oregon.
13 *Morning Oregonian*, July 2, 1902.
14 *Morning Astorian,* July 3, 1902.
15 *Morning Oregonian*, July 2, 1902.
16 *Oregon Mist*, June 27, 1902.
17 "Major Crimes in Columbia County", *Columbia County History*, Vol. 2, 1962, p. 51. I have not been able to verify this. He may have said this out of bitterness at his son's death or it may have been the truth.

Chapter Forty-Two

State of Oregon v. A. L. Belding 1903

Alfred Lester Belding had been waiting for this day, July 11, 1902, to arrive for months. A few moments earlier he had received word that his wife, Sylvia Maude Belding, her parents and her new lover, George "Gyp" Woodward, were together at Lemuel and Deborah McCroskey's home. Carefully, he loaded a Smith and Wesson pistol and a Colt revolver and at 9 p.m. walked to the small house on Fifth and Flanders Street. On the porch he met his son, six year-old Eddie Belding and talked to him for a few minutes, before sending him inside to go to bed.

Just as Eddie scampered into the house Gyp Woodward stood in the doorway and confronted Belding. Belding knew Woodward was Maude's lover and with her parent's blessing was getting ready to file for divorce. Before Woodward could say anything, Belding drew his Colt revolver and shot the man in the chest. Maude, startled at the sound of the shot, came out into the hallway and saw Belding. Before she could run, he shot her through the heart. His 25-year-old wife died instantly.[1] Belding walked down the hall, met Maude's mother, Deborah McCroskey, age 61, and again, with one shot killed another victim. Only one person remained—Lemuel McCroskey, his father-in-law. Lemuel had seen Belding shoot his wife and pulled his own pistol, getting at least one shot off before Belding shot him three times. One bullet passed through his left arm, another nicked his neck and another hit him in the side. Belding didn't know it at the time, but the last shot would have killed McCroskey except it hit the man's watch and ricocheted off to the side.

Never worrying a minute about the terrified little boy hiding in his room, Belding left the house and walked across the street into the Lake Charles Saloon and telephoned the Portland Police, told them what he had done and offered to wait there until someone arrived. In the meantime, he ordered a drink for himself and another for a friend he recognized there.

When the police arrived Belding voluntarily offered his guns and confessed to killing all four people. Later, he was furious to discover Lemuel McCroskey wasn't dead, just severely wounded. The 60-year-old eventually recovered enough to testify against his son-in-law at the trial.

Lester Belding and Maud McCroskey were married in 1895 when she was 17 years old and Belding was 23. Their son, Edward Lester Oliver Belding, was born a year later on September 27, 1895.[2]

Multnomah County District Attorney George E. Chamberlain (later to serve as Oregon's governor and U. S. senator) was in charge of the prosecution. He decided to try Belding for the murder of Deborah A. McCrosky, his mother-in-law, first. The trial started on September 9, 1902. The most difficult time in the whole trial was when Belding's six-year old son, Eddie, testified how his father fired three shots at him as he ran screaming away.[3] The twelve men chosen for the jury were John Bird, Owen Carraher, Philip Holbrook, N. A. Jensen, Sam M. Lacy, E. B. Madden, George Robertson, James Shaunessy, F. M. Sutford, Isaac S. Thomas, William M. Taylor, and John Winters.[4]

Dan R. Murphy, Belding's attorney, pled Belding not guilty by reason of insanity. Those testifying at the trial included Portland City police officer Bailey who arrested Belding, P. A. Foster, a black barber who was standing on the sidewalk and saw Belding shoot Gyp Woodward, and Detective Frank Snow, who caused a mild sensation when he pulled out his loaded pistols in the crowded courtroom. Detective Snow recalled seeing Belding smoking in the opium dens several times in the recent past. Doctor Harry Lane was the last person to testify and to the defendant's disappointment, he testified that he didn't believe Belding was insane at the time of the murders.[5] Barely an hour after the jury left the courtroom they returned with a verdict of "guilty in the first degree."

On September 26, 1902 Lester Belding, age 31, was sentenced to hang on October 31 by circuit court Judge M. C. George.[6] A few days before the scheduled event, Multnomah County Sheriff Storey came out with a novel idea. He proposed to set up a paid subscription list for the benefit of Eddie Belding, the soon-to-be orphan now living at the Boys and Girls Aid Society. Members of the public wanting to attend the hanging would pay $5 each to receive an invitation to the execution and the proceeds would go for the child's support. The sheriff withdrew his proposal when various citizens expressed disapproval of the idea. Instead, the execution remained private with only officials and reporters being allowed to view the event.

Belding's attorney, Dan R. Murphy, quickly filed an appeal, which delayed the execution. There wasn't much chance of Belding escaping punishment as the district attorney still had two murder indictments against Belding in reserve.

Meanwhile, Belding sat in the Multnomah County Jail and waited.

Morning Oregonian, March 27, 1903
Alfred L. Belding.

After a few months his bravado vanished and he started regretting his past indiscretions and started yearning for freedom. He hatched a plot to escape involving a gullible young lady by the name of Cora Dawson, who was known as Belding's long time mistress. Thinking that Belding was soon to hang and feeling sorry for him, the police guards rarely searched her and let her have close visiting privileges with the murderer. Belding sent a note to a friend with a released prisoner, a dope addict named "Spider," on December 28, 1902. Fortunately, Jailor Jackson noticed something was up and had the man intercepted by Portland Detectives Kerrigan and Frank Snow.

The friend was to be given $50 to buy guns and ammunition. He was to hide them in a safe place to wait for Belding's escape and give Cora another package containing red pepper and a pair of blackjacks, which she was to hide under her corset. When next she visited Belding she would blind the jailor with the red pepper, give Belding and George Smith, another murderer waiting in the jail, the blackjacks and they would escape to British Columbia. The sheriff's office was quickly notified of the plot and set police in place ready to capture the conspirators when Cora arrived.

Unfortunately, The *Morning Oregonian* reported the plot early and scared off the conspirators. The rival Portland newspaper, The *Oregon Daily Journal*, was aware of the plot and had agreed to print the news after the conspirators were arrested. On December 31, 1902,

The *Daily Journal* printed the entire contents of Belding's note (omitting the name of the friendly conspirator) detailing the plot.

However, Belding hadn't bothered to tell Cora about his plans. When he was confronted with the note he laughed and maintained it was all a joke meant to encourage his friends to give him money to buy extra comforts in jail. It had the opposite effect. Cora left Portland for San Francisco the next day and reportedly married soon after.[7] Belding's few remaining friends decided to terminate their relationships in case he tried to implicate them in some other scheme. In the last month of his life he was lonely and scared as he read the Bible and experienced a spiritual conversion.

Belding's appeal was denied and on January 29, 1903 the Supreme Court notified Multnomah County that the verdict was affirmed. Belding was sentenced to hang on February 20 but the governor granted a thirty-day reprieve.

On March 27 Belding finally faced his last day. He spent his last hours conferring with Father Gartland, a Catholic priest. At 6:22 a.m. Sheriff William Storey unlocked the cell door and asked Belding if he would listen to the reading of the warrant.

"I waive its reading," Belding said.

"Will you have anything to say on the gallows?" asked the Sheriff.

"I care to say nothing," he replied.

After Belding was taken from the jail three cuffs were found in his cell with a long message written on them to his sister and her husband. Removable cuffs and collars were used in those days to keep dress shirts looking clean and new. In the letter he declared, "She (his late wife) was made a tool of by designing people. Then why should I not prefer to see her in her grave than know that she was living in shame?"[8]

The scaffold was the same one Wade and Dalton had been executed on a year earlier. The scaffold was arranged so that the body would fall straight down for five feet and remain suspended about two feet above the ground. No one knew who really sprung the trap because three ropes were fastened in such a way that no one could tell which rope really controlled the deadly trapdoor. Each rope was held by a different man and, as the signal from the sheriff was given, all pulled together. Two traps had been built into the scaffold so Wade and Dalton could be hanged simultaneously.[9] Belding was led to the trapdoor on the right facing the spectators. After his arms and legs were secured the sheriff again asked if Belding had anything to say. Again Belding refused. Just before Sheriff Storey pulled the black cap over his head, Father Gartland reached up and pulled a small silver cross out of Belding's pocket.

The Father raised the small cross to Belding's lips and said, "In Jesus."

"In Jesus," Belding repeated.

At 6:30 a.m. the trapdoor opened and Belding fell hard through the hole. Unfortunately he didn't fall straight through and bounced a little as he went. He hit the side of his head on the edge of the trapdoor just before he died.

Seventeen minutes later the murderer was pronounced dead. Before an hour passed he was buried in Calvary Cemetery.[10]

The authorities had issued an invitation to the local medical students to witness the execution and all present and possible students answered the invitation. As Belding

Oregon State Sheriffs' Association
Multnomah County
Sheriff W. A. Story

swung at the end of the rope Doctor Littlefield invited the medical students to come forward and listen to the poor man's heart slowly come to a halt. Instantly he was pushed, shoved and jostled as students clamored to get close enough to listen. Nearly 250 people witnessed the execution and shortly after the body was removed someone mounted the scaffold and cut down the hangman's rope. He cut it into little pieces and after filling his pockets threw them into the crowd below, nearly causing a riot as men scrambled to catch the gruesome mementos.[11]

The official execution witnesses were W. N. Chambers, Doctor P. S. Langworthy, C. Minsinger, Emil Gluloch, Doctor T. D. Perkins, Fred T. Merrill, W. R. Cody, H. Smith, Joseph L. Reed, Richard Meilke, George H. Torgler and T. W. Hollister.[12]

Little Eddie Belding was sent to live with Mr. and Mrs. Ed Nodine, Belding's sister and brother-in-law.

A trusty made the final comment as he watched the hanging from the jail. " It's hard enough to croak when you don't know it's coming, ain't it?' said the trusty. "But it's skitterish when a fellow wakes up in the morning and knows that at the same time the next day he'll be a dead one."[13]

References

1895 Oregon State Census, Multnomah County, Oregon.

City of Portland Birth Index, Oregon State Archives, Salem, Oregon.

City of Portland Death Index, 1881-1905, Oregon State Archives, Salem, Oregon.

Humbird, Jim. "When Hangings Were a Major Pastime." *Oregonian* (Portland, Oregon) September 3, 1939.

Morning Oregonian (Portland, Oregon) March 27, 1903, March 28, 1903.

Oregon Daily Journal (Portland, Oregon) September 9, 1902, September 10, 1902, September 11, 1902, September 12, 1902, September 24, 1902, October 18, 1902, October 20, 1902, October 27, 1902, October 28, 1902, December 31, 1902, March 26, 1903, March 27, 1903.

State of Oregon v. A. L. Belding, No. 5934, File No. 03343, Journal entry: Vol. 15, p. 462, Oct. 22, 1902, Oregon Supreme Court Appeals file, Oregon State Archives, Salem, Oregon.

Chapter 42 notes

1 City of Portland Death Index, 1881–1905, Oregon State Archives, Salem, Oregon.

2 City of Portland Birth Index, Oregon State Archives, Salem, Oregon.

3 *Oregon Daily Journal* (Portland, Oregon) September 11, 1902.

4 *Oregon Daily Journal*, September 10, 1902.

5 Doctor Lane was Portland mayor from 1905-9 and U.S. Senator from 1913-17.

6 State of Oregon v. A. L. Belding, No. 5934, File No. 03343, Journal entry: Vol. 15, p. 462, Oct. 22, 1902, Oregon Supreme Court Appeals file, Oregon State Archives, Salem, Oregon.

7 *Morning Oregonian* (Portland, Oregon) March 27, 1903.

8 *Oregon Daily Journal*, March 27, 1903.

9 *Morning Oregonian*, March 27, 1903.

10 *Morning Oregonian*, March 28, 1903.

11 *Oregon Daily Journal*, March 27, 1903.

12 Ibid.

13 *Oregon Daily Journal*, March 26, 1903

Chapter Forty-Three

State of Oregon v. Edward Elliot Lyons 1903

The hanging of Edward Lyons was one of the fastest pieces of justice in nineteenth century Oregon history. It was only seventy-one days from the day the bullet flew to the day the scaffold trapdoor opened. The prisoner had a working knowledge of the Bible and garnered some sympathy when his last words were, "God forgive you people, for you know not what you do."[1]

It all started on July 6, 1902, when Elliot Lyons got involved with a group of men who stole two horses in Jackson County from Frank M. Ferguson. Jackson County issued a warrant for his arrest on December 19, 1902. Lane County Sheriff William Withers knew that Lyons' parents, wife and siblings lived at Walton on the Siuslaw River about thirty miles west of Eugene and figured Lyons would return there. Withers was 43 years old and was well respected by everyone who knew him. It was dusk on the evening of February 5, 1903, when Sheriff Withers and two deputies arrived at the home of Lyons' parents. Withers ordered Deputy C. W. Cornelius and Constable Jack Smith to guard the back door. What happened in the next few minutes is somewhat confusing.

Sheriff Withers entered the front door and stepped into a very dark sitting room with no light or lamps except what emanated from a feeble fireplace. Some sources say Elliot Lyons was in the sitting room with the rest of the family and some sources say he was farther back in the kitchen. In any case a struggle ensued and in the confusion Lyons made a fatal decision. Both his parents immediately started yelling and begging the sheriff to have pity on their son. Lyons heard the racket from the kitchen where he was sitting with his pregnant wife and ran down the hallway leading to the front door. Withers was holding his gun in his right hand and grabbed Lyons with his left, all the while demanding the man surrender before someone got hurt. Mrs. Lyons was behind her husband and in trying to help him knocked the gun out of the sheriff's hand. Lyons pulled a 38-caliber pistol out of his pants and fired. The bullet hit the sheriff in the neck and lodged in the spinal column. Lyons ran out the front door and escaped heading east through the mud, snow and timber toward Eugene. Sheriff Withers died thirty-six hours later. Withers and Lyons had at one time been friends, and may have been related. The shooting wasn't planned or premeditated. Even Frank Withers, his son, thought that the shooting was more of an accident than a murder.[2]

A $1,000 reward was offered for the killer's capture. Four days later, Lyons was recognized in Creswell where he was trying to board a freight train and arrested peacefully. He had spent the last four days staggering around Lane County in the freezing cold with nothing to eat. Eight men shared the reward.[3]

Elliot Lyons was a familiar figure in Lane County. He had been a Deputy sheriff in 1896 under Sheriff A. J. Johnson when he was caught stealing a $10 gold coin (eagle) paid by G. W. Kirk for his taxes. He served time in the Oregon Penitentiary from March 14, 1897 to August 4, 1897, for larceny.[4] In that case, Governor Lord had shown pity on the man and pardoned him six months early. Here he was, six years older, but not much wiser.

On March 2, the Lane County Grand Jury handed down an indictment for first-degree murder against Elliot Lyons. His wife was also arrested as an accessory but her attorney, James K. Weatherford of Albany, got her released on a $1,000 bail bond.[5] Because of her pregnancy the charges were eventually dropped.

George B. Dorris was appointed by the county to defend Lyons. District Attorney George M. Brown and Deputy District Attorney Lawrence T. Harris headed the prosecution.[6] The trial lasted one day—March 4. Twenty minutes after the jury left, it returned and handed its guilty verdict to Judge Hamilton.[7] The jurors were W. F. Gilstrap, D. McCrady, Amos Wilkins, Walter Blachly, Jerry Atkinson, Thomas Brown, J. R. Sellers, H. J. Hillegas, Lincoln Taylor, Marion Smith, J. D. Campbell, and W. H. Kay.[8]

At 10 a.m. on March 6, Lyons stood in front of the courtroom with his hat in his hand ready to hear his sentence, and Judge J. W. Hamilton asked if he had anything to say.

"I don't know why I fired the shot." He shifted his weight from one foot to another and grimaced awkwardly over the words. "I hesitated a long time and he (Withers) ought to have seen my gun. I think Smith (Constable) is to blame," he frowned with his usual bitter expression and continued, "for he was standing at the back window and could not have helped from seeing me with the pistol. He ought to have come in and I wouldn't have fired. I . . . I didn't mean to do it."[9]

Judge Hamilton wasn't impressed with Lyons' excuse.

> *"It will not do for you to say that the crime was the fault of any other man or person. You said 'any person attempting to get the drop on you does not value his life,' or words to that effect. You took life under this circumstance and you alone are responsible . . . The sentence of this court is that on Friday, April 17 between the hours of 9 a.m. and 4 p.m. in the courtyard of the jail situated at the county seat of Lane County, Oregon witnessed by at least 12 bona fide citizens of the county, you hang by the neck until dead. May God have mercy on your soul."*[10]

Oregon State Sheriffs' Association
Lane County
Sheriff William Withers

Oregon State Sheriffs' Association
Elliot Lyons

The days quickly passed while Lyons waited in his jail cell. He spent considerable time studying his Bible and meeting with three local ministers. The morning of April 17, he ate a hearty breakfast of ham, eggs and coffee, dressed slowly and shaved carefully, leaving only his mustache, as usual. At 9:15 Sheriff Fisk unlocked the cell door and everyone prepared to leave the jail.

The procession leaving the jail consisted of the 37-year-old prisoner, Lane County Sheriff Fred Fisk, Deputy Harry Brown, Wallace Chamberlain, Shelton Jenkins, J. J. Elwood, John Jones and

$500 REWARD.

Sheriff's Office, Eugene, Feb. 5, 1903.

Arrest for assault with intent to kill and probably murder, description: Elliott Lyons, age about 38 years; height 5 feet, 8 inches; weight 165 pounds; complexion light; hair light brown or flaxen; blue eyes; dim cut scars on right index finger; cut scar back of right thumb; white scar outside of left elbow; cut scar first toe right foot; well built. May have darkened or blacked hair and eyebrows.

The above-described man shot and probably fatally wounded Sheriff W. W. Withers of Lane County, Oregon, on the evening of Feb. 5th, while the latter was endeavoring to arrest him on a warrant for horse stealing. I hold a warrant and want this man bad. Arrest and hold him and wire me. All information thankfully received.

FRED FISK, Deputy Sheriff, Lane Co., Oregon.

Oregon State Sheriffs' Association
Reward poster issued for Elliot Lyons.

Reverends H. A. Green and F. E. Billington.[11] In front of the gallows twelve men watched the execution and signed as witnesses on the death warrant. They included Michael Schneider, H. A. Vincent, R. M. Murphy, J. N. McPherson, M. F. Casteel, H. M. Milliorn, Fred B. Bellman, H. E. Underwood, John Stewart, L. N. Roney, J. M. Stafford, and I. P. Inman.[12]

Reverend Green spoke for Lyons as the black cap was pulled over his head and the hangman's knot was tightened around his neck.

"Mr. Lyons wishes to thank all his friends who have been so kind as to call upon him during his imprisonment, all relatives for their sympathy, and the officials who have shown him kind consideration. He has professed religion and is penitent. He has confessed his crime and may God receive his soul as it leaves this earth."

Doctor F. M. Day and Doctor D. A. Paine pronounced Lyons dead at 9:31a.m. His wife and brother, Benton Lyons, signed for the body after the hanging and he was buried at the Eugene I.O.O.F. Cemetery.

A week before the hanging Roy Hurlburt was arrested without incident on a farm north of Eugene on the charge of horse stealing. He was part of the gang that Lyons joined back in the fall of 1902 when the whole story began.

Seven years after the execution Ida J. (Lyons) Robertson wrote a letter to the Lane County clerk asking him to release Lyon's revolver, knife and any other property to Charles W. Lyons. Charles signed a receipt for the property.[13]

This was the second and last hanging in Lane County. Sheriff Withers was in charge of the hanging in 1899 when Claude Branton was hanged. No one ever thought another man would hang for Withers murder.

References

Baker, Dean. "Death by Hanging." *Register Guard* (Eugene, Oregon) April 4, 1976.

Daily Eugene Guard (Eugene, Oregon) March 3, 1903, March 6, 1903, March 16, 1903, April 17, 1903, April 18, 1903.

Maxwell, Ben. "Frontier Hangings Were Gala Occasions in Salem." *Capital Journal* (Salem, Oregon) January 30, 1952.

Oregon Journal (Portland, Oregon) April 16, 1903, April 17, 1903.

Oregonian (Portland, Oregon) April 9, 1903.

Oregon State Penitentiary Records, Inmate Case File #3804, E. E. Lyons, Oregon State Archives, Salem, Oregon.

"Scrapbook 310," p. 6, Oregon Historical Society, Portland, Oregon.

State of Oregon v. E. E. Lyons, Lane County Circuit Court Case Files, #3989, and #4989 Lane County Courthouse Archives, Eugene, Oregon.

State of Oregon v. Ida Lyons, Lane County Circuit Court Case File #4993, Lane County Courthouse Archives, Eugene, Oregon.

Chapter 43 notes

1 *Oregon Journal* (Portland, Oregon), April 17, 1903. This was only nine days longer than it took to hang Thomas Smith in 1866, 37 years earlier. It also tied with the time it took to hang Wade and Dalton in 1902.

2 Dean Baker, "Death by Hanging" *Register Guard* (Eugene, Oregon) April 4, 1976.

3 *Daily Eugene Guard* (Eugene, Oregon), March 16, 1903.

4 Oregon State Penitentiary Records, Inmate Case File #3804, E. E. Lyons, Oregon State Archives, Salem, Oregon.

5 *Daily Eugene Guard*, March 6, 1903.

6 Lawrence Harris was a member of the state house of representatives for many years and in 1905 was appointed circuit court judge for the second judicial district. In 1914 he was appointed associate justice of the Oregon Supreme Court.

7 *Daily Eugene Guard*, April 17, 1903.

8 State of Oregon v. E. E. Lyons, Lane County Circuit Court Case File #4989, Lane County Courthouse, Eugene, Oregon.

9 *Daily Eugene Guard*, March 6, 1903.

10 Ibid.

11 *Oregon Journal*, April 17, 1903.

12 State of Oregon v. E. E. Lyons, #4989.

13 Ibid.

Chapter Forty-Four

State of Oregon v. George Smith 1903

Being a black man on the western frontier wasn't an easy thing. By the time George Smith was born in 1873 Kansas, the Civil War was over and he was a free man. As a young man he didn't choose his friends wisely and on Monday, November 25, 1889 16-year old George and his pal, John Berry, were convicted of larceny in Multnomah County.

Smith and Berry were originally accused of "assault and robbery, and being armed with a dangerous weapon." Smith must have been an accomplice, rather than the main perpetrator, because Berry was sentenced to four years in the Oregon State Penitentiary and Smith sentenced to three. Smith was released on June 17, 1891.[1] He moved back to Portland where his mother, Mrs. E. Williams, and his sister lived. According to the 1900 Census there were 1,105 Blacks living in Oregon, or .27 percent of the state's population.[2]

The Portland *Oregonian* of July 1893 reported that Smith was a familiar figure in the jail and various courtrooms around the city. "All his troubles seem to arrive from the fact that he has a good-looking white wife, and he is very proud of her." While the couple was walking on Pine Street, a gentleman sitting on a nearby bench, M. Dougherty, remarked to his friend, "Well, what do you think about that?"[3] Smith was so incensed he pulled a knife and attacked the man. Bystanders pulled him off and assault charges were filed against him.

During the trial, Smith testified that he and Annie were married on May 17, 1900.[4] They moved around between Portland, Astoria and Spokane. Annie Smith previously had lived in a house of ill repute and, eventually she left Smith and returned to her old habits. The move was precipitated by Smith's involvement in the case of the State of Oregon vs. Gladisee. He was a witness for the state and the defendant hired another black man, Ed "Kansas" Potella, to harass Smith. Kansas started hanging around Annie and eventually persuaded her to leave Smith and move into a room over the Boston Saloon at Davis and Second Streets in the north end of Portland.

Oregon Daily Journal, June 5, 1903
George Smith

The different cultures and races mixed freely in the red-light section of Portland.[5] The district catered to prostitution, gambling, drinking and drugs of all kinds. Whether Annie was a prostitute during her marriage to Smith is unknown, but there is little doubt that Kansas was serving as her pimp after she left Smith's home.

Kansas caught Smith alone one evening and pistol-whipped him unconscious in the street. On August 21, 1902, Annie warned him that Kansas was looking to kill him. Smith bought passage on a steamer to Astoria and tried to persuade Annie to move with him but she refused. The next day Smith went to Annie's room, supposedly to give her some keys. As they stood talking in the doorway Smith spotted a man crouching behind a bureau and without thinking pulled his revolver and shot. In his panic he fled down the stairs, across the street and into the Sportsman Saloon.[6]

Unfortunately, for Smith, Carl Quall, a 19-year-old farmer from Minnesota, was sitting outside the employment office across the street from the Boston Saloon. He heard the pistol shot and a woman's scream. When Smith came running out, he followed him and gave directions to police officers Kitsmiller and Roberts.

The police immediately arrested Smith and took him to the Portland City Jail where they stashed him in the little cell next to Chief Dan McLaughlin's office called the "sweatbox." Besides being an uncomfortable place to stay, it was the most heavily guarded cell in the jail. Less than a year earlier Alonzo Tucker, a black man, had been lynched while being held in the Coos Bay jail.[7] Chief McLaughlin wanted no repetition of that in Portland.

The first confession was a rambling account of an unnamed "uncle" shooting Annie. Chief McLaughlin thought the story so unreasonable he put Smith back in the cell to think it over. After about fifteen minutes Smith asked to speak with the chief again.

"I want to tell you all the truth about that. I lied to you before. Now I want to tell you the whole truth."

"Go ahead and tell me."

"I want you to take me out of here into your office and I will tell you the truth." So the jailor escorted Smith into Chief McLaughlin's office where Deputy District Attorney John Manning and the Chief listened to the second confession.

"I want to tell you the whole truth about it. There was nobody in this thing but me. I went up there and talked to Annie and tried to get her to come home and she would not come and I shot her."

"Why did you do it, George?"

"She was gone away with another man and wouldn't come home with me."[8]

Anna Maytod Smith died on August 21, 1902. She had been born in Oregon and was only 30 years old.[9]

Smith, age 30, was held in the city jail until October 13, 1902, when his trial started. Charles A. Petrain and W. T. Hume were appointed to defend him. M. C. George was the presiding judge. George E. Chamberlain, Multnomah District Attorney (later elected Governor and asked to commute Smith's sentence) served as the prosecutor.[10] The twelve jurors were Chauncey Ball, William M. Cake Sr., Owen Carraher, A. M. Cummings, Norman Darling, Sam M. Lacy, John Landigan, Hans Larsen, James Shaunessy, F. M. Sutford, William M. Taylor, and J. Winters.[11]

Smith testified in his own defense and tried to persuade the jury that he shot in self-defense and accidentally killed Annie. That might have been easier to believe if Carl Quall hadn't testified that he overheard Smith threaten to "get some white person" the night before the murder and seen him the next day run away right after the shot was fired. For certain Kansas and Smith hated each other, but there seemed to be a lot of doubt that Smith was in "imminent danger" when he fired the fatal shot. Eight days later, the jury found George Smith guilty of murder in the first degree, and Judge M. C. George sentenced him to hang on Friday, December 19, 1902.[12]

Attorney Petrain filed an appeal to the Oregon Supreme Court, which postponed the hanging. In the appeal it was noted that Chauncey Ball, a juror at the trial, was so ill the last couple days of the trial that the jury reached a verdict in record time because they were afraid he'd die. He "was frequently attended by his physician . . . and was compelled to lie upon a lounge in the courtroom during the trial . . . and during the deliberation of the jury the said juror, Ball, was compelled to recline upon said lounge and unable to participate in the deliberation."[13]

Besides having an incompetent and ill juror, there was evidence of possible perjury. C. E. Thompson, a bartender, signed an affidavit saying he was sick and confined to bed during Smith's

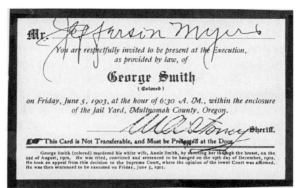

Oregon Historical Society
Invitation to the hanging of George Smith.

trial and didn't know his testimony was necessary. He refuted C. A. Quall's testimony that Smith had a pistol on August 22, the night before the murder. He remembers Smith being in the bar but did not see the gun or hear Smith threaten to kill anyone.

After due consideration the court denied the request and ruled in favor of the lower court. Smith was again sentenced to hang on June 5, 1903.[14] By then the new law limiting hangings to the penitentiary was in effect. Smith's case was the first to challenge it. Governor George Chamberlain signed the bill on February 17, 1903, and it went into effect on May 18, 1903. However, the closing section of the act had two new sentences added: "Any warrant issued prior to the taking effect of this measure, shall be executed by the Sheriff. This act shall not be construed to affect the execution of any warrant issued prior to the taking effect of this measure."[15]

The scaffold used to hang A. L. Belding was still in the jail yard so Sheriff William A. Storey had few preparations to make. He ordered a new 3/4-inch hemp rope made especially for the purpose and attached it to the scaffold. Three men were assigned to pull the three ropes inside the courthouse. Again no one knew who would really pull the rope attached to the trap.

While Smith waited in jail he kept busy doing a little twisting and tying a few knots as he knitted shawls and blankets for the wives and families of the jailors. Jailor D. D. Jackson told the newspaper reporters, "He has been here longer than any man that we have in the jail and he is one of the best prisoners we have had. He does not blame anyone for his trouble, but says that he brought it all upon himself."[16]

Governor Chamberlain refused to commute Smith's sentence and most people did not expect him to do so. He noted Smith had been in the penitentiary for assault with intent to rob, and said that if Smith had borne a good reputation there might be some reason for clemency in this case. He believed that "Smith had a mind, which would permit him to commit a crime of this nature, and that Smith deliberately murdered his wife because her affections had been estranged".[17]

At 6:30 a.m. on June 5, the jailhouse door opened and Smith walked out of his jail cell for the last time. He followed the sheriff and his deputies, brave and smiling up the scaffold steps and stood at military attention while his arms were tied behind his back. Besides Smith and Sheriff Storey, there were twelve other men seated on the scaffold: Reverend C. B. F. Moore of the Zion African Methodist Episcopal Church; Deputies Herman Schneider, Lou Harlow, Johnson and Stott; Sheriff Harvey Kimball Brown of Baker County; Sheriff Worth Houston of Linn County; Sheriff M. P. Burnett of Benton County; Sheriff Alfred H. Huntington of Baker County; Sheriff C. Sam Smith of Crook County; Oregon State Penitentiary Supt. James, and Guard Curtis.[18]

Certainly Smith had better manners than the men watching him. One reporter was appalled. "Those holding invitations to the hanging were admitted through the east entrance to the courthouse and had to show their cards before they were allowed to pass. The action of several before the gates leading into the scaffold pen were opened was far from manly. Curses, coarse jokes and bestial jibes were to be heard and the air reeked of tobacco smoke and drink-tainted breath. There were one or two who staggered."[19]

The twelve men assigned to the sheriff's jury were C. W. Cornelius, S. K. Hollister, W. R. Littlefield, W. S. Drake, A. T. Meyers, George Sunderland, Henry D. Griffin, John Cardano, E. M. Lance, R. O. Scott, P. P. Hiedel and F. W. Hollister.[20] Smith's body was laid in a coffin and immediately released to his mother. Deputy Sheriff Schneider gave portions of the rope to bystanders who wanted a little souvenir. Altogether it cost Multnomah County $650 to prosecute and hang George Smith.[21]

The spring of 1903 had been a busy year for Oregon's hangmen. Three murderers had challenged the law and lost.

References

Aaron, Louise. "This Was Portland." *Oregon Journal* (Portland, Oregon) January 26, 1958.

Bellesiles, Michael A. ed. *Lethal Imagination: Violence and Brutality in American History*. N.Y.: New York University Press, 1999.

Century Edition of the American Digest. A complete digest of all reported American cases from the earliest times to 1896, Vol. 26, St. Paul: West Publishing, 1901.

City of Portland Death Index, 1881-1905, Oregon State Archives, Salem, Oregon.

Humbird, Jim. "When Hangings Were A Major Pastime." *Oregonian* (Portland, Oregon) September 3, 1999.

McKanna, Clare V. *Homicide, Race and Justice in the American West, 1880-1920*. Phoenix: University of Arizona Press, 1997.

McLagan, Elizabeth. *A Peculiar Paradise*. Eugene: Georgian Press, 1980.

Morning Oregonian (Portland, Oregon) July 14, 1893, March 31, 1903, April 1, 1903, June 5, 1903.

Oregon Daily Journal (Portland, Oregon) June 5, 1903.

Oregon State Penitentiary Records, Inmate Case File #2274, George Smith, Oregon State Archives, Salem, Oregon.

State of Oregon v. George Smith, No. 5952, File No. 03446, Journal Entry: Vol. 15, p. 501, Feb. 9, 1902, Oregon Supreme Court Appeals file, Oregon State Archives, Salem, Oregon.

Chapter 44 notes

1 State of Oregon v. George Smith, No. 5952, File No. 03446, Journal Entry: Vol. 15, p. 501, February 9, 1902, Oregon Supreme Court Appeals file, Oregon State Archives, Salem, Oregon.

2 Elizabeth McLagan, *A Peculiar Paradise,* (Portland: Georgian Press, 1980) p. 185.

3 *Morning Oregonian* (Portland, Oregon) July 14, 1893.

4 State of Oregon v. George Smith.

5 Elizabeth McLagan, p. 91.

6 Clare V. McKanna, *Homicide, Race and Justice in the American West, 1880-1920* (Phoenix: University of Arizona Press, 1997) p. 55. "Interracial homicides involving black perpetrators and white victims can be divided into three basic categories: saloon-related fights, disputes involving women, and robberies."

7 Elizabeth McLagan, pp. 135-6.

8 Michael A. Bellesiles, ed, *Lethal Imagination: Violence and Brutality in American History*, N.Y.: (New York University Press, 1999) p. 301. "The Negro Would Be More Than an Angel to Withstand Such Treatment" by Jeffrey S. Adler. "African American men increasingly grew jealous of their lovers or enraged when relationships ended, and they murdered their lovers."

9 City of Portland Death Index, 1881-1905, Oregon State Archives, Salem, Oregon.

10 It's not often that the same man who prosecutes a criminal has the ultimate right to commute his sentence. Whatever his personal reasons for refusing to help Smith, his public reason was consistent with his past and future actions.

11 State of Oregon v. George Smith.

12 Ibid.

13 Ibid.

14 Ibid.

15 *Morning Oregonian*, April 1, 1903.

16 *Morning Oregonian*, June 5, 1903.

17 Ibid.

18 *Oregon Journal* (Portland, Oregon) June 5, 1903.

19 Ibid

20 State of Oregon v. George Smith.

21 *Oregon Journal,* June 5, 1903.

Chapter Forty-Five

State of Oregon v. Pleasant Armstrong 1904

Baker County Sheriff Harvey Kimball Brown had a big problem on his hands at 2 a.m. on March 2, 1903. At least 150 armed and masked ruffians had surrounded the county jail and were demanding the release of Pleasant Armstrong so they could lynch him.[1] Baker City had a long history of vigilante action but Brown was determined to keep such a thing from happening while he was sheriff.

Armstrong had shot his sweetheart, Minnie Ensminger, on December 25, 1902, and had been waiting in jail until he could be tried in the circuit court. Earlier that evening several anonymous phone calls warned Deputy Sheriff Snow that trouble was brewing and frantically they searched for a safe place they could stash Armstrong. At last they found the perfect location—the county clerk's vault. It was the size of a small room and once locked no one could get in, or out. While members of the lynch party searched the jail and courthouse, Sheriff Brown hid Armstrong inside the safe. The next day he hurriedly got an order from a judge and sent Armstrong to safety in Portland. For the first time in Baker County history "Judge Lynch" was denied his prey.

Sheriff Brown didn't protect Armstrong because he was innocent. Too many people saw Armstrong shoot the pretty teacher twice in the chest.[2]

Pleasant and Minnie first met in February 1900 and had become engaged. In the fall of 1902, while he was away working in the Maxwell Mine, Minnie wrote him a letter breaking their engagement, and saying, "that she never could become his wife in this world; that

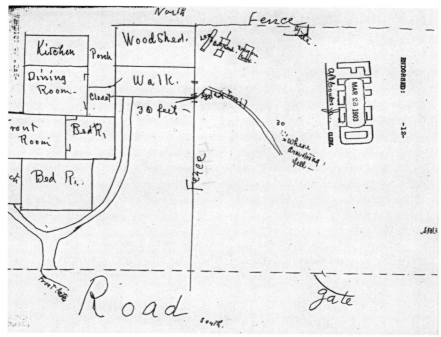

Exhibit A, State of Oregon v. Pleasant Armstrong
Map of house and property where Millie Ensminger was murdered.

she would rather die than go back on him."[3] Her parents were well known and respected in the North Powder area of Baker County and wanted more for their daughter than being the wife of a barely literate miner. When they asked her to end the relationship she honored their request.

Armstrong immediately quit his job and returned to Baker City where he had a friend purchase a .44 caliber Colt revolver for him on December 16. Knowing Minnie would be at Haines and attend the Redding Ranch Christmas Eve dance he decided to confront her there. That night he played his violin until 10 p.m. when he went into a back room and rested for a couple hours. With his black hair and dark eyes the 25-year-old was a handsome young man and his talent with the fiddle made him popular at parties. Minnie's sister, Blanche, spoke to him briefly when she handed him his overcoat just before he left the building ahead of Minnie and her family. Shortly after midnight on December 25, they left the dance and walked across the yard to their waiting sleigh.

Armstrong jumped out of the darkness just outside the gate nearly thirty feet from the party, and without saying a word to anyone, fired his Colt revolver. The first shot went through Minnie's chest and spun her around. The second entered her back and she crumpled to the ground with a scream of pain.[4] After he shot the girl, he attempted to kill himself, but only managed to gouge some hair and skin off his head. He was immediately arrested and jailed.

When asked why he shot her he said, "I loved this girl more than anyone else in the world. I loved her when I fired the shot. I entertained no hate or malice toward her. While I was laying on the lounge I meditated on self-destruction. I never thought of killing the girl. I don't know what made me kill the young lady. I tried to kill myself."[5] Minnie Ensminger died two days later on Saturday, December 27, 1902, after suffering intense pain.

Armstrong's lawyer, George J. Bentley, filed a request for a change of venue with Circuit Court Judge Robert Eakin (the same judge that signed the order sending Armstrong to Portland for safe-keeping after the lynching affair), but was denied. The actual trial started March 23, 1903. It took three days to choose a jury and Armstrong was returned from Portland with plenty of deputies guarding him. The twelve jurors chosen were Frank Jasper, L. P. Makinson, Henry Moody, W. A. Moore, Frank Geldness, James Fulp, George Gillett, Joe Wilson, Charles Marville, Albert Boyer, William Samples, and W. F. Cropp, foreman.[6]

Samuel White, the district attorney, and his assistant, A. B. Winfree, made a good case of premeditated murder against Armstrong.[7] He offered as evidence a map of the murder site and Armstrong's note, written December 21 from Rock Creek, Oregon asking Minnie to meet him before December 25.[8] Defense Attorney Bentley tried his best to convince the jury that Armstrong's mind became unhinged when Minnie broke their engagement and, at best, he was guilty of second-degree murder. Armstrong's tearful testimony on March 27 had nearly everyone in the courtroom in tears. He swore that he didn't mean to kill her. He had meant only to say good-bye to her and shoot himself.

The jury began its deliberations the evening of Friday, March 27. It was out all night and the next morning requested a meeting with the judge. They wanted to know what "constituted reasonable doubt", because one of the jurors was holding out for second-degree murder.[9] On Saturday, March 28, at 1:30 p.m., the jury returned a verdict of first-degree murder against Armstrong.[10] Maybe it was the fact that he shot her twice point-blank that convinced the jury to believe his actions and not his words. Judge Eakin sentenced him to hang on May 8, 1903. Defense Attorney Bentley immediately filed an appeal for a new trial with the Oregon Supreme Court, which postponed the hanging.

Meanwhile Sheriff Brown had his hands full in Baker County. In the middle of July a strange woman, eventually identified as Mrs. Cora Rockwell, a Christian Scientist, began hounding the authorities with a wild story concerning Pleasant Armstrong. She insisted that she was a member of the U. S. Secret Service and had evidence that someone other than Armstrong had killed Minnie Ensminger. Instead, Armstrong was under the hypnotic influence of this "red-handed murderer" and his gang. She believed that the Blue Beard family was responsible for this and many other murders and disappearances in Baker County.[11]

Oregon State Sheriffs' Association
Pleasant Armstrong

When Armstrong was told about the woman he ordered Deputy Bill Lachner to "keep that woman out of here with her dope dreams. I want some more of that tea, Bill."

The Supreme Court denied the appeal and Armstrong stood in front of Judge Eakin again on December 12, 1903. There was some confusion about the change in the law setting the place of the execution. Judge Eakin gave a written opinion similar to the one in Belding's case—the law in effect at the time of the murder would be applied. That meant Armstrong would hang in Baker County instead of at the penitentiary. The court set January 22, 1904, as the big day.

The newspapers covered Armstrong's last twenty-four hours minute by minute. His two brothers arrived from Waltsburg, Washington to see him about 10:30 a.m. the day before the hanging, and they visited together for the last time. That night he played his violin for two hours just as he had for every previous evening. In the months before his hanging he enjoyed turkey dinners, cigars, and visits from ministers, reporters and women.[12]

The scaffold was built in the center of the west side of the enclosure at the south side of the courthouse. The enclosure was thirty-two feet wide by sixty feet long. The three-foot square trap door was situated in the middle of the ten by twelve-foot floor of the scaffold.[13] A network of ropes was attached to the trigger, hiding the identity of the person pulling the real rope. A new rope with a hangman's noose at

Gallows at Baker City used to hang Pleasant Armstrong.

the end was stretched and draped over the joist or scantling. The slightest stretching or giving of a rope prolonged the suffering of the criminal. Even a second of additional suffering was too much, so it was "customary to stretch the rope to the full limit so that when the drop falls it snaps the victim's neck like a cable".[14] Although the sheriff gave out engraved invitations to anyone who requested one, there were many people in the enclosure who did not have invitations.

At 7 a.m. Armstrong stood on the scaffold ready to pay for his crime. He seemed more cheerful than anyone else standing in the cold mud and pouring rain.[15] Sheriff Brown, Deputy Sheriff William, Deputy J. Lachnor and Oregon Penitentiary Superintendent C. W. James and Father Olivetti preceded Armstrong up the thirteen steps of the scaffold. Behind him stood Multnomah County Sheriff William Storey, Union County Deputy Sheriff Johnson, Malheur County Sheriff James E. Laurence, Washington County, Idaho Sheriff Adams, La Grande City Marshal Louis Rayburn, Multnomah County Deputy Sheriff Snider and Colonel James A. Painting of Baker City.

Deputy Jesse Snow summoned men from the bystanders to serve as witnesses. They included A. B. Davis, James York, Sr., H. K. Fisher, D. L. Moomaw, H. E. McCulloch, J. T. Parkinson, C. F. Slade, George C. Hyde, H. A. Mitchell, A. T. Merwin, J. S. Kenyon and G. W. Vanderwall.[16]

The execution proceeded as planned and Armstrong died at exactly 7:04 a.m. Souvenir hunters surged over the scaffold after the body was removed. A man from Rock Creek was the only one to get a piece of the rope before a deputy rescued it.[17]

Armstrong's dead body was taken to the local undertaker, Fred Eppinger, and throngs of people filed through to view the remains. He was buried the next day in the Baker City Catholic Cemetery.

The event testified to the law's ability to bring a criminal to justice in Baker County. Outraged communities no longer had to depend on "Judge Lynch" to ensure righteous punishment, but instead needed only to wait for the law to take its course.

Oregon State Sheriffs' Association
Baker County Sheriff
H. K. Brown

References

Andrews, Wesley. "Baker City in the Eighties." *Oregon Historical Quarterly*, Vol. 50, June 1949.

Haskell, Scottie, Baker City, Oregon, provided copy of invitation to hanging.

Herald (Baker City, Oregon) April 21, 1903, August 24, 1903, April 1, 1903, April 29, 1903, May 1, 1903, July 18, 1903, July 26, 1903, July 28, 1903, November 20, 1903, November 24, 1903, November 29, 1903, January 18, 1904, January 21, 1904, January 22, 1904.

Oregonian (Portland, Oregon) March 28, 1903, March 29, 1903, March 30, 1903, April 1, 1903.

State of Oregon v. Pleasant Armstrong, No. 6071, File No. 03600, Journal entry: Vol. 16, p. 66, January 20, 1904, Oregon Supreme Court Appeals file, Oregon State Archives, Salem, Oregon.

The History of Baker County Baker County Historical Society, Baker City: Taylor Publishing Company, 1986.

Chapter 45 notes

1 *Herald* (Baker City, Oregon) January 22, 1904.

2 *The History of Baker County*, Baker County Historical Society (Baker City: Taylor Publishing Company, 1986).

3 *Oregonian* (Portland, Oregon) March 28, 1903.

4 *Herald*, January 22, 1904.

5 Ibid.

6 State of Oregon v. Pleasant Armstrong, No. 6071, File No. 03600, Journal entry: Vol. 16, p. 66, Jan. 20, 1904, Oregon Supreme Court Appeals file, Oregon State Archives, Salem, Oregon.

7 *Herald*, January 22, 1904.

8 State of Oregon v. Pleasant Armstrong, Exhibits A and B.

9 *Oregonian*, March 29, 1903.

10 *Herald*, January 22, 1904.

11 *Herald*, July 18, 1903, and July 28, 1903.

12 Wesley Andrews, "Baker City in the Eighties", *Oregon Historical Quarterly*, Vol. 50, June 1949, p. 96.

13 *Herald*, January 21, 1904.

14 Ibid.

15 Herald, January 22, 1904.

16 Ibid.

17 Ibid.

Chapter Forty-Six

State of Oregon v. Daniel Norman Williams 1905

The last case is the most famous case of all. It set a legal standard still cited today by appeal lawyers around the United States. It challenged the way the legal system viewed expert medical testimony, the definition of "corpus delicti," and the way defense lawyers conducted their defense cases. Yet, the case would never have gone to court if a clerk in the U.S. District Attorney's office hadn't remembered a beautiful young woman filing on a homestead claim.

Late in 1900, Norman Williams presented a letter to the clerk in the U.S. Attorney's office. It was dated June 23, 1900, and allegedly signed by Alma Nesbitt relinquishing her homestead claim. Giving up the claim allowed Williams to buy the land bordering his. The land office didn't know it at the time but, because of an inaccurate survey, William's house had accidentally been built on Alma's land. The office clerk, remembering the pretty lady, told U. S. Attorney for the District of Oregon, John H. Hall, that he suspected the letter was a fraud and Hall sent for the original claim. After comparing the two signatures it was obvious that someone other that Alma Nesbitt had signed the note.[1] On October 29, 1903, the federal grand jury heard testimony from U.S. Attorney John H. Hall. The subsequent indictment against Norman Williams started the investigation into Alma's disappearance.

Louise Nesbitt, age 69, and her daughter, Alma Nesbitt, age 31, had been missing since the winter of 1900.[2] Louise's son and Alma's brother, George Nesbitt, happened to see a copy of the federal indictment published in the *Oregonian* on October 29, 1903, which stated

Norman Williams was wanted for forging the name of Alma Nesbitt to a homestead relinquishment.[3] George had kept several letters from Williams stating that his mother and sister had disappeared without a trace and he didn't know where they were. Even though both women had been prolific letter writers to friends and family, no one had heard from them since March 8, 1900. It seemed strange to him that Williams was now trying to present a letter from Alma dated almost four months later. He decided to go on a trip to investigate.

On February 7, 1904, George Nesbitt, of Kirkham, Iowa, arrived in Hood River, Oregon and made arrangements to go see Norman Williams' property with Albert K. Stranahan, the local livery stable owner.[4] What they found, four years after the women disappeared, was a revelation. Inside a small shed they dug up the soft earth of a grave-shaped depression containing chunks of long gray hair and a piece of scalp with long brunette hair still attached. Taking the hair, a piece of broken pottery and the blood-soaked gunnysacks back to Hood River, George Nesbitt made a long overdue visit to the office of Wasco County District Attorney, Frank Menefee.

Menefee was a meticulous, tenacious, and shrewd litigator. Conferring with U. S. Attorney John Hall in Portland, and a host of other Hood River authorities, Menefee put together the strings of a circumstantial case against Williams ranging from Nebraska, to a lonely Hood River homestead, up to British Columbia, back to Portland, and finally to Bellingham, Washington. It was a snowball of a case: starting out the size of a fist, the evidence kept sticking together until it was the size of a house and its momentum was overwhelming.

After putting it all together, Menefee presented his case to the Wasco County grand jury, which returned an indictment on April 27, 1904, charging Daniel Norman Williams with the first-degree murder of Louise and Alma Nesbitt. Williams was located and arrested in Bellingham, Washington where he was living with his sixth wife. A trial was set for May 23, 1904, in The Dalles, county seat of Wasco County, with Judge Bradshaw officiating.[5]

Williams hired Henry E. McGinn, a renowned criminal defense lawyer, to represent him with the $2,500 from the life insurance policy insuring his fifth dead wife. McGinn decided to use a typical defense, but in an entirely unique way. He had Williams plead not guilty based on the theory that there can be no conviction if there is no murder, and there is no murder if there is no body. Such a defense rested on the definition of "corpus delicti." He called no defense witnesses and Williams didn't testify. However, he did a great deal of objecting and a thorough job of cross-examination.

282

Because the facts of the case were so complex and intertwined, District Attorney Menefee constructed his case carefully and completely. He planned for each witness's testimony to present the facts one step at a time, until the wall was so high McGinn couldn't begin to break it down. Menefee planned to prove that "circumstantial evidence alone could be sufficient to prove death. He said that where such evidence was forthcoming and where there was no reasonable doubt that murder had been committed, it was not necessary to find the body of the victim."[6] And what the witnesses presented was damning.

Oregon State Sheriffs' Association
Daniel Norman Williams

Alma had left Omaha, Nebraska, with her fiancé, Norman Williams, and come to Oregon to file adjoining homestead claims near Hood River in May 1899. On June 10 Alma filed the papers for her homestead in The Dalles. She then worked in Portland for a short time and on July 25, 1899, Norman Williams and Alma Nesbitt were married in Vancouver, Washington. What Alma apparently didn't know was that Williams was still married. They kept their marriage secret so as not to lose either one of their claims, as a married couple could only keep one claim, not two.

After the wedding, they traveled back to Wasco County. Alma began working as a housekeeper in The Dalles at the home of Judge and Mrs. A. S. Bennett in May 1899 until her mother, Louise Nesbitt, arrived in October 1899. Both women then went to Portland and stayed at the Winters Hotel where Alma got another job as a housekeeper. They stayed there until March 7, 1900, when they returned to her homestead. Ironically, Williams later tried to persuade Judge Bennett to defend him for Alma's murder. Bennett told the *Daily Journal*, "I will undertake the defense of no man whom I think is a red-handed murderer."[7]

On February 7, 1900, the women traveled to Portland where they lived together in a boarding house with Williams only a frequent visitor. On March 8, 1900, all three left Portland together on the train and arrived in Hood River late that evening. For some unknown reason they didn't stay in town that night but rented a buggy and, even though it was a terribly rainy and stormy night, they drove the twenty miles to Norman Williams' homestead. That was the last time anyone ever saw Louise or Alma Nesbitt, dead or alive. But Williams was seen coming back into Hood River the next morning at 8 a.m. When asked where the women were, he said they had left on the train going west. Unfortunately, the only train going west had already left at 5:30 a.m.

The Dalles, Oregon, *July 15th* 1905

Mr. *Martin White*

You are hereby invited to be present and witness the execution of NORMAN WILLIAMS on

Friday, July 21st, 1905,

at the hour of 6 o'clock, a. m., within the enclosure of the Wasco County Jail Yard in The Dalles, Oregon.

R. C. Sexton

Sheriff of Wasco County, State of Oregon.

NOT TRANSFERABLE. Present this card for admittance.

☞Norman Williams was convicted of the crime of murder in the first degree for the killing of one, Alma Nesbitt, at Hood River, Oregon. Convicted May 28, 1904. Re-sentenced, after appeal, June 10, 1905.

Oregon State Sheriffs' Association
Invitation to hanging of Norman Williams.

Prosecutor Menefee knew that the bloody hair was the key to proving Williams murdered the women that night. His trump card at the trial was Doctor L. Victoria Hampton, a young Portland chemist and microscopist. A lady scientist was practically unheard of in Oregon, particularly in the very rural area of Wasco County.[8] Using her microscope she was able to verify that the brown hair was still attached to bloody skin and scalp. Proving that the sacks were soaked in human blood, instead of horse blood, took a lot more work. This was the first time Doctor Hampton had used the "serum" test, newly developed in Germany and published in 1903, to determine whether old blood was human or animal. This was only her third court appearance as an expert witness and McGinn tried his best to confuse her. It was a lost cause. Nothing fazed her—not even questions asked by the jurors. Her testimony was devastating. Menefee rested his case.

Defense attorney Henry E. McGinn called no witnesses nor did he let Williams testify. He didn't try to disprove any facts in the case, or question the purported motives attributed to his client. He built his case on one idea and one idea only. There could be no murder without a body, and a couple pieces of hair wasn't enough to constitute a body.

On May 27, 1904, the attorneys gave their closing statements and the jury left the courtroom. Three and a half hours later, at 8 p.m., it returned with a verdict of "guilty of murder in the first degree."[9] It only took three ballots to get a unanimous vote and the jury had time to eat dinner too. Five days later, Norman Williams was sentenced to hang on Friday, July 22, 1904. D. D. Jackson, the county jailer, welcomed Williams back to his cell in the Wasco County Jail.

Henry McGinn immediately filed an appeal with the Supreme Court of the State of Oregon. The justices denied the appeal on March 15, 1905, and the case was sent back to Wasco County Circuit Court for judgment. The case set a precedent still cited today. "Where, as here, the circumstances point with one accord to the death of the person alleged to have been murdered, the finding of fragments of a human body, which are identified as part of the body of the alleged victim, will be sufficient, if believed by the jury, to establish the fact of death, when this is

Trial record, State of Oregon v. Daniel Norman Williams
Document from Sheriff F. C. Sexton verifying that Norman Williams was hanged.

the best evidence that can be obtained under the circumstances."[10] McGinn's desperate defense based on the lack of a body failed. The judge gave Norman Williams until July 21, 1905, to get his affairs in order.

By then newspaper reporters had investigated most of Williams' life discovering that, in reality, he was an ex-con from Nebraska who had served four years of an eight-year sentence for assaulting a neighbor woman in Chadron County, Nebraska.[11] By 1904 it was established that he had been married six times and his wives had a distressingly short lifespan after marrying him. At least three wives died under suspicious circumstances. He forgot to get a divorce from his Nebraska wife, before he left Omaha with Alma. Following a consistent pattern, as soon as Alma disappeared, Williams met another young woman in Bellingham, Washington and married her. A short time later she died and an autopsy showed a very unhealthy amount of arsenic in her system. His sixth wife, 25-year-old Anna Ziveney, was arrested as an accomplice in the land fraud case. When she found out Williams still had a wife living in Nebraska, she filed for divorce while Williams sat in the Wasco county jail waiting to be hanged. She should have known better. He'd had her lie to U.S. Attorney John Hall about seeing Alma Nesbitt back in March 1900—after Louise and Alma Nesbitt were already dead. Besides the suspicious death of his wives, Williams was also suspected of murdering an elderly couple, Jesse and Martha Tuman in Muscatine, Iowa in August 1902.[12] Sheriff Sexton and Sheriff J. D. Stuart of Muscatine County, Iowa, determined that the "Dan Williams" wanted in that case matched the description of Daniel Norman Williams in the Nesbitt case.

His description certainly matched. "One Dan Williams. About five feet nine inches tall, heavy set, chunky with square shoulders. Weight about 185 or 190 pounds. Has rather large, full, oval face, large hands and wrists and big lips. Dark, sandy complexion; light mustache, probably smooth shaven now. Eyes gray or blue. Bald on top of head. Brown hair, streaked with gray. Prominent chin. Friendly manner. Walks slow and slouchy. Never bites tobacco; always cuts it with a knife. He is about 45 to 50 years old."[13]

Sheriff Sexton issued engraved invitations to the hanging to various officials and chose his witnesses for the hanging: C. A. Borders of The Dalles, R. H. Darnielle of the Dalles, N. C. Evans of Hood River, W. J. Harriman of The Dalles, W. E. Huskey of Mosier, J. W. Moore of Hood River, C. D. Morgan of Mosier, A. C. Parrott of Hood River, Doctor Siddell of The Dalles, G. D. Woodworth of Hood River, and John Wood of Kingsley.[14] Two women standing behind the second story windows of the courthouse, and 100 men inside the enclosure, watched the hanging.

Norman Williams was the last man hanged outside the penitentiary, so a little bit of the penitentiary was brought to him. Wasco County officials had the official state hangman's rope sent to them and strung up on the gallows. Williams was the eighth man to be hanged with that particular piece of rope.[15]

The hanging took place in The Dalles inside the walls surrounding the scaffold next to the jail. Wasco County Sheriff, Felix C. Sexton, pulled the pin at exactly 6:15 p.m. on July 21, 1905, according to the death certificate.[16] Williams refused to admit his guilt even to the priest, Father Desmarais, who prayed for him.[17] No one ever knew exactly how old he was. His self-made biography said he was born in 1867, but the records from Nebraska made him older than that and he looked at least 55. He was buried in the Catholic Cemetery in a plain pine box.

The event hardly raised a ripple in the town. On the day of the hanging *The Morning Oregonian* stated, "So completely separated from the daily life of the people here was the carrying out of the law's decree this morning in the courthouse yard that visitors to The Dalles noted nothing out of the ordinary with the citizens as they went about their business. No maudlin sentimentalism toward the murderer was ever shown here."

The era of the "necktie parties" was over.

References

Holbrook, Stewart. *Wildmen, Wobblies and Whistle Punks*. Corvallis: Oregon State University Press, 1992.

Lavender, David. *Land of Giants*. Garden City, New York: Doubleday, 1956.

Morning Oregonian (Portland, Oregon) February 9, 1904, April 28, 1904, May 31, 1904, July 21, 1905, July 22, 1905, July 29, 1905.

Daily Journal (Portland, Oregon) April 24, 1904, April 28, 1904, April 29, 1904, May 28, 1904.

State of Oregon v. Norman Williams, No 6254, File No. 04060, Journal entry: Vol. 16, p. 483, September 13, 1904, Oregon Supreme Court Appeals file, Oregon State Archives, Salem, Oregon.

Chapter 46 notes

1 Stewart Holbrook, *Wildmen, Wobblies and Whistle Punks* (Corvallis: Oregon State University Press, 1992) p. 282.

2 State of Oregon v. Norman Williams, No. 6254, File No. 04060, Journal entry: Vol. 16, p. 483, Sept. 13, 1904, Oregon Supreme Court Appeals file, Oregon State Archives, Salem, Oregon.

3 *Morning Oregonian* (Portland, Oregon) July 21, 1905.

4 *Morning Oregonian*, February 9, 1904.

5 State of Oregon v. Norman Williams.

6 *Morning Oregonian*, May 31, 1904.

7 *Daily Journal* (Portland, Oregon) April 28, 1904.

8 Stewart Holbrook, p. 283.

9 State of Oregon v. Norman Williams.

10 State of Oregon v. Norman Williams.

11 *Daily Journal*, April 28, 1904.

12 Ibid.

13 Ibid.

14 *Morning Oregonian*, July 29, 1905. The newspaper article says twelve men were chosen but only eleven are listed.

15 *Morning Oregonian*, July 22, 1905.

16 Ibid.

17 David Lavender, *Land of Giants* (Garden City, New York: Doubleday, 1956) p. 190. This seems to be the same priest noted by Lavender as Father Demers who arrived in Oregon in 1838. By this time he must have been at least 85 years old.

Epilogue

I have extracted the following summary from the individual cases covered in *Necktie Parties*.

All of the hangings in Oregon during this time period were of men between the ages of 18 and 61. In four cases pairs were hanged. They killed together and they died together. They were men—overwhelmingly middle class and native born of Euro-American descent. There was one each of the following nationalities: Irish, Norwegian, German, Finnish, and Polish. Four were Native American, two were African American, and three were Chinese. The average age of the men was 34.95 years. The youngest was Lloyd Montgomery at age 18 and the oldest was William Landreth at age 61.

Many of the cases involved the abuse of alcohol, which shouldn't be too surprising. Violence and alcohol are still common companions today. Saloons, particularly in Portland, served as community social centers for many of the young, single men, and many carried guns, or had easy access to guns. Of the fifty cases in *Necktie Parties*, alcohol was involved in at least nine.

Eleven out of fifty men went to the noose maintaining their innocence. There was enormous pressure from families, authorities and society for convicted murderers to confess at the end. In many cases these men had led respectable and responsible lives until a single traumatic moment changed everything. In some cases the men initially took responsibility for their actions and only later tried to deny or excuse their guilt.

There were, of course, many men sentenced to hang who somehow did not. A few died of natural causes before the appointed day.[1]

Sometimes, a convict managed to commit suicide before the state could do the deed for him.[2] Somehow that was considered more honorable and less humiliating than hanging. Hanging was supposed to be a humiliating punishment. Convicted murderers occasionally escaped from the county jails and were never seen again.[3] Of course, the avenue of last resort was the governor's decision to commute a sentence from death to life imprisonment. In a few cases suspects were convicted, appeal granted and acquitted in a second trial.

One might expect the oldest and most populated counties to have the highest number of executions, and certainly Multnomah County, created in 1854, had the most hangings. Of the first nineteen counties created prior to 1859 when Oregon became the thirty-three state, two of the oldest counties had no hangings: Tillamook and Umpqua/Douglas. By 1905, when the last county hanging took place, there were thirteen counties that had no legal hangings: Umpqua/Douglas, Harney, Gilliam, Klamath, Lake, Lincoln, Malheur, Morrow, Sherman, Tillamook, Union, Wallowa, and Wheeler. Below is a chart listing the number of hangings that occurred in each county:

Multnomah – 13	Jackson – 3
Polk – 5	Coos – 2
Marion – 5	Clatsop – 2
Linn – 4	Josephine – 2
Wasco – 4	Lane – 2
Grant – 3	

The following counties had one hanging each: Baker, Benton, Columbia, Curry, Grant, Umatilla, Union, Washington and Yamhill.[4]

There were fifty-five victims killed by the fifty convicted murderers. Adult males were most often the victims. Fifteen women and two children were killed. The most common weapon was a gun. Eight used a knife, eight used their hands, two used a rock, one used an ax, and one used a stick. Stranger murders were very uncommon. Eighteen killed their wife or a family member.

Grouping the murders by motive was problematic. It wasn't unusual for a man to have several reasons for committing a murder thereby making it difficult to pick just one. At least six categories emerged:

Murder as part of a robbery or over money – 19
Murder as the result of uncontrollable rage – 13
Murder as a consequence of envy – 9
Murder over property or land – 4

Murder of an enemy or antagonist – 3
Murder as the result of trying to escape the law – 1

One would expect the number of hangings to increase as the population of Oregon increased but that was not the case. The *Oregon Blue Book* states that Oregon's population was 12,093 in 1850 (70 percent were men) and 413,536 in 1900. Surprisingly the number of county sponsored hangings remained about the same during each decade until 1901 when a dramatic increase occurred.

Between 1850 and 1860 there were 11 hangings.
Between 1861 and 1870 there were 6 hangings.
Between 1871 and 1880 there were 7 hangings.
Between 1881 and 1890 there were 10 hangings.
Between 1891 and 1900 there were 11 hangings.
Between 1901 and 1905 there were 8 hangings.

There were no hangings between June 1866 and December 1876. Verifying that fact required many hours spent reading seven years of microfilmed newspapers in the Knight Library at the University of Oregon. Fortunately, on January 1, 1874, the Portland *Oregonian* began publishing an annual review of the previous year's major news events including murders and hangings.

As you read the previous stories I hope you experienced in a small way the flavor of life in nineteenth century Oregon and better understood why society's acceptance of capital punishment by hanging changed over time. History has much to teach us. It is our heritage and our burden. As a society we can choose to rise above the horrors of the past or to repeat them. Capital punishment and hangings will always be a subject full of controversy. Hopefully these stories will add to that controversy and provide knowledge to enlarge that dialogue.

1 State of Oregon v. A. H. Hinch. He killed Andrew Wikman on June 1, 1892, and died in Coos County jail of heart disease while waiting to hang. He was 58 years old.
2 *Mountain Sentinel* (Union, Oregon) May 25, 1893. Also the *Oregonian* (Portland, Oregon) October 19, 1884 when Lee Song hung himself in his jail cell.
3 State of Oregon v. Samuel G. Brown, Douglas County Circuit Court Case File No. 103-2, August 4, 1873, Douglas County Courthouse, Room 101, Roseburg, Oregon.
4 See Hugo Bedau, "Capital Punishment in Oregon, 1903-1964", *Oregon Law Review*, Vol. 45, (1965) p. 7 for his analysis of the period's fifty-eight death sentences by county.

Appendix A

The Case of Berry Way in an 1863 Miner's Court

Sometimes it was difficult to distinguish the line between legal and illegal hangings. The term actually comes from the southern version of do-it-yourself mob violence as practiced by Colonel Charles Lynch of 1780 Virginia.[1] A lynching was usually the result of a community's loss of trust and faith in the legal system. Some parts of Oregon were so wild and sparsely populated that residents were used to taking care of themselves in the most expedient manner possible. At other times mobs gathered and not even a respected lawman could keep the violence in hand.

In 1863, Canyon City had Berry Way, a suspected highwayman, under arrest. A mob gathered and Way was in serious danger of being lynched until Ike Hare gave an eloquent speech and persuaded the mob to wait until a trial could be held. "Yes, gentlemen," he said. "We will give him a fair and impartial trial. We know him to be guilty, and we will hang him anyway."[2]

Frank Gallagher, from San Francisco, operated a pack train between Portland, The Dalles and Canyon City, and supplied the miners of eastern Oregon with vitally needed supplies. Unfortunately, such pack trains were prime targets of thieves and highwaymen. Gallagher was a good-hearted chap, so when Berry Way asked to ride along with him between Canyon City and The Dalles, Gallagher agreed.

On Wednesday, May 1, 1863, a group of travelers found Gallagher's body a short distance from Cherry Creek on the trail between The Dalles and Canyon City.[3] He had been shot through the head and robbed of everything except his pants. Gallagher was known to be carrying $900 in gold dust.[4] He left a wife and young child living in Portland.[5]

Meeting Berry Way along the trail, someone recognized Gallagher's stolen pack outfit and reported the matter to Wasco County Deputy Sheriff Frank McDaniels in Canyon City. McDaniels was the closest lawman available as Wasco County stretched from the Cascade Mountains all the way east to the Oregon border and all the land south of the Washington border. Wasco County Sheriff N. Olney had to depend on deputies like Frank McDaniels to enforce the law outside the county seat, The Dalles.

McDaniels deputized five or six men to go with him. They overtook Way between Juniper Flat and Canyon City and arrested him on Sunday, May 10, 1863, about ten miles from Canyon City.[6]

He was scheduled for questioning in front of a judge on Monday, but the witnesses hadn't arrived from The Dalles yet, so he was handcuffed and locked in a log house on Canyon Street guarded by McDaniels and John Kingsbury. During the night both men fell asleep and Way escaped.

The uproar that followed resembled an anthill stirred with a stick. McDaniels was so embarrassed he even offered $250 of his own money as a reward. Eight days later, word came that Way had been spotted in Auburn, Oregon located on Burnt River. Sheriff McDaniels and Charles McNelly now began a torturous two weeks of riding horseback over some of the most isolated and rugged desert in Oregon. They followed Way's trail over the Snake River at Olds Ferry and into Idaho, traveling to Placerville, Bannock City, Grimes Creek, and Fort Logan. Finally on Monday, May 25, McDaniels and four others snuck up on Berry Way as he slept. They relieved him of his revolvers, tied him up, and headed back to Canyon City.

Finally, early on Wednesday, June 3, they arrived home, exhausted, but triumphant, and ready to start the business of trials and witnesses. However, the mob in Canyon City had other ideas. At 3 p.m. that afternoon there was a public meeting. Mr. Ike Hare was chosen chairman and George Woodman was chosen secretary.[7] M. B. F. McClure gave a little speech and asked the audience whether they should hang Way or give him a trial. The 460 men crammed into the saloon voted for a trial. Immediately the crowd filed across the street to the Fashion Saloon where Way was being held and demanded the deputy sheriff release him.

Sheriff McDaniels stood alone in front of the mob. "I can't release him. I took an oath to protect and to see that the law is sustained. Everyone go home now and let the law do its job."

Because of the respect everyone had for him the crowd grumbled, but dispersed, and Way was safe for the moment. Later that day McDaniels left the saloon and was seized by a group of men intent on holding a trial immediately. They kept him locked away until after the hanging. Sadly, another highwayman, Van Tichnor, shot Sheriff Frank McDaniels to death two months later on August 6, 1863, in Canyon City, Oregon.[8]

The prisoner was taken to John Fenessey's home where a temporary sheriff, and twelve jurymen were chosen. Mr. George Woodman acted as prosecutor and Mr. Grey acted as defense counsel. John Strowbridge, local justice of the peace, read several witnesses' statements he had taken before Way's escape. Other witnesses testified, and Way was questioned thoroughly by both temporary attorneys.[9]

Following the rather standardized and expected ritual, the trial finally concluded at midnight and the jury retired to a separate room. Half an hour later the jury came back with a verdict of guilty. In another show of democracy at work the crowd voted to wait until 2 p.m. the next day to hang Way. Two dozen trusted bystanders were chosen to guard the prisoner until then.

On Thursday, June 4, 1863, nearly 800 men crammed into the small town of Canyon City. With a guard of thirty-six men flanking him, Berry Way was marched half a mile to the hastily erected gallows with its "California Collar" (normally called the hangman's noose) hanging from the scaffold.[10] Reverend Knight begged him to confess, but Way refused.

Facing the audience of nearly 1,000 men, Way stood cool and calm on the scaffold. "I'm innocent of the charges against me. It's a hard thing to be hung for a crime I'm not guilty of. Sheriff McDaniels and Kingsbury are innocent of helping me escape." The prisoner's comments about McDaniels and Kingsbury pleased the crowd immensely. However that pleasure did not stop the hanging from taking place.

The mob went to great effort to give themselves the illusion of legitimacy. Why didn't they just wait for the law to take its course? Was it because The Dalles was the county seat—so far away—and the prisoner's fate would be up to men they didn't trust? Were they just too close to their wagon train roots and slipped too easily back into that unnecessary informality?

Ignoring the citizens' use of illegal violence, the Oregon Legislature created Grant County a few months later in 1864. Canyon City was named its county seat.

Way's skull is on display in the Grant County Museum.

References

"Affiliated Societies–Grant County Historical Society." *Oregon Historical Quarterly*, Vol. 54, June 1953.

Daily Oregonian (Portland, Oregon) May 5, 1863, June 12, 1863, August 17, 1873, August 25, 1873.

Friedman, Lawrence. *Crime and Punishment in American History.* N. Y.: Basic Books, 1993.

Helm, Mike, ed. *Conversations with Bullwhackers, Muleskinners, Pioneers, Prospectors, '49ers, etc.* Jefferson: Rainy Day Publishers, 1981.

Wicks, Ned. "49ers, The Dalles, Oregon." *Oregon Journal* (Portland, Oregon) February 8, 1927, March 4, 1927.

Notes

1 Lawrence M. Friedman, *Crime and Punishment in American History* (N.Y: Basic Books, 1993) p. 189.
2 "Affiliated Societies – Grant County Historical Society", *Oregon Historical Quarterly*, Vol. 54, June 1953, p. 154.
3 *Daily Oregonian* (Portland, Oregon) May 5, 1863.
4 Mike Helm, ed., *Conversations with Bullwhackers, Muleskinners, Pioneers, Prospectors, '49ers, etc.* (Jefferson: Rainy Day Publishers, 1981) p. 211.
5 *Daily Oregonian*, May 5, 1863.
6 *Daily Oregonian*, June 12, 1863.
7 Ibid.
8 *Daily Oregonian*, August 17, 1863.
9 Friedman, p. 182. Vigilantes sometimes ran "trials," heard witnesses, and reached verdicts. There were, to be sure, not many acquittals at these "trials."
10 *Daily Oregonian*, June 12, 1863.

The Author

Diane Goeres-Gardner is a fifth gen-
eration Oregonian whose ancestors
came to the region in 1852, settling in
Tillamook County. She is the author of
several published articles on Oregon
history and winner of the 2001
Southern Oregon University Walden
Fellowship. She also captured first
place in the narrative division of the
2002 Oregon State Poetry Contest,
sponsored by the Oregon State Poetry
Association.

A retired reading instructor, school
administrator and mother of two
daughters, Diane lives in the Umpqua
Valley with her husband and "my little
shadow, Cody Dog."

Index

297

Belt, Walter C. 169
Benglesdorff, Gus 191
Bennett, A. S. 283
Bennett, Columbus 196
Bennett, Homer 253
Bennett, W. J. 120
Bennett, William Hardin 8
Benson, Charles 120
Benson, Henry L. 196
Bentley, George J. 276
Benton 218
Benton County 43, 44, 45, 71, 116, 121, 140, 141, 142, 181, 272
Bergman, A. 153
Berry, John 268
Berry, M. P. 63
Besser, L. 88
Bethel, Albert 51
Billington, F. E. 266
Bilyeau, L. 208, 213
Bin, Wong 98
Bing, Mah 151
Bird, John 258
Blachly, Walter 264
Blake, Mary 242
Blakely, Sheriff James xv
Blakeley, W. W. 253
Blakely, William 218, 232
Blanchet, Father Francois Norbert 128
Blue River 204
Bogart, Charles 178
Boggs, Elias 145
Bogue, C. E. 242
Bohannon, J. S. 143
Boise, Judge Reuben 12, 15, 30, 36, 46, 57, 66, 70, 86, 118, 133, 135, 136, 137, 143, 145
Bond, Looney 47
Bondy, L. H. D. 106
Bonser, James 8
Bonser, John 7, 8
Bonser, Elizabeth 7
Bonser, Martha Jane 9
Bonser, Stephen 8
Boon, John 30
Borders, C. A. 286
Borland, J. D. 51
Boston Saloon 269
Boswell, Ed 191
Bothwick, A. E. 88
Botsford, Charles xiv
Bowditch, J. T. 125
Bowman, Jacob 125
Boyer, Albert 276
Boys and Girls Aid Society 258
Brach, Peter 171
Bradbury, C. M. 7

Bradbury, Charles 7
Bradbury, Edward 8
Branton, Caroline 212
Branton, Clarence 202, 212, 218
Branton, Claude viii, ix, 201, 202, 203, 204, 205, 206, 207, 208, 209, 210, 211, 212, 213, 214, 215, 216, 217, 218, 219, 232, 266
Branton, S. C. 218
Brazee, Louis 161, 163
Brenen, D. B. 24
Brenan, Paul 88
Bridge Creek 50, 102
Bridges, Daniel 78
Bridges, G. H. 3
Bridges, John B. 248
Briedwell, J. W. 134
Briggs, C. H. 253
Briggs, N. P. 43
Bristol, J. N. 106
Bristow. S. D. 186
Broche, Peter 169
Brooks, W. W. 146
Brown, Archie vii, 84, 85, 86, 87, 89, 91, 94
Brown, George 35
Brown, George M. 209, 213, 240, 241, 264
Brown, Harry 265
Brown, Harvey Kimball 272, 274
Brown, J. G. 93, 143
Brown, John J. 196
Brown, Thomas 92, 264
Brown, William 118
Brownsville 65, 66, 68, 70, 175, 177, 178, 179, 180, 182, 183, 184
Brunk, Thomas W. 227
Bryant, O. J. 253
Bryant, Z. T. 71
Billington, F. E. 266
Bunker, Al 26
Bunker Hill Coal Mine 252
Bunker Hill Road 252, 254
Burch, J. W. 12
Burke, Thomas 85
Burkhalter, Alexander 230
Burnes, W. P. 94
Burnett, H. G. 39, 70
Burnett, Judge George 179, 223, 228, 230, 231, 232
Burnett, M. P. 272
Burns, Robert 35, 36
Burns, Rose 116
Burnside, D. W. 167
Burnsides, David 19
Burrows, William E. 243
Bus, Gus 253
Butler, I. M. 232
Butler, Otis D. 143, 233
Butz, Harry S. 227

Gilham, William 2, 3
Gilkey, Fred 175
Gillespie, Coalman viii, ix, 238, 239, 240, 241, 242, 243, 244
Gillett, George 276
Gillett, W. L. 168
Gilliam County 201, 202, 208, 220
Gilliam, Smith 14
Gillihan, Martin 8
Gilman, Fidelia 159
Gilman, J. M. 88
Gilman, John F. viii, 155, 156, 157, 159, 160
Gilmore, John 255
Gilmour, John 8
Gilstrap, W. F. 264
Ging, Lung 151
Gird, William 19
Glass, J. W. 182
Gliniecki, Mrs. Frank 253
Gluloch, Emil 261
Godfrey, J. B. 253, 255
Goff, S. 12
Gold Beach 238, 239, 240, 241, 242, 243, 244
Golden, Charles B. 78
Gong, Chee viii, 149, 150, 151, 152
Good Samaritan Hospital 150
Goodyear, Mrs. M. J. 126
Gordan, John 152
Gore, E. E. 26
Gore, E. T. 253
Gotha, W. N. 46
Gothard, Samuel 35
Goucher, G. W. 137
Graham, C. J. 88
Graham, C. M. 253
Graham, Harry 219
Grand Army of the Rebuplic 114
Grandy, B. W. 191
Grant County 62, 63, 64, 100, 249, 293, 294
Grant, William 231
Grants Pass 185, 186, 188, 194, 195, 196, 198, 199, 200
Grass Valley 202
Grave Creek 124, 126
Graves, T. J. 146
Graves, T. N. 137
Gray, G. G. 191
Gray, J. D. 126
Green Mountain 161
Green. Courtland ix, 201, 202, 203, 204, 205, 206, 207, 208, 209, 210, 211, 212, 213, 215
Greenbacks 63
Green, H. A. 266
Greenwood Cemetery 167

Gregory, Thomas 24
Gregory, W. M. 106
Gribble, C. H. 163
Gridley, John A. 126
Gridley, Louisa 126
Griffin Hardware Company 218
Griffin, G. W. 218
Griffin, Henry 162
Griffin, Henry D. 272
Griffin, John S. 9
Griffis, J. H. 125
Grigsby, Levi 126
Grimes, W. R. 167
Gross, George 209
Groves, John F. 120, 145, 146, 232
Guptill, E. W. 157

H

Hale, Milton 70
Haley, P. W. 47, 48, 146
Hall, George A. 255
Hall, Gilbert 78
Hall, Henry 120
Hall, John F. 156
Hall, John H. 227, 230, 234, 281, 282, 285
Hall, L. D. 57
Hall, L. M. 232
Hall, Samuel 24, 26
Halpruner, D. J. 112
Hamilton, J. M. 71
Hamilton, J. W. 156, 213, 242, 264
Hamilton, John 3, 4
Hamilton, L. 225
Hamilton, William 1, 2, 5, 6
Hamilton, William J. 4, 5
Hamlin, James 24
Hampton, L. Victoria 284
Handsaker, Jno. 219
Hanley, John A. 128
Hanna, H. K. 125, 187, 196, 197, 198
Hannah, Emma 179, 184
Hansen, Caroline 166, 167, 168, 171, 172
Hansen, John viii, ix, 163, 164, 166, 167, 169, 170, 171, 172
Hansen, Martin 166, 169
Hansen, Victor 167, 168, 169, 172
Harding, B. F. 2
Harding, Sterling F. 137
Hare, Ike 291
Hare, Joseph 238, 242
Hargadine, Robert 24
Harlocker, Lintner 158
Harlow, Lou 272
Harms, John 13
Harper, George 35
Harper, Mrs. L. 157
Harpool, F. H. 134
Harriman, W. J. 286

Mayfield, William 126
McArthur, L. L. 80, 103
McBride, James 9
McBride, Thomas A. 163, 168, 170, 253, 254
McCain, James 134, 179
McCarty, Edward 24
McClure, M. B. F. 292
McCormack, J. T. 157
McCormack, W. R. 76
McCormick, Hugh 164, 168
McCrady, D. 264
McCroskey, Deborah 257
McCroskey, Lemuel 257, 258
McCroskey, Maud 258
McCulloch, H. E. 278
McDaniel, Amanda 123, 124, 125, 126, 130
McDaniel, Holt 227
McDaniel, John 125
McDaniel, Lewis 123, 124, 125, 129, 130
McDaniels, Frank 292, 293
McDermitt, Charles 233
McDonough, James 125
McDowell, Charles 182
McFadden, O. B. 26
McFarland, Warren 240
McFeron, James A. 180, 182, 183
McGinn, Henry E. 150, 282, 284
McGowen, Angus 51
McGuhen, John 242
McGuire, H. P. 112
McGuire, J. 163
McHargne, G. W. 249
McIntyre, John 120
McKay, Harry 248
McKay, James 252, 253
McKay, James K. 252
McKay, Nancy 29
McKay, Thomas 29, 31
McKenzie Bridge 203, 207, 209, 210
McKenzie River 201, 202
McKenzie Toll Road 204
McKenzie, John 242
McKercher, Daniel B. 175, 176, 178, 179, 183
McKercher, John 183
McKinley, Joshua 2
McKinnie, A. 150
McKnight, Frank 178
McLaren, A. P. 255
McLaughlin, Dan 226, 227, 246, 269
McLaughlin, John 128
McLean, William 248
McMullen, David 208
McNeily, Charles 298
McPherson, J. N. 266
McPherson, W. A. 120
McPherson, Preston 209

McQuate, John 80
McTimmonds, Tracy 230
Mead, James 120
Meek, Alice 50
Meek, Emily 50
Meek, George W. 49, 50
Meek, Isabel 50
Meek, Margaret 50
Meek, Samuel 50, 51
Meek, Sarah 50
Meek, Schuyler 50
Meeker, Isaac 70
Megerie, George 125
Meilke, Richard 261
Melson, Alta 185
Melson, Edna 185
Melson, Lemuel 185
Melson, Mary 185
Melson, Virgil 185
Merrill, David xxii
Merrill, Fred T. 261
Merrill, Roscoe R. 243
Menefee, George 282
Mervin, A. T. 278
Methodist Mission School 29
Meyers, A. T. 272
Michelbach, J. 82
Michell, John 80
Middleton, Frank 27
Miles, W. A. 255
Millard, John 70
Miller, Alf 240
Miller, B. F. 126
Miller, Charles 123
Miller, Ed 84
Miller, Fred 186
Miller, George 70
Miller, Joaquin 50
Miller, John R. 243
Miller, Kate Pringle 59
Miller Miriam 143
Miller, Wilbur 143
Miller, William H. 80
Miller, William M. 126
Miller, William R. 242, 243
Millican, Laurence 204, 210
Millican, Walter 210
Million, Bennett 39
Milliorn, H. M. 266
Minsinger, C. 261
Minto, John 119
Mirgus, H. 255
Mitchell, H. A. 278
James Mitchell 230, 231
Mitchell, John H. 33
Mitchell, Mrs. James 231
Mitchell, R. H. 255

Wilson, Jared 253
Wilson, Joe 276
Wilson, R. P. 8
Wilson, S. W. 134
Wilson, W. C. 186
Wilson, William 8
Wimple, Adam vii, xviii, 16, 17, 19, 20, 21, 95
Wimple, Mary Allen 16, 17, 19, 20
Winchester, Oregon 47
Winfree, A. B. 276
Wingate, G. 164
Winship, John 47
Winsor, Charles S. 242, 243
Wintermiere, Charles 207
Winters, J. 270
Winters, John 258
Winton, F. D. 163, 170
Wire, M. C. 119
Wiseman, J. J. 231
Withers, Frank 264
Withers, William W. 206, 211, 216, 219, 263
Witt, William 208
Wolcott 92
Wolverton, Charles E. 216
Wonder (ship)
Wood, Adeline 21
Wood, John 286
Wood, Reece H. 51
Wood, W. A. 253
Woodman, George 292, 293
Woodmen of the World 211
Woodruff, Delos 242, 243
Woods, George L. 150

Woods, L. N. 147, 225
Woodsides, Jacob 4
Woods 223
Woodward, George "Gyp" 257, 258
Woodworth, G. D. 286
Wren, William W. 242
Wright, Ben 239
Wright, Colonel 26
Wright, C. S. 164
Wright, William W. 134
Wyckoff, Emma Finn 204
Wyckoff, John 203
Wyckoff, James 204

Y

Yamhill County 13, 93, 131, 132, 133, 140, 141, 142, 249
Yenke, Alfred 110, 111, 112, 114
Yik, Lee 149, 150, 151, 153
Ying, Chin Sue 96, 98
Yok, Kang 153
Yoran, Silas M. 209, 214
York, James Sr. 278
York, W. B. 186
You, Lum 100
Young, Andrew 168
Young, J. B. 218

Z

Zan, James C. 248
Zeller, Eva 253
Zion African Methodist Episcopal Church 272
Ziveney, Anna 285
Zumwalt, Charles 240

Related Titles from
CAXTON PRESS

Holy Rollers:
Murder and Madness in Oregon's Love Cult
T. McCracken & R. Bloggett
ISBN 0-87004-424-9 308 pages paper $16.95

Manhunt: The Pursuit of Harry Tracy
Bill Gulick
ISBN 0-87004-392-7 250 pages paper $18.95

Outlaws of the Pacific Northwest
Bill Gulick
ISBN 0-87004-396-x 216 pages paper $18.95

Oregon's Golden Years
Miles F. Potter
ISBN 0-87004-254-8 181 pages paper $14.95

On Sidesaddles to Heaven
The Women of the Rocky Mountain Mission
Laurie Winn Carlson
ISBN 0-87004-384-6 256 pages paper $19.95

Early Oregon Days
Edwin D. Culp
ISBN 0-87004-314-5 185 pages paper $22.95

For a free catalog of Caxton books write to:

CAXTON PRESS
312 Main Street
Caldwell, ID 83605-3299

or

Visit our Internet Website:

www.caxtonprinters.com

Caxton Press is a division of The CAXTON PRINTERS, Ltd.